Monetary and Financial Cooperation in East Asia

Monetary and Financial Cooperation in East Asia

The State of Affairs after the Global and European Crises

Edited by
Masahiro Kawai, Yung Chul Park, and Charles Wyplosz

UNIVERSITY PRESS

OXFORD
UNIVERSITY PRESS

Great Clarendon Street, Oxford, OX2 6DP,
United Kingdom

Oxford University Press is a department of the University of Oxford.
It furthers the University's objective of excellence in research, scholarship,
and education by publishing worldwide. Oxford is a registered trade mark of
Oxford University Press in the UK and in certain other countries

© Oxford University Press 2015

The moral rights of the authors have been asserted

First Edition published in 2015

Impression: 1

All rights reserved. No part of this publication may be reproduced, stored in
a retrieval system, or transmitted, in any form or by any means, without the
prior permission in writing of Oxford University Press, or as expressly permitted
by law, by licence or under terms agreed with the appropriate reprographics
rights organization. Enquiries concerning reproduction outside the scope of the
above should be sent to the Rights Department, Oxford University Press, at the
address above

The views in this publication do not necessarily reflect the views and policies of the Asian
Development Bank Institute (ADBI), its Advisory Council, ADB's Board or Governors, or the
governments of ADB members.

ADBI does not guarantee the accuracy of the data included in this publication and accepts no
responsibility for any consequence of their use.

By making any designation of or reference to a particular territory or geographic area, or
by using the term "country" or other geographical names in this publication, ADBI does not
intend to make any judgments as to the legal or other status of any territory or area.

You must not circulate this work in any other form
and you must impose this same condition on any acquirer

Published in the United States of America by Oxford University Press
198 Madison Avenue, New York, NY 10016, United States of America

British Library Cataloguing in Publication Data
Data available

Library of Congress Control Number: 2014953040

ISBN 978-0-19-871415-6

Printed and bound by
CPI Group (UK) Ltd, Croydon, CR0 4YY

Links to third party websites are provided by Oxford in good faith and
for information only. Oxford disclaims any responsibility for the materials
contained in any third party website referenced in this work.

Contents

List of Figures	vii
List of Tables	ix
Abbreviations	xi
List of Contributors	xv
1. Introduction *Charles Wyplosz*	1
2. Financial and Monetary Cooperation in East Asia *Masahiro Kawai and Yung Chul Park*	11
3. International Financial Integration and Crisis Intensity *Andrew K. Rose*	52
4. Lessons from the European Public Debt Crisis *Charles Wyplosz*	79
5. A View from ASEAN *Chalongphob Sussangkarn and Worapot Manupipatpong*	102
6. A View from the People's Republic of China *Yongding Yu*	133
7. A View from Japan *Masahiro Kawai*	158
8. A View from the Republic of Korea *Yung Chul Park and Chi-Young Song*	198
Index	223

List of Figures

2.1	Gross capital inflows in East Asia excluding Japan	13
2.2	Export growth in East Asia	14
2.3	GDP growth in East Asia	15
2.4	Real effective exchange rates of the East Asian economies	17
2.5	Current account surpluses of East Asian economies	21
2.6	East Asia's trade and GDP growth, 2000–12	24
2.7	East Asia's foreign direct investment flows, 2000–12	28
2.8	Scope of concluded FTAs in East Asia total, 2000–12	31
2.9	Structure of the Chiang Mai Initiative	36
2.10	Development and deepening of Asian corporate bond markets, 2011	42
2.11	Share of intraregional portfolio investment in debt	43
3.1	The progressive recession	59
3.2	Insulation from the current account	60
3.3	Asset exposure to the United States	64
3.4	Asset exposure to Japan	65
3.5	Asset exposure to the Republic of Korea	65
3.6	Asset exposure to the People's Republic of China	66
3.7	Bank exposure to the United States	67
3.8	Bank exposure to Japan	67
4.1	Exchange rate volatility before and during the crisis	84
4.2	Change in exchange rate volatility and the exchange rate regime	84
4.3	The AMU exchange rate, 2000–14	89
4.4	Regional real exchange rate dispersion	90
4.5	Change in trade between 2007 and 2009	91
5.1	Exchange rate trends	114
5.2	Euro trade effects	124
6.1	The fluctuations of ASEAN+2 currencies against the US dollar, yen, and euro	140

List of Figures

6.2	Fluctuation of East Asian currencies against the US dollar	140
6.3	Fluctuation of East Asian currencies against the euro	141
7.1	Nominal yen appreciation matched by relative price deflation	162
7.2	Japan's current account and its composition	166
7.3	Real effective exchange rates of the yen, BIS data, and for automobiles	169
7.4	Production of non-tradable goods relative to tradable goods, nominal and real	170
7.5	Japan's MOF intervention in the foreign exchange market	171
7.6	Nominal exchange rates of the yen against the won and other currencies	174
7.7	Correlation of GDP growth rates between Japan and major economies	180
8.1	Trend of foreign exchange reserves in the Republic of Korea	200
8.2	Sovereign spreads: foreign currency denominated sovereign bond spreads (vs. US Treasury note)	202
8.3	CDS premium on the Republic of Korea government bond	202
8.4	Stock price movements in East Asia	203
8.5	Exchange rates against the US dollar of East Asian economies	204
8.6	Changes in stock price and exchange rates in the Republic of Korea	204
8.7	Fluctuations of the won/dollar exchange rate since the breakout of the global financial crisis	207
8.8	Frequency of the Republic of Korea's interventions in the won/dollar foreign exchange market	209
8.9	Won/dollar exchange rate flexibility index	210
8.10	Nominal and real effective exchange rates of the Republic of Korea won	210

List of Tables

2.1	Fiscal policy in major East Asian countries, 2009 and 2010	19
2.2	Destination of East Asia's exports by stages of production, 1995–2012	25
2.3	Sources and destinations of East Asia's foreign direct investment flows, 2003–12	29
2.4	Financial contributions and voting powers under the Chiang Mai Initiative Multilateralization	38
2.5	IMF classification of East Asian exchange rate regimes, 2012	45
3.1	Crisis manifestations	55
3.2	MIMIC model estimates with only control variables	58
3.3	Adding multilateral financial linkages, 2006	61
3.4	Adding bilateral financial linkages, 2006	63
3A	Data sample	77
4.1	Change in trade between 2007 and 2009	90
4.2	Correlations of changes between 2007 and 2009 of exports with various measures of exchange rate movements	92
4.3	Currency swap arrangements during the crisis	93
5.1	Ratio of exports of goods and services to GDP	111
5.2	Bank capital to assets ratio	112
5.3	Foreign reserves and potential short-term liabilities	113
5.4	Total ASEAN trade, 2008–9	114
5.5	ASEAN real GDP growth, 2006–11	115
5.6	Intra-East Asian trade shares	116
6.1	Weights of currency changes in East Asian currencies explained by the US dollar, euro, and yen	141
6.2	Trade growth of East Asian economies, 1996–2012	143
7.1	Internationally coordinated intervention for the yen	172
7.2	Currency distribution of reported foreign exchange market turnover	175
7.3	Estimated shares of currency areas of major currencies, 1970–2007	177
7.4	Ranking of global financial centers, March 2007–September 2013	183

List of Tables

8.1	Effects of change in the RMB/US dollar exchange rate on East Asian currencies	213
8A.1	Rate of renewal of foreign loans at the Republic of Korea banks	221
8A.2	Exports by principal commodity, 2007	221
8A.3	Frequency of the Republic of Korea's interventions in the won/US dollar foreign exchange market	221

Abbreviations

ABCDE	Annual Bank Conference on Development Economics
ABF	Asian Bond Funds
ABMI	Asian Bond Markets Initiative
ACBF	ASEAN Central Bank Forum
ACU	Asian currency unit
ADB	Asian Development Bank
ADBI	Asian Development Bank Institute
AEC	ASEAN Economic Community
AFMM	ASEAN Finance Ministers Meeting
AFTA	ASEAN Free Trade Area
AMF	Asian monetary fund
AMO	Asian monetary organization
ASA	ASEAN Swap Arrangement
ASEAN	Association of Southeast Asian Nations[1]
AMRO	ASEAN+3 Macroeconomic Research Office[2]
ASFOM	ASEAN Senior Finance Officials Meeting
ATIGA	ASEAN Trade in Goods Agreement
BEC	Broad Economic Categories
BIS	Bank for International Settlements
BNM	Bank Negara Malaysia
BOJ	Bank of Japan
BPA	Bilateral Payments Arrangement
BRICS	Brazil, Russian Federation, India, People's Republic of China, and South Africa
CDS	credit default swap

[1] The ASEAN members are Brunei Darussalam, Cambodia, Indonesia, Lao PDR (People's Democratic Republic), Malaysia, Myanmar, the Philippines, Singapore, Thailand, and Viet Nam.
[2] The ASEAN+3 countries comprise the ten ASEAN member states plus the PRC, Japan, and Republic of Korea.

Abbreviations

CEPT	Common Effective Preferential Tariff
CLMV	Cambodia, Lao PDR, Myanmar, and Viet Nam
CMI	Chiang Mai Initiative
CMIM	Chiang Mai Initiative Multilateralization
CMIM-PL	CMIM Precautionary Line
CMIM-SF	CMIM Stability Facility
COFAB	Committee on Finance and Banking
CPI	consumer price index
CPIS	Coordinated Portfolio Investment Survey
DSGE	dynamic stochastic general equilibrium
EADS	East Asian dollar standard
EAS	East Asia Summit
ECB	European Central Bank
ECU	European Currency Unit
EFSF	European Financial Stability Fund
EMS	European Monetary System
EMU	Economic and Monetary Union
ERM	Exchange Rate Mechanism
ERPD	Economic Review and Policy Dialogue
ESM	European Stability Mechanism
EU	European Union[3]
EMEAP	Executives' Meeting of Asia-Pacific Central Banks
FCL	Flexible Credit Line
FDI	foreign direct investment
FSA	Financial Services Agency
FTA	free trade agreement
FSB	Financial Stability Board
G20	Group of Twenty[4]
GMS	Greater Mekong Subregion
IBA	International Bankers Association of Japan

---

[3] 'EU-27' denotes the 27 countries (Austria, Belgium, Bulgaria, Cyprus, Czech Republic, Denmark, Estonia, Finland, France, Germany, Greece, Hungary, Ireland, Italy, Latvia, Lithuania, Luxembourg, Malta, the Netherlands, Poland, Portugal, Romania, Slovakia, Slovenia, Spain, Sweden, and the United Kingdom) constituting the EU from January 1, 2007 until July 1, 2013 when Croatia joined as the 28th member.

[4] The G20 members are Argentina, Australia, Brazil, Canada, PRC, France, Germany, India, Indonesia, Italy, Japan, Republic of Korea, Mexico, Russian Federation, Saudi Arabia, South Africa, Turkey, the United Kingdom, the United States, and the European Union.

Abbreviations

IMF	International Monetary Fund
JGB	Japanese government bond
KOSPI	Republic of Korea Composite Stock Price Index
LNG	liquefied natural gas
MIMIC	Multiple Indicator Multiple Cause
MNC	multinational corporation
MOF	Ministry of Finance
MU	Ministerial Understanding
NAFTA	North American Free Trade Agreement
NDF	non-deliverable forward
NIE	newly industrialized economy
NIIP	net international investment position
OCA	Optimum currency area
PBOC	People's Bank of China
PPI	producer price index
PRC	People's Republic of China[5]
PRTSS	Pilot RMB Trade Settlement Scheme
PTA	preferential trade agreement
QE	quantitative easing
QQE	quantitative and qualitative easing
RCEP	Regional Comprehensive Economic Partnership
REER	real effective exchange rate
RIETI	Research Institute of Economy, Trade and Industry
RMB	renminbi
ROW	rest of the world
TPP	Trans-Pacific Partnership
VAR	vector autoregressive

[5] In this book, references to the People's Republic of China may according to context include or exclude Hong Kong, China, for which economic and financial statistics are often given separately and which on many bodies has its own separate representation.

List of Contributors

Masahiro Kawai, Project Professor, Graduate School of Public Policy, University of Tokyo, Japan, and former Dean, Asian Development Bank Institute, Tokyo, Japan

Worapot Manupipatpong, former Director of Capacity Building and Training, Asian Development Bank Institute, Tokyo, Japan

Yung Chul Park, Distinguished Professor, Division of International Studies, Korea University, Seoul, Republic of Korea

Andrew K. Rose, Professor of Economic Analysis and Policy, Haas School of Business, University of California, Berkeley, United States

Chi-Young Song, Professor, Department of Commerce and Finance, Kookmin University, Seoul, Republic of Korea

Chalongphob Sussangkarn, Distinguished Fellow, Thailand Development Research Institute, Bangkok, Thailand

Charles Wyplosz, Professor of International Economics and Director of the International Center for Money and Banking Studies, The Graduate Institute, Geneva, Switzerland, and Centre for Economic Policy Research, London, United Kingdom

Yongding Yu, Academician, Chinese Academy of Social Sciences, and former Director-General, Institute of World Economics and Politics, Chinese Academy of Social Sciences, Beijing, People's Republic of China

1

Introduction

Charles Wyplosz

This book brings together papers presented in Seoul in December 2010 at a conference organized by Yung Chul Park from Korea University and Masahiro Kawai from the Asian Development Bank Institute (ADBI). This was a time when the Great Financial Crisis that reached its climax with the collapse of Lehman Brothers in September 2008 was considered successfully controlled, except in the Eurozone, where the sovereign debt crisis was building momentum. Since then, the European crisis has surged to the forefront, raising a host of questions about monetary integration, in Europe as well as in East Asia. For this reason, and also because things have moved further in East Asia, the papers were thoroughly revised in late 2013.

The originality of this book is that various authors have been asked to look at financial cooperation in East Asia from their own country perspectives after global shocks led to deep rethinking of the very principles that shape practice. East Asian countries have been discussing monetary and financial coordination for more than a decade, sometimes with the aim of following in the footsteps of European monetary integration, but have achieved relatively little in substance. Obviously, national interests and objectives differ from country to country, but these differences tend to be kept implicit. The East Asian authors in this volume do not hesitate to describe what they believe motivated their policymakers. Two non-Asian authors look at East Asia from their respective US and European perspectives.

Another important aspect of this collection of essays is the timing. It is commonplace to consider that the two historic crises—the Great Financial Crisis and the ongoing Eurozone sovereign debt crisis—will have deep and lasting negative consequences for East Asia's quest for monetary integration. All authors agree that views about East Asian monetary and financial cooperation have changed. While there is little disagreement that integration has been pushed onto the back burner, views about what it will mean in practice are somewhat different. Concluding that the euro experiment looks more like a failure than the success that it was sometimes touted to be, at least as a world-leading currency, the Asian authors anticipate an acceleration of the emergence of the People's Republic of China (PRC) as a world power, while the non-Asian authors are not so sure.

The present chapter offers a synthetic overview of these contributions. It does not intend to introduce each chapter, nor does it attempt to cover all the issues touched upon by the contributors. The objective is to provide an assessment of some key issues.

1.1 The US Crisis and Exchange Rate Cooperation

East Asian financial institutions have had no or negligible exposure to the US sub-primes or even to the US or European financial institutions that were seriously shaken by the crisis. In part, this is a consequence of the East Asian crisis of 1997–8, which instilled a great dose of prudence in managing risk in the region. Along with the rapid expansion of intraregional trade centering on the PRC, this led to the "decoupling theory," the view that East Asia would not feel in any serious way the impact of the 2008 financial crisis. This theory has proven deceptive. A deep recession in the region's main export markets could only have an adverse impact on economic growth in East Asia. While this was obvious, less straightforward consequences have materialized with direct implications for monetary and financial cooperation.

One after another, starting with Japan in the 1960s, all East Asian countries have adopted an export-led strategy. The details of what this strategy entails have varied from one country to another, but the common implication is that growth in the region was intimately linked to growth in the US and Europe. The crisis has now brought home the very real possibility that these rich markets may be unstable and even that "lost decades" of sluggish growth cannot be ruled out. Indeed, it is a stylized fact that banking and financial crises can lead to protracted periods of slow growth (Reinhart and Rogoff 2009). This realization has led to a reconsideration of the export-led strategy. Many East Asian countries, including the PRC, have now come to embrace the concept of rebalancing growth, according to which future growth will depend less on the economic health of the US and Europe and more on domestic demand. Rebalancing, however, appears to have different meanings in different countries.

For the PRC and its huge population, rebalancing means an increase of spending on non-traded goods. This immediately raises two separate questions. First, how to generally boost domestic demand. Second, how to shift demand toward non-traded goods. Given that investment already amounts to half of GDP (gross domestic product), the first question calls for more consumption. This, in turn, requires a change in income distribution toward households and the build-up of a social safety net. The second question implies the need for an increase in the prices of traded goods relative to non-traded goods, which typically follows from a lasting real exchange rate appreciation. Much of the global hassle will diminish if the PRC de-emphasizes external competitiveness.

The ASEAN countries too were hit through their trade links, not only to the West but also to the PRC. Once again they found themselves in an uncomfortable spot. Quantitative easing (QE) and other non-conventional monetary policies in the US and Europe have put upward pressure on their exchange rates. The announced end of QE—the tapering decision of the Federal Reserve—has had the opposite effect. The Chinese policy of re-pegging the renminbi (RMB) has meant that the ASEAN countries, which often compete with the PRC, first found themselves at a competitive disadvantage just when some of their main export markets were softening. Monetary cooperation, once again, came to the fore. The PRC's response is that many of its own exports incorporate components from the other East Asian countries, which also assemble other components produced in the PRC, so that in the end intraregional exchange rate fluctuations matter little. This "benign neglect" view of the region's economic giant is a natural source of friction, which may lead to the disintegration of ASEAN+3 by precipitating the formation of a renminbi area. At this stage this and other important problems related to regional economic integration are left unattended.

This is the view of Japan, the other regional economic power, but with a different twist. The yen is the currency that initially appreciated most. Through regional intra-firm trade of industrial components in which it is also deeply involved, Japan was partially protected from yen overvaluation, but this is partial at best because Japan is an export powerhouse in its own right. For this reason, Japan was unhappy that the yen appreciated greatly while other Asian currencies remained in the RMB's orbit. Then, as a consequence of Abenomics, a radical shift in macroeconomic policies, the yen promptly depreciated, raising eyebrows throughout the region.

Like the ASEAN countries, Japan is in favor of some form of regional monetary and exchange rate policy coordination, but which one? Japan has clearly indicated that it does not intend to give up on exchange rate flexibility, supplemented by occasional interventions, and it still hopes that other countries will link their currencies to the yen. The ASEAN members, on the other hand, would favor some collective arrangement. They are mostly concerned with the RMB as they regard the PRC as more of a competitor than Japan, which is more advanced and whose labor costs are on a different scale. Japan's concern is less about the level of its exchange rate than about intraregional volatility. This is why Japan wishes the other countries to adopt a form of basket pegging, though it has been unclear on the constituents of the basket it favors. With the PRC uninterested and Japan unwilling to lead by example, this otherwise reasonable proposal is not taken to heart.

The Republic of Korea offers yet another perspective. Its experience during the Great Financial Crisis has been chastening. In terms of economic and financial development, it stands between Japan and the other countries of the region. Its large corporations have become global players, sometimes even displacing US and Japanese incumbents at the high-technology end of goods markets. But these successes are limited to a small number of goods and firms. Financial globalization has progressed significantly, allowing the Republic of Korea to benefit from foreign direct investment from the rest of the world. At the same time, its financial markets remain small relative to global flows. As a big fish in a small pond, it has limited financial wiggle room; indeed, the Republic of Korea's was the worst-hit economy in the region during the Great Financial Crisis. When the US and Europe went into recession, the trade impact was concentrated and brutal for a few very large firms. Foreign investors thought it prudent to remove their liquid investments and to hedge long-run positions; given the relatively small size of local financial markets, even modest retrenchment had large effects. As momentum picked up, the won came under pressure. The Bank of Korea discovered how quickly foreign exchange reserves can be exhausted. In the end the won lost more than 30 percent of its pre-crisis value. This event has reinforced the Republic of Korea's interest in monetary coordination, but its analysis is the same as that of the ASEAN countries: the lack of joint leadership by the PRC and Japan means that, eventually, East Asia will become an RMB area. But the Republic of Korea does not want to and perhaps cannot politically be part of the area. In order to stay out of this area and preserve its political independence, the Republic of Korea is destined to adopt a relatively free-floating regime. At the same time it has been promoting a pooling of foreign exchange reserves as a source of liquidity support in the region, an issue to which I return below.

1.2 The European Sovereign Debt Crisis and Monetary Cooperation

Until the sovereign debt crisis, the process of European monetary integration was often seen as a possible blueprint for East Asia. Although the region's political make-up meant that East Asia was unlikely to follow that route (Park and Wyplosz 2010), the perceived success of the euro was seen as an encouragement to deepen monetary coordination in the region. The sovereign debt crisis has radically changed that perception.

Introduction

All countries of the region now consider that the euro experiment has failed. The widely shared analysis is that monetary cooperation is much more demanding than had hitherto been believed. For years, East Asian countries were unwilling to consider the kind of sovereignty losses that had been accepted in Europe and this unwillingness persists to this day. Yet they still entertained the hope that a softer version of monetary cooperation was possible. Collective stabilization of intraregional exchange rates was a widely shared objective. It was an elusive objective, but one that could eventually be pursued more decisively. This quest has now been abandoned. Even if East Asia does qualify as a common currency area—and it does not—giving up economic and political sovereignty, even partially, has long been too demanding to be considered seriously beyond vague official declarations. Now that the Eurozone crisis has shown that monetary and financial integration requires deep sovereignty transfers, even the rhetoric is being phased out. Out of realism or diminished expectations, East Asia's agenda has shifted. The shift, however, may well be too radical. East Asian countries are likely to continue to build an institutional foundation for financial rather than monetary integration. In this regard, they have a lot to learn from the European experience. The European crisis is the result of imperfections of the Eurozone architecture, which could be remedied without deeper sovereignty losses. The generally held view that the Eurozone is on a path to disintegration does not necessarily represent the most likely prospect. Yet, the spell has been broken, maybe because this now offers an easy way out for governments that failed to make progress over more than a decade.

1.3 Reserves Pooling

The East Asian crisis left countries in the region with the conviction that they should avoid, in the future, a position where they need International Monetary Fund (IMF) support because they resented—and still do—the conditions that were then imposed. One consequence has been the accumulation of foreign exchange reserves seen as self-insurance against speculative attacks. Another consequence has been efforts to pool foreign exchange reserves. The response has been the Chiang Mai Initiative (CMI), a network of bilateral swap agreements. Over time the amounts involved have been increased and bilateral swaps replaced with multilateral arrangements—a process called CMI Multilateralization or CMIM.

Yet the total amount, US$240 billion, is small and CMIM suffers from a birth defect. In order to garner support from the US and the IMF, which had vetoed an earlier Japanese proposal to set up an Asian monetary fund, it has been agreed that swaps above 20 percent of the country quota can only be activated when the beneficiary country signs an IMF program. Given the widespread distrust of IMF conditionality, this clause in effect renders CMIM useless. This was illustrated in 2009 when the Republic of Korea found itself once again facing a speculative attack. Rather than applying for CMIM swaps, it asked for and obtained a swap arrangement directly from the Federal Reserve.

This episode has not been lost on East Asian policymakers. The Republic of Korea is now arguing for a more extensive swap network, both among East Asian countries and with the developed countries. The ASEAN countries are proposing to reduce, in gradual steps, the CMIM link to IMF programs. The fact that the Eurozone has created its own monetary fund offers a new opportunity to move in that direction, a wish long thwarted by the US and the IMF. An implication is that surveillance would then be exercised at the regional level. A first step in this direction has been to create a permanent unit, the ASEAN+3 Macroeconomic Research Office (AMRO). Based in Singapore, AMRO will feed the high-level Economic Review and Policy Dialogue (ERPD) meetings, and it could, over time, take over conditionality as part of CMIM lending.

1.4 The Debt Crisis and Foreign Exchange Reserves

Prior to the Great Financial Crisis, the East Asian countries had accumulated about US$4 trillion worth of foreign exchange reserves. The Republic of Korea experiment should remind them of the limits of self-insurance, but ASEAN and the Republic of Korea may have drawn the opposite conclusion. Despite the heavy cost of accumulating them, they seem to believe that large reserves can help and are needed, especially since CMIM is likely to be of limited help. The key question is whether the PRC will change its policy.

With more than US$3 trillion, the PRC holds about half of the world's foreign exchange reserves. Whether it has accumulated reserves for self-insurance or for mercantilist reasons—a byproduct of the export-led strategy—is a controversial issue, largely because intentions are in the eyes of the beholders. What is clear is that the PRC has discovered the "wealthy man curse": so much wealth must be carefully invested and managed. For a long time, the PRC kept the bulk of its reserves in the liquid and safe form of US government bonds. In many respects, this is one reason why the PRC has been so reluctant to let the RMB appreciate vis-à-vis the US dollar. Indeed, such an appreciation results in valuation losses on the books of the People's Bank of China (PBOC). Even though these are only paper losses as long as the reserves are held, they represent a political embarrassment that can have domestic political consequences. In addition, the PRC has been burnt by the fate of the quasi-public US agencies, Fannie Mae and Freddy Mac.

A response has been to diversify its assets, but there are few safe and liquid assets in large amounts. The next best instruments were Eurozone public debt instruments. Soon after the PRC had embarked on this diversification route with great fanfare, the European sovereign debt crisis started to unfold. Debt defaults are no longer ruled out. This may even apply to the US federal government if the stalemate between Democrats and Republicans lasts longer. All of a sudden, the PRC has realized that being so rich in reserves may be dangerous. One response has been to acquire Japanese government bonds, but the Japanese government is the most indebted government in the world. Another response is a push toward RMB internationalization (see section 1.5). The rebalancing policy is yet another response. If the PRC gives up on its export-led growth strategy, it may be willing to let the RMB appreciate to the point where it no longer runs a current balance surplus. In the short run, expectations of RMB appreciation fuel capital inflows and therefore a balance of payments surplus. In the longer run, when the RMB is no longer seen as undervalued, the balance of payments could become balanced or even in deficit if private savings decline.

1.5 Financial Markets and Renminbi Internationalization

Yet another response of the PRC to its foreign exchange reserves conundrum comes under the label of RMB internationalization, meaning the promotion of its currency for use internationally, starting mostly in East Asia. In fact, that strategy is seen in the PRC as providing an answer to many of the issues raised so far.

To start with, the practical obligation of holding reserves in assets denominated in US dollars is seen as one manifestation of the dollar's status as the international currency. Proposing to end this "unipolar" situation has a strong appeal in most parts of the world. Projections of the size of its economy over twenty or fifty years invariably suggest that the PRC is the next giant and that its currency stands to challenge the dollar's supremacy.

The PRC authorities have shown keen interest in this development and are now promoting "RMB internationalization." They encourage trade invoicing and eventually settlement in RMBs. They expect that this will eliminate exchange rate uncertainty for their commercial traders. However, this reasoning overlooks the basic fact that one side of any trade deal involving two currencies must bear the exchange rate risk. That side provides an implicit insurance and this insurance must be priced. Chinese traders may convince their counterparts to bear the risk but there will be an implicit cost.

The PRC's well-planned efforts to internationalize the RMB are not only likely to bring disappointing results, but they also face a number of hurdles. The limited extent of RMB convertibility implies that the authorities must manage the wider use of the RMB in international trade and financial transactions. While this may bring some early results, further progress cannot just be the result of administrative or political actions. A currency can only become truly international as the result of widespread market acceptance.

This may be why the PRC authorities now report that their goal for RMB internationalization is initially focused on East Asia. This being primarily a political objective, the results depend on political acceptability. Taking advantage of disappointments with regional monetary and financial cooperation as well as with the European blueprint, the PRC authorities are presenting RMB internationalization as a substitute. If a growing number of countries in East Asia price and pay for intraregional trade in RMB and if the RMB remains stable vis-à-vis the dollar and the euro, then the PRC will next encourage more countries to peg their currencies to the RMB.

Quite predictably, Japan is unenthusiastic and sees RMB internationalization as a long-run proposition, at best. The Republic of Korea too is dubious and sees the RMB area as likely to prevail in ASEAN, Taipei,China, and Hong Kong, China, but not in the Republic of Korea and Japan. The ASEAN countries do not seem convinced either, however. They accept that the PRC is and will increasingly be the dominant economic player in the region, but they are eager to keep a distance. To that effect, they suggest that India—the next economic giant—and Australia be brought into the picture.

1.6 Crisis and Trade

The rebalancing response to the crisis involves attempts both to build up domestic demand for domestic goods and to increase intraregional trade. More generally, diversifying trade partners is seen as a desirable strategy. This has led all countries in the region to seek free-trade agreements (FTAs).

The ASEAN countries have been most active. They started long ago with the ASEAN FTA and have progressed to the point where they are getting close to a customs union and now negotiate collectively. They have reached FTAs with the "Plus Three" countries: the PRC, Republic of Korea, and Japan. They also look at the greater region, having concluded FTAs with India, Australia, and New Zealand. The "Plus Three" have been trying to reach bilateral FTAs among themselves, but as long as they are mired in territorial disputes it will take many years—if ever—to conclude their negotiations for a PRC–Japan–Republic of Korea (CJK) FTA.

1.7 Conclusions

The contributions collected in this volume cover many more issues, including efforts to build up regional financial markets, starting with bonds, and the various institutional arrangements developed to that effect over a long period of time. Indeed the architecture of East Asian monetary and financial cooperation is as complex and multi-faceted as it is ineffectual. Ever since the inception of the CMI in 2000, East Asia's political leaders have been trying to deepen cooperation without giving up sovereignty. Since this is impossible, knowingly or not, they have built up cooperation processes and forums with little influence. Symbols have trumped action.

The ineffectiveness of cooperation has been made plain by the financial crisis. The European sovereign crisis has made cooperation far less attractive than it used to be. East Asia is now engaged in a search for alternative collective purposes. Rebalancing regional spending has been the first answer. Although rebalancing does not directly concern monetary and financial cooperation, it matters indirectly. It means that the long-dominating focus on exchange rates vis-à-vis the US dollar and the euro is becoming less relevant while regional exchange rate stability is being brought forward, which means more cooperation. Similarly, the discovery that "safe assets", possibly even including US public debt instruments, are not so safe after all is shaking long-held convictions. The quest for foreign exchange reserves is bound to become less attractive and far more complicated. It reinforces the view that exchange rates need to be kept as competitive as before, relative to non-regional currencies.

It also means that the East Asian countries wish to change the global monetary and financial architecture that they regard as a relic of the times when the West was the dominant power. They are gradually discovering that such changes will be painfully slow. As a result, they will endeavor to develop their own financial markets, an issue discussed at some length in most contributions to this book.

These efforts, however, are heavily shaped by the fact that only two countries, the PRC and Japan, can ever hope to be global players. More precisely, Japan is already a global player but of diminishing importance as its economic size has been stagnant for two decades and its demography implies a continuous decline. This leaves the PRC as the bright spot for the future, but doubts have been raised as to whether it could sustain the rapid growth of the past while addressing the deterioration in distributive equity. In addition to its declining demography, the PRC will need an extensive financial reform if it ever wants to become a leading financial power. Many in the region doubt that the PRC has the political ability to do what it takes to move in this direction. Most countries also fear the PRC's hegemony.

This is exemplified by the current policy of RMB internationalization. Trumpeted by the PRC authorities as the first step in transforming regional monetary and financial cooperation, RMB internationalization is a government-led effort in an area that can only be market-driven. Early successes are the result of administrative measures; more progress will be difficult to sustain in the same way.

At the end of the day, East Asia's conundrum is clear: there can be no regional monetary and financial cooperation without Chinese leadership, but the PRC does not feel it has to promote regional economic integration. All it has to do is to wait as other countries come into its fold one by one. The PRC already feels that it is too powerful to have any need to negotiate with its trading partners. It believes that its continuing growth and transformation will turn East Asia into a PRC economic and monetary area. The ASEAN countries dislike this prospect and look to India and other countries for a possible counterweight, but eventually economic interests will outweigh their concerns about the PRC's domination. Japan is determined not to join the PRC economic area. The Republic of Korea faces the same choice, but will have to remain outside the area as long as the PRC continues to prop up the Democratic People's Republic of Korea regime. Given this security constraint, its strategy has been to deepen and diversify its trade and financial relations with countries in other regions through forming FTAs, as it has with the US and EU. The Eurozone crisis has taken the wind out of regional monetary cooperation, but a new concept is not in sight.

References

Park, Yung Chul, and Charles Wyplosz. 2010. *Monetary and Financial Integration in East Asia: The Relevance of European Experience*. Oxford: Oxford University Press.

Reinhart, Carmen, and Kenneth Rogoff. 2009. *This Time Is Different: Eight Centuries of Financial Folly*. Princeton, NJ: Princeton University Press.

2

Financial and Monetary Cooperation in East Asia

Masahiro Kawai and Yung Chul Park

2.1 Introduction

The global financial crisis of 2007–9 did not originate in East Asia, and East Asian economies largely avoided direct losses from holdings of toxic assets, as well as liquidity or solvency crises. Nevertheless, East Asian economies were hit hard by the downturn in export demand, and, in some cases, by turbulence in foreign exchange and capital markets resulting from a sudden stop in the inward flow or withdrawal of capital. Although the region made a V-shaped economic recovery, the longer-term implications of the crisis for East Asia's economic and financial future are greater than the short-term ones.[1]

East Asian economies were major players in the widening global imbalance in the period leading to the global financial crisis. The global slowdown of economic growth following the crisis heightened the need to rebalance growth toward greater reliance on domestic and regional demand. Growth rebalancing requires not only growth that is consistent with smaller external imbalances and less dependent on net exports to the West, but also growth that avoids a build-up of internal imbalances.

The global payments imbalance was a reflection of US overspending and East Asia's (and oil producers') underspending relative to their respective outputs. The global imbalance has already been reduced substantially since the outbreak of the global financial crisis as a result of the implosion of US

[1] In this chapter East Asia refers to the People's Republic of China (PRC) including Hong Kong, China; Japan; the other advanced economies of East Asia (Republic of Korea, Singapore, and Taipei,China); and the nine other ASEAN member states besides Singapore (Brunei Darussalam, Cambodia, Indonesia, Lao PDR, Malaysia, Myanmar, the Philippines, Thailand, and Viet Nam).

consumption and investment, which more than offset the sharp rise in the fiscal deficit of the US. The large current account surplus in the People's Republic of China (PRC) in the pre-global financial crisis period—reaching more than 10 percent of GDP in 2007—has been reduced largely due to the rise in domestic fixed investment, facilitated by real effective appreciation of the renminbi (RMB). To make this rebalancing process sustainable, adjustment in both the demand side and the supply side of the economy would be required.

To achieve a balanced pattern of growth, which would contribute to stable and sustainable growth both in the region and globally, the East Asian economies need to focus on policies to address both demand-side management and supply-side structural changes. These would include nationally appropriate policies and regional coordination of policies in various areas. This chapter discusses the importance of regional monetary and financial cooperation. It reviews major macroeconomic developments, trade patterns and free-trade agreement (FTA) initiatives, financial market deepening and financial cooperation initiatives, and examines exchange rate policies in East Asia before, during, and after the 2007–9 global financial crisis. The chapter is intended to set the stage for the country studies that follow.

Section 2.2 reviews the impact of the global financial crisis on the East Asian economies, their economic recovery, and the progress of economic rebalancing in the post-crisis period. Section 2.3 examines patterns of trade and foreign direct investment (FDI) in East Asia, the region's emergence as Factory Asia, and recent FTA initiatives. Section 2.4 discusses recent progress on regional financial market deepening and financial cooperation, focusing on local currency bond market development, regional economic and financial surveillance, and short-term liquidity support. Section 2.5 investigates exchange rate policy issues in East Asia. Section 2.6 concludes the chapter.

2.2 Macroeconomic Developments

2.2.1 *Pre-Crisis Macroeconomic Conditions*

In the years just prior to the global financial crisis, East Asian economies generally enjoyed high growth, bolstered by capital inflows from the developed economies and strong export performance. Real GDP growth was led by the PRC, which averaged 11.8 percent in 2005–7. Growth in ASEAN countries averaged 6.1 percent during the period, and that of the region's other advanced economies was 6.3 percent. The PRC's merchandise export growth also led the way, averaging 27 percent over the years, while growth for ASEAN averaged 15 percent.

Financial and Monetary Cooperation in East Asia

East Asia saw substantial increases in current account surpluses: 10.1 percent of GDP for the PRC, 8.3 percent for the ASEAN economies as a whole, and 7.1 percent for East Asia's other advanced economies. This clearly reflected the rise in global payments imbalances during the period, led by the rising current account deficit of the US. Along with these very favorable growth conditions, inflation pressures were also building. Again, this was most notable in the PRC, where consumer price index (CPI) inflation increased to 4.8 percent in 2007 versus 1.8 percent in 2005. Inflation conditions among ASEAN economies were variable, and the average inflation rate actually fell in 2007, partly reflecting a temporary decline in oil prices. Finally, gross capital inflows to East Asia (excluding Japan) rose strongly during the period, almost doubling from 7.1 percent of GDP in 2004 to 12.3 percent of GDP in 2007 (Figure 2.1). This reflected confidence about emerging East Asia's growth prospects.

Japan's situation differed markedly from those of other East Asian economies, as it had already endured a decade and a half of slow and intermittent growth following the collapse of its own asset price bubble, which had peaked in 1989–90. Plunging real estate prices, deleveraging, and a very strong yen fed into a prolonged weak demand, and outright deflation appeared first in 1996, and then on a more prolonged basis starting in 1999. As a result, the Bank of Japan (BOJ) adopted quantitative easing (QE) for the first time in 2001. Japan saw a period of sustained growth in 2002–7, partly as a result of an upturn in exports due to the global economic recovery following the dot-com bubble

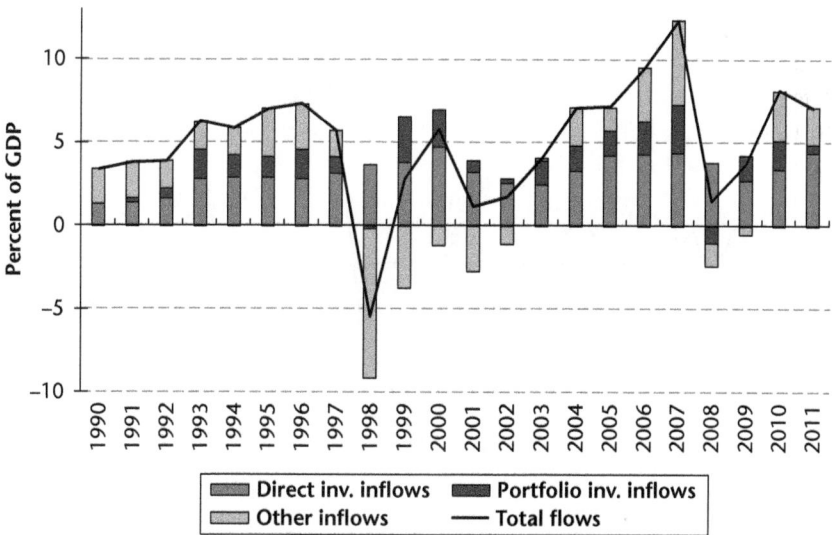

Figure 2.1. Gross capital inflows in East Asia excluding Japan (% of GDP)
Source: CEIC database, available at <http://ceicdata.com> (accessed October 25, 2013).

burst in 2000–1, and substantial progress in the adjustment of banks' and corporations' balance sheets, partly due to policies under the Koizumi government. As a result, Japan managed to achieve average real GDP growth of 1.7 percent in 2005–7, and even briefly escaped from deflation in 2008.

Japan also differed from other East Asian economies in the rapid build-up of government debt in the pre-crisis period, reflecting shortfalls in tax revenues, the large expenses of numerous fiscal stimulus packages, and rising pension and health costs associated with a rapidly aging society. The ratio of gross government liabilities to GDP rose from 65 percent in 1990 to 162 percent in 2007, while net liabilities rose from 13 percent to 80 percent over the same period. This high debt level posed the debt sustainability problem.

2.2.2 Impacts of the Global Financial Crisis

During the last quarter of 2008, following the September collapse of Lehman Brothers, East Asia took a turn for the worse: many economies slid into a deep recession, and the Republic of Korea and Indonesia faced significant financial shocks. Although the degree of the decline differed from country to country, from September 2008 to the second quarter of 2009 all East Asia's economies saw their export growth plunging into negative territory (Figure 2.2) and, in most cases, falling output (Figure 2.3), in some cases quite sharply. Reflecting

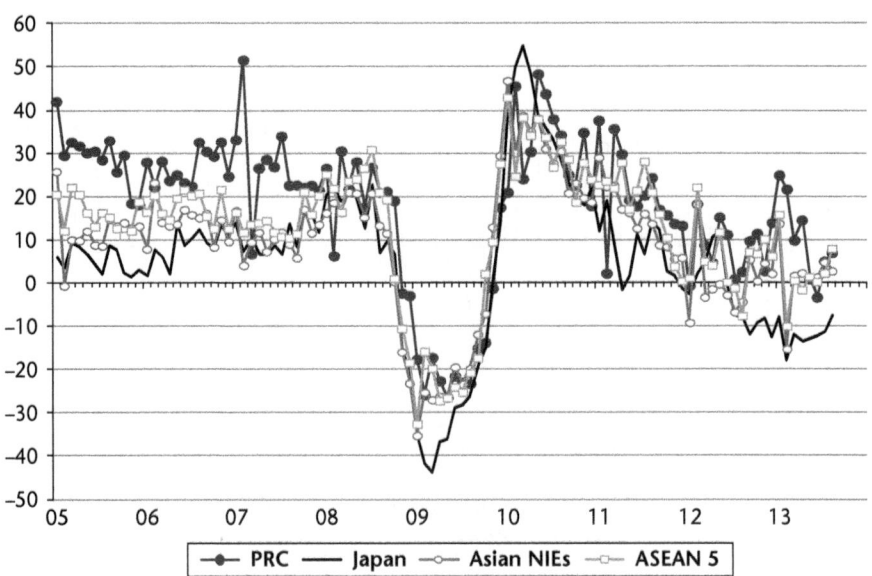

Figure 2.2. Export growth in East Asia (year-on-year percentage change)
Source: CEIC database, <http://ceicdata.com> (accessed October 25, 2013).

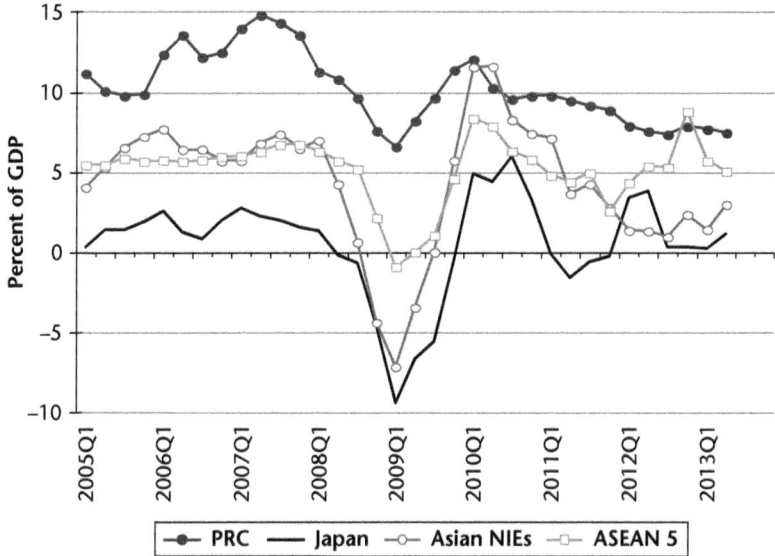

Figure 2.3. GDP growth in East Asia (year-on-year percentage change)
Source: CEIC database, <http://ceicdata.com> (accessed October 25, 2013).

the collapse of domestic demand and exports, and a steep fall in the prices of oil and other raw materials, import demand plummeted more throughout the region. As a result, practically all East Asian economies were generating trade surpluses during the same period. Not surprisingly, inflation rates fell and, in Japan, deflation returned. The East Asian economies were impacted via both the trade and financial channels.

TRADE CHANNEL
The crisis hit East Asia mainly via the trade channel. Not only the size of exports relative to GDP but the product structure of exports also mattered in transmitting the external shocks. As shown by Blanchard (2009), economies that concentrated heavily on a limited number of manufactured export goods, which are highly cyclical, were hit harder by the crisis than those with a diversified mix of export products. Japan, the Republic of Korea, Singapore, and Taipei,China, whose exports were heavily concentrated in manufactures, experienced a somewhat deeper slowdown than other economies such as Indonesia and the Philippines, which exported relatively more agricultural goods, resources, and other non-manufactured products. Given that the income elasticity of import demand is typically higher for manufactured than non-manufactured imports (Goldstein and Khan 1985), a global recession would therefore bring down export earnings of economies such as Japan,

the Republic of Korea, and Taipei,China more than those of other economies. However, the general pattern of decline (and subsequent recovery) was very similar across economies.

The overall severity of the impact of the crisis varied by country according to the growth rates exhibited in Figure 2.3. The ASEAN 5 coped with the crisis better than other neighboring countries as, in aggregate, they registered positive growth in 2009. The GDP of the PRC grew 9.1 percent in 2009, partly as a result of stimulus measures described in section 2.2.3. East Asia's other advanced economies were battered severely by the crisis, reflecting their high export exposures and related impacts on private capital investment. The negative impact on Japan was even more severe than those on East Asia's other advanced economies but from a lower growth base.

FINANCIAL CHANNEL

The region's banking sector was not heavily loaded with nonperforming assets—certainly not large enough to threaten its solvency or systemic risk. Nor did it indulge in acquiring US toxic assets. Maturity and currency mismatches in the balance sheets, which were at the root of the insolvency of many banks and other financial institutions during the 1997–8 Asian financial crisis, had been by and large under control. Governance, transparency, and the financial soundness of the corporate sector had all improved. On macroeconomic policy, greater flexibility of foreign exchange rates throughout the region should be given some credit for softening the impact of the liquidity crunch, although it could not avert a run on central bank reserves in the Republic of Korea. The depreciation of the region's currencies against the US dollar during the height of the crisis subsequently helped to improve competitiveness of exports to propel East Asia's recovery.

Nonetheless, East Asia's financial markets displayed considerable instability following the outbreak of the global financial crisis. Stock prices nosedived throughout the region and real effective exchange rates, except for the Japanese yen (which appreciated) and those pegged to the dollar, generally depreciated against the US dollar and exhibited increased degrees of volatility until the second quarter of 2009 (Figure 2.4). Sovereign spreads over US Treasuries widened dramatically, and credit default swap (CDS) premiums, a measure of the quality of financial liabilities, also soared, before dropping early in 2009.

The strength of the yen resulted both from the "flight to quality" away from risky financial assets as a result of the financial crisis and also from the narrowing of interest rate differentials as the US Federal Reserve, the Bank of England, and the European Central Bank all slashed their policy rates to near zero in an effort to jump-start their economies. As a result, the yen appreciated steadily from 123 yen/dollar in mid-2007 to only 77 yen/dollar in January 2012, a cumulative 60 percent appreciation in nominal terms and 26 percent

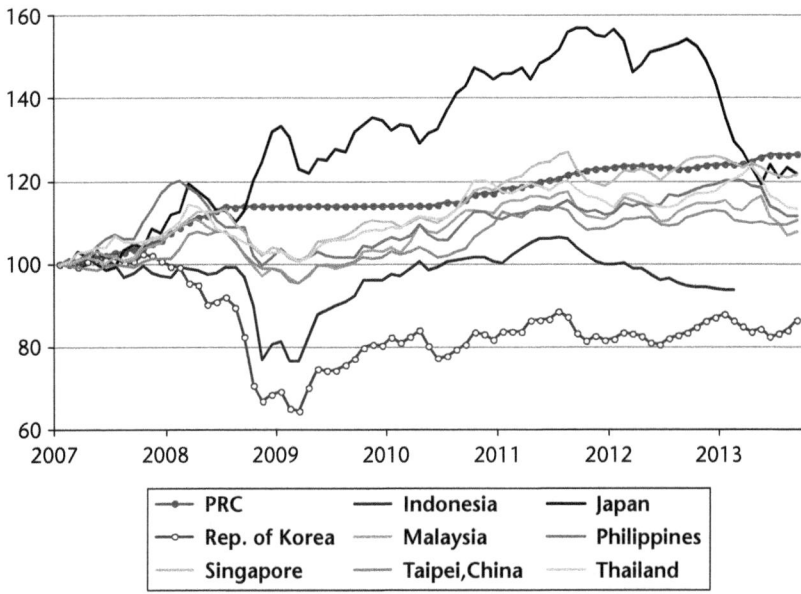

Figure 2.4. Real effective exchange rates of the East Asian economies
Note: Index Jan. 2007=100.
Source: BIS.

in real effective terms. This had a huge and sustained deflationary impact on the Japanese economy, so that the sharp rebound of growth in 2010 had no observable impact on improving inflation.

In this bleak crisis landscape, banks and other financial institutions cut back their lending operations by recalling existing loans as the availability of both local and foreign currency liquidity evaporated, future economic prospects looked dim, and their losses were piling up. Most damaging was the drying up of trade credits, which further reduced sagging exports. Some countries such as the Republic of Korea suffered large capital outflows, as many foreign investors were liquidating their holdings of local financial assets to buy into more liquid assets (such as US Treasuries) and to cover their losses back home. Amid the financial deterioration, most East Asian economies held up well, but the Republic of Korea could not ward off a liquidity squeeze in the fourth quarter of 2008: during this period, it saw a massive depreciation of its currency and reserve losses, and was on the verge of a currency crisis.

2.2.3 Economic Stimulus Responses

Once the magnitude of the global financial crisis became apparent, many East Asian economies aggressively eased monetary and fiscal policies to combat the effects of declining exports. The call of the G-20 nations for coordinated monetary and fiscal easing helped create the environment for such measures.

MONETARY POLICY MEASURES

Almost all central banks in the region eased monetary policy following the Lehman shock. Japan still maintained the legacy of an easy monetary policy it had inherited from the beginning of the decade. Most other economies in East Asia, on the other hand, came into the onset of the global financial crisis with substantially tighter monetary policies, as they were concerned about the inflationary consequence of overheating and rising commodity prices given rising inflation from 2007 to mid-2008.

The subsequent softening of energy and commodity prices, especially after the Lehman shock, allowed monetary authorities to cut policy interest rates aggressively, aided by the substantial monetary policy space they possessed in terms of the level of policy interest rates. They adopted not only conventional but also unconventional monetary policies. As conventional policies, for example, the PBOC halted the gradual renminbi (RMB) appreciation policy, re-pegged it to the US dollar, reduced reserve requirements, and removed limits on credit growth, which led to an extraordinary expansion of bank lending in the first quarter of 2009. As unconventional policies, the BOJ slightly raised monthly outright purchases of government bonds from 1.2 trillion yen per month (which had been set in October 2002) to 1.4 trillion yen in December 2008. Bank Indonesia extended the term for fine-tuning operations, as well as for foreign exchange swaps, relaxed conditions for access to its liquidity facility, and began to purchase bankers' acceptances for exporters. The Bank of Korea escaped from a mini-currency crisis partly by arranging a currency swap amounting to US$30 billion with the US Federal Reserve.

FISCAL POLICY MEASURES

Given the unprecedented collapse of real economic activity, many governments in the region, as elsewhere, resorted to aggressive easing of fiscal policy. As a result, the fiscal positions deteriorated sharply throughout East Asia in the final quarter of 2008, and further in 2009. The sharpest deteriorations from 2008 to 2009 were experienced by Malaysia, Japan, and Singapore. Except in Japan, such an active use of countercyclical fiscal policy was a radical departure from the fiscal conservatism that had characterized the economic policy-making of most East Asian economies. In fact, excluding Japan, East Asian economies had not used countercyclical fiscal policy actively except at the time of the Asian financial crisis of 1997–8.

It is not easy to estimate the size of the fiscal stimulus package, net of the automatic stabilizers and the spending or tax reduction measures that had already been planned; the announced spending increase in some cases also

Table 2.1. Fiscal policy in major East Asian countries, 2009 and 2010 (% of GDP, change with respect to pre-crisis year 2007)

	2009		2010	
	Overall balance	Crisis-related discretionary fiscal measures	Overall balance	Crisis-related discretionary fiscal measures
PRC	−4.8	−3.1	−4.8	−2.7
Indonesia	−1.4	−1.4	−0.9	−0.6
Japan	−7.4	−2.4	−7.5	−1.8
Republic of Korea	−6.2	−3.6	−6.2	−4.7

Source: Estimates from IMF (2009), Annex Table 3.2.

included prospective contributions from the private sector and amounts which were not actually implemented. The International Monetary Fund (IMF 2009) estimated that the size of the crisis-related discretionary fiscal measures relative to 2007 was particularly large in the PRC (3.1 percent and 2.7 percent of GDP in 2009 and 2010) and the Republic of Korea (3.6 percent and 4.7 percent of GDP) (see Table 2.1). Even Japan's figures were higher than the G-20 average (2.0 percent of GDP in 2009 and 1.6 percent of GDP in 2010) (Horton 2010), despite the limitations on its fiscal space described in section 2.2.1.

The aggressive use of countercyclical fiscal policy appears to have had a measure of success in pulling the economies out of the deepest recession in recent decades. Using a sample of 26 economies and regions, Park et al. (2010) find some evidence that fiscal policy had a marginally significant impact on supporting aggregate demand in East Asia, but not in other economies. While general government expenditure or revenue had no statistically significant effect, an interaction term between government expenditure and the dummy variable for developing Asia had a significant effect upon the gap between predicted GDP and actual GDP during the recent global financial crisis.[2]

Nevertheless, the fiscal measures in some cases had potentially negative longer-term consequences. In particular, the PRC's well-publicized stimulus package of 4 trillion yuan was largely driven by provincial-level infrastructure investment spending financed by bank loans and other sources. As a result, the share of gross fixed capital investment in GDP jumped from 39 percent in 2007 to 46 percent in 2009, a level that was unlikely to be sustainable. Along with this, growth of the broad money supply M2 accelerated sharply by an unprecedented 26.5 percent in 2009, while total bank loans rose even more, up 29 percent in the same year, almost twice the average growth rate of the

---

[2] The sample consists of eighteen G20 economies (all except for the European Union and Saudi Arabia); Hong Kong, China; Malaysia; the Philippines; Singapore; Taipei,China; and Thailand.

previous three years. Financing by the "shadow banking" sector also grew rapidly. These trends have raised concerns about the risk of a real estate bubble and a potential sharp increase in non-performing loans later on, especially if GDP growth slows markedly.

2.2.4 Post-Crisis Developments and Challenges

ECONOMIC RECOVERY

East Asia made a rapid V-shaped recovery beginning in 2009. This no doubt was partly due to the monetary and fiscal stimulus measures adopted in the region, but also and perhaps mainly to the recovery of export growth, reflecting the end of economic contraction in the US and Europe. At the same time, East Asia saw the return of foreign capital inflows into the region.

The rapid recovery of East Asia raises an important question as to how a region that had been buried deep in a slump could make such a quick turnaround to break out of the recession ahead of other regions. One could argue that unlike the 1997–8 Asian financial crisis, the epicenter of the crisis was located outside of the region and hence East Asia bore less of the burden of resolving it. East Asia excluding Japan suffered a transitory external shock that it could absorb more readily than a decade earlier, as its economy had built up enough resilience through extensive reforms of its financial, corporate, and public sectors.

Japan's economy also recovered beginning in 2009, showing a pattern similar to those of other East Asian economies, but from a lower base. Its GDP rose by 4.7 percent in 2010. However, the recovery trend was dealt a harsh blow by the Great East Japan Earthquake of March 2011, which developed into the "triple-disaster" encompassing earthquake, tsunami, and meltdown of the nuclear reactors at Fukushima. The tsunami and earthquake caused widespread disruptions in Japan's delicate supply chain networks, which suffered from a lack of alternative suppliers of critical parts and components, especially in the important automobile and electronics sectors. Japanese companies were able to recover from these shocks relatively quickly, but the impacts of the nuclear disaster were longer-term, and included the worsening of the trade balance because of the need to import mineral fuels, as nuclear power plants all over Japan were shut down due to concerns about safety. As mentioned above, Japan's economy was also hit by the steady appreciation of the yen until late 2012 when the first announcements of "Abenomics" policies were made.

PROGRESS OF ECONOMIC REBALANCING

Although there is considerable debate about the degree to which global current account imbalances in the pre-crisis period contributed to the development of the global financial crisis, there is little disagreement that a return in East Asia to the status quo ante of export-led growth accompanied by large current account surpluses is neither advisable nor feasible. Lower growth rates in the US and Europe look likely to persist for some time, so their markets will not be able to absorb East Asian products as much as before. East Asian economies need increasingly to rely on domestic and regional demand.

East Asian economies have already seen significant declines in their current account surpluses, especially those of the PRC and Japan, which respectively fell to only 2 percent and 1 percent of GDP in 2012 (Figure 2.5). For the PRC, this reflected a number of factors, including relatively sluggish growth of exports since the crisis, real effective appreciation of the RMB, and a rise in domestic demand led by fixed investment. For Japan, this partly reflected the surge in mineral fuel imports and yen appreciation. The surplus for the ASEAN 5 countries also fell dramatically. That for East Asia's other advanced economies has remained relatively high, mainly reflecting large surpluses in Singapore and Taipei,China. The main question is whether this external rebalancing will persist.

The PRC economy perhaps faces the biggest challenge in rebalancing growth in multiple dimensions. The contribution to growth from net exports to GDP was unsustainably large in the pre-crisis period, but the role of net exports declined and the contribution of fixed investment rose after the

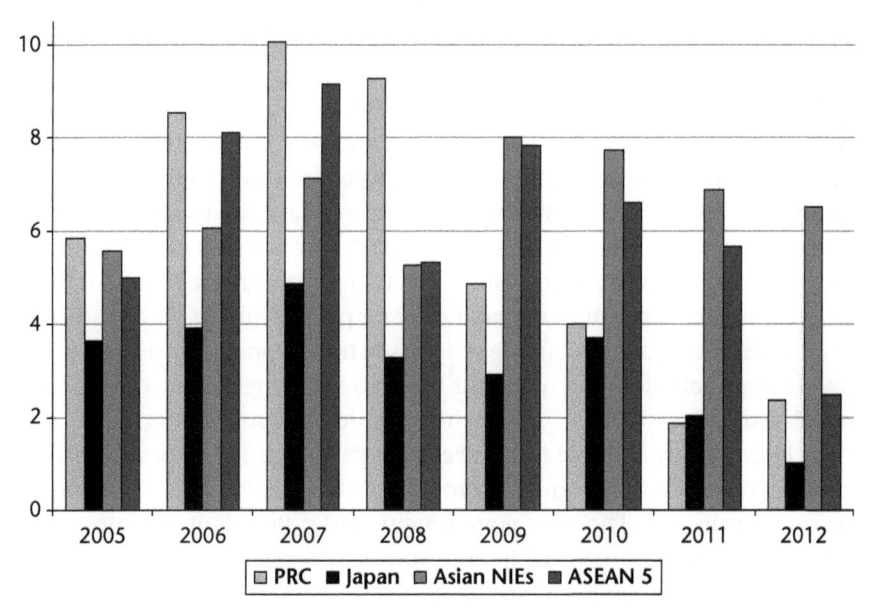

Figure 2.5. Current account surpluses of East Asian economies (% of GDP)
Sources: CEIC Database Co., <http://www.ceic.com> (accessed October 25, 2013).

Lehman collapse. But the ratio of household consumption to GDP fell to about 35 percent, an exceptionally low level. This raised many concerns about the sustainability of the PRC's growth, since high rates of capital investment—reaching 48 percent of GDP in 2010–13—were accompanied by declining returns to capital and a massive rise in debt in the economy. The rise of off-balance-sheet liabilities by provincial governments and the rapid development of the "shadow" banking system in response to repressed deposit rates in the banking sector are of particular concern. Essentially, the external imbalance has been replaced by the internal imbalance—excessively high investment-to-GDP ratios and the build-up of financial imbalances through shadow banking activity.

MACROECONOMIC POLICY CHALLENGES

In the post-global financial crisis era, East Asian economies must find new ways to achieve sustained economic growth. They need to raise productivity through innovation and structural reforms. Japan is trying to exit from the "two lost decades," while many developing East Asian economies are trying to escape from the "middle-income" trap.

One of the key recent developments is the adoption of policies under Japanese Prime Minister Shinzo Abe aimed at eliminating deflation and restoring growth in Japan, which have come to be known as "Abenomics." These include the "three arrows" of easy monetary policy, "flexible" fiscal policy, and growth-oriented structural policies. In anticipation of aggressive monetary easing measures, the yen began to weaken and stock prices began to rise even before the implementation of a new monetary policy framework with an inflation target of 2 percent under the new BOJ Governor Haruhiko Kuroda in April 2013. The weaker yen helped Japanese export firms to raise yen-based profits and the higher stock prices helped to boost consumer spending. The government also announced a fiscal stimulus package worth about 1 percent of GDP, as well as a number of growth-oriented policies including participation in the Trans-Pacific Partnership negotiations and labor market reforms. The government attempts to tread a delicate path of steady fiscal consolidation to stabilize government debt levels while supporting self-sustaining growth of private domestic demand through implementation of the "third arrow"—structural policies—under the pressure of population aging.

The PRC authorities have recognized that its economy needs to migrate to a path of lower but higher-quality growth, of the order of 7.0–7.5 percent for the coming decade. The new government under President Xi Jinping and Premier Li Keqiang is expected to push forward a series of reforms to shift the economy to sustainable growth. Reforms will focus on six major areas, including cutting red tape to reduce the role of the government in the private sector, improving the fiscal system to rebalance the revenue-raising and expenditure responsibilities of central and local governments, a range of financial reforms, pricing reform for energy and resources, and giving migrant workers access to the same public services that are available to urban residents, in order to promote inclusive growth and urbanization (HSBC 2013). As with Abenomics, it is still too early to tell what the final results will be.

The Republic of Korea's recent growth performance has been mixed, as a strong rebound of 6.3 percent in 2010 was followed by a slowdown to only 2 percent growth in 2012. Consumption growth slowed markedly, while fixed capital investment fell in both 2011 and 2012. Economic growth would have been slower had it not been supported by a robust expansion of exports and a large increase in the current account surplus. There are concerns about continuing stagnation in the real estate market and the associated decline in CPI inflation, potentially building up deflationary pressures. Also, the Republic of Korea needs to improve its productivity and competitiveness. The prospect of rapid aging of the population also presents challenges for fiscal policy management.

ASEAN economies have fared relatively well in the post-crisis period, with an average growth rate of 4.5 percent in 2010–12. They face three major challenges—achieving deeper economic integration, raising competitiveness, and promoting sustainable and inclusive development. The ASEAN Economic Community (AEC) to be built by 2015 is a key institution for meeting these challenges. It will expand the economies of scale and accelerate investments in physical capital, technology, and people and thus sustain growth, productivity, and efficiency. Although the development gap between the more advanced economies and the less developed economies including Cambodia, Lao PDR, Myanmar, and Viet Nam is still large, the AEC can help narrow that gap.[3] For example, the share of the four less developed economies to total ASEAN GDP has increased from 3.4 percent in 1990 to 8.8 percent in 2013. Infrastructure connectivity across and within countries is vital in facilitating regional integration by reducing logistics and trade costs.

2.3 East Asia's Trade and Investment and Free-Trade Agreement Initiatives

2.3.1 *Trade Patterns*

Despite the global financial crisis, East Asia saw an expansion of trade within the region and with the rest of the world by more than 240 percent, from

---

[3] The four are referred to as the CLMV countries.

US$2.9 trillion in 2000 to US$9.9 trillion in 2012. As a result, East Asia's share in world trade has grown from 23 percent in 2000 to 31 percent in 2012. The expansion of East Asia's trade volume has nevertheless not been smooth, with considerably more volatility than GDP growth (see Figure 2.6). The crash of the dot-com bubble in 2000–1 led to the first contraction of both imports and exports and the subsequent decline of GDP growth in East Asia. Annual trade growth accelerated again in 2002 and remained above 15 percent for the period 2003 to 2008. East Asia consistently recorded a trade surplus, which widened until 2007 when exports exceeded imports by 14.5 percent.

Declines in GDP growth during the global financial crisis brought this upward trend to a sudden stop. Both exports and imports dropped in East Asia by more than 17.0 percent from 2008 to 2009, taking both flows back to lower levels than in 2007. The crisis also reduced the trade surplus from US$444 billion to US$319 billion. However, already in 2010 the region's trade rebounded strongly (by 30.0 percent) and outweighed the losses incurred in the previous year. In 2011, East Asia's trade further expanded by almost 20 percent. For the year 2012, trade growth significantly slowed down due to macroeconomic uncertainties and the recession in several European countries. As a result, during the years 2009 to 2012 East Asia's trade surplus remained rather small. In 2012 trade growth remained below GDP growth—as in 2001 and 2009—for the third time in the last twelve years (Figure 2.6).

It is revealing to go one level deeper and analyze how trade in goods has developed before, during, and after the crisis. Table 2.2 lists East Asia's export volumes with the regional economies, the US, the EU, and the rest of the world by commodity group for the years 1999–2000 to 2011–12. Based on the

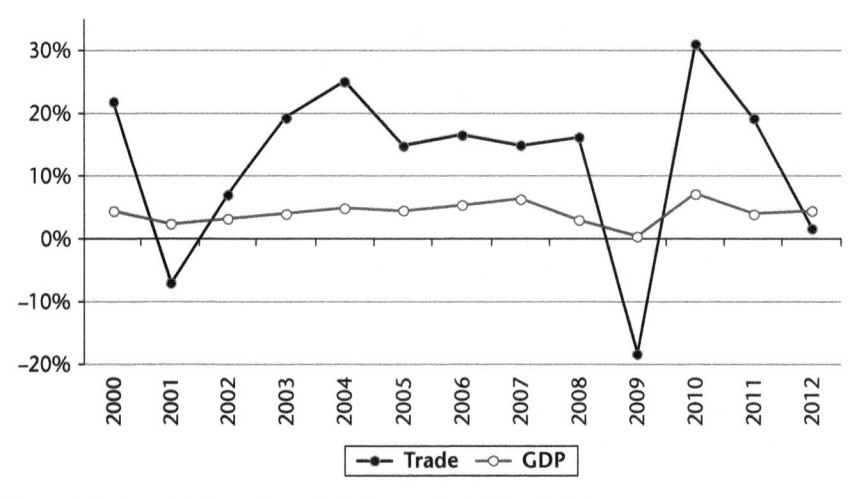

Figure 2.6. East Asia's trade and GDP growth, 2000–12 (%)
Source: Authors' calculations using UN Comtrade and World Bank WDI databases.

Table 2.2. Destination of East Asia's exports by stages of production, 1995–2012 (US$, % in parentheses)

Stages of production	Destination	1999–2000	2001–2	2003–4	2005–6	2007–8	2009–10	2011–12
Primary goods	East Asia	72.6 (64.1)	79.9 (64.7)	106.9 (63.6)	157.3 (62.7)	226.2 (60.7)	233.4 (61.5)	356.0 (64.0)
	US	9.4 (8.3)	9.6 (7.8)	12.6 (7.5)	19.6 (7.8)	25.3 (6.8)	23.6 (6.2)	29.0 (5.2)
	EU-27	8.8 (7.8)	9.1 (7.4)	12.5 (7.4)	18.8 (7.5)	30.8 (8.3)	28.9 (7.6)	36.3 (6.5)
	ROW	22.4 (19.8)	24.8 (20.1)	36.2 (21.5)	55.0 (21.9)	90.4 (24.3)	93.5 (24.6)	134.7 (24.2)
	Total	113.2 (8.1)	123.4 (8.5)	168.2 (8.3)	250.7 (8.9)	372.7 (10.0)	379.4 (10.1)	556.0 (11.2)
Intermediate goods	East Asia	333.8 (50.6)	363.3 (54.6)	547.7 (57.8)	745.3 (56.6)	947.4 (55.0)	973.4 (56.0)	1,285.5 (55.8)
	US	123.4 (18.7)	107.7 (16.2)	126.9 (13.4)	168.6 (12.8)	190.4 (11.0)	170.3 (9.8)	229.7 (10.0)
	EU-27	89 (13.5)	82.5 (12.4)	115.4 (12.2)	161.7 (12.3)	224.2 (13.0)	207.8 (12.0)	251.6 (10.9)
	ROW	113.4 (17.2)	112.2 (16.9)	158.0 (16.7)	240.2 (18.3)	361.4 (21.0)	386.7 (22.2)	535.9 (23.3)
	Total	659.6 (47.1)	665.7 (46.0)	948.0 (46.9)	1,315.8 (47.0)	1,723.4 (46.1)	1,738.2 (46.2)	2,302.7 (46.2)
Capital goods	East Asia	87.0 (31.0)	102.2 (35.4)	161.6 (38.3)	226.8 (37.6)	300.8 (36.7)	335.7 (39.1)	474.8 (42.1)
	US	75.1 (26.7)	71.8 (24.9)	94.5 (22.4)	128.4 (21.3)	148.5 (18.1)	144.0 (16.8)	182.8 (16.2)
	EU-27	58.4 (20.8)	58.9 (20.4)	83.1 (19.7)	121.0 (20.1)	167.2 (20.4)	154.3 (18.0)	176.5 (15.6)
	ROW	60.5 (21.5)	55.8 (19.3)	83.2 (19.7)	126.3 (21.0)	204.2 (24.9)	225.2 (26.2)	294.1 (26.1)
	Total	281.0 (20.1)	288.7 (20.0)	422.4 (20.9)	602.5 (21.5)	820.7 (22.0)	859.2 (22.8)	1128.2 (22.6)
Consumption goods	East Asia	82.8 (23.8)	91.6 (24.8)	122.4 (25.3)	147.6 (23.3)	193.4 (23.6)	203.2 (25.8)	271.4 (27.2)
	US	128.7 (37.0)	139.2 (37.7)	159.5 (32.9)	198.7 (31.4)	218.9 (26.7)	197.4 (25.1)	230.5 (23.1)
	EU-27	73.1 (21.0)	71.5 (19.4)	104.3 (21.5)	139.4 (22.0)	173.9 (21.2)	162.0 (20.6)	185.6 (18.6)
	ROW	62.8 (18.1)	66.5 (18.0)	98.5 (20.3)	146.9 (23.2)	232.5 (28.4)	224.1 (28.5)	310.2 (31.1)
	Total	347.4 (24.8)	368.8 (25.5)	484.7 (24.0)	632.6 (22.6)	818.7 (21.9)	786.7 (20.9)	997.7 (20.0)
All goods	East Asia	576.2 (41.1)	637.0 (44.0)	938.6 (46.4)	1,277.1 (45.6)	1,667.8 (44.6)	1,745.6 (46.4)	2,387.6 (47.9)
	US	336.6 (24.0)	328.4 (22.7)	393.5 (19.4)	515.3 (18.4)	583.2 (15.6)	535.4 (14.2)	672.1 (13.5)
	EU-27	229.4 (16.4)	221.9 (15.3)	315.3 (15.6)	440.8 (15.7)	596.1 (16.0)	553.0 (14.7)	650.0 (13.0)
	ROW	259.1 (18.5)	259.3 (17.9)	375.9 (18.6)	568.3 (20.3)	888.5 (23.8)	929.6 (24.7)	1,274.8 (25.6)
	Total	1,401.3 (100)	1,446.6 (100)	2,023.3 (100)	2,801.5 (100)	3,735.6 (100)	3,763.6 (100)	4,984.5 (100)

Note: Numbers in parentheses for East Asia, US, EU-27, and ROW are percentage (%) shares of the total of each category of goods. Numbers in parentheses for total are percentage (%) shares of the total of all goods.

Source: Authors' calculations using UN Comtrade data.

same data, Table 2.2 also shows the percentage shares of East Asia's exports for each of the four commodity groups with the four destinations, expressed in two-year averages. The commodity groups are based on the Broad Economic Categories (BEC) classification (developed by the United Nations) which classifies traded goods by stages of production. Primary goods include food and beverage, fuel, lubricants, and primary industrial supplies for industry. Intermediate goods include processed goods mainly for industry and parts and components for capital goods and transport equipment. Capital goods include machinery and equipment used by producers as inputs for production. Consumption goods are household goods and government final product purchases.

The first striking observation is that intermediate goods account for the lion's share of the region's exports. In 2011–12 intermediate goods represented almost 46 percent of all exports, whereas primary goods represented around 11 percent, capital goods 23 percent and consumption goods 20 percent. The share of intermediate goods in exports was even higher for intraregional trade. In 1999–2000 it stood at 51 percent of the total intermediate goods export and in 2011–12 it grew to almost 56 percent. The high level of intermediate goods exports clearly shows that the region has established itself as a "Factory Asia" (Baldwin 2006) with value chains that are well integrated across economies in the region.

One of the unique features of East Asian trade is the so-called "triangle trade" (Baldwin and Kawai 2013). This is where sophisticated parts and components are exported from industrialized to less industrialized nations in the region, and are then assembled into final goods for rich-nation markets. Although this started as a simple triangle, typically with goods exported from Japan to ASEAN (and more recently to the PRC as well) and then on to the US, Europe, and Japan, the pattern has become far richer. While the most sophisticated components still come from the advanced industrialized nations in the region, many parts and components are produced by the emerging market economies and sold to each other. As is known by now, this trade pattern has been created initially by FDI activities of global multinational corporations—Japanese, European, and the US—and more recently by firms from within emerging East Asia. In this context it is interesting to observe that the share of capital goods traded within East Asia has increased from 31 percent in 1999–2000 to almost 42 percent in 2011–12. "Factory Asia" seems to source its machinery increasingly from the region itself.

The table holds another interesting insight. When comparing the evolution of East Asia's exports in the four product groups during the last several years, one observes that intraregional exports continuously increased. The financial crisis slowed down intraregional biannual trade growth to a one-digit level compared to a solid two-digit level prior to the crisis. In contrast, exports to the EU and the US in all four commodity groups declined in 2009–10 to a similar extent. However, except for primary goods the rebound of exports in 2011–12 was more marked for the US than for the EU.

It appears that the EU had maintained its relative importance as East Asia's export destination until the global financial crisis, but its importance has since declined. In contrast, the US had substantially lost its importance as an export destination for East Asia well before the crisis, which only accelerated this declining trend. The last decade has seen a reduction in "triangle trade" and substantial diversification of East Asia's trade partners. The overall trade effect of the global financial crisis was thus that East Asia continued its regional economic integration through greater intraregional trade, whereas the US and EU lost part of their importance as export destinations.

This reorientation can be observed most strongly for capital goods, where East Asia increased its share of intraregional exports by 11.1 percentage points and of exports to the rest of the world by 4.6 percentage points. Today, the EU and the US hold a share of 31.8 percent compared to 47.5 percent in 1999–2000. In the case of intermediate goods, East Asia reduced its exports of intermediate goods to the US and the EU by over 11 percentage points and increased its exports within the region and toward the rest of the world by over 5 percentage points. Finally, for consumption goods the shares of these two exports markets decreased from 58.0 percent to 41.7 percent over the same time period, and East Asia increased exports to the rest of the world by 13 percentage points over the past twelve years. The global financial crisis has accelerated a decline in the importance of the US as an export destination for East Asia's exports and, together with the subsequent economic crisis in southern Europe, has led to a decline in the EU's share of East Asia's exports. These exports have been reoriented toward countries within the region and in the rest of the world.

2.3.2 Foreign Direct Investment in East Asia

FDI has historically played a key role in East Asian economic development. By attracting FDI, East Asian economies have been able to supplement domestic capital accumulation, absorb technology spillovers, and achieve rapid industrialization and economic growth. More recently, FDI has been instrumental in the development of Factory Asia. Growing outward FDI from the region to other parts of the world has been a relatively recent phenomenon, with the exception of Japan.

PATTERNS OF FDI IN EAST ASIA

In the past decade, both East Asia's inward and outward FDI have grown dramatically (see Figure 2.7). This reflects the region's continued attractiveness as a destination for FDI, as well as its rising importance as a source of FDI

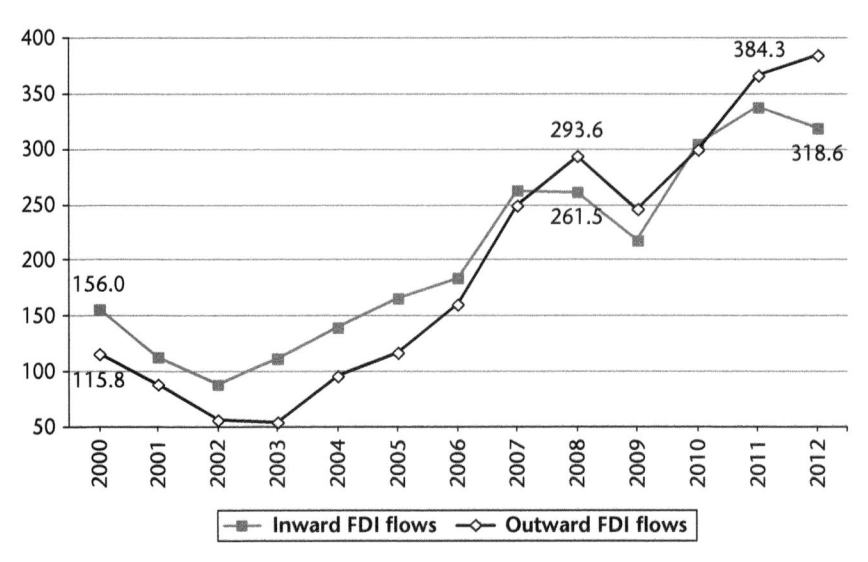

Figure 2.7. East Asia's foreign direct investment flows, 2000–12 (US$ billion)
Source: Authors' calculations using UNCTAD FDI database.

for the global economy. Between 2000 and 2012, the annual flows of inward FDI to East Asia increased by more than 100 percent, from US$156 billion to US$319 billion. Even more striking was the rise of outward FDI, which over the same time period leaped by more than 230 percent, from US$116 billion to US$384 billion, overtaking inward FDI in 2008.

The upward march of FDI activity in East Asia did not by any means follow a steady drumbeat. Just as previously observed with trade flows, East Asia's FDI flows were punctuated by the boom-and-bust cycles of the global economy. In the run up to the 2000–1 dot-com crash and the 2007–9 global financial crisis, both inward and outward FDI could be seen to rise in tandem before collapsing as the global economy stuttered. It appears that outward FDI rises more sharply than inward FDI during booms.

Between 2003 and 2007, outward FDI grew at nearly twice the rate of inward FDI, rising at a frenetic annual average of 47 percent as compared to inward FDI's very respectable 24 percent. In the onset of the global financial crisis, inward FDI was first to dip (−0.4 percent), and outward FDI continued to grow at a decelerated pace (17.8 percent). Both forms of FDI activity fell in 2009 to a similar extent (16–17 percent). In the subsequent rebound, outward FDI was slower to rally, but when it did it accelerated faster than inward FDI (22 percent versus 11 percent per annum). Finally, in 2012 there was a repeat of the 2008 trend—that is, while inward FDI fell (−6 percent) outward FDI continued to grow, though at a decelerated pace (5 percent).

Noting that the economic shocks over the past twelve years originated in two of the major source economies of FDI to East Asia, it may not be surprising that inward FDI closely followed the economic situation in these economies. However, the observed lag in the region's outward FDI in reaction to external disturbances, as well as its buoyancy, might indicate that the regional economies are rising in resilience to external shocks. Taking the analysis a step deeper to look at the sources and destinations of East Asia's FDI, one can observe that the traditional East Asian FDI patterns are rapidly evolving.

SOURCES AND DESTINATIONS OF FDI

Table 2.3 summarizes the sources and destinations of East Asia's greenfield FDI as a share of total flows. As in trade shares, two-year averages are again used, but for simplicity only key periods are displayed in the table. Looking at the first three columns, we observe that intraregional FDI is the single largest source of FDI for East Asia compared to the FDI flows coming from the EU, the US and the rest of the world.

Furthermore, the share of intraregional FDI has been continuously growing: Between 2003–04 and 2011–12, East Asia's intraregional share of inward FDI expanded by 2.6 percent points from 34.9 percent to 37.5 percent. Over the same time period, the EU-27's share of East Asia's inward FDI followed a V-shaped trajectory, falling from 28.3 percent to 23.2 percent before rebounding to 28.0 percent. In contrast, the US share of East Asia's inward FDI continued to decline over the sample period, falling from 22.6 percent to 17.8 percent. The economic uncertainties in the Eurozone may have prompted several EU economies to reorient a greater share of their FDI to East Asia, in order to take advantage of the more favorable growth prospects in the region. Conversely, in the aftermath of the financial crisis, the US may have sought to refocus investments in its domestic economy.[4]

Table 2.3. Sources and destinations of East Asia's foreign direct investment flows, 2003–12 (% of total)

Partner economy	Share of inward FDI to East Asia			Share of outward FDI from East Asia		
	2003–04	2007–08	2011–12	2003–04	2007–08	2011–12
East Asia	34.9	35.4	37.5	54.3	51.3	41.3
EU-27	28.3	23.2	28.0	6.6	7.3	13.4
US	22.6	20.7	17.8	6.4	3.7	8.7
ROW	14.3	20.6	16.8	32.7	37.7	36.7
Total	100.0	100.0	100.0	100.0	100.0	100.0

Note: Data captures only greenfield investments.
Source: Authors' calculations using FDI Markets data.

---

[4] According to FDI Markets data, between 2007–8 and 2011–12, the share of US investments in its domestic economy as a percentage of FDI outflows rose from 32.9% to 44.5%.

Another insight from the table is that regional economies are still the preferred destinations for FDI originating from East Asia, accounting for 41 percent of outward FDI. However, this has been decreasing. Between 2003–4 and 2011–12, East Asia's share of the region's outward FDI fell by 13 percent points. This indicates greater diversification of East Asia's outward FDI to extraregional economies. The largest beneficiary of East Asia's reorientation is the EU. Over the sample period, the EU-27 more than doubled their share from 6.6 percent to 13.4 percent (an increase of 6.8 percentage points), while the US and the rest of the world increased their shares by 2.3 percentage points (to 8.7 percent) and 4.0 percentage points (to 36.7 percent) respectively. It is noteworthy that East Asia's outward FDI had already been trending toward extraregional destinations and the recent economic shocks have not reversed this trend.

What might be the driver for East Asia's outward FDI? The traditional motivations for FDI include accessing markets and taking advantage of lower factor costs. More recently, South–North FDI has also been associated with the extension of upstream control over value chains and acquisition of new technology (Rasiah et al. 2010).

Overall, the EU and US may be diminishing in importance as sources of FDI for East Asia, while intraregional FDI has been rising in prominence. As East Asian countries diversify their outward FDI toward extraregional destinations, the EU and US have received an increasing share of FDI from the region. While the global and European financial crises have not reversed these trends, the difficulties in Europe may have prompted a reorientation of EU FDI to East Asia.

2.3.3 *East Asia's Free-Trade Agreements*

The reorientation of East Asia's trade and investment flows can be explained to a certain extent by the spread of free-trade agreements in the region. FTAs were largely absent in East Asia until the turn of the millennium. As Figure 2.8 shows, the number of concluded FTAs in East Asia as a group rose from only three to twenty-two between 2000 and 2005 and further to sixty-nine in 2012. Of these, sixty-four FTAs are currently in effect. This figure compares with 266 worldwide according to the World Trade Organization's (WTO's) counting.

The global financial crisis appears not to have affected the spread of FTAs in the region, which can be explained by different factors. First, it usually requires several years to negotiate an FTA. Second, the impact of a downward economic swing on the negotiations is rather unclear. On the one hand, it might delay the negotiations as more urgent economic policy decisions need to be made. On the other hand, an economic downturn might accelerate the negotiations in order to provide fresh impetus for the economy through trade expansion.

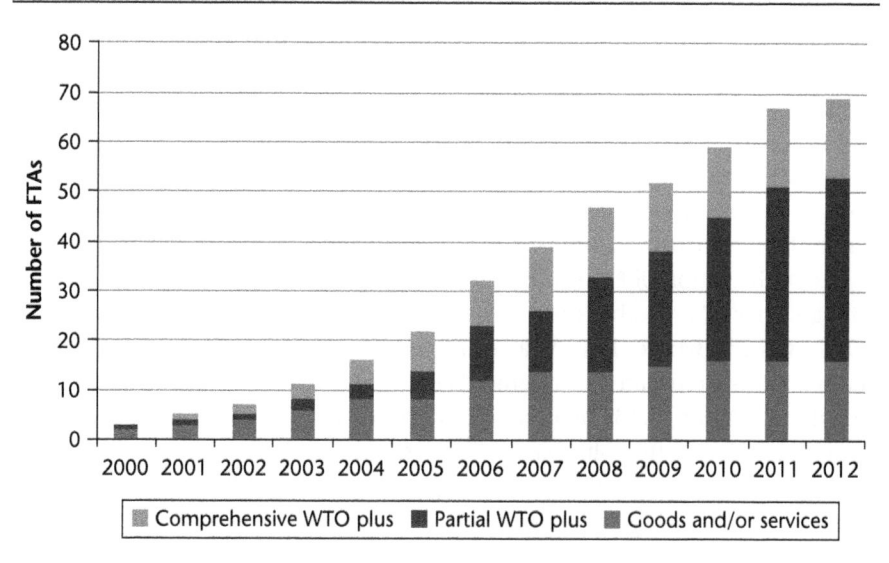

Figure 2.8. Scope of concluded FTAs in East Asia total, 2000–12 (no. of FTAs)
FTA = free-trade agreement.
Source: Baldwin and Kawai (2013); ADB, Asian Regional Integration Center (ARIC Website).

SCOPE OF FTAs

Figure 2.8 shows the number and scope of FTAs in East Asia concluded between 2000 and 2012. To assess the scope, all FTAs are divided into three categories: (i) narrow agreements that deal with goods and/or services only; (ii) somewhat broader agreements covering goods, services, and some Singapore issues ("partial WTO-plus");[5] and (iii) comprehensive agreements covering goods, services, and all four Singapore issues ("comprehensive WTO-plus"). Those FTAs shown in categories (ii) and (iii) may be considered WTO-plus FTAs. The scope of concluded agreements reflects a combination of economic interests, competitiveness strength, and negotiation capacity.

It is striking that early East Asian FTAs seemed to be concerned largely with goods and services. From the mid-2000s onward, however, significantly more emphasis was given to broader agreements with WTO-plus elements. Interestingly, with the onset of the financial crisis in 2007, almost all new FTAs went beyond liberalizing goods and services. The share of the first category stagnated, whereas partial and comprehensive WTO-plus FTAs continued to grow. By 2012, 16 FTAs (23 percent of the total) were goods and/or services only, 37 FTAs (54 percent) were partial WTO-plus, and 16 FTAs (23 percent) were comprehensive WTO-plus. This shift toward more wide-ranging agreements

---

[5] Singapore issues include investment, trade facilitation, competition policy, and government procurement.

might reflect the need for deeper integration to further stimulate trade and growth when faced with uncertain economic prospects. For example, competition policy and investment provisions are integral ingredients in facilitating FDI flows and the development of supply chains. Inclusion of provisions on trade facilitation and logistics development would help lower transaction costs in conducting trade. Cooperation provisions are intended to stimulate technology transfer and industrial competitiveness.

The proliferation of FTAs in East Asia is likely to be sustained. It is estimated that another 87 are either under negotiation or proposed (Baldwin and Kawai 2013). On the whole, East Asia seems to be opting for bilateral rather than more complex plurilateral agreements because the former tend to be easier to negotiate.[6] As of 2013, bilateral FTAs comprised 76 percent of East Asia's concluded FTAs, while plurilateral FTAs comprised the remainder.

The most important bilateral FTA negotiations in East Asia in terms of economic weight take place among the PRC, Japan, and the Republic of Korea. The PRC–Republic of Korea FTA negotiations were officially launched in May 2012 and the first stage of the negotiations (modalities) was completed in September 2013. In the second-phase negotiations the two countries are reported to have agreed in principle on trade liberalization in 2014. In contrast to these fast-advancing negotiations, the Japan–Republic of Korea FTA negotiations have not made much progress since they started in October 2003. The official negotiations were suspended in November 2004 and since then no bilateral negotiation has taken place. However, negotiations on a trilateral FTA among the PRC, Japan, and the Republic of Korea started in November 2012. Once concluded, the trilateral FTA would cover 70 percent of Asia's GDP and 20 percent of the world's total. The second round of the trilateral FTA talks was held in August 2013. The negotiations could take a few years given the size of the involved countries and their divergent interests. It is noteworthy to mention that these negotiations have been held despite long-standing territorial and history issues which could potentially hamper economic cooperation.

RCEP AND TPP

The most comprehensive plurilateral agreements currently under negotiation in the region are the ASEAN Framework for a Regional Comprehensive Economic Partnership (RCEP) and the Trans-Pacific Partnership (TPP) Agreement.

East Asian countries agreed to begin negotiations for an RCEP among the ASEAN+6 countries (the ten ASEAN member countries plus Australia, the PRC, India, Japan, the Republic of Korea, and New Zealand). The first negotiation

---

[6] Bilateral FTAs refer to agreements between two countries. Plurilateral FTAs involve more than two countries, or one or more countries and a trading bloc (such as ASEAN), or two trading blocs (such as ASEAN and EFTA). See also Baldwin and Kawai (2013).

started in November 2012 with the aim of completion by the end of 2015. The RCEP covers trade in goods and services, investment, economic and technical cooperation, intellectual property, competition, dispute settlement, and other issues. The intention of the participating countries is that it should have broader and deeper engagement than the existing ASEAN+1 FTAs.[7] Numerical results by Kawai and Wignaraja (2008) based on a computable general equilibrium (CGE) model show that the ASEAN+6 FTA scenario would offer large gains to world income, while the losses to non-members (such as the US) would be relatively small.

The TPP started as the Pacific Four (P4) Agreement, a plurilateral FTA among Brunei Darussalam, Chile, New Zealand, and Singapore that came into force in May 2006.[8] Since the US announced in 2008 its intent to begin comprehensive negotiations with the P4 economies to join the agreement, seven more countries—Australia, Canada, Japan, Malaysia, Mexico, Peru, and Viet Nam have joined the talks. Under the current membership TPP would cover 41 percent of world GDP and 12 percent of world trade. In September 2013, the Republic of Korea announced its interest in joining the negotiations. There has also been speculation about the PRC expressing interest in joining the TPP negotiations. If the Republic of Korea and the PRC were both to join TPP, then the trade deal would cover more than half of world GDP and the trade share would increase to 24 percent.

The goal of the TPP would be to achieve a comprehensive twenty-first century FTA covering not only goods tariff reductions and services trade liberalization but also a large number of WTO-plus issues, such as investment, public procurement, competition policy (including state-owned enterprise reform), environmental and labor standards, intellectual property, sanitary and phytosanitary measures, and technical barriers to trade. Regarding market access, in principle all tariffs are to be eliminated. Non-tariff barriers to trade would be substantially reduced and behind-the-border regulatory reforms would be pursued to make domestic markets open and transparent.

2.4 Regional Financial Cooperation

Regional financial cooperation has been pursued in East Asia on three fronts: (i) regional economic surveillance (under the Economic Review and Policy Dialogue (ERPD) supported by the ASEAN+3 Macroeconomic Research Office

---

[7] Existing ASEAN+1 FTAs refer to the ASEAN's FTAs with Australia–New Zealand, the PRC, India, Japan, and the Republic of Korea.
[8] The agreement eliminated 90% of all tariffs among member economies upon entry into force and will completely eliminate all trade tariffs by 2015.

(AMRO)); (ii) regional short-term liquidity support facility (the Chiang Mai Initiative (CMI)); and (iii) local currency bond market development.

2.4.1 ERPD and AMRO

The ERPD was introduced in 2000 as a regional economic surveillance process to promote macroeconomic and financial stability in the region, particularly to prepare liquidity assistance under the CMI. It was designed to prevent financial crises through the early detection of irregularities, vulnerabilities, and systemic risks and the swift implementation of remedial policy actions. It was intended to facilitate analysis of economic and financial conditions of the global, regional, and individual economies; monitoring of regional capital flows and financial market developments; and provision of policy recommendations for undertaking necessary national policies as well as joint actions on issues affecting the regional economies. The expectation was that countries would implement better macroeconomic and financial sector policy at the national level as a result of peer pressure, and would pursue policy coordination if needed.

Without strong supporting institutions for regional surveillance, however, the ERPD process was not as successful as initially expected, although gradual improvements were made over time. Another problem was the absence of central bank governors in the process, even though central bank contribution to the process was considered necessary.[9] Recognizing these problems, the ASEAN+3 authorities created the AMRO, a surveillance unit in charge of regional economic surveillance, in Singapore and replaced the finance ministers' meetings by joint meetings for both the finance ministers and the central bank governors starting in May 2012.

The ERPD is now considered an integral part of the Chiang Mai Initiative Multilateralization (CMIM), a multilateralized version of the regional short-term liquidity facility. AMRO's task is to enhance the effectiveness of the surveillance mechanism and the decision-making process for the CMIM.

To play a significant role for the CMIM, AMRO aims to become strong in its surveillance function and build technical competence in establishing the pre-qualification criteria of CMIM crisis prevention and management function. AMRO has made good progress in its initial years of operation. Nonetheless, AMRO does not seem to have sufficient resources and has yet to establish a long-term development plan, clear targets and milestones. Once AMRO is able

---

[9] Accordingly, central bank deputy governors were brought in to the ASEAN+3 finance deputies' meetings. Central bank governors in the region have been collaborating with each other through the Executives' Meeting of Asia-Pacific Central Banks (EMEAP), which is separate from the ASEAN+3 finance ministers' process.

to achieve appropriate levels of technical capabilities and credibility, it can serve CMIM as a credible secretariat.

AMRO will have to work closely with the Asian Development Bank (ADB) and the IMF. The ADB provides technical inputs into the ERPD process of the ASEAN+3 finance ministers and central bank governors. The IMF will also have to be involved if a large-scale financial crisis breaks out, as the required resources will likely be far greater than those provided by the CMIM and bilateral financing assistance. AMRO may also wish to build good working contacts with other relevant agencies, such as the BIS, the World Bank, the ASEAN Secretariat and bilateral donor agencies.

2.4.2 Chiang Mai Initiative and its Multilateralization

CHIANG MAI INITIATIVE

The Chiang Mai Initiative is a regional short-term liquidity support facility intended to prevent and manage currency crises or crisis contagion. It started as a combination of (i) a network of bilateral swap agreements (BSAs) among the Plus Three countries—the PRC, Japan, and the Republic of Korea—and between one of these Plus Three countries and selected ASEAN members and (ii) the ASEAN Swap Arrangement (ASA).

The CMI was designed as a regional liquidity support facility to provide short-term US dollar liquidity to any of its member countries experiencing a balance of payment crisis. It was intended to supplement the existing international financial arrangements and was designed to be closely linked to the IMF (see below). Because of this, the US and the IMF cautiously welcomed the initiative. The representative of the US Treasury at the ADB Annual Meeting noted that a regional initiative such as the CMI could be constructive if it were supportive of prompt financial and economic adjustment. An IMF representative also welcomed the CMI's intention to work with the IMF.[10] The total amount of swaps under the CMI, before its multilateralization, was US$90 billion. The various bilateral amounts are shown in Figure 2.9.

An important feature of the CMI was that crisis-affected members requesting short-term liquidity support could immediately obtain financial assistance up to an amount equivalent to 10 percent (later raised to 20 percent) of the maximum amount that could be borrowed, and that the remainder was to be provided to the requesting member under an IMF program.[11] Thus the CMI was closely linked with an IMF program and its conditionality. The CMI's link with the IMF was designed to address the concern that the liquidity shortage

---

[10] See Henning (2002), Chapter 3.
[11] This portion of the CMI that could be mobilized without involving the IMF was called the IMF-delinked portion. It was set initially at 10% and was raised to 20% in May 2005.

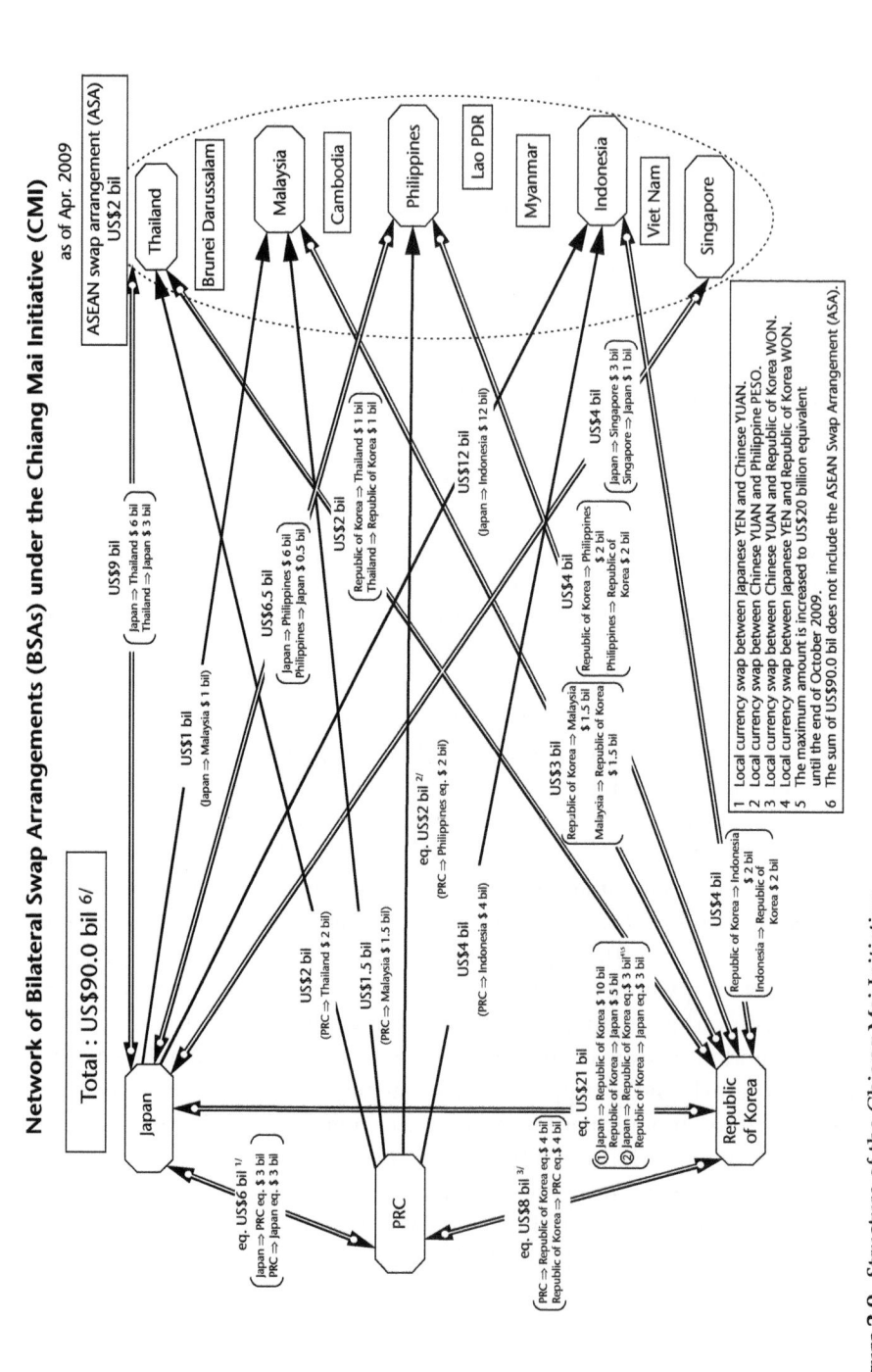

Figure 2.9. Structure of the Chiang Mai Initiative

Source: Ministry of Finance, Japan.

of a requesting country might be due to fundamental policy problems, rather than a temporary liquidity shortage, and that the potential moral hazard problem could be significant in the absence of rigorous conditionality. Essentially, the CMI was intended to be used for crisis lending and hence required conditionality. The perceived lack of the region's capacity to formulate and enforce effective adjustment programs in times of crisis was a major reason for requiring the CMI to be linked to IMF programs.[12]

CHIANG MAI INITIATIVE MULTILATERALIZATION
Given the cumbersome nature of the multiplicity of bilateral agreements it was decided to multilateralize the CMI, in the form of a self-managed reserve pooling arrangement governed by a single contractual agreement. Negotiations to finalize the CMIM were not straightforward, particularly on member contributions and voting weights.[13] However, these were mostly concluded by May 2009 with some final revisions in 2010. The CMIM came into effect and replaced the CMI in March 2010.[14] The member contributions, purchasing multiples,[15] borrowing limits, and voting weights are summarized in Table 2.4.

The total size of the CMIM was set initially at US$120 billion, with 80 percent contributed by the Plus Three countries and 20 percent by ASEAN countries. In May 2012, the CMIM was further modified. The size was doubled to US$240 billion, with the same contribution shares, purchasing multiples and voting weights as in the table. The IMF-delinked portion was raised to 30 percent of a country's quota, with a target of 40 percent to be achieved in the future. The maturity of the swap was set at one year for the IMF-linked portion with two possible renewals, and six months with three renewals for the IMF-delinked portion. This swap, called the CMIM Stability Facility (CMIM-SF), was intended for crisis response. At the same time, to address the concern that the CMI was ineffective in preventing a currency crisis, a crisis prevention facility, called the CMIM Precautionary Line (CMIM-PL), was

---

[12] Japan and the PRC, as potential creditor countries, argued that the CMI's IMF link was essential. Some potential borrower members, such as Malaysia, argued that the CMI should not be linked to IMF programs. In the end, the intent of potential creditor members prevailed.

[13] Japan and the PRC worked together, despite their rivalry, in the process of establishing the CMIM. In deciding on the financial contribution among the CMIM members, upon which the borrowing ceiling and voting shares were determined, the Japanese and PRC authorities, after long and protracted negotiations, agreed to contribute the same amount (32%) with the premise that the PRC's contribution included Hong Kong, China's 3.5%. Both Japan (whose contribution share exceeded the PRC's share, excluding Hong Kong, China, of 28.5%) and the PRC (which with Hong Kong, China secured the same share as Japan's), along with the Republic of Korea (which obtained a 16% contribution share in the CMIM, much larger than its economic weight), achieved their respective objectives after this remarkable political compromise. See Kawai (2014).

[14] However, the ASEAN Swap Arrangement components of the CMI remained in force.

[15] A member's contribution times its purchasing multiple equals the maximum amount that it can draw from the CMIM.

Table 2.4. Financial contributions and voting powers under the Chiang Mai Initiative Multilateralization

Members	Financial contributions US$ billion (%)	Purchasing multiple	Borrowing limits US$ billion (%)	Voting powers (%)
Plus Three	192.0 (80.00)		115.2 (47.72)	71.59
PRC	76.8 (32.00)		38.4 (15.91)	28.41
PRC excl. Hong Kong, China	68.4 (28.50)	0.5	34.2 (14.17)	25.43
Hong Kong, China	8.4 (3.50)	2.5	4.2 (1.74)	2.98
Japan	76.8 (32.00)	0.5	38.4 (15.91)	28.41
Republic of Korea	38.4 (16.00)	1.0	38.4 (15.91)	14.77
ASEAN	48.0 (20.00)		126.2 (52.28)	28.41
Brunei Darussalam	0.06 (0.025)	5.0	0.30 (0.12)	1.16
Cambodia	0.24 (0.100)	5.0	1.20 (0.50)	1.22
Indonesia	9.104 (3.793)	2.5	22.76 (9.43)	4.37
Lao PDR	0.06 (0.025)	5.0	0.30 (0.12)	1.16
Malaysia	9.104 (3.793)	2.5	22.76 (9.43)	4.37
Myanmar	0.12 (0.050)	5.0	0.60 (0.25)	1.18
Philippines	9.104 (3.793)	2.5	22.76 (9.43)	4.37
Singapore	9.104 (3.793)	2.5	22.76 (9.43)	4.37
Thailand	9.104 (3.793)	2.5	22.76 (9.43)	4.37
Viet Nam	2.00 (0.833)	5.0	10.00 (4.14)	1.85
ASEAN+3 Total	240.0 (100.00)		241.4 (100.00)	100.00

Source: The Joint Ministerial Statement of the 13th ASEAN+3 Finance Ministers' Meeting, May 2, 2010, Tashkent, Uzbekistan; ADB.

adopted, again with a maturity of six months for the IMF-delinked portion and one year for the IMF-linked portion, with a maximum duration of two years for both cases. The qualification criteria were based on five policy areas: (i) external position and market access, (ii) fiscal policy, (iii) monetary policy, (iv) financial sector soundness and supervision, and (v) data adequacy. A country cannot draw on CMIM-SF and CMIM-PL at the same time, and the maximum drawing in either case is the country's swap quota.

The maximum quota that a country can draw from the CMIM equals its contribution multiplied by its purchasing multiple. The voting weights are determined by giving each country 1.6 basic votes plus the number of votes equal to the number of billions of US dollars that it contributes to the pool. Consensus is required for fundamental issues, such as size, contribution, purchasing multiples, membership, and terms of swaps. Swap issues, including approval of swap, renewal, and default, are to be decided by two-thirds weighted majority vote.

Even with the increase in the size of CMIM and the IMF-delinked portion, the delinked amount available to a country is unlikely to be sufficient for either crisis response or prevention. For example, the delinked amounts available for Thailand and the Republic of Korea would be US$9.01 billion and US$15.36 billion, respectively, even if the delinked portion were to be raised to 40 percent. These are small compared to the IMF package of US$17.2 billion that Thailand obtained in 1997, or compared to the bilateral swap arrangement of US$30 billion that the Republic of Korea secured from the US Federal Reserve during the global financial crisis.[16] So for the current structure of CMIM to be effective, the IMF-linked portion would have to be mobilized, but this raises the issue of "IMF stigma" which made CMI ineffective during the global financial crisis. A redesign of the IMF link is needed if CMIM is to become more useful to countries in the region.

CMIM could be redesigned as an integrated crisis prevention (provision of temporary foreign exchange liquidity support) and crisis response (for cases of currency crises requiring strong macroeconomic adjustment policies) mechanism. One reform idea would be to provide CMIM liquidity to a country, facing temporary foreign exchange liquidity shortage such as an unexpected episode of rapid short-term capital outflows, without any IMF link or conditionality up to the full amount of the country's swap quota, if the country passed the CMIM pre-qualification criteria. Quick access to a sufficient amount of swap line is important to gain market confidence and stabilize the situation—as happened in the Republic of Korea during the global financial crisis. If the problem persisted after using the CMIM swap for (say) six months, then it would be likely to be a crisis situation rather than a temporary liquidity shortage, and thus policy adjustments might be required.[17] Removing the IMF link altogether would make it much more attractive for countries to access the full amount of the CMIM swap.

The IMF could be invited when it became apparent that the situation was not a temporary liquidity shortage but rather a currency crisis requiring both larger amounts of liquidity support than those provided under the CMIM and also significant macroeconomic policy adjustments. If the required liquidity support were small and within the swap limit, then CMIM support should be provided to an eligible country without involving the IMF but with macroeconomic policy conditions. Only when the crisis were large-scale or covered multiple countries would CMIM be advised to work with the IMF. In this way CMIM would be the first line of defense for temporary foreign exchange liquidity shortage problems and small currency crises requiring macroeconomic policy adjustments, with the IMF joining to deal with large-scale crisis situations.

In a currency crisis, the issue of policy conditions would arise. Here, the current voting weights might need to be adjusted. The decision rule is a two-

---

[16] See Park and Song in this volume on the Republic of Korea's swap arrangement with the US Federal Reserve.
[17] The period before macroeconomic policy adjustments were required could be decided appropriately.

thirds weighted majority. Presently, the Plus Three countries have 71.6 percent of the votes (Table 2.4).

2.4.3 Asian Bond Market Development

LOCAL-CURRENCY BOND MARKETS FOR ASIAN ECONOMIES

It was the 1997–8 Asian financial crisis that made the region's policymakers and market participants fully acknowledge the importance of local-currency bond markets in East Asia. Previously, East Asian economies excluding Japan had depended on foreign currency-denominated short-term loans to fund long-term domestic investment, thus giving rise to a "double mismatch" problem (both a currency and a maturity mismatch). Consequently, once foreign loans were not rolled over, the value of East Asian economies' currencies started to decline sharply, causing currency crises. Policymakers and market participants came to recognize the need to create a balanced financial system by developing markets for local currency-denominated long-term bonds, thereby channeling the region's savings into long-term investment in the region. It was also believed that such a mechanism would help resolve the double mismatch problem faced by these East Asian economies, and remedy their financial systems' excessive reliance on banks.

There are four other reasons why the bond market has taken on greater importance for East Asia in recent years. First, the dynamic economic growth in emerging East Asia—such as the PRC and ASEAN member states—is expected to require large funding for corporate investment, thereby raising the role played by bond markets. Second, because it is becoming increasingly important to invest in Asian infrastructure projects for development, environmental preservation, and disaster risk preparedness, bond markets have a meaningful role to play in facilitating fundraising throughout the region. Third, multinational corporations—particularly Japanese and the Republic of Korea—setting up operations in emerging East Asian economies can rely on bond markets to raise long-term funds in local currencies. Fourth, bond markets are gaining importance as a venue for relatively secure long-term investment of assets when these economies are establishing pension management and insurance institutions, and the expanding numbers of middle-income earners have been accumulating wealth.

According to ADB and ADBI (2009), Asian demand for infrastructure development—including energy, transportation, telecommunication, and water and sanitation systems—is expected to total US$8.3 trillion between 2010 and 2020, which amounts to about US$750 billion annually. Given the need to invest not only in infrastructure but also in environmental preservation and in projects to build a low-carbon and disaster-proof economy in emerging East Asia, a very large amount of development funds will need to be raised. While it is essential to obtain funding from official sources, public funds alone will not suffice, making private-sector participation indispensable, particularly through bond markets.

DEVELOPMENT OF THE ASIAN BOND MARKET

To date, steady progress has been achieved in the development and deepening of the Asian bond market. This is supported by both the Asian Bond Markets Initiative (ABMI) and the Asian Bond Funds (ABF) project.[18] The former represents an initiative undertaken by finance ministers of ASEAN+3 countries, while the latter has been undertaken by the Executives' Meeting of the East Asia-Pacific Central Banks (EMEAP), an organization made up of eleven central banks in East Asia and the Pacific.

Significant headway was made by the EMEAP which set up the ABF, with the objective of creating an environment to help private-sector financial institutions introduce investment trusts tracking the Asian bond market. Another initiative that has achieved progress is the task of establishing the Credit Guarantee and Investment Facility (CGIF) under the ABMI's policy efforts. Its objective is to provide credit enhancement to corporate issuers with weak, but investment-grade credit ratings in the East Asian region. The launch of the CGIF is designed to boost the issuance of corporate bonds, thus facilitating increased activity in the primary corporate bond market.

These policy efforts have contributed to the expansion of the primary market for sovereign bonds and quasi-sovereign bonds, allowing market participants to construct a benchmark yield curve. However, the development of corporate bond markets is lagging behind. Figure 2.10 plots data available for local currency-denominated corporate bonds outstanding as a percentage of GDP for 2011 around the world, including the OECD countries and major emerging economies (vertical axis) against per capita GDP for the same year (horizontal axis). The center line represents the average for all sample economies and dotted lines show one standard deviation, upward and downward, from the average. These lines indicate that the higher the per capita income level of an economy, the deeper is its corporate bond market. They also

---

[18] The Asian Bond Markets Initiative (ABMI) was adopted in August 2003 under the auspices of the ASEAN+3 finance ministers to develop local-currency denominated bonds. The EMEAP-led central bank process launched ABF programs to facilitate local-currency bond market development, particularly its ABF-2 in 2004. Two notable developments have been made under the ABMI. First, the ASEAN+3 Bond Market Forum, comprising bond market experts from the region, was launched in September 2010 as a common platform to foster standardization of market practices and harmonization of regulations on cross-border bond transactions in the region. Second, the Credit Guarantee and Investment Facility (CGIF) was set up as a trust fund of the ADB with an initial capital of US$700 million in November 2010, with the objective of boosting local-currency corporate bond markets through providing credit enhancement for corporate issuers having weak but investment-grade credit ratings who would otherwise have difficulty tapping local bond markets.

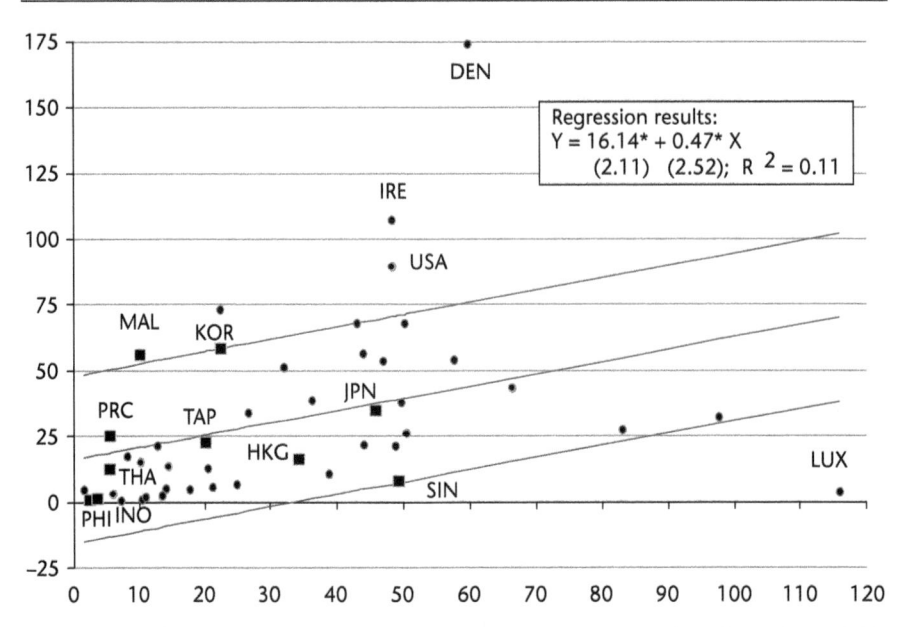

Figure 2.10. Development and deepening of Asian corporate bond markets, 2011 (% of GDP)

Source: Constructed by the authors using data from BIS, IMF.

highlight that the size of the bond market in the Republic of Korea and Malaysia is significantly greater than the sample average, while countries like India, Indonesia, and the Philippines are trailing behind the international average. Thus even though the Asian bond markets have developed significantly to date, the level of corporate bond market development still varies greatly from one economy to another.

Another notable feature is that the level of cross-border bond transactions conducted within East Asia is extremely low. Data for 2011, displayed in Figure 2.11, show that the majority of cross-border bond transactions undertaken by East Asian investors were for investment in North American and European bonds, with a mere 30 percent for investment in Asian bonds. This is because the Japanese investors, the biggest in the region, were much less active investing in emerging East Asian bonds. This is in stark contrast to the situation in Europe, where close to 70 percent of cross-border bond investment was made in European bonds. While Asia's percentage of intraregional bond investment compares favorably with that of North America (21 percent), it should be noted that in North America, US bond investors' exposure to Canada and Mexico is relatively low as US investment is global. Overall, while intra-Asian bond investment has increased in recent years, it has yet to reach a meaningful level, leaving a significant potential upside for the coming years.

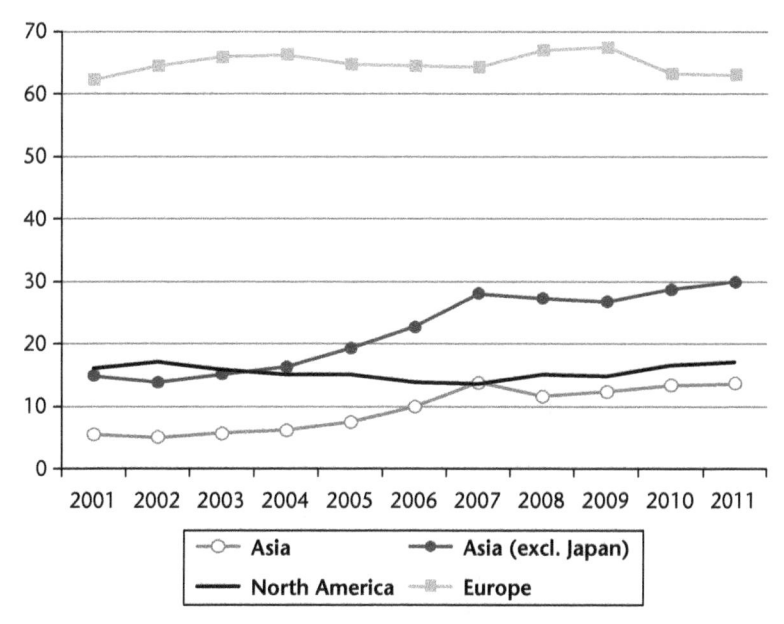

Figure 2.11. Share of intraregional portfolio investment in debt (%)
Source: Coordinated Portfolio Investment Survey (CPIS), IMF (2013).

BOND MARKET COOPERATION IN EAST ASIA

Regional financial cooperation aimed at developing the Asian bond market has, to date, been driven by public-sector groups such as the ASEAN+3 finance ministries and the EMEAP central banks. Going forward, however, efforts to strengthen financial cooperation will have to be undertaken mainly by private-sector entities (issuers, investors, intermediary firms, securities exchanges, and credit rating agencies). The newly launched ASEAN+3 Bond Market Forum is expected to play an important role in this respect.

One challenge that will need to be addressed is the promotion of bond market integration in the East Asian region. For this purpose, a series of measures are needed such as expanding corporate bond markets, diversifying the investor base to bring in market liquidity, liberalizing cross-border capital transactions, and strengthening and harmonizing market infrastructure such as regulations, rules, and practices. In particular, it will be essential for capital flow regulations and foreign exchange controls to be relaxed, and for rules, systems, and accepted market practices to be harmonized.

Further progress is needed to build a market infrastructure for cross-border securities settlement, which so far has been conducted by international operators (such as Euroclear and Clearstream) as well as by US and European financial institutions that provide global custodian services. While such conventional international settlement methods are efficient, Asian investors are exposed to significant risk—known as Herstatt Risk—arising from time zone differences. Indeed, it is challenging to recover money from a counterparty financial institution that has run into financial difficulties or gone bankrupt during the creditor's non-business hours. Given the expected large volume of cross-border securities transactions conducted within East Asia, it will be desirable to establish a system across East Asia that will allow investors to settle cross-border securities transactions during business hours.[19]

2.5 Exchange Rate Policy in East Asia

2.5.1 Exchange Rate Regimes

East Asia exhibits a rich set of diverse foreign exchange rate regimes. As shown in Table 2.5, according to the IMF survey of the East Asian exchange rate regime in 2012 the spectrum ranges from the US dollar peg of Hong Kong, China at one end to free floating of Japan at the other. In between there are other types of intermediate regimes chosen by different economies.

Movements of the exchange rates—in both nominal and real effective terms—of these economies have displayed considerable divergence. Independently of their chosen exchange rate regimes, however, many of these economies have managed to accumulate sizeable current account surpluses.

From the early 1990s the total surplus of ASEAN+3 as a whole soared to reach almost 7 percent of total GDP in 2007 before beginning a precipitous descent, settling at 2 percent in 2012. Much of the rise and fall has come from current account developments in the region's two largest economies—the PRC and Japan.

The PRC revalued its currency against the US dollar and at the same time exited from a dollar peg in July 2005 and began to allow a gradual currency appreciation. However, in the summer of 2008, it returned to a US dollar peg to prevent the erosion of its export competitiveness, even before many of its competitors in the region began to suffer from a sharp depreciation of their currencies after the collapse of Lehman Brothers. Two years later, the PRC abandoned the peg once again, making its US dollar exchange rate more flexible. The IMF classifies the PRC's exchange rate regime as a crawl-like arrangement. Since returning to a more flexible rate regime, its nominal effective exchange rate has appreciated by more than 10 percent (as of July

---

[19] There are also continuous discussions on other issues such as cross-border issuance and investment, enhancing credit ratings, and securitization.

Table 2.5. IMF classification of East Asian exchange rate regimes, 2012

Monetary policy framework		Exchange rate arrangements						
		Currency board	Conventional peg	Stabilized arrangements	Crawl-like arrangements	Other managed arrangements	Floating	Free floating
Exchange rate anchor	US dollar	Hong Kong, China		Cambodia				
	Composite	Brunei Darussalam		Viet Nam		Singapore		
	Other							
Monetary aggregate target					PRC			
Inflation-targeting framework							Indonesia, Republic of Korea, Philippines, Thailand	
Others				Lao PDR		Malaysia, Myanmar		Japan

Source: IMF's De Facto Classification of Exchange Rate Arrangements and Monetary Policy Frameworks, April 2012.

2013). Although it is difficult to present any reliable empirical evidence, the currency appreciation since 2005 may have facilitated a sharp decline in the current account surplus.

The Japanese yen is the only freely floating reserve currency in the region. Although it has all the prerequisites of a regional anchor, it has not been widely used as an invoicing and settlement currency. The yen experienced a period of sustained appreciation from early 2006 until October 2012, even during the global financial crisis and despite the triple disaster that hit the eastern part of Japan in 2011. However, the yen's value against the US dollar began to fall in October 2012, mostly as a result of market expectations and the BOJ's implementation of quantitative and qualitative monetary policy easing (QQE) in April 2013. Over the following year its value fell by more than 22 percent in real effective terms. Although it is too early to judge, it is expected that the success of Abenomics, coupled with the normalization of US monetary policy, will sustain the yen's depreciation at least until the BOJ reverses its monetary policy to exit from QQE.

In the aftermath of the 1997-8 financial crisis, the Republic of Korea managed a regime of inflation targeting with floating, in the form of a market-determined exchange rate system with interventions aimed at smoothing out the volatility of the won. From 2003 to 2007 the currency continuously gained on the US dollar. Like many other currencies of East Asia's emerging economies it experienced a huge depreciation against the US dollar after the collapse of Lehman Brothers in 2008. It has recovered from the global financial crisis, but there is the suspicion that the Republic of Korea's policy authorities are intervening to resist appreciation when its current account surplus is large and growing. Unable to stimulate domestic demand, the country is not likely to forsake its dependence on exports for growth.

The latest semi-annual US Treasury report on global exchange rates came out with the warning that all three countries—the PRC, Japan, and the Republic of Korea—should not try to hold down the value of their currencies to gain a competitive advantage in world markets.

Three of the five founding members of ASEAN—Indonesia, the Philippines, and Thailand—are floaters, if not "clean" floaters. Singapore and Malaysia have been on a managed arrangement. Notwithstanding their disparate exchange rate regimes, the nominal as well as real effective exchange rates of these countries have (except for Indonesia) moved closely with one another. Although there is no reliable evidence, either the authorities of these countries have intervened in the foreign exchange markets to prevent any loss of export competitiveness vis-à-vis other neighboring countries or market forces have allowed close co-movements of their bilateral exchange rates.

2.5.2 Efficacy of Currency Floating for Emerging East Asia

Ten years after recovering from the 1997–8 financial crisis, many East Asian emerging economies were hammered by the contagion of the US-originated global financial crisis. US dollar liquidity evaporated, pushing some of these economies to the edge of financial meltdown, as was the case in the Republic of Korea. Before the financial crisis ran through its course of recovery, the global economy was hit by the Eurozone sovereign debt and banking crisis, plunging it into an enduring slow growth and financial instability.

Unable to put together a proper mix of macroeconomic policies, the US and the European central banks began printing large sums of money to prevent any further setback in growth and employment, flooding the global financial markets with liquidity. Some of the excessive liquidity also inundated financial markets in East Asian economies, causing currency appreciation and low interest rates unwarranted by domestic economic conditions. In the meantime, the US Federal Reserve began tapering the quantitative easing (QE) in 2013. Concerns about the adverse consequences of the tapering have reverberated throughout East Asian emerging economies, causing capital outflows and currency depreciation. How should then the East Asian emerging economies brace themselves for this inevitable outcome, which is likely to set off another round of financial turbulence in their domestic financial markets?

A conventional prescription would advocate greater nominal exchange rate flexibility. This recipe may not necessarily work. Park and Wyplosz (2012) show that when market participants overreact and herd on to the exit from an external shock such as the QE tapering, the nominal exchange rate could easily be on an implosive trajectory, provoking more capital outflows.

Most emerging economies in East Asia have taken steps to liberalize and open their financial markets since the 1997–8 financial crisis. This has enabled many of these economies to forge closer and more extensive ties with global financial markets. This development may well have compromised their monetary independence even when their exchanges rates are market-determined.

In a recent paper, Rey (2013) argues that a global financial cycle—that is, the co-movement in capital flows, asset prices, and credit expansion across both developed and emerging economies—makes these economies lose their monetary independence, unless they are prepared to institute capital controls. Capital controls, once a taboo in the lexicon of the IMF, are now widely accepted throughout the emerging world as an additional means of controlling the volatility of capital flows under certain conditions endorsed by the IMF (see Ostry et al. 2010). The problem is that many of the known control measures may not be as effective as they are made out to be.

As shown by Kawai and Lamberte (2010) and Park and Wyplosz (2012), emerging economies may have a number of instruments at their disposal to control capital inflows. However, this does not necessarily mean that they can also control capital outflows. To be sure, some of the measures could keep foreign capital longer than otherwise in the domestic economy, but when foreign lenders stop renewing their loans and foreign financial investors start selling off their holdings of local financial assets, the potential amount of capital outflows can be the existing stock of all foreign liabilities. No measure of capital control—direct or indirect—will be effective in slowing down outflows when market participants panic or overreact to, for example, shocks emanating from developed countries.

The preceding argument does not necessarily mean that free floating has no place in managing capital account transactions. Instead, it underscores the peril of blind belief in the efficacy of free floating. Different measures of capital control with a flexible exchange rate system may work in different countries. What is emphasized here is that there does not appear to be a one-size-fits-all buffer capable of blocking vagaries of international financial markets in the emerging world. Each emerging economy in East Asia will need to construct its own macroeconomic policy framework that works in insulating itself from the adverse consequences of external shocks such as the tapering of the QE.

2.5.3 Scope for Exchange Rate Policy Coordination

In recent years, a number of economists and institutions from the region have proposed a basket of regional currencies known as the ACU index—a weighted average of East Asian currencies—as an indicator of the extent of overvaluation or undervaluation against the regional average for the purpose of regional economic surveillance and exchange rate policy coordination (see Kawai 2009). Although different authors use different procedures, Ogawa and Shimizu (2005), Gupta (2012), and Pontines (2013) all show a widening deviation in the exchange rate movements of the East Asian currencies in recent years.[20] This misalignment is attributed to the different exchange rate regimes, with diverse policy objectives, of the countries whose currencies are included in the unit.

Pontines (2013) claims that his ACU index could be used for surveillance and, by implication, for exchange rate policy coordination. As Kawai and Takagi (2012) point out, ASEAN+3 may need a framework for exchange rate policy coordination incorporating an ACU and its deviation indicator, if it is serious about stabilizing bilateral exchange rates among its members. To be

---

[20] In his estimation of an ACU index, Pontines (2013) finds emergence of two contrasting groups of currencies: one group of strong currencies consisting of the renminbi, the yen (until October 2012), and the baht and another group including weak currencies, such as the Indonesian rupiah, the Republic of Korea won, and Philippine peso.

effective, exchange rate policy coordination will need more than a framework and an anchor. The reason is that joint action in the region has been stifled by the difficulty of reaching consensus on the modality of the surveillance and enforcement mechanism required for efficient policy coordination among the members.

In view of the travails of the Eurozone as a monetary union, it is not clear whether the members of ASEAN+3 would see enough merit in stabilizing their mutual exchange rates. Even if they did, they might not be willing to delegate even a small part of monetary policy sovereignty to a regional institution. They have yet to nurture the sense of a common destiny vital to successful policy coordination. In principle, they may all realize the need for closer policy coordination, but in reality few members of ASEAN+3 would want any regional organization—such as AMRO—to tell them that their currencies were over- or undervalued vis-à-vis other currencies, let alone to subject them to exchange rate adjustments.

Given the high and rising degree of economic and financial interdependence in the region, it is important for the East Asian economies to nurture the sense of importance of working together. To manage rising capital flow volatility and maintain macroeconomic and financial stability the region's policymakers need to strengthen policy dialogue and peer reviews, including on exchange rate issues. This could induce relevant policymakers to adjust policies so that all the countries concerned could be better off.

2.6 Conclusion

This chapter has reviewed major macroeconomic developments, trade patterns and FTA initiatives, regional financial integration and cooperation, and exchange rate policies in East Asia before, during and after the 2007–9 global financial crisis. The region made a rapid V-shaped recovery from the financial crisis owing mainly to the restoration of stability in the US and European economies and the subsequent recovery of export growth. A strong rebound of trade has facilitated East Asia's economic integration through intraregional trade and the growth of outward FDI. The economic recovery has been accompanied by reductions in external imbalances but, in some countries, at the cost of rising internal imbalances.

To achieve balanced and sustainable growth, the East Asian economies need to address major policy challenges. These include supporting supply side adjustment to raise productivity, especially in the service sector; expanding the effective regional market size via a region-wide FTA; developing and deepening financial markets to mobilize Asian savings to finance long-term investment and to raise resilience to future financial shocks and crises;

achieving macroeconomic and financial stability through effective monetary policy, macroprudential policy, fiscal policy, and management of exchange rates and capital flows; and enhancing regional economic and financial cooperation to strengthen policy coordination in various areas.

The chapter argues for the creation of the RCEP, i.e. an East Asia-wide free-trade area among the ASEAN+6 countries, further progress on Asian bond market development as a private-sector-driven process, a more effective policy dialogue exercise supported by an enhanced ASEAN+3 Macroeconomic Research Office (AMRO), a redesign of the Chiang Mai Initiative Multilateralization (CMIM) as a crisis prevention and management mechanism, and more effective exchange rate policy coordination to cope with further financial integration in the region.

References*

ADB and ADBI. 2009. *Infrastructure for a Seamless Asia*. Manila: Asian Development Bank and Tokyo: Asian Development Bank Institute.

Baldwin, Richard. 2006. "Multilateralising Regionalism: Spaghetti Bowls as Building Blocs on the Path to Global Free Trade." *World Economy* 29(11): 1451–1518.

Baldwin, Richard, and Masahiro Kawai. 2013. "Multilateralizing Asian Regionalism." ADBI Working Paper No. 431. Tokyo: Asian Development Bank Institute. <http://www.adbi.org/working-paper/2013/08/15/5857.multilateralizing.asian.regionalism/>.

Blanchard, Olivier. 2009. "Emerging Market Countries in the Crisis." Keynote address delivered at the ABCDE Conference (June 22–24), Seoul.

Goldstein, Morris, and Mohsin S. Khan. 1985. "Income and Price Effects in Foreign Trade." In *Handbook of International Economics*, edited by Ronald Winthrop Jones and Peter B. Kenen. Amsterdam: Elsevier.

Gupta, Abhijit Sen. 2012. "Exchange Rate Coordination in Asia: Evidence Using the Asian Currency Unit." ADBI Working Paper No. 356. Tokyo: Asian Development Bank Institute.

Henning, C. Randall. 2002. *East Asian Financial Cooperation*. Policy Analyses in International Economics 68. Washington, DC: Institute for International Economics.

Horton, Mark. 2010. "Fiscal Policy after the Crisis." A paper presented at the ADBI conference on Global Financial and Economic Crisis: Fiscal Policy Issues after the Crisis (January 19). Tokyo.

HSBC. 2013. "Our Multi-asset View of the Third Plenum: China's Turning Point?" Hong Kong, China: Hong Kong and Shanghai Banking Corporation. <https://www.research.hsbc.com/midas/Res/RDV?p=pdf&key=ekkrZAi0aX&n=390208.pdf>.

IMF. 2009. "The State of Public Finances Cross-Country Fiscal Monitor." IMF Staff Position Note SPN/09/25 (November), Fiscal Affairs Department. Washington, DC: International Monetary Fund.

* The Asian Development Bank recognizes China by the name People's Republic of China.

IMF. 2013. Coordinated Portfolio Investment Survey (November 13). International Monetary Fund. <http://cpis.imf.org/>.

Kawai, Masahiro. 2009. "An Asian Currency Unit for Regional Exchange-Rate Policy Coordination." In *Fostering Monetary and Financial Cooperation in East Asia*, edited by Duck-Koo Chung and Barry Eichengreen pp. 73–112. Singapore: World Scientific.

Kawai, Masahiro. 2014. "From the Chiang Mai Initiative to an Asian Monetary Fund." Processed, Graduate School of Public Policy, University of Tokyo.

Kawai, Masahiro, and Mario Lamberte, eds. 2010. *Managing Capital Flows: Search for a Framework*, Cheltenham: Edward Elgar.

Kawai, Masahiro, and Shinji Takagi. 2012. "A Proposal for Exchange Rate Policy Coordination in East Asia." In *Monetary and Currency Policy Management in Asia*, edited by Masahiro Kawai, Peter Morgan, and Shinji Takagi. Cheltenham: Edward Elgar.

Kawai, Masahiro, and Ganeshan Wignaraja. 2008. "EAFTA or CEPEA: Which Way Forward?" *ASEAN Economic Bulletin* 25(2): 113–39.

Ogawa, Eiji, and Junko Shimizu. 2005. "A Deviation Measurement for Coordinated Exchange Rate Policies in East Asia." RIETI Discussion Paper Series 05-E-017.

Ostry, Jonathan D., Atish R. Ghosh, Karl Habermeier, Marcos Chamon, Mahvash S. Qureshi, and Dennis B.S. Reinhardt. 2010. "Capital Inflows: The Role of Controls." IMF Staff Position Note SPN10/04. Washington, DC: International Monetary Fund.

Park, Donghyun, Seok-Kyun Hur, Shikha Jha, and Pilipinas F. Quising. 2010. "Did Fiscal Stimulus Lift Developing Asia out of the Global Crisis?: A Preliminary Empirical Investigation." A paper presented at the Conference on the Global Financial and Economic Crisis, organized by Asian Development Bank Institute, Policy Research Institute of the Ministry of Finance of Japan, and Hitotsubashi University, the Center for Intergenerational Studies-International Development Research Centre (January 19), Tokyo.

Park, Yung Chul, and Charles Wyplosz. 2012. "International Monetary Reform: A Critical Appraisal of Some Proposals." ADBI Working Paper No. 364. Tokyo: Asian Development Bank Institute.

Pontines, Victor. 2013. "How Useful Is an Asian Currency Unit (ACU) Index for Surveillance in East Asia?" ADBI Working Paper No. 413. Tokyo: Asian Development Bank Institute.

Rasiah, Rajah, Peter Gammeltoft, and Yang Jiang. 2010. "Home Government Policies for Outward FDI from Emerging Economies: Lessons from Asia." *International Journal of Emerging Markets* 5(3/4): 333–57.

Rey, Hélène. 2013. "Dilemma, Not Trilemma: The Global Financial Cycle and Monetary Policy Independence." A paper presented at the Federal Reserve Bank of Kansas City's Jackson Hole Symposium *Global Dimensions of Unconventional Monetary Policy* (August 22–24).

3

International Financial Integration and Crisis Intensity

Andrew K. Rose

3.1 Introduction

The purpose of this chapter is to analyze the causes of the 2007–9 financial crisis, with a special focus on the role of international financial integration. In particular, I ask the question "Did countries with deeper international financial ties experience more (or less) intense crises?" This is an interesting question, since a number of authors have asserted that crises can be imported or exacerbated through international financial linkages. A finding that more integrated countries suffered worse recessions implies that policymakers should think twice before encouraging deeper financial ties between countries. This topic is of special importance in Asia, which is slowly continuing its movement toward deeper regional monetary and financial ties.

I use a number of different of measures of both multilateral and bilateral financial linkages on a large cross-section of countries. There is a special focus on Asian economies; I ask whether countries with stronger financial ties to the People's Republic of China (PRC), Japan, and the Republic of Korea were affected more (or less) than countries with weaker ties. For contrast, I compare the importance of these linkages to linkages with the United States, both through the private sector (cross-holdings of bank-loans and assets) and through the public sector (access to a Federal Reserve swap line). This allows me to contrast the importance of intra-regional linkages with US connections. Throughout, I control for a number of domestic determinants of crisis intensity using sources of vulnerability that have worked well in the literature. Methodologically, I treat crisis intensity as a latent variable that can only be measured with error. Accordingly, I use a Multiple Indicator Multiple Cause (MIMIC) model to link together the causes and consequences of the crisis.

My empirical findings are weak, since it is not easy to model the causes of the 2008–9 crisis in a way that works well for a large number of countries. Richer countries were harder hit, as were countries with larger current account deficits. There is some evidence that tighter credit market regulations also moderated crisis intensity. However, none of the six measures of multilateral financial integration I use is significantly correlated with crisis intensity across countries. I also employ seventeen measures of bilateral financial integration, and find only weak signs of significance.

Curiously, countries with stronger bilateral financial ties to the United States experienced milder crises, though the same is not true of countries that are more integrated with the large Asian economies. This is interesting both because the crisis first broke out in the United States and because of the special financial role that the United States plays in the world and especially in Asia. It also underlines the continuing importance of the United States in global financial markets.

In the main, I find little evidence that countries which were more deeply financially integrated experienced substantially worse recessions. This is actually a strong result, since eminent scholars (including Stiglitz, Rodrik, Bhagwati, and others) have criticized financial integration primarily because it is said to be associated with volatility. However, the absence of any clear linkage between international financial integration and the most profound business cycle of generations constitutes a strong counter-argument.

In the next section I review the data set that I use and discuss my empirical strategy more broadly. The results of a baseline empirical specification (including only domestic factors) are contained in section 3.3. The next section assesses the empirical importance of international financial linkages in understanding crisis incidence, and constitutes the most important section of the chapter. I find evidence that closer financial linkages with the United States (but not the Republic of Korea, the PRC, or Japan) seem to have alleviated the intensity of the 2007–9 crisis. Section 3.5 is more speculative and focuses on the special role of the United States. It brings the preceding analysis to bear on two important policy-related questions: what are the challenges to US-led global financial stability, and how should the United States view continued East Asian monetary and financial cooperation? The chapter ends with a brief summary and conclusion.

3.2 Data: Identifying Cross-Country Differences in Crisis Severity

I am interested in examining a broad cross-section of countries,[1] including all those dramatically affected by the crisis and also (as controls) a number of others not affected as badly. Since the incidence of the crisis was notable among high-income countries, I include all of them as well as a large number of developing countries. In particular, I examine all countries with real GDP per capita of at least US$10,000 in 2003. To this set of countries, I add those with real GDP per capita of at least US$4,000 and a population of at least one million.[2] After eliminating countries with missing data, I am left with a sample of eighty-five economies (see Data Appendix, Table 3A).

Identifying the incidence of any financial crisis (currency, asset, banking, or other) across countries is no simple matter, let alone determining its severity (e.g. Berg et al. 2004). Any reasonable methodology should take into account the fact that potentially serious measurement error is inherently present.

Mine is a non-structural approach. In particular, I consider four observable indicators of the crisis, and model the incidence and severity of the crisis as being a latent variable that is manifest through these variables (though only imperfectly). When measuring these manifestations of the crisis, I restrict myself insofar as possible to data from 2008–9.[3]

Real GDP growth is an obvious indicator of the crisis, and I used the backcasts for 2008–9 real GDP growth that were available in late April 2010 from the Economist Intelligence Unit. Since financial variables are intrinsically forward-looking and the crisis was financial in nature, I also use three different manifestations from important financial markets. In particular, I use 2008–9 changes in: (a) the national stock market (measured in local currency, from national sources); (b) the multilateral (SDR) exchange rate (from the IMF's International Financial Statistics), measured as the price of a SDR; and (c) the two-year difference in country credit ratings (between March 2008 and March 2010) as measured by *Euromoney*. The latter range in principle from 0 to 100; in March 2010, the most highly ranked countries were Norway (94.1), Luxembourg (92.4), and Switzerland (90.7), while the lowest-ranked countries were Haiti (18.4), Swaziland (26.0), and Ecuador (28.0).[4] The data set is presented in more detail in the Data Appendix.

---

[1] I refer below to all these entities as 'countries' simply for the sake of convenience even though some (e.g. Hong Kong, China) are not.
[2] The Penn World Table Mark 6.2, which I use, ends in 2004 and has a number of missing values for that year, hence the choice of data for 2003. The measure of income in the PWT6.2 is "rgdpl." US$4000 is approximately the cut-off for World Bank "upper middle income" countries.
[3] I restrict my attention to crisis causes from 2006 and earlier to avoid any overlap between causes and consequences of the crisis, with the one exception of the Federal Reserve swap lines.
[4] 'To obtain the overall country risk score, *Euromoney* assigns a weighting to seven categories. These are political risk (30% weighting), economic performance (30%), debt indicators (7.5%), debt

One could reasonably dispute the relevance of these particular manifestations of the crisis. Why not de-mean the 2008–9 growth rate by subtracting some earlier growth rate? For that matter, why not use the output gap, or the consumption growth rate instead? Why three financial indicators instead of more or less, and why those indicators? I employ the MIMIC methodology precisely to acknowledge such measurement issues.

The four measures of the consequences (and manifestations) of the crisis are presented for sixty economies in Table 3.1, sorted by the size of the 2008–9 stock market decline. These four variables collectively seem to deliver a reasonable view of the economies most affected by the crisis. For instance, Iceland appears as a country dramatically affected by the crisis in all four sectors, as do Ukraine, Estonia, Latvia, Ireland, and the UK. But Asian economies were not particularly hard hit; while the PRC experienced the most severe stock market decline, its bond ratings improved and real GDP growth was phenomenal. Japan, on the other hand, experienced a large decline in its stock market, a decline in its bond ratings, and a severe recession (though its currency appreciated as the "carry trade" ended). Indonesia, the Republic of Korea, Malaysia, Taipei,China, and Thailand are in the sample but are not listed in Table 3.1 since their stock market declines were relatively mild.

Table 3.1. Crisis manifestations (top 60 economies ranked by equity decline, 2008–9 changes)

	2008–9 changes in	Stock market	Euromoney credit rating	SDR exchange rate	Real GDP
1	Iceland	−91.4	−23.4	100.3	−5.6
2	Russian Federation	−81.2	−1.6	22.2	−2.7
3	Bulgaria	−75.8	−6.4	1.7	0.7
4	United Arab Emirates	−69.9	−4.4	−0.8	4.5
5	Cyprus	−66.9	−1.0	1.4	1.8
6	Macedonia (FYR)	−64.3	−3.7	1.6	4.1
7	Slovenia	−64.1	−4.0	1.4	−4.6
8	Croatia	−61.7	5.2	1.3	−3.5
9	Greece	−58.3	−9.8	1.4	−0.0
10	Bermuda	−57.3	−15.3	−0.8	0.4
11	Ireland	−57.1	−15.3	1.4	−9.8
12	Latvia	−53.9	−15.8	0.2	−21.8
13	Romania	−52.3	−6.6	18.6	−0.5
14	Ukraine	−51.2	−8.3	56.9	−13.0
15	Lithuania	−49.1	−11.0	1.2	−12.6
16	Bahrain	−47.1	−2.1	−0.8	9.4
17	Italy	−46.6	−7.7	1.4	−6.3

(continued)

in default or rescheduled (5%), credit ratings (7.5%), access to bank finance/capital markets (10%), and discount on forfeiting (10%). Further details are available at <http://www.euromoney.com/Print.aspx?ArticleID=2404432>.

Table 3.1. Continued

	2008–9 changes in	Stock market	Euromoney credit rating	SDR exchange rate	Real GDP
18	Finland	−46.2	−4.1	1.4	−6.7
19	Kuwait	−46.0	−6.7	4.2	6.7
20	Belgium	−46.0	−7.8	1.4	−2.2
21	Estonia	−45.5	−12.1	1.3	−17.2
22	Austria	−44.8	−5.8	1.4	−1.8
23	Saudi Arabia	−44.5	−3.1	−0.8	4.6
24	Luxembourg	−43.3	−7.5	1.4	−4.8
25	Egypt	−40.7	−1.8	−1.1	12.2
26	Slovakia	−40.1	5.8	1.4	1.2
27	Czech Republic	−38.4	0.6	0.8	−1.8
28	People's Rep. of China	−38.3	4.3	−7.3	19.1
29	Netherlands	−37.9	−7.1	1.4	−2.1
30	Portugal	−35.0	−11.2	1.4	−2.7
31	Costa Rica	−34.7	1.1	12.6	1.5
32	Japan	−34.0	−9.2	−19.9	−6.3
33	Kazakhstan	−32.9	−6.7	22.4	4.5
34	France	−32.2	−6.2	1.4	−1.9
35	Malta	−29.9	−0.8	1.4	−0.7
36	Oman	−29.5	−2.4	−0.8	16.7
37	New Zealand	−29.4	−6.6	6.4	−1.2
38	Germany	−28.6	−6.5	1.4	−3.8
39	Norway	−28.4	−3.4	6.0	0.3
40	Poland	−27.6	−4.2	16.1	6.8
41	Qatar	−27.4	4.4	−0.8	24.2
42	United States	−24.6	−9.0	−0.8	−2.0
43	Switzerland	−24.4	−5.6	−9.2	0.3
44	Bahamas	−24.3	−9.1	−0.8	−5.5
45	Denmark	−24.1	−4.8	1.4	−5.8
46	Australia	−24.0	−5.4	−2.5	3.7
47	Spain	−23.5	−9.9	1.4	−2.7
48	El Salvador	−23.4	−3.4	−0.8	−1.2
49	Barbados	−22.4	−6.2	−0.8	−4.9
50	Ecuador	−22.2	−5.7	−0.8	6.2
51	Jamaica	−22.1	−3.7	25.5	−4.1
52	Trinidad & Tobago	−22.1	−8.5	−0.3	−0.1
53	Hong Kong, China	−20.0	−1.3	−1.4	−0.7
54	Peru	−19.0	3.1	−4.3	10.8
55	United Kingdom	−18.8	−9.5	22.7	−4.4
56	Singapore	−18.7	−7.0	−3.4	−0.6
57	Hungary	−17.8	−6.6	8.1	−5.7
58	Morocco	−17.7	−0.7	1.1	11.1
59	Canada	−17.4	−4.1	5.1	−2.2
60	Namibia	−16.9	7.2	7.5	2.3

3.3 Results: A Baseline Domestic Model

My primary interest is in linking crisis incidence to its causes. We know that most countries went into serious recession after the worldwide financial crisis which followed the bankruptcy of Lehman Brothers in September 2008. The question is whether we can map plausible cross-country indicators of vulnerability before Lehman to crisis intensity afterwards. To avoid endogeneity issues, I restrict myself to data from 2006 and earlier for crisis determinants (sources of vulnerability). I link 2006 causes of the crisis with 2008–9 measures of its intensity using a Multiple Indicator Multiple Cause (MIMIC) model.

The Methodology Appendix describes the MIMIC model. It posits that a crisis severity (measured with the four indicators listed above) is explained by its intensity. Crisis intensity is a non-observed variable that is explained, in turn, by some observed indicators of vulnerability. The model assumes that causes have the same impact on intensity in all countries and, similarly that intensity has the same effect on consequences. These assumptions allow the effect of causes on the unobserved intensity to be identified. I distinguish between domestic and international causes of the crisis.

In Rose and Spiegel (2010, 2011, 2012), we examined more than 140 possible domestic determinants of the crisis suggested by the literature and other researchers.[5] We found that only three variables worked with any plausible consistency for the 2007–9 crisis; the natural logarithm of 2006 real GDP per capita; the degree to which capital markets were tightly regulated in 2006 (a variable measured by the Fraser Institute and disseminated by the Heritage Foundation); and the 2006 current account, measured as a fraction of GDP. I include all three as controls in the analysis which follows. Most sources of vulnerability suggested by researchers simply do not line up well in the data for more than a couple of countries; I ignore such variables in what follows.[6]

My analysis is cross-sectional in nature, and is focused deliberately on a period of time when we know that there was a major financial/economic crisis affecting a large number of countries. That is, I make no attempt at all to model the timing of the crisis. I consider the latter to be a more challenging objective than mine, which is merely to study the incidence of the 2007–9 crisis across countries.

In Table 3.2, I report MIMIC estimates of the effect of the three previously indicated potential causes of the crisis and the four default indicators as measures of crisis manifestations. Standard errors are recorded in parentheses, and coefficients significantly different from zero at the 0.05 (0.01) level are marked by one (two) asterisk(s). I also provide sensitivity analysis in Table 3.2. First, I drop the exchange rate indicator from the four manifestations of the crisis, since some countries use the exchange rate as a tool of monetary policy (especially in Asia). Second, I restrict the sample of countries

---

[5] As well as a large number of financial and macroeconomic features, this work extensively tests a variety of measures of international trade linkages; they typically have little effect in explaining crisis incidence across countries.

[6] This means in practice that I ignore measures of bank leverage, real estate and other asset prices, measures of indebtedness, and so forth; the interested reader is referred to Rose and Spiegel (2010, 2011, 2012).

Table 3.2. MIMIC model estimates with only control variables

Control	MIMIC default	Drop exchange rate conseq.	Asia-Pacific	OLS growth	OLS stocks
Log (2006 real GDP p/c)	−12.6** (4.36)	−13.5** (4.4)	−6.0 (3.2)	−3.0** (0.8)	−13.2** (3.9)
2006 credit market regulation	−2.5 (3.5)	−2.0 (3.5)	−0.4 (3.1)	−2.2** (0.7)	−1.4 (2.8)
2006 current account (% of GDP)	0.56* (0.26)	0.53* (0.26)	−0.22 (0.27)	0.21** (0.06)	0.53* (0.25)

Note: Coefficients, with standard error displayed in parentheses. Coefficients significantly different from zero at 0.05 (0.01) significance level marked by one (two) asterisk(s). Each of the cells in the two left columns represents MIMC estimation on cross-section; each of the cells in the two right columns represents OLS estimation on cross-section (regressand in column header), with intercept not recorded and robust standard errors. Default: 4 consequences (2008–9 change in stocks, 2008–9 growth, 2-year change in Euromoney rating, 2008–9 exchange rate change), fixed loading on stocks. Adaptive quadrature estimation; 85 observations.

used for the estimation to the twenty-two economies in Asia or the Pacific, as well as the United States.

The final two columns at the extreme right-hand side of Table 3.2 record regression coefficient estimates from a simple linear model that links directly the potential causes to the outcomes, thus side-stepping the unobserved intensity variable (and therefore the MIMIC procedure). There are two columns of results at the right of Table 3.2, for two key regressands which I use on the left-hand side of (3): (a) the 2008–9 real GDP growth rate; and (b) the 2008–9 growth rate of the stock market.

The results of Table 3.2 echo those of Rose and Spiegel (2010). Real GDP per capita has a negative and significant effect since richer countries were systematically hit more intensely than poorer countries. This negative relationship can also be seen in Figure 3.1, which scatters the four different manifestations of the 2007–9 crisis (on the four y-axes) against the log of real GDP per capita (on the x-axis). Figure 3.1 also demonstrates clearly the variation in the intensity of the crisis across countries. While many countries experienced stark stock market declines, quite a few national stock markets actually rose over 2007–9.[7] The same spread is apparent in GDP growth, exchange rate depreciations, and country credit rating changes.

The degree of credit market regulation (much emphasized by Giannone et al. 2010) also has a negative effect on crisis intensity, indicating that looser credit market regulation might have exacerbated the financial crisis. However, this effect is not always statistically significant at conventional levels.

Finally, the coefficient on the current account term is generally significantly positive, indicating that countries with current account surpluses generally

---

[7] The Tunisian stock market rose by over 100% during the period.

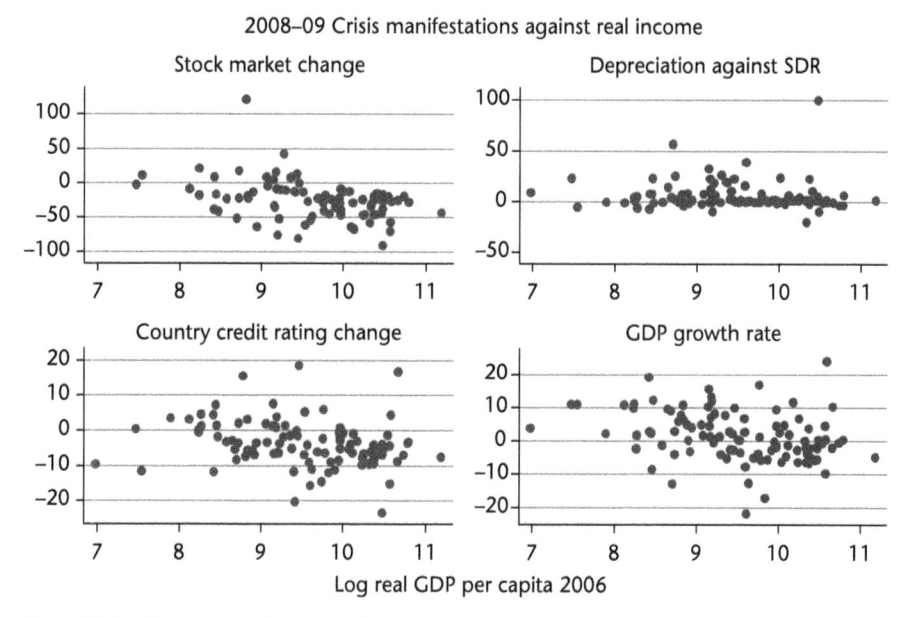

2008–09 Crisis manifestations against real income

Figure 3.1. The progressive recession

had milder crises than countries entering with large current account deficits. The positive relationship between the current account and crisis indicators can also be seen in Figure 3.2, which is the analogue to Figure 3.1 but uses the current account (measured as a percentage of GDP) on the x-axis in place of real income.

All these results fall into line with those in the existing literature (discussed in Rose and Spiegel 2010). The results seem generally insensitive to the econometric perturbations that I consider, though (unsurprisingly) nothing is statistically significant when I throw away three-quarters of my sample and restrict my attention to the United States and Asian/Pacific countries. This gives me some confidence that the underlying econometric model of crisis incidence—the *ceteris paribus* conditions from a statistical viewpoint—seems reasonable. The question to which I now turn is whether measures of international financial linkages matter, above and beyond these underlying domestic factors.

3.4 Results: How Important are International Financial Linkages?

As potential causes of the crisis, I now add international financial linkages to the default MIMIC model of Table 3.2. I begin with a variety of measures of multilateral integration before considering bilateral measures.

Andrew K. Rose

2008–09 Crisis manifestations against current account

Stock market change

Depreciation against SDR

Country credit rating change

GDP growth rate

Current account % GDP 2006

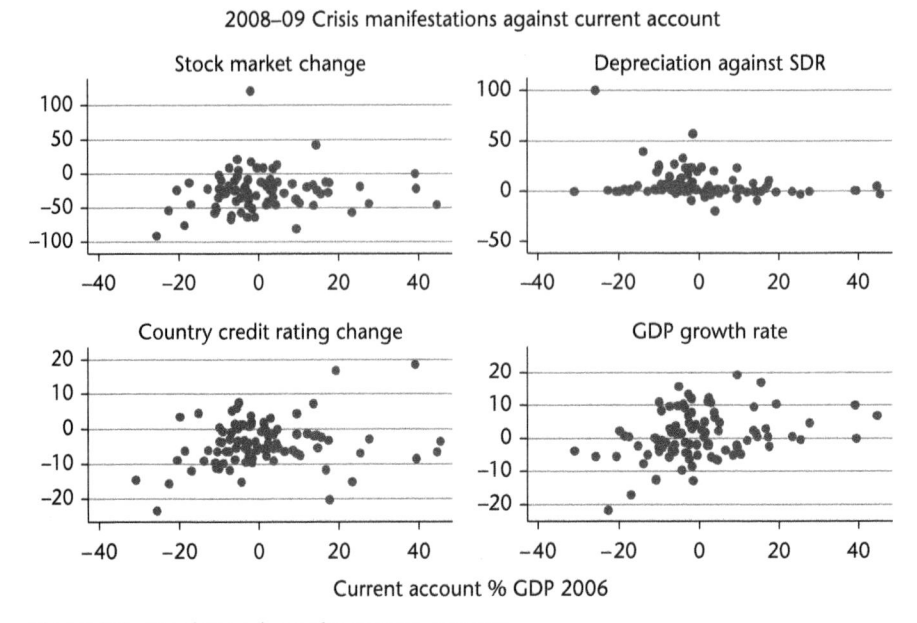

Figure 3.2. Insulation from the current account

Since there is no single perfect measure of integration, I test a number of variables that have been used in the literature. My only requirement is that the measure be quantifiable and available for a large number of countries in 2006; both stock and flow measures are included. The measures that I examine include: (a) net foreign assets; (b) external debt; (c) short-term external debt; (d) financing via international capital markets; and (e) international reserves. All five of these proxies are measured in 2006 as ratios to domestic GDP. I also include a dummy variable for countries that were part of a monetary union in 2006. I proceed by adding, one by one, each of these six measures of international financial integration to the default MIMIC model of Table 3.2. The coefficient estimates for the different measures of international financial integration are tabulated in Table 3.3. Standard errors are recorded parenthetically, and the four columns to the right of the "MIMIC Default" estimates present sensitivity analysis along the same lines as Table 3.2.

The results of Table 3.3 are generally poor; they provide little indication that standard measures of multilateral international financial integration affected crisis incidence, at least after the three domestic factors of Table 3.2 are taken into account. Of the thirty estimates, only one is significantly different from zero at the 1 percent significance level, and an additional pair at the 5 percent significance level. The ratio of short-term external debt to GDP takes a

International Financial Integration and Crisis Intensity

Table 3.3. Adding multilateral financial linkages, 2006

Multilateral linkages	MIMIC default	Drop exchange rate conseq.	Asia-Pacific	OLS, growth	OLS, stocks
Net foreign assets/GDP	−8.3 (6.3)	−8.6 (6.3)	3.9 (4.8)	0.29 (1.28)	−9.0 (8.0)
Debt/GDP	0.11 (0.31)	0.03 (0.32)	0.05 (0.10)	0.00 (0.04)	0.01 (0.31)
Short-term external debt/GDP	−1.0 (0.8)	−1.0 (0.8)	−5.6** (1.4)	−0.36* (0.14)	−0.98 (0.55)
Financing via international capital markets/GDP	−0.9 (1.1)	−1.0 (1.1)	−1.8* (0.8)	0.12 (0.18)	−1.11 (0.86)
Reserves/GDP	−0.2 (0.2)	−0.2 (0.2)	0.3 (0.2)	−0.00 (0.03)	−0.18 (0.16)
Currency union member	−3.9 (7.5)	−4.6 (7.5)	n/a	−0.48 (1.41)	−4.3 (4.4)

Note: Coefficients, with standard error displayed in parentheses. Coefficients significantly different from zero at 0.05 (0.01) significance level marked by one (two) asterisk(s). Each of the cells in the two left columns represents MIMC estimation on cross-section; each of the cells in the two right columns represents OLS estimation on cross-section (regressand in column header), with intercept not recorded and robust standard errors. Default: 4 consequences (2008–9 change in stocks, 2008–9 growth, 2-year change in Euromoney rating, 2008–9 exchange rate change), fixed loading on stocks. Three control causes (log 2006 real GDP p/c, 2006 credit market regulation, 2006 current account % GDP) included in all runs but not recorded. Adaptive quadrature estimation.

consistently negative sign (and is large economically and statistically when the sample is restricted to the Asian/Pacific countries), indicating that countries more exposed to short-term foreign obligations experienced more intense crises; these findings echo Blanchard et al. (2010). However the effect of this source of vulnerability is statistically weak, in part because it is only available for developing countries.

Given the weak evidence that indicators of multilateral financial integration affected crisis severity, I now turn my attention to bilateral linkages. Those results are presented for seventeen measures of bilateral linkages (all the relevant ones available, to the best of my knowledge) in Table 3.4, which is analogously formatted to Table 3.3. There are three basic variables which are available for a large number of countries in 2006: (a) data on international cross-holdings of assets, taken from the Coordinated Portfolio Investment Survey (CPIS) collected by the IMF (and others); (b) data on consolidated international banking claims collected by the Bank for International Settlements (BIS) and others; and (c) the fractions of public and publicly-guaranteed debt denominated in different currencies, collected by the World Bank (and others).

The CPIS data set covers total portfolio assets and assets broken down into various asset classes; accordingly, I examine cross-holdings of both total and long-term debt, as well as total asset cross-holdings. These are available for four countries of relevance to this study: the three large regional economies of Japan, the Republic of Korea, and the PRC, as well as the United States. The United States remains the anchor of the international financial system in a number of different metrics (it provides a disproportionate amount of the world's international reserves), and is the monetary anchor of choice in much of East Asia. The United States is also of special interest because the financial crisis first broke out there, in the late summer of 2007, and also because of the unexpected and dramatic appreciation of the US dollar through the peak of the crisis in 2008. By examining linkages between Asian countries, the United States, and the three most important regional economies, I should be able to pin down more precisely the nature of the linkage between crisis incidence and financial integration.

The first row of Table 3.4 adds to the default specification (of Table 3.2) the share of external assets (taken from the IMF's 2006 CPIS data set) that are held in the United States. At the end of 2006, Canada held a total of US$633.05 billion externally in total portfolio investments, of which some US$325.84 billion (or 51.5 percent) were held in the United States. Canada was thus more heavily exposed to US financial risk than, say, the UK, which held only 26.6 percent of its external financial assets in the United States. The top left cell in Table 3.3 displays the estimated marginal effect of the share of foreign assets held in the United States on the unobserved crisis intensity.[8] The coefficient is positive and significantly different from zero at the 0.05 level; countries with more exposure to US financial assets seem to have experienced less intense crises. Dropping the exchange rate manifestation of financial crises does not substantially change the size or significance of the coefficient, although it fades in both economic and statistical significance when the sample is restricted to the Asian/Pacific economies. While the CPIS share of US assets matters in an OLS regression of stock market growth, it does not when real GDP growth is the regressand.

The next rows of Table 3.4 sequentially add the remaining measures of bilateral financial linkages, for different countries and asset classes. In total, there are twelve different measures of CPIS financial linkages (three asset classes for each of four countries). They all tell the same story in essence. First, there is weak evidence that more exposure to the United States actually alleviated the intensity of the financial crisis, as manifest in positive and significant coefficients in Table 3.4. This result does not depend much on the precise asset class considered. Second, exposure to either Japanese or the Republic of Korea's assets never has a consistent or significant effect on crisis intensity across countries. Third, the sample of Asian/Pacific economies never delivers statistically significant coefficients, possibly because the sample of countries is so small. Finally, there is weak evidence that countries with greater exposure to Chinese assets experienced higher growth in both real GDP and stocks, though this finding is sensitive and driven by a few outliers.

---

[8] The number of observations varies by cause because of data availability.

Table 3.4. Adding bilateral financial linkages, 2006

Bilateral linkages	Exposure to	MIMIC default	Drop exchange rate conseq.	Asia/Pacific	OLS, growth	OLS, stocks
CPIS asset share	United States	0.44** (0.12)	0.48** (0.12)	0.10 (0.12)	0.02 (0.03)	0.48** (0.10)
	Japan	1.5 (1.2)	1.9 (1.2)	0.11 (0.61)	0.36 (0.20)	1.9 (1.5)
	Republic of Korea	0.26 (2.80)	0.3 (3.1)	4.7 (2.6)	−0.18 (0.61)	0.5 (2.9)
	People's Rep. of China	4.7 (7.8)	4.7 (7.8)	1.5 (2.8)	2.79** (0.56)	4.7 (4.2)
CPIS debt share	United States	0.39** (0.11)	0.43** (0.11)	0.17 (0.14)	0.02 (0.03)	0.44** (0.09)
	Japan	−0.62 (1.27)	−0.59 (1.34)	0.0002 (0.0007)	0.39 (0.22)	−0.60 (1.52)
	Republic of Korea	−0.38 (2.56)	−0.27 (2.54)	2.3 (2.1)	−0.10 (0.41)	−0.2 (2.2)
	People's Rep. of China	1.0 (1.2)	1.0 (1.2)	0.4 (1.0)	0.40** (0.08)	1.06* (0.44)
CPIS long debt share	United States	0.38** (0.12)	0.44** (0.12)	0.26 (0.19)	0.02 (0.03)	0.45** (0.10)
	Japan	−1.74 (1.5)	−1.6 (1.6)	0.0001 (0.0009)	0.16 (0.22)	−1.6 (1.7)
	Republic of Korea	0.17 (2.05)	0.30 (2.04)	2.4 (1.7)	−0.08 (.30)	0.3 (1.6)
	People's Rep. of China	1.1 (1.1)	1.0 (1.1)	2.0 (3.4)	0.43 (.07)	0.98* (0.47)
BIS consolidated banking share	United States	191. (122.)	202. (122.)	−224. (212.)	−13.6 (18.8)	207.** (69.)
	Japan	59. (48.)	57. (49.)	−18. (33.)	10.0** (3.8)	57** (18.)
% PPG debt in $	United States	0.11 (0.24)	0.08 (0.23)	n/a	−0.01 (0.04)	0.07 (0.25)
% PPG debt in yen	Japan	0.15 (0.50)	0.12 (.50)	−0.11 (0.27)	0.10 (0.09)	0.10 (0.28)
Federal Reserve swap line	United States	7.2 (8.1)	7.2 (8.2)	−1.7 (7.0)	−0.8 (1.6)	7.5 (6.7)

Note: Coefficients, with standard error displayed in parentheses. Coefficients significantly different from zero at 0.05 (0.01) significance level marked by one (two) asterisk(s). Each of the cells in the two left columns represents MIMIC estimation on cross-section; each of the cells in the two right columns represents OLS estimation on cross-section (regressand in column header), with intercept not recorded and robust standard errors. Default: 4 consequences (2008–9 change in stocks, 2008–9 growth, 2008–9 exchange rate change), fixed loading on stocks. Three control causes (log 2006 real GDP p/c, 2006 credit market regulation, 2006 current account % GDP) included in all runs but not recorded. Adaptive quadrature estimation.

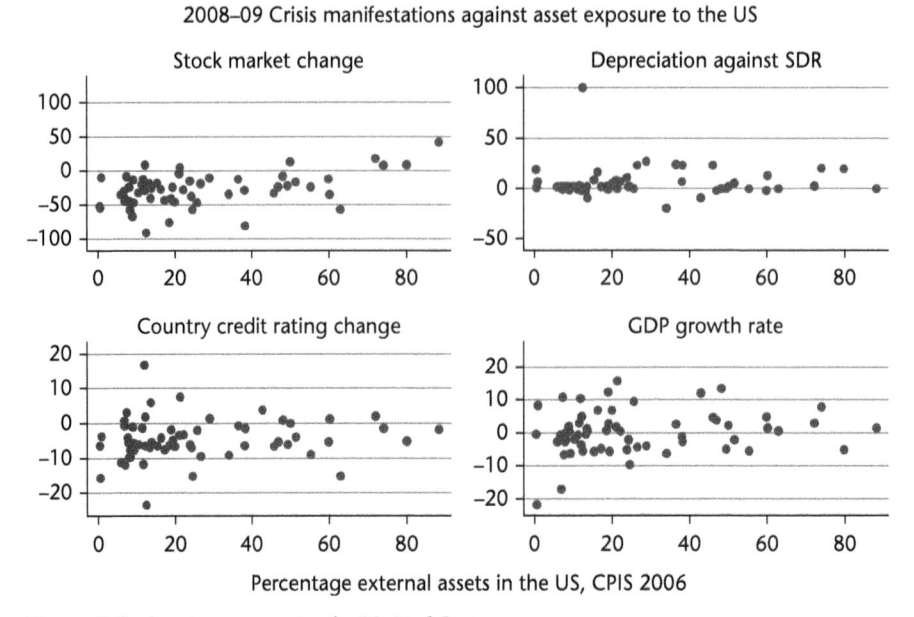

Figure 3.3. Asset exposure to the United States

The result that countries with greater exposure to US assets experienced less severe crises may seem initially surprising, especially given the widespread chatter in the popular press about toxic US assets. However, it seems to be loosely present in the data and is not a mere statistical illusion. Figure 3.3 provides simple scatter-plots of the four manifestations of the crisis graphed against the share of external assets held in the United States. Countries that had larger shares of their 2006 foreign wealth in the United States seem systematically to have experienced smaller stock market declines in 2008.[9] The relationship is loose, if also apparently linear. Analogues for the three Asian regional economies of interest are in Figures 3.4–3.6.

Next, I narrow my interest to the banking sector and take advantage of data on consolidated banking statistics produced by the BIS. These data cover banks' on-balance sheet financial claims on foreign countries, and thereby provide a measure of the exposures of lenders' national banking systems. The data set I use covers contractual lending by the head office and all its branches and subsidiaries on a worldwide-consolidated basis, so that they are net of inter-office accounts, and are reported on an ultimate risk basis.[10] I average the

---

[9] Venezuela, Mexico, Colombia, Bermuda, and Costa Rica all had more than 60% of their foreign assets in the United States, and had relatively small stock market declines compared with countries with less than 10% of their foreign wealth invested in the United States (which include Romania, Latvia, Czech Republic, Estonia, Spain, Austria, and Cyprus).

[10] Further details are available at <http://www.bis.org/statistics/consstats.htm>.

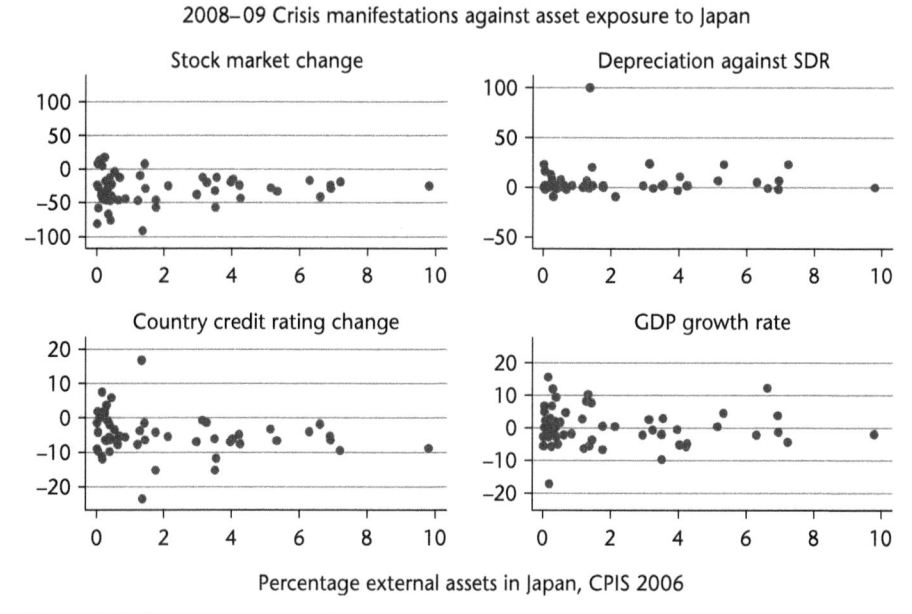

International Financial Integration and Crisis Intensity

Figure 3.4. Asset exposure to Japan

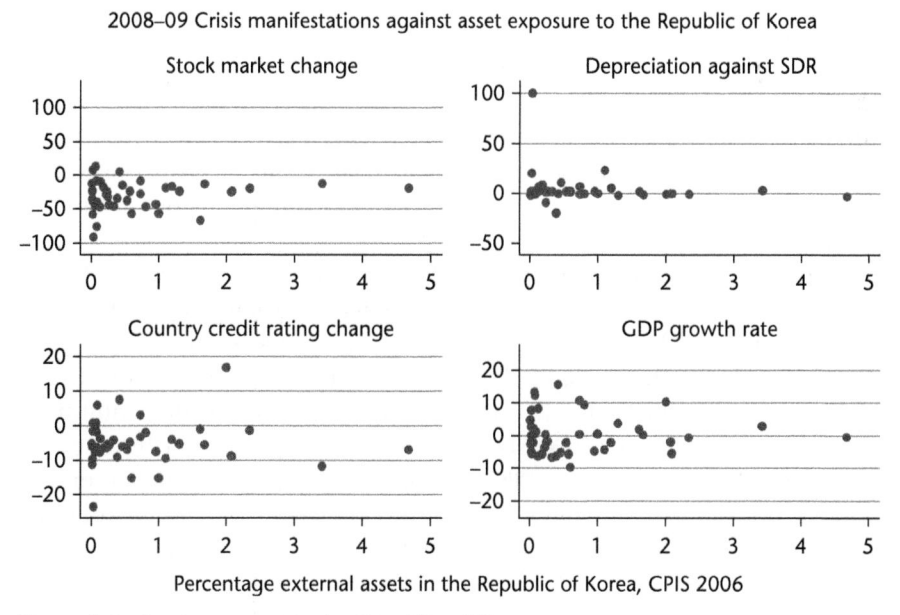

Figure 3.5. Asset exposure to the Republic of Korea

65

Andrew K. Rose

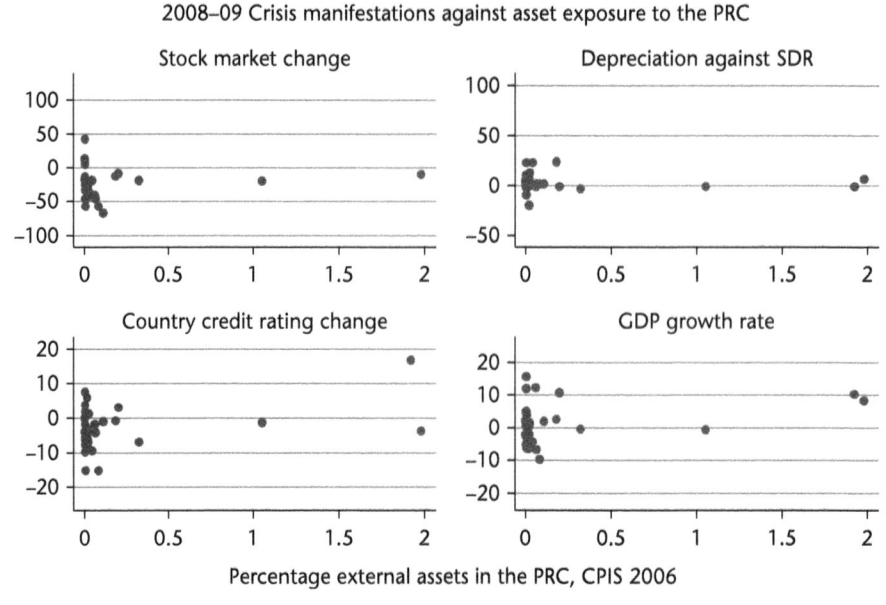

2008–09 Crisis manifestations against asset exposure to the PRC

[Four scatter plots: Stock market change, Depreciation against SDR, Country credit rating change, GDP growth rate — all plotted against Percentage external assets in the PRC, CPIS 2006]

Figure 3.6. Asset exposure to the People's Republic of China

quarterly 2006 data, and normalize individual countries' exposure to the United States and Japan by dividing by total foreign exposure.[11] However, I am unable to find consistent effects from foreign bank exposure to the crisis measures. The effect is significantly positive for US exposure when OLS is used with stock market growth as the dependent variable, but it is insignificantly different from zero in the four other perturbations and inconsistent in sign. The coefficients for Japanese exposure are somewhat stronger and positive for both OLS regressions, but are insignificantly different for all three MIMIC models. The fragility of these results is shown in Figures 3.7 and 3.8, which show that a few outliers are especially important for the BIS series in the case of Japan.

My next pair of bilateral financial linkages is taken from the World Bank's Global Development Finance data set. Both refer to the currency composition of public and publicly-guaranteed (PPG) debt; I have shares of PPG debt denominated in both yen and US dollars. I add both of these series to the basic specification of Table 3.2, and record the estimates in the penultimate rows of Table 3.4. There seems to be no strong consistent relationship between crisis intensity and the share of PPG debt denominated in either dollars or yen.

In the bottom row of Table 3.4, I add the coefficients for a binary dummy variable whose value is one if the Federal Reserve extended a swap line to the

---

[11] These data are not reported to the BIS for the PRC and the Republic of Korea.

International Financial Integration and Crisis Intensity

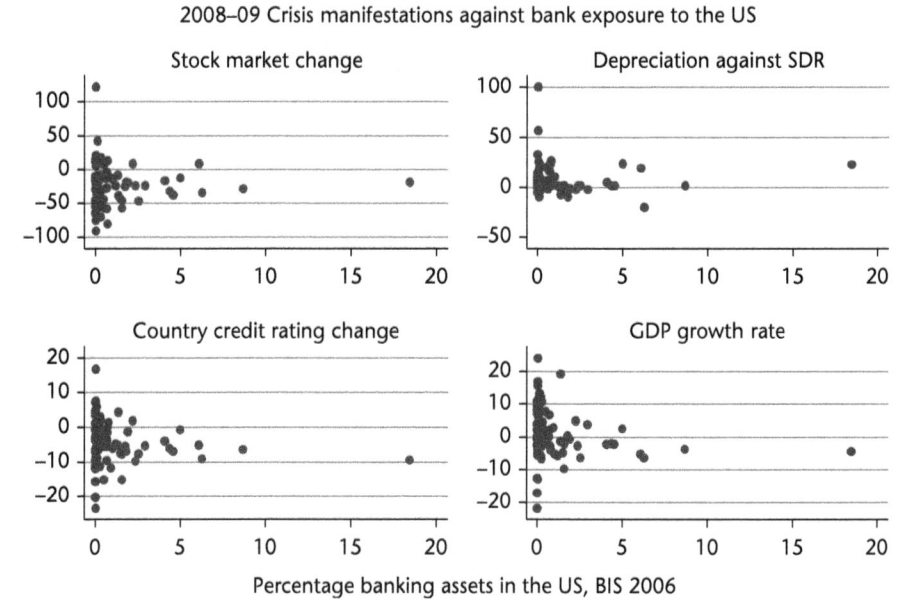

2008–09 Crisis manifestations against bank exposure to the US

Percentage banking assets in the US, BIS 2006

Figure 3.7. Bank exposure to the United States

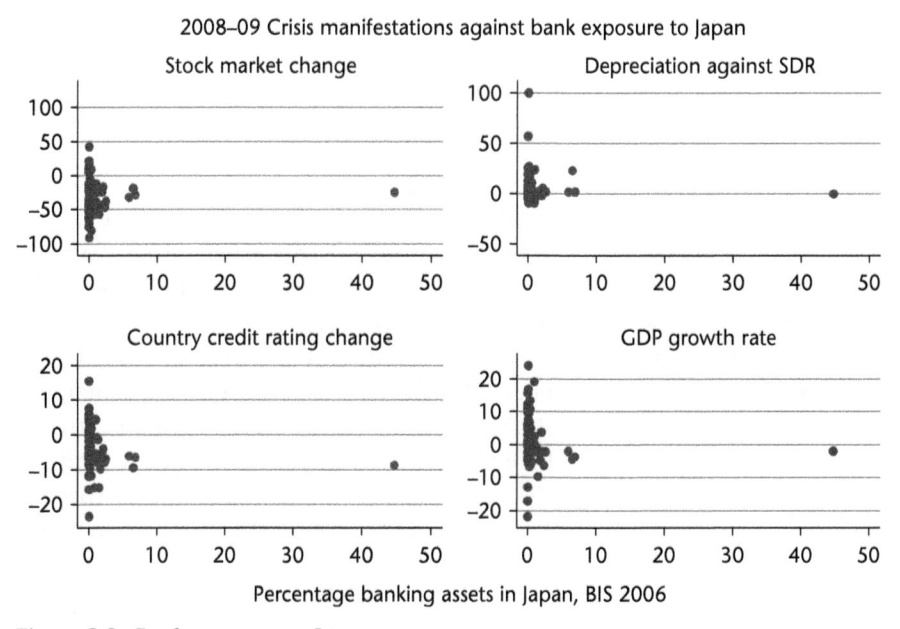

2008–09 Crisis manifestations against bank exposure to Japan

Percentage banking assets in Japan, BIS 2006

Figure 3.8. Bank exposure to Japan

country and zero otherwise. These liquidity swaps were first created by the Federal Reserve in December 2007 and were eventually extended to a total of fourteen central banks by late October 2008. Since these bilateral swaps were explicitly created as part of the endogenous policy response to the crisis the coefficients may be seriously affected by simultaneity bias. Thus the reported correlations reported should be viewed as just that; non-structural correlations. Perhaps unsurprisingly, none of them are significantly different from zero at any conventional level of confidence.

Succinctly, while there is some evidence that countries with tighter financial linkages to the United States experienced milder crises, the same cannot be said of countries more closely tied to the larger Asian economies. Of course, finding a lack of evidence that financial integration can be tied to crisis incidence does not mean that no linkage exists.[12] A subtler researcher could find it, perhaps with a different model or data set. Still, the fact that I have searched unsuccessfully for a linkage in a variety of different ways lends some validity to the exercise.

3.5 Policy Implications and Interpretation

In this section, I extrapolate from the results of the previous section and bring the evidence to bear on a couple of important policy-relevant issues. I ask two related questions. First, what are the challenges to US-led global financial stability? Second, what is a reasonable US view of continued East Asian monetary and financial cooperation?

3.5.1 *Challenges to US-Led Global Financial Stability*

The results from section 4 offer some evidence that countries with closer ties to the United States experienced milder crises, *ceteris paribus*. There is little comparable evidence of the importance of linkages to the other countries I examine, the larger East Asian economies. Does this constitute definitive proof that a financial Pax Americana persists of late?

Certainly it is reasonable to consider challenges to US-led global financial stability. For one thing, a number of the findings in section 3.4 are of marginal (and sometimes negligible) statistical significance. It is particularly striking that the existence of Federal Reserve swap lines do not seem to have mattered in a purely statistical sense. Then again, the coefficients indicate that the existence of swap lines seems to have been economically beneficial to the

---

[12] I thank Josh Felman for pointing this out to me forcefully.

countries that received them, though the effects were not estimated very precisely. In any case, it is perhaps more striking that no one else offered them, an implicit but strong signal of the continuing unique role of the United States in the global financial system. There are many other such indications. The IMF remains an American creature, with an American veto, an American senior Deputy Managing Director, and, in many ways, an American mindset. The United States continues to play a leading role in both the other Bretton Woods institutions and the new developing institutions of the G20 and Financial Stability Board (FSB).

More generally there are few rivals to the United States. Continuing European and Japanese fiscal stresses lead one to believe that no rich country will pose a serious challenge to US leadership in the financial sphere any time soon. The ambitious agenda necessary for Japan to establish financial leadership in East Asia laid out by Kawai (Chapter 7 in this volume) underlies the fact that US financial hegemony in the region is unlikely to be challenged in the near future. Political paralysis in both Japan and Europe deepens this conviction. Other rich countries which are in better economic shape (such as Canada, Sweden, and Australia) are simply too small to be viable competitors. Many developing countries weathered the 2008–9 financial storm better than their richer counterparts, most notably the PRC, India, and Brazil. Still, no developing country with a dependent monetary policy, immature financial system, or significant capital restrictions poses a serious threat to the United States' financial leadership any time soon; many emerging markets have all three. So there do not seem to be obvious foreign competitors to US-led global financial stability.[13]

This broad-brush picture seems even more plausible when it is examined in even slightly finer detail. Consider the important sector of banking, and East Asia, the most obvious potential regional economic rival to the United States. After the 1997–8 crisis there was certainly banking reform in East Asia, though it was limited. This is clearly manifest in the fact that European and US banks continue to dominate the list of the world's largest banks (measured by assets), more than a decade after the Asian crisis. A few Japanese banks remain in the list, and Chinese banks have entered of late. This underlines the point that access to large integrated markets seems to matter a lot. The world's biggest bank is French, and the Netherlands, Switzerland, Belgium, and Denmark all have top-fifty banks; economies can be small and host big banks if they have access to large markets. However, there is no contender from the Republic of

---

[13] The financial situation is thus broadly comparable to the importance of the United States on the real side of the economy, as pointed out by Yu (Chapter 6 in this volume).

Korea; Hong Kong, China; or Singapore.[14] So the patterns indicate that access to a large internal or integrated center (in the case of the Europeans) seems to matter a lot for banking. Given the lack of any serious policy moves toward deeper integration in East Asia (see section 3.5.2), East Asian banks (especially those outside Japan and the PRC) do not seem likely to pose a serious threat to the status quo any time soon.

The same is true of most capital markets in East Asia, especially outside Japan (for Japanese markets, see Chapter 7 in this volume). Asian markets have evolved in the past fifteen years, but remain underdeveloped compared to the United States. Governance problems—especially the rights of creditors and shareholders—remain generic. Capital accounts have not been fully liberalized, in part to protect exchange rate stability. Since exchange rate stability is still widely (though not universally) seen as a driver of export and overall economic growth, US capital markets seem unlikely to be challenged by Asians in the short run.

So, there is no obvious alternative to US-led global financial stability. This does not mean that no problems exist; there is no guarantee of global financial stability. A different way to say this is that the biggest possible threat to US-led financial supremacy is probably the United States. Eichengreen (2011) writes convincingly that the primary fear of the United States in this sphere is itself. Continued fiscal stress may slowly be starting to undermine the financial credibility of the United States. The Republican Party refuses to raises taxes and has not specified substantial proposals for spending cuts, while the Democratic Party remains addicted to government spending and has never presented a credible alternative. Meanwhile, the US government and external indebtedness have both continued to climb for more than a decade. This depressing state of affairs reminds one of Kindleberger's (1973) insights that interwar financial chaos in the 1930s took place in the policy vacuum between British- and US-led global financial leadership.

3.5.2 *Continued East Asian Monetary and Financial Cooperation: US View*

Americans have little to fear from East Asia (or indeed, the rest of the world) insofar as rivalry for financial leadership is concerned, at least in the short run. Indeed, it seems safe to think that the United States welcomes further Asian efforts toward integration. The main problem is that these efforts seem to be too slow and too shallow.[15]

---

[14] I draw on data from *Global Finance* (<http://www.gfmag.com/tools/best-banks/10619-worlds-50-biggest-banks.html#axzz1FSdFXUzA>).

[15] Park and Wyplosz (2008) provide a lucid introduction to recent events.

Consider efforts aimed at deepening and integrating financial markets in East Asia. Official policy initiatives in this forum have been among the more successful undertaken since the 1997–8 crisis. Most notably, Asian bond markets continue to grow and deepen as a result of policy. Much effort has gone into creating Asian index bond funds that can be used easily by the private sector, but these efforts have not yet borne much fruit. The first Asian bond fund (ABF1) was created in 2003, while another followed in 2005. But while the Asian bond markets initiative is welcome, these markets still have a long way to go before they acquire the depth and resilience of the US Treasury markets. More generally, a number of related difficulties persist: capital is far from completely mobile in the region, the governance structures differ a lot across countries, and more generally there is a large national component associated with capital returns in East Asia. More analysis is provided by Kawai (Chapter 7 in this volume).

The other big official success exists on the intra-regional monetary front. The most important is a set of international reserve swaps and repurchase agreements for emergency assistance (initially bilateral, later multilateral). The Chiang Mai Initiative was begun in 2000 by the ASEAN countries along with their three larger economies to the north (the PRC, Japan, and the Republic of Korea, collectively ASEAN+3). But the CMI has not really been put to the test and can certainly not be considered a proven success at this point, as pointed out by Yu (Chapter 6 in this volume). Indeed, Park and Song (Chapter 8 in this volume) state that "Although it was in dire need for liquidity in 2008, [the Republic of] Korea simply did not consider approaching the CMIM [Chiang Mai Initiative Multilateralization]." Much of it is reliant on the still-despised IMF; a country that wishes to move beyond an initial CMIM tranche must have an IMF program in place. More importantly, most East Asians now hold so many reserves individually that they do not really need access to the resources of the CMIM.

In terms of more conventional monetary frameworks, Asia continues to move slowly. An Asian system of fixed exchange rates, let alone an Asian currency union, Asian currency unit, or Asian monetary fund still seems far away. ASEAN surveillance, such as it is, has even less effect on domestic policies than IMF surveillance. This is part of a long tradition of deference to domestic interests; ASEAN countries are generically touchy about intrusive interventions with their neighbors.

If anything, East Asian countries have moved away from closer international monetary ties over the last decade, an observation consistent with the skepticism of Park and Song (Chapter 8 in this volume). A number of important East Asian economies (including Indonesia, the Republic of Korea, the Philippines, and Thailand) have engaged in domestic inflation targeting; this typically entails exchange rates that float (albeit not freely). This domestically-oriented monetary policy is perhaps the diametric opposite of the European experience of increasingly close monetary integration, which eventually led to monetary union. Inflation targeting has proven to be sustainable and successful in East Asia, as it has elsewhere in the world; no country has switched away from inflation targeting as a result of the 1997–8 "Great Recession." Even economies that do not formally practice inflation targeting (such as Japan, Singapore, and Taipei,China) maintain exchange rate regimes with considerable flexibility. Official moves toward deeper monetary integration in East Asia (for instance, as discussed by Kawai in Chapter 7 of this volume) seem increasingly unlikely. It is also notable that where Asians continue to care about their exchange rates, they are often most concerned with the bilateral dollar rates (most overtly in the cases of Hong Kong, China and the PRC).

To summarize, East Asia is moving slowly on most financial and monetary fronts. This is largely because it is part of an evolving Darwinian process that seems to work. The Asian financial crisis of 1997–8 led to looser monetary stances (avoiding pegged exchange rates) and financial development (most notably shunning short-term foreign debt which lead to well-known problems with maturity and currency mismatch). The crisis also encouraged East Asia to accumulate large war-chests of international reserves. While some of the latter can then be shared, in practice there seems little reason to do so. One of the big lessons from the 1997–8 crisis seems to be that East Asian countries should be more self-reliant in monetary and financial matters. No government wishes to return cap in hand to the IMF. This nationalistic bent is the opposite of financial integration, and is likely to continue. Consistent with the results of section 3.4, many countries seem to be taking the message that less financially integrated countries (such as the PRC and India) did better through the 2008–9 crisis. If this lesson is broadly swallowed, it will slow regional integration even further.

Official Asian efforts to integrate financial and monetary policies have been halting and of limited efficacy. I agree with Park and Song (Chapter 8 in this volume) that further dramatic integration efforts in East Asia seem unlikely. Insofar as further Asian integration is desirable, it seems that the lowest-hanging fruit will be on the real side of the economy. Official efforts to loosen trade barriers seem, if anything, to be lagging behind those in financial and monetary markets; a significant Asian customs union seems far away now. As McKinnon has long pointed out, freer trade tends to precede financial and monetary development; the European single market of 1992 preceded EMU (Economic and Monetary Union) by years. If one issue tends to unite economists (especially US-trained economists) it is that trade barriers are typically harmful and counterproductive.

Insofar as East Asian officials wish to seize the policy initiatives, regional trade liberalization seems to be a more effective use of official effort than integration on the financial or monetary fronts. Such a reorientation might have dramatic effect, as the recent NAFTA example shows. In the case of East

Asia, trade is becoming increasingly tightly integrated, but mostly as the result of technological rather than policy-driven initiatives. That is, Asian trade integration has been mostly driven by "natural" rather than "unnatural" causes, to use Samuelson's terminology. If there is a trade-off between the two, renewed efforts toward regional trade liberalization seem more likely to enhance welfare than official efforts to deepen Asian financial or monetary integration.

3.6 Summary and Conclusion

The international financial crisis and global recession that hit much of the world in 2008–9 was the most severe for three generations. It seems to be a "natural experiment" to deepen our understanding of the importance of international financial linkages. The fact that the crisis occurred recently allows us to see if the impact of increasing financial integration is actually visible in the data. I am particularly interested in seeing if countries that were more deeply integrated in international finance and banking experienced systematically more (or less) severe financial crises, after taking into account other domestic factors of relevance.

I use a flexible econometric methodology that takes into account the facts that the intensity of the crisis varies across countries, is only imperfectly measured, and may have multiple causes and manifestations. I rely on my previous work (with Spiegel) and the literature to model the national causes of the crisis, using data from 2006 and earlier on real GDP per capita, the tightness of financial market regulation, and the current account. Above and beyond these national causes, I search for evidence that the incidence and intensity of the 2008–9 financial crisis across countries was systematically linked to their degree of international financial integration.

I find little evidence that multilateral financial linkages across countries help explain the incidence or intensity of the crisis. There is some evidence that countries with stronger bilateral linkages with the United States weathered the crisis better, though it is by no means enough to be conclusive. There is no comparable (let alone superior) indication that countries with closer financial ties to any of the three regional East Asian powers (the PRC, Japan, and the Republic of Korea) fared better. Thus, even though the financial crisis originated in the United States in 2007, my results are quite consistent with the enduring financial importance of the United States.

Where does one end up as a result of all this? It is often said that financial integration may have long-term benefits (in the form of greater risk diversification, a more efficient allocation of capital, and so forth), but certainly has short-term costs in the form of greater exposure to crises and associated business cycle volatility. In this chapter, I have searched for but found no evidence of the latter; more financially integrated countries do not seem to have suffered more during the most serious macroeconomic crisis in decades. This leads one to conclude that the costs of international financial integration may have been overstated; if they were not great during the Great Recession, when could we ever expect them to be larger? Since long-term benefits are often undervalued by myopic policy makers, I conclude that further steps toward international financial integration continue to seem reasonable (though further integration may be even more beneficial). Succinctly, one of the minor lessons from the Great Recession is that continuing international financial integration both within Asia and between Asia and the United States seems warranted.

Acknowledgments

This chapter draws on contemporaneous research with Mark M. Spiegel of the Federal Reserve Bank of San Francisco; I thank him for our collaboration now published in Rose and Spiegel (2010, 2011, 2012). I also thank Josh Felman and Charles Wyplosz for comments. A current version of this paper, key output, and the main Stata data set used are available at <http://faculty.haas.berkeley.edu/arose>.

References

Aigner, Dennis J., Cheng Hsiao, Arie Kapetyn, and Tom Wansbreek. 1984. "Latent Variable Models in Econometrics." In *Handbook of Econometrics II*, edited by Zvi Griliches and Michael D. Intriligator, pp. 1321–93. Amsterdam: Elsevier Science.

Berg, Andrew, Eduardo Borensztein, and Catherine Patillo. 2004. "Assessing Early Warning Systems: How Have They Worked in Practice?" IMF Working Paper No. WP/04/52, March.

Blanchard, Olivier, Hamid Faruqee, and Mitali Das. 2010. "The Initial Impact of the Crisis on Emerging Market Countries." Unpublished.

Breusch, Trevor. 2005. "Estimating the Underground Economy using MIMIC Models", Working Paper, Australian National University.

Eichengreen, Barry. 2011. *Exorbitant Privilege*. New York: Oxford University Press.

Gertler, Paul J. 1988. "A Latent Variable Model of Quality Determination." *Journal of Business and Economic Statistics* 6: 97–107.

Giannone, Domenico, Michele Lenza, and Lucrezia Reichlin. 2010. "Market Freedom and the Global Recession." *IMF Economic Review* 59(1): 111–35.

Goldberger, Arthur S. 1972. "Structural Equation Methods in the Social Sciences." *Econometrica* 40: 979–1001.

Kindleberger, Charles P. 1973. *The World in Depression*. Berkeley: University of California Press.

Park, Yung Chul, and Charles Wyplosz. 2008. *Monetary and Financial Integration in East Asia*. European Economy Economic Papers 329. Brussels: European Commission, Directorate-General for Economic and Financial Affairs.

Rabe-Hesketh, Sophia, Anders Skrondal, and Andrew Pickles. 2004a. "Generalized Multilevel Structural Equation Modeling." *Psychometrika* 69(2): 167–90.

Rabe-Hesketh, Sophia, Anders Skrondal, and Andrew Pickles. 2004b. "GLLAMM Manual." UC Berkeley Biostatistics Working Paper 160.

Rose, Andrew K., and Mark M. Spiegel. 2010. "Cross-Country Causes and Consequences of the 2008 Crisis: International Linkages and American Exposure." *Pacific Economic Review* 15(3): 340–63.

Rose, Andrew K., and Mark M. Spiegel. 2011. "Cross-Country Causes and Consequences of the Crisis: An Update." *European Economic Review* 55(3): 309–24.

Rose, Andrew K., and Mark M. Spiegel. 2012. "Cross-Country Causes and Consequences of the 2008 Crisis: Early Warning." *Japan and the World Economy* 24(1): 1–16.

Methodology appendix: Linking incidence and causes with the MIMIC model

The MIMIC model was introduced to econometrics by Goldberger (1972); see also Aigner et al. (1984) and Gertler (1988). The model consists of two sets of equations:

$$y_{i,j} = \beta_j \xi_i + v_i \tag{1}$$

$$\xi_i = \gamma_k x_{i,k} + \zeta_i \tag{2}$$

where: $y_{i,j}$ is an observation on crisis indicator j for country i, $x_{i,k}$ is an observation for potential crisis cause k for country i; ξ_i is a latent variable representing the severity of the crisis for country i; β and γ are vectors of coefficients; and v and ζ are mutually uncorrelated well-behaved disturbances with zero means and constant variances.[16] Equation (1) links J consequences and manifestations of the crisis (denoted by y) to the unobservable measure of crisis severity. In practice, I model this measurement equation using the (J = 4) indications of the crisis (the 2008–9 national changes in: (a) real GDP, (b) the stock market, (c) the credit rating, and (d) the exchange rate). The second equation models the determination of the crisis as a function of K causes (x's, dated 2006 or earlier).

By substituting (2) into (1), one derives a model which is no longer a function of the latent variable ξ. This MIMIC model is a system of J equations with right-hand-sides restricted to be proportional to each another. These proportionality restrictions constrain the structure to be a "one-factor" model of the latent variable; with the addition of normalization, they achieve identification of the parameters in (1) and (2). One of the features of the MIMIC model is that it explicitly incorporates measurement error about a key variable—the incidence and severity of the crisis—in a non-trivial and plausible way. Indeed, this is one of the attractions of the MIMIC model.[17]

I estimate my MIMIC models in STATA with GLLAMM; Rabe-Hesketh et al. (2004a, b) provide further details. The iterative estimation technique begins with adaptive quadrature which is followed by Newton-Raphson.[18] I normalize and achieve identification by imposing a factor loading of unity on the stock market change.[19]

---

[16] The normalization implies that the latent variable estimate should be interpreted as decreasing in crisis severity.

[17] Much of the previous literature on the determinants of financial crises (e.g. Berg et al. 2004) has used discrete characterizations of economies as being in or out of crisis, either in an ad hoc way or based on some objective criteria; this variable is then treated as observed without error. In actuality, the severity of a crisis is likely to be a continuous variable, and one that is only observed with error. The MIMIC framework accounts for both measurement error and continuity.

[18] Occasionally I use a different iterative technique to achieve convergence.

[19] I follow Breusch (2005) in choosing to load first on the stock market because it delivers a better fit in a bivariate regression than our three other crisis indicators.

Data appendix

Table 3A. Data sample

Argentina	Finland	Lebanon	Russian Federation
Armenia[a]	France	Lithuania	Saudi Arabia
Australia[a]	Georgia[a]	Luxembourg	Singapore[a]
Austria	Germany	Macedonia	Slovakia
Barbados	Greece	Malaysia[a]	Slovenia
Belgium	Guyana	Malta	South Africa
Botswana	Hong Kong, China[a]	Mauritius	Spain
Brazil	Hungary	Mexico	Sri Lanka[a]
Bulgaria	Iceland	Morocco	St. Kitts and Nevis
Canada	Indonesia[a]	Namibia	Swaziland
Chile	Iran	Netherlands	Sweden
China, People's Rep. of[a]	Ireland	New Zealand[a]	Switzerland
Colombia	Israel	Norway	Thailand[a]
Costa Rica	Italy	Oman	Trinidad and Tobago
Croatia	Jamaica	Panama	Tunisia
Cyprus	Japan[a]	Papua New Guinea[a]	Turkey[a]
Czech Rep.	Kazakhstan[a]	Paraguay	United Kingdom
Denmark	Republic of Korea	Peru	Ukraine
Ecuador	Kuwait	Poland	United States[a]
Egypt	Kyrgyz Rep. [a]	Portugal	Uruguay
El Salvador	Latvia	Romania	Venezuela
Estonia			

Note: [a] indicates an Asian/Pacific economy.

Key data sources

Many of the data series were extracted in June 2010 from the World Bank's World Development Indicators.[20] Other key data sets are listed below. The entire (STATA 10.0) data set is available at http://faculty.haas.berkeley.edu/arose/MIMIC2Data.zip.

– National sources

Percentage change in 2008, 2009 broad stock market index

– International Monetary Fund, International Financial Statistics

Percentage change in 2008, 2009 SDR exchange rates

– *Euromoney* magazine

Country credit ratings

– International Monetary Fund, CPIS

Table 8: International cross-holdings of portfolio assets, debt, long-term debt

---

[20] This includes series on: population; real GDP per capita; current account/GDP; stock market capitalization/GDP.

– Bank for International Settlements, Consolidated Banking Statistics

2006 ultimate risk basis financial claims

– World Bank, Global Development Finance

Percentages of public and publicly-guaranteed debt denominated in dollars and yen in 2006

– US Federal Reserve website

Swap line data available at http://www.federalreserve.gov/monetarypolicy/bst_liquidityswaps.htm

4

Lessons from the European Public Debt Crisis

Charles Wyplosz

4.1 Introduction

Exchange rates are uniquely ubiquitous. They matter for trade, they affect capital flows, they impact domestic inflation, and they redistribute income, wealth, and purchasing power within and across countries. It is no surprise therefore that no government can ignore its exchange rate, even if it is committed to let it float freely. At the same time, there is no universally perfect way of dealing with the exchange rate. Decades of experimentation with all sorts of arrangements leave us with a better understanding of what different regimes achieve (see, e.g. Reinhart and Rogoff 2004) but also that regime choices involve complex trade-offs. East Asian economies[1] are well aware of both the importance of the exchange rate and of the difficulty of choosing a regime. Most economies of the region have grown at record speed over the last decades, largely as the result of increasingly deeper integration both with each other and with the rest of the world. As a result the exchange rate has become a crucial strategic variable as well as the source of serious disturbances, well illustrated by the 1997–8 crisis.

The response to this crisis has been to seek monetary integration at the regional level. The prime motivation was to reduce vulnerability to the sometimes erratic behavior of financial markets and to build a system of mutual support at the regional level. Several landmark agreements have followed. The Chiang Mai Initiative (CMI) aimed at pooling foreign exchange reserves. Over the years, it has been expanded both in size and in ability to respond to needs, as explained by Kawai and Park (Chapter 2 in this volume). From a web of

---

[1] In this chapter, 'East Asia' refers to the ASEAN+3 group, generally with the addition of Hong Kong, China and Taipei,China.

bilateral swap arrangements it has become a common pool, now called Chiang Mai Initiative Multilateralization (CMIM). All along it was realized that mutual assistance requires mutual surveillance. Initially, the task was implicitly delegated to the IMF as the Economic Review and Policy Dialogue (ERPD) process was very unstructured and informal. More recently, it was decided to strengthen the process by setting up a permanent secretariat, the AMRO, to operate from Singapore. Over time, if AMRO grows in size and influence, this may come to be recognized as instrumental.

This chapter asks whether the global economic and financial crisis which started in 2007 has affected the cooperation path in East Asia and, if so, how. One often-noted aspect is that East Asia has not been decoupled from these far-away events. This confirms that the growth strategy of increasing economic and financial integration with the rest of the world has become deep and entrenched. Equally important is the fact that most East Asian economies have quickly bounced back, relatively unscathed. This indicates that East Asia is no longer at the periphery of the globalized economy but has become one of its nodes, in fact the fastest-growing node. What remains to be seen is whether it is also a resilient node. Here the jury is still out.

Another aspect of the crisis is how it has played out in Europe, especially in the Eurozone. Until the crisis, East Asian policymakers and many observers have looked at the European experience as a sort of blueprint of regional economic and monetary integration, even though it has long been understood that this experience cannot simply be transferred (Park and Wyplosz 2010). Lingering doubts about European banks and the ongoing public debt crisis are now seen as warning signals—in fact a reminder—that the European construction is not quite a perfect blueprint. The implications for East Asia need to be spelled out, perhaps more carefully than they have been so far.

Finally, the crisis has triggered new thinking toward a rebalancing of growth in East Asia, with more emphasis on domestic demand. For a region that has relied on export-led strategies this may be a major turning point. Paradoxically, perhaps, this would make East Asia more similar to Europe than it has been so far. Blueprint or not, such a rebalancing is likely to raise the importance of regional cooperation in both trade and exchange rate policies.

The policy implications, developed in some detail in this chapter, emphasize two main considerations. First, the Great Moderation years are gone; we have rediscovered that international financial markets are, and will remain, inherently unstable. This concerns exchange rates as well. It follows that the choice of an exchange rate regime very much remains a live key issue. In particular, regions characterized by a high degree of economic and monetary integration may wish to limit exchange rate volatility. The case for monetary integration is strengthened by globalization. Second, the European debt crisis has shown the importance of well-crafted arrangements. East Asian economies have so far dutifully practiced constructive ambiguity as they made vows to deepen monetary cooperation. As they now realize the depth of commitments required to actually cooperate, they are fast retrenching from ambitious plans.

The next section draws some general lessons from the crisis. Section 4.3 examines how the crisis played out in East Asia. Section 4.4 compares monetary policy coordination in East Asia and in Europe during and in the aftermath of the crisis.

4.2 General Lessons from the Crisis

The global economic and financial crisis calls for a rethink of previous views and policy strategies. As convincingly argued by Reinhart and Rogoff (2010), the crisis is not undermining macroeconomic theory. In many respects, it was a classic credit boom-and-bust cycle. The lessons lie rather in the details, more precisely in the so far understudied interconnections between specific aspects of financial markets and macroeconomic developments. This section focuses on regional monetary integration. It asks whether some previously reached conclusions require revisiting. It examines monetary policy strategies, the ever-complex relationship between monetary and fiscal policies, and the importance of collective fiscal discipline in regional integration.

4.2.1 Monetary Policy and the Exchange Rate

By the time the crisis hit, conventional wisdom was that flexible inflation targeting, whether explicit or implicit, was the most appropriate monetary policy strategy.[2] This strategy emphasized that central banks should use the short-term interest rate as their instrument and focus on what they can actually achieve, namely price stability in the long run. The strategy also argued that central banks should avoid committing to objectives that are highly desirable but largely beyond their reach or in contradiction with their core duty, price stability. Still, flexibility was allowed for in the sense that central banks accepted the need to design the path to and around price stability in a way that would minimize output (and unemployment) fluctuations around a trend that was outside their remit.

As just stated, the flexible integration strategy is not really undermined by the crisis. The challenge concerns what is not stated, namely that central banks can no longer ignore financial stability, i.e. the evolution of asset prices.

---

[2] For a careful statement, see Gerlach et al. (2009).

When this point was made long ago (Cecchetti et al. 2000), central banks strongly objected (Bean 2004; Bernanke 2002). They argued that dealing with asset prices would distract them from their core responsibility and that in any case they only had one instrument, the interest rate, which was inappropriate to deal with asset price misalignments and, anyway, could be used to achieve only one objective, price stability.

Asset price misalignments, which can grow into bubbles, undoubtedly lie at the root of the crisis. Someone, therefore, must accept some responsibility for dealing with this major source of instability. The new emerging consensus takes an intermediate position (Svensson 2010). It accepts that central banks cannot excuse themselves from financial stability, if only because financial conditions affect the transmission of monetary policy. It admits that the interest rate is too blunt an instrument to prick bubbles without imposing severe costs on the economy. It notes that financial stabilization policy takes the form of regulation, which should be designed to deal with asset price misalignments. This emerging consensus calls therefore for central banks to carefully monitor asset price movements and, when need be, call upon the financial market regulators to take action (Blinder et al. 2013).

The exchange rate is a particular asset price. As such it can be misaligned and the source of macroeconomic instability, as the Asian crisis illustrated. The very old debate about the choice of an exchange rate regime can be seen as a special case of the debate on the role of asset prices in the formulation of monetary policy, with one difference: while central banks cannot directly control most asset prices,[3] they can control the nominal exchange rate. To do so, however, they must completely abandon the interest rate instrument unless they set up effective capital controls. In principle, they could still pursue an inflation-targeting strategy, using the exchange rate as an instrument. Several central banks actually claim to do so, including those of Indonesia and the Republic of Korea according to Genberg and He (2009). For that to be the case, the exchange rate should be changed at a frequency similar to that at which interest rates are adjusted when they are the policy instrument. Because anticipated exchange rate changes tend to be foreseen by the markets, which then actively take open positions, occasional discrete changes are not manageable, at least when the capital account is free. A managed float may offer the suitable room for flexibility, but other difficulties arise because of the ubiquitous nature of exchange rates and because of their highly visible distributional effects. In addition, a main virtue of the inflation-targeting strategy is that central banks can explain how their policy actions relate to their inflation forecasts, to the point where their actions are forecastable. There is little

---

[3] The exception is very short-term bonds.

indication that inflation targeters who manage their exchange rates actually relate exchange rate movements to inflation forecasts. It follows that they cannot exploit the transparency that is the hallmark—and a key advantage—of the inflation-targeting strategy.

The tension between exchange rate stability and the monetary policy strategy has been heightened during the financial crisis. Economic and financial turmoil spreads partly through the exchange rate but not all exchange rates have been free to move and transmit the shock. An intriguing aspect of the European experience is that, indeed, exchange rate stability has been achieved at the cost of a public debt crisis, an issue taken up in section 4.2. Absorbing some of the pressure through the exchange rate, on the other hand, affects trade competitiveness. This may hurt trade both directly via exchange rate volatility, and indirectly if it generates political frictions that encourage protectionist measures.

The data presented in Figure 4.1 provide information on exchange rate volatility among developed and emerging market economies. It displays the coefficient of variation of monthly nominal effective exchange rates over two subperiods: before (2000:1 to 2007:6) and after (2007:7 to 2010:9) the financial crisis. The first period is associated with the Great Moderation, which includes the financial turmoil of 2001–2. It may be surprising to note that exchange rate volatility has declined over the post-crisis periods in a large number of economies. Notable exceptions are Japan, the Republic of Korea, and the United Kingdom, which underwent strong appreciation (Japan) or depreciation (the Republic of Korea and UK) since mid-2007.[4]

The various outcomes described in Figure 4.1 reflect both varied local conditions—like the role of the banking sector in the UK—and global patterns—for example, the strong appreciation of the Swiss franc. Of interest here is the role played by the monetary policy strategy. Using a coarse definition of the exchange rate regime (pegged vs. floating), Figure 4.2 plots the *change* in volatility (after 2007:6 *minus* before), as displayed in Figure 4.1. For the economies classified as floaters, changes in volatility are fairly evenly spread, with about as many increases as decreases. For the fixers, however, volatility declines are more frequent and larger than increases.

The message here is not that the flexible inflation-targeting strategy has been a source of exchange rate volatility, but simply that central banks can reduce exchange rate fluctuations only if they mean to. In addition, while there is no evidence that exchange rate volatility has increased among floaters

---

[4] Effective exchange rate movements are partly driven by fluctuations of partner country currencies. This is an unavoidable "noise" when characterizing individual country exchange rate developments. The alternative is to look at bilateral rates, like exchange rates vis-à-vis the US dollar or the euro, but then the reference currency plays an even larger role.

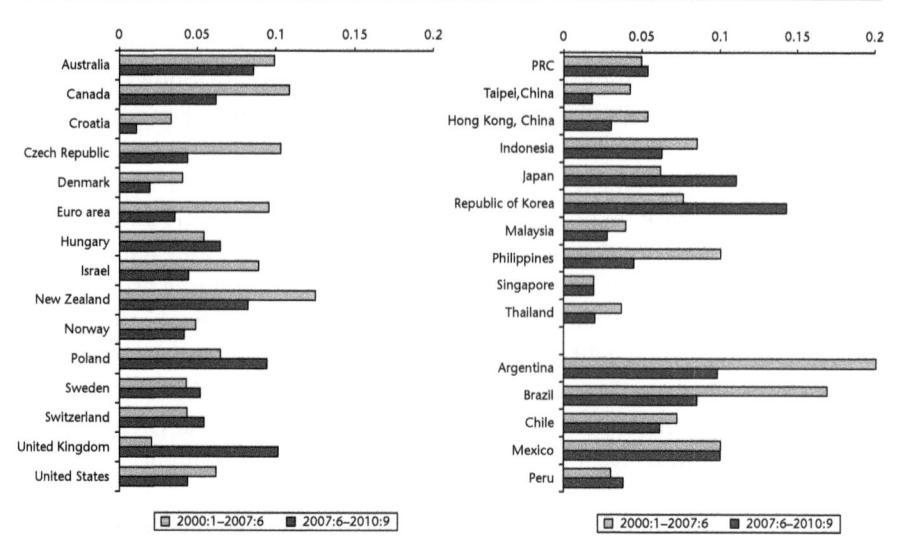

Figure 4.1. Exchange rate volatility before and during the crisis
(Coefficient of variation of nominal effective exchange rates, monthly data)
Source: Author's calculation using BIS data.

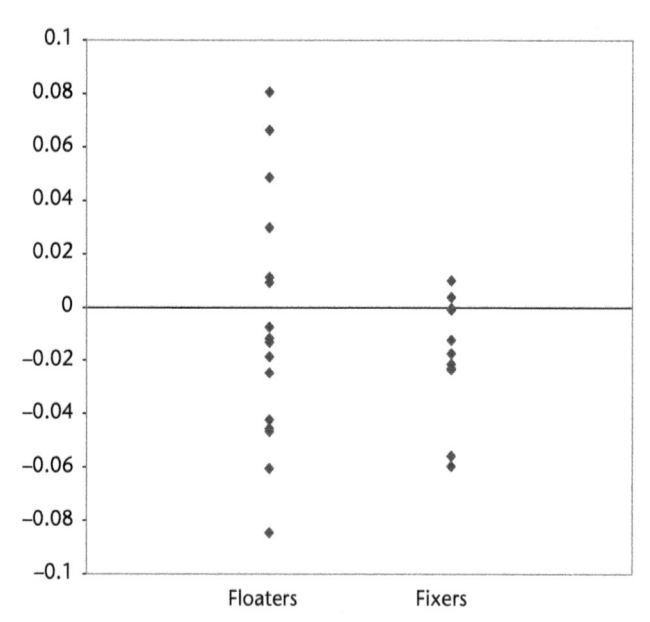

Figure 4.2. Change in exchange rate volatility and the exchange rate regime
Note: Economies classified as fixers are Denmark; the PRC; Hong Kong, China; Indonesia; Malaysia; Philippines; Singapore; Thailand; and Peru.
Source: Figure 1 and the 2007 update of the Reinhart-Rogoff fine classification (using 10 and above to classify floaters).

during the financial crisis, volatility has mostly declined among fixers. These observations provide additional support to the view that central banks ought to be concerned with exchange rates, over and beyond the impact that they directly have on price inflation.

4.2.2 Monetary Policy in a Low-Inflation Environment

One of the surprises of the crisis is the speed at which policy interest rates have reached the zero lower bound in the advanced economies and in a few emerging market economies. Part of the reason is that real interest rates were low to start with, maybe too low. But another reason is that nominal interest rates are unavoidably low in a low-inflation environment.

The switch to unconventional monetary policies represents an effort to recover some effectiveness at the zero lower bound. A growing theoretical and empirical literature debates the effectiveness of quantitative and qualitative easing on the real economy.[5] The analysis largely focuses on financial markets as channel of transmission. Yet, unconventional monetary policies could also act through their impact on the exchange rate since they consist in increasing the volume of domestic currency, a step that most exchange rate models would associate with a depreciation. In addition, the liquidity that commercial banks absorb can travel and become a source of potentially disruptive capital flows. This has led to a vigorous debate among policymakers as actions by the developed countries (the US, the UK, and Japan) have created serious disturbances in the emerging market countries.

For East Asia, the effects are both global (actions by the Federal Reserve and the Bank of England) and regional (actions by the Bank of Japan). This is yet another example of why some form of cooperation is desirable. The US Fed has clearly indicated that it understands the impact of QE and its end on other countries but that there is little it can do about it. Within East Asia, both trade and financial integration raise the strength of these effects. As exchange rate movements disturb the profitability of new trade—value chains—the desirability of monetary policy cooperation rises.

4.2.3 Strategic Dominance

Before the crisis, it was generally admitted that central bank independence was highly desirable and actually achieved in nearly all developed as well as in several emerging market countries (see e.g. Arnone et al. 2009). The crisis has

---

[5] For the US case, a good representative sample is Walsh (2009), Cúrdia and Woodford (2010), Krishnamurthy and Vissing-Jorgensen (2011), and Thornton (2013). For the UK experiment, see Breedon et al. (2012) and for Japan, see Ueda (2012).

challenged this view. The extensive asset purchase programs of the Fed have resulted in holdings of large stocks of risky assets. Both the action itself and the possibility that the Fed may suffer large losses potentially undermine its independence. In a spectacular reversal of its stated policy, the European Central Bank (ECB) has undertaken to acquire public debts in a joint bid with European governments to relax pressure on the Greek and other governments. More generally, central banks have undertaken large-scale operations, including bank rescues and large-scale acquisitions of treasury bonds, which have blurred the frontier between monetary and fiscal policy. These may well have been decisions taken independently in exceptional circumstances. Yet, these are decisions that most central banks would have rather not taken, and reveal the extreme pressure under which they had to operate. It is precisely in such times that high-level principles—such as a central bank's ability to let its government deal with the consequences of its policies—are tested.

The delicate nature of this issue is captured by the principle of strategic dominance.[6] As explained by Canzoneri et al. (2001), the fiscal and monetary authorities are bound by a joint budget constraint. Current total public indebtedness, the sum of the public debt and of the money base, must be matched by present and future net receipts, the present discounted value of the sum of budget surpluses and income from seigniorage. Several implications follow. First, the government and the central bank are jointly responsible for upholding the value of total public indebtedness. Second, there is no possible way of disentangling this joint responsibility because total indebtedness includes the government debt and the money supply (the liability side of the central bank's balance sheet). Indeed, and this is the third implication, if markets conclude that the future net receipts are insufficient, the market value of total public indebtedness declines. This can affect the value of the public debt, or the value of money through inflation and exchange rate depreciation, or both simultaneously. No matter how independent it is, the central bank cannot extricate itself from this joint budget constraint. It may independently and voluntarily accept to do its share of the financing of the public sector; this is the case of fiscal dominance. Alternatively, monetary dominance means that the central bank remains steadfast in the face of fiscal indiscipline, but it must then accept a public debt crisis, most likely along with a decline in the market value of money through an exchange rate depreciation and, maybe, an eventual inflation surge.

---

[6] All too often, the strategic dominance question is associated with the fiscal theory of price determination. The price effect of fiscal dominance is just one model-based aspect of the wider issue of who, the government or the central bank, undertakes to meet the overall budget constraint of the public sector.

Lessons from the European Public Debt Crisis

The European experience provides a striking illustration of this struggle for dominance. The ECB was widely seen as the most independent central bank of the world, because an international treaty that can only be changed with unanimous support of all member countries, a most unlikely step, guarantees its status. The threat of debt default in one country, Greece, fed fears of contagion to other countries and an all-out attack on the euro. The ECB caved in when it agreed to buy public debts under visible government pressure. Although it claimed that Greece was a "special and unique case," the ECB went on buying large quantities of Italian and Spanish debt. In many respects, the US Fed went further down the same road by financing bank bailouts and absorbing the federal debt to an extent that would have never been imagined beforehand. Much the same applies to the Bank of England, which famously started out by denying any responsibility when several British banks started to tank, and to the Swiss National Bank—another staunchly independent central bank—that ended up creating a special fund to absorb the toxic assets accumulated by the private bank UBS. The Bank of Japan had traveled this road long before; although it has become constrained by the large public sector debt, it has resumed its large-scale purchases of Japanese government bonds as part of Abenomics, a government inspired change of macroeconomic policy. There is nothing untoward in these actions but they show that central bank independence is not a black-and-white issue.

The implications for international coordination are vast and complicated. Central banks cannot make unconditional commitments, even if they are technically fully independent. There will always exist situations where their actions will be constrained by the sustainability of their national public debt. In theory, this implies that any agreement on monetary policy cooperation must include safeguards regarding the accumulation of public debt. But monetary policy cooperation is an order of magnitude easier, politically and technically, than fiscal policy cooperation. Indeed, monetary policy involves "simple" decisions on the interest rate and it is carried out by (mostly) independent bureaucrats, with limited effects on income distribution. Fiscal policy, on the other hand, involves a very large number of parameters (spending and taxing items) that all redistribute income and are therefore deeply ingrained in political considerations. In addition, the effects of fiscal policy actions are less well known and therefore open to many controversies.

The current travails within the Eurozone well illustrate the extreme difficulties of fiscal policy coordination, even when the objective is merely the achievement of some degree of budgetary discipline. Broader fiscal coordination efforts aimed at macroeconomic burden-sharing have failed in the Eurozone and were also non-existent at the height of the crisis in 2008-9. Much the same applies to global fiscal coordination. The last attempt goes back to the Louvre and Plaza agreements of 1985 and is widely seen as a failure, if only because the agreements were reached too late and therefore proved to be pro-cyclical (see Kenen et al. 2004).

4.3 East Asian Exchange Rates during the Crisis

Unlike banks in Europe, East Asian banks had not accumulated significant amounts of toxic US or local assets. This observation led to the deceptive presumption that the East Asian economies would de-link from the rest of the world and escape unhurt. The presumption ignored the trade and financial links that were bound to transmit at least part of the shock.

From the viewpoint of regional coordination, the question was whether the impact would pull East Asian exchange rates apart, whether this could reach dangerous proportions and, if so, whether the regional mechanisms in place would help cushion the blow. As an importer of a shock originating elsewhere, it was likely that the region would see a deterioration of its current account balances as exports to the countries most affected would decline. The consequent impact on domestic growth and imports would limit, but generally not eliminate, the current account deterioration.

What about the exchange rates? One could argue that a current account deterioration should be accompanied by exchange rate depreciation, but exchange rates are relative variables. The US and Europe, being at the center of the crisis, should have undergone a depreciation vis-à-vis the countries only indirectly affected. This, in fact, is the channel through which their current account balances should have improved, cushioning—or, equivalently, spreading—the blow. East Asia, in other words, stood to be a "collateral victim" of the crisis through declining exports, first on account of declining demand in the developed countries, second on account of the equilibrating role of exchange rate appreciation. Then, with growth returning to the US and monetary policy being normalized, the exact opposite should have occurred.

This is exactly what happened. Current accounts generally declined, except in economies that were more seriously impacted by the crisis (Indonesia, the Republic of Korea, Taipei,China, and Thailand). As shown in Figure 4.3, which displays the value of the synthetic Asian monetary unit (AMU) in terms of a basket of US dollars and euros, collectively, East Asian exchange rates appreciated by 15 percent between August 2007 and the summer, when the Fed "tapering" announcement triggered a reflux.[7]

Yet, the fate of individual exchange rates has been varied. Relative to the US dollar, on the way up the Japanese yen appreciated by more than 25 percent,

---

[7] AMU is a trade-weighted basket of the currencies of 14 economies (ASEAN+3 and Hong Kong, China).

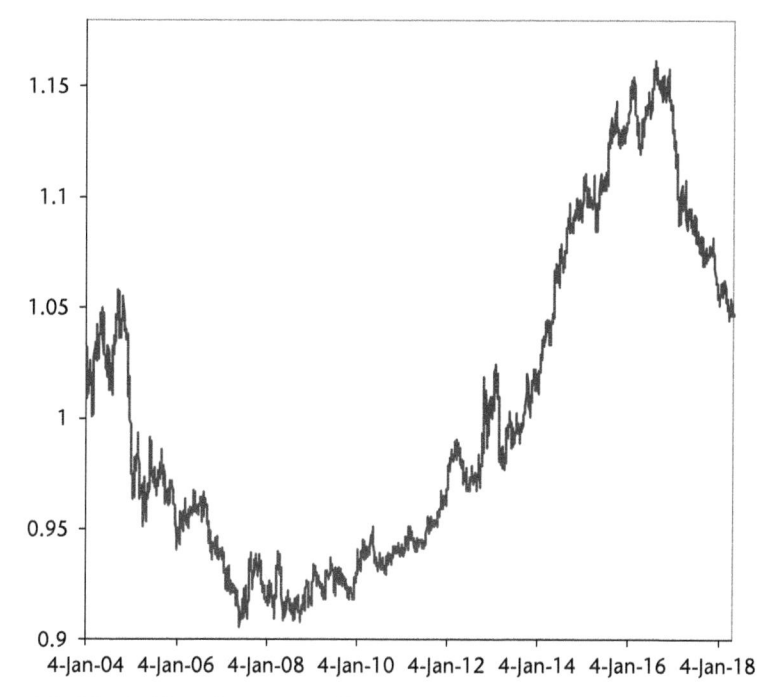

Figure 4.3. The AMU exchange rate, 2000–14
Source: RIETI.

while the Republic of Korea won depreciated by more than 30 percent. For cooperation purposes, it is useful to look at fluctuations within the region. Rather than looking at the whole matrix of bilateral rate correlations, Figure 4.4 uses exchange rates vis-à-vis the AMU, a regional basket that can be used as a common reference. This allows neutralizing the collective evolution displayed in Figure 4.1. The figure presents the coefficient of variation of AMU exchange rates over the last decade.[8] The increase in dispersion—which starts in early 2007—is clear. It is to be contrasted with the low dispersion that prevailed in the years of the Great Moderation, even through the turmoil that accompanied the 2000–1 stock market crisis in the developed countries.

Thus East Asian economies were dragged into the worldwide recession mostly through their exports; an important question is what happened to regional trade. Given the importance of trade in intermediate parts, regional trade was bound to decline as well. In fact comparing total merchandise exports in 2009 to 2007, East Asian exports declined by 6.7 percent, less than the 10.9 percent

---

[8] The exchange rates of Indonesia, Lao PDR, and Myanmar are excluded because they have undergone large idiosyncratic changes that cloud the pattern.

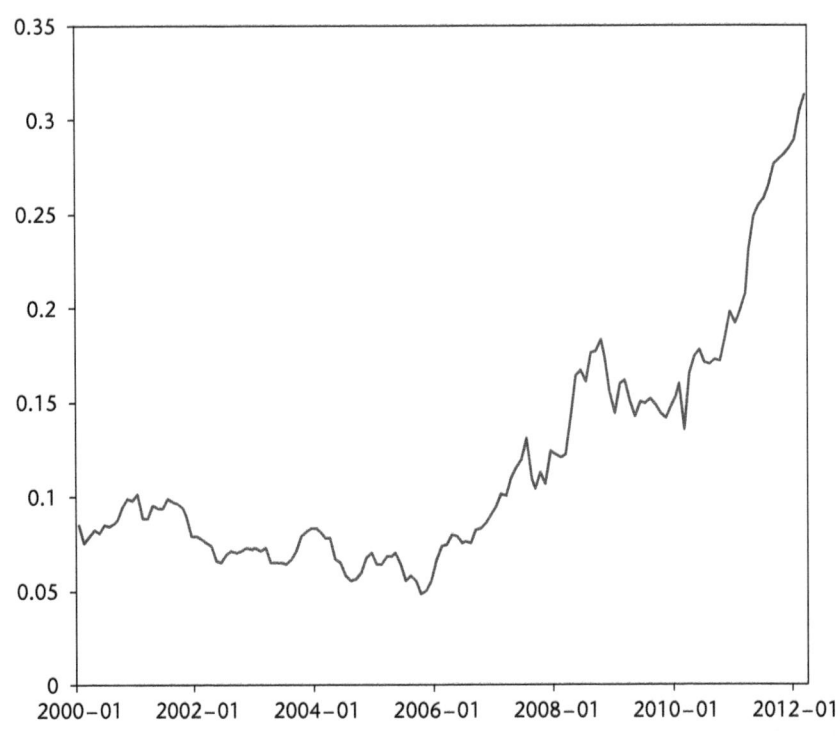

Figure 4.4. Regional real exchange rate dispersion

Note: coefficient of variation of ASEAN+3+Hong Kong, China (excluding Indonesia, Myanmar, and Lao PDR) real exchange rates vis-à-vis AMU, normalized to 100 over the sample period.

Source: Author's calculation using data from RIETI. Real effective exchange rates are computed using the divergence indicator.

Table 4.1. Change in trade between 2007 and 2009 (US$, % change)

World exports	−10.9
ASEAN+5 exports	−6.7
ASEAN+5 exports to the rest of the world	−8.4
ASEAN+5 exports to the ASEAN+5	−5.0

Note: ASEAN+5 is ASEAN+3 plus Hong Kong, China and Taipei,China.
Source: ADB calculations from *Direction of Trade*, IMF.

fall in total world exports. Furthermore, Table 4.1 shows that East Asian exports to the region declined by less than exports to the rest of the world.

This general pattern, however, conceals important divergences among individual economies. While exports declined by more than 15 percent in Japan and Taipei,China, they increased in some smaller and less integrated economies such as Lao PDR, Myanmar, and Viet Nam, as well as in Indonesia. As Figure 4.5 shows, export fallbacks to the region and to the rest of the world

Lessons from the European Public Debt Crisis

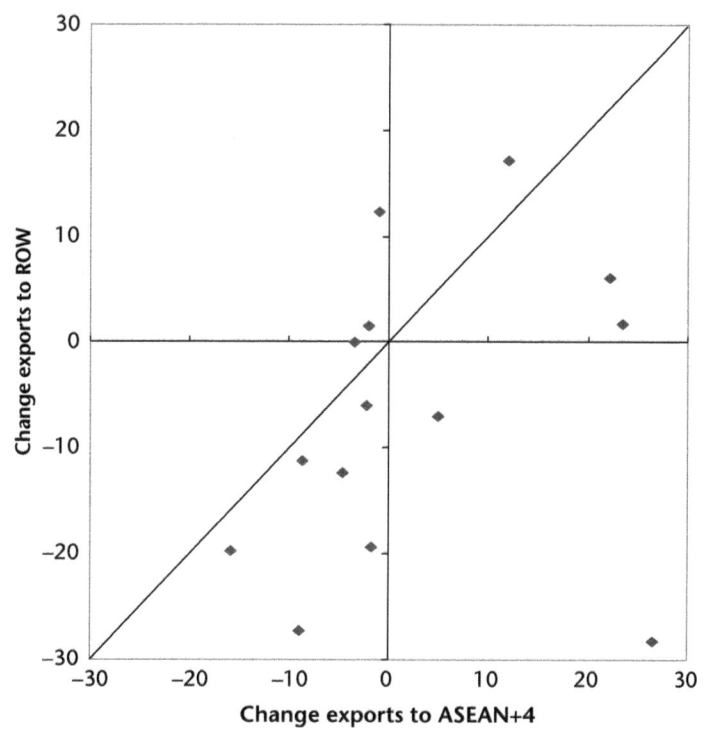

Figure 4.5. Change in trade between 2007 and 2009
(US$, % change of exports)
Source: Author's calculations from ADB data.

are positively correlated, but not very strongly so. For the majority of economies whose overall exports declined, the fall was typically smaller within the region than towards the rest of the world; exceptions are the PRC and Thailand.

An important question is whether the relative pattern of exports can be explained by the behavior of exchange rates. A complete answer to this question would require separating out the effect of exchange rates on exports from the reverse effect, from export performance to exchange rate. Looking at one event—the crisis—and at the limited sample of East Asian economies precludes a formal analysis. Accordingly, the evidence presented in Table 4.2 is tentative. The table displays unconditional correlations of the measured changes in exports displayed in Figure 4.5 with a number of measures of exchange rate behavior: the change in the real effective exchange rate (from July 2007 to September 2010), its volatility over the crisis period July 2010 to September 2010, and the change in volatility between the crisis period and the period January 2000 to June 2007. There is no clear picture emerging when using all economies for which effective exchange rate data are available. If we

Table 4.2. Correlations of changes between 2007 and 2009 of exports with various measures of exchange rate movements

	Ten economies		Without Taipei,China	
	Exports to region	Exports to ROW	Exports to region	Exports to ROW
Change in real exchange rate	0.144	0.007	−0.180	−0.127
Exchange rate volatility	0.081	−0.081	−0.185	−0.193
Change in exchange rate volatility	−0.090	−0.112	−0.341	−0.192

Notes: The ten economies are the PRC; Hong Kong, China; Republic of Korea; Indonesia; Japan; Malaysia; Philippines; Singapore; Taipei,China; and Thailand. As in Figure 4.1, the exchange rate volatility is computed using monthly real effective exchange rates, taking the coefficient of variation for each member over the subperiods 2000:1 to 2007:6 and 2007:7 to 2010:9.

Source: Changes in exports, see Figure 5; Exchange rate measures: BIS (an increase represents an appreciation).

consider Taipei,China as an outlier, however, some tentative conclusions emerge.

The first row in Table 4.2 indicates that declines in exports are positively associated with real exchange rate appreciation. This would suggest that the economies whose real exchange rates appreciated suffered deeper declines in exports, both compared to other East Asian economies and to the rest of the world (ROW). The two next rows associate export declines with exchange rate volatility, both during the crisis period and when comparing pre- and post-crisis volatility.

Although the causality implicit in this interpretation should be seen as nothing more than an informed guess, these results suggest that the exchange rates did not protect the Asian economies from the crisis, quite to the contrary. Where exchange rates have been reasonably flexible, this could be the consequence of destabilizing capital flows. Elsewhere, this could reflect inappropriate policy choices. At any rate, the impression is that there is room to improve upon the explicit or implicit exchange rate policies adopted during the crisis in the region.

4.4 Monetary Cooperation in East Asia and in Europe

4.4.1 *The East Asian Experience*

In the midst of a violent global crisis, the rise in exchange rate volatility, evidenced in Figure 4.1, was probably unavoidable. A natural question is whether the coordination mechanisms put in place following the 1997–8 crisis nevertheless helped to smooth these fluctuations and their impacts. A striking observation is that a number of support mechanisms were arranged, both within and from outside the region, but that the CMIM was not

Table 4.3. Currency swap arrangements during the crisis (US$ billion)

	PRC	Hong Kong, China	Indonesia	Japan	Republic of Korea	Malaysia	Singapore	US Federal Reserve	Total reserves
PRC	–						22		2,416
Hong Kong, China	29	–							256
Indonesia	24		–	18	2				64
Japan				–	20			60	1,022
Republic of Korea	35			20	–			30	270
Malaysia	13					–			95
Singapore	22						–	30	188

Note: The table reports swaps that provide funds from the economy in the top row to the economy in the first column. The last column reports foreign exchange reserves at the end of 2009.
Source: ADB.

activated. Table 4.3 shows that, double-counting bidirectional swaps, extra-CMIM swaps within the region totaled US$205 billion. The Federal Reserve pledged up to US$90 billion.[9] All in all, the regional swaps represent about 4.75 percent of the reserves of the seven economies involved.

It might come as a surprise that the CMIM, whether in its previous or in its multilateralized version, has not been invoked. The reason seems to be that significant amounts are only available to countries that simultaneously borrow from the IMF, under its conditionality. This reflects the well-known contradiction that CMI was set up to avoid applying to the IMF for support and that, yet, IMF conditionality is required to activate the swaps.

It might also be surprising that some countries that have vast foreign exchange reserves sought swap agreements with the US Federal Reserve. They were not alone: the ECB and Switzerland also established swap lines with the Fed, even though they too hold large amounts of foreign exchange reserves. This may reflect the fact that, in the face of resolute market pressure, virtually no amount of reserves is sufficient (Jeanne and Wyplosz 2003). On the other hand, large reserves may deter, temporarily at least, market pressure.[10] This may be why the authorities were eager to advertise that they were acting cooperatively and could up the markets' ante. At any rate, the case-by-case approach and the recourse to the US have shown that monetary cooperation in East Asia is not yet operational in a crisis context.

---

[9] The US$30 billion to the Republic of Korea and Singapore is the total amount available for both countries.

[10] In a multiple-equilibria situation, the size of reserves may affect which equilibrium market participants converge to.

93

4.4.2 The European Experience

The contrast with Europe is clear, although Europe also met the limits of its own arrangements. The monetary union completely shelved its member countries from exchange market pressure and the single currency mostly appreciated during the financial crisis. But all is not perfect in the European monetary union, far from it. Indeed, with the exchange channel securely locked, pressure on individual countries operated through their public debt markets. A number of countries have faced, and still face, a situation where they find it very difficult, at times even impossible, to finance their budget deficits and to refinance their maturing public debt. A striking aspect of this crisis is its contagious nature. It started with the Greek debt, which is high but not particularly out of line with those of other developed countries, and then affected Ireland, Portugal, Italy, and Spain, bypassing several other countries also facing high and rising public indebtedness but that do not share the euro.

The European debt crisis has revealed a fault line of the monetary union, with potential implications for other regions contemplating deep monetary integration.[11] The unique feature of the Eurozone has always been that it involved a complete transfer of sovereignty in the monetary policy domain but that fiscal policies remain national. Yet, monetary stability cannot be sustained in the absence of fiscal discipline, a point made clear by the issue of strategic dominance (see section 4.1.3). The response to this contradiction has been the Stability and Growth Pact, the combination of a surveillance mechanism and assorted sanctions. The pact, however, has failed repeatedly, precisely because it is bedeviled by the sovereignty issue. As a result fiscal discipline has not been established.

The response to the debt crisis was momentous in many ways. European leaders quickly concluded that the Greek debt crisis was a matter of collective responsibility, transforming a local issue into a Eurozone-wide issue. They then bailed out Greece—providing €110 billion under IMF conditionality—in what was a violation of the spirit of the Maastricht Treaty's no-bailout clause. Facing contagion, they have established the European Financial Stability Fund (EFSF), authorized to borrow from the markets to bail out other countries. The EFSF was due to be a temporary operation but, as the crisis lingered and spread, a new permanent institution was created, the European Stability Mechanism (ESM), to take over from the EFSF.

The EMS is best seen as a European Monetary Fund. Like the IMF, the EMS lends under strong conditionality. The EFSF/ESM experience is that conditionality is stronger than at the IMF. As of late 2013, the EFSF/ESM has not

---

[11] It is sometimes argued that the crisis is also a proof that Europe is not an Optimum Currency Area (OCA). While that may well be, the crisis is largely unrelated to this feature but rather is due to an improper treatment of the need for collective fiscal discipline.

shown show any flexibility, as the IMF routinely does. One reason is that the arrangement is much more politicized than the IMF, making it difficult to admit errors.

This episode illustrates a general principle: economic integration is a dynamic process whereby each integrative step calls for more integration. Starting with a tariff union, European countries moved to a common market, which then underpinned the search for internal exchange rate stability. The system of fixed exchange rates then made way for a monetary union, which is now calling for some form of a fiscal union or, at least, mutual guarantees on public debts.

The contrast with the events in East Asia is striking. When tensions rose, East Asian countries did not invoke the CMIM coordination mechanism but sought bilateral agreements or external support. In Europe, the crisis revealed the need for a stronger form of coordination, which was rapidly undertaken.

4.5 The Case for Monetary and Financial Cooperation Revisited

The general case for economic cooperation has long been made both in theory (key references are Hamada 1976, 1985; Cooper 1968; and Mundell 1961) and in practice, including for East Asia (see e.g. Frankel and Wei 1995 and Kawai 2002). It is well understood that the exchange rate is a crucial channel of transmission of economic and financial disturbances, and that some of its fluctuations are helpful in the sense that they help to restore equilibrium while others are disturbing the pre-existing equilibrium, for example in the case of self-fulfilling crises. It is also clear that any bilateral exchange rate belongs to two countries, so any desired reaction to its fluctuations requires some degree of cooperation. Cooperative arrangements that help to sort out desired from undesired exchange rate fluctuations are inherently desirable.

4.5.1 Regional Cooperation

This general observation applies to regions where a high level of economic and financial integration has been achieved or is deemed desirable. There are at least five good reasons for regional cooperation.

First, the new trade theory explains well why trade links tend to be deeper with neighboring countries. Since generally "finance follows trade," deeper trade links foster a deepening of financial links. This is why exchange rates tend to matter more at the regional than at the global level.

Second, bilateral cooperation on exchange rates is an unavoidable source of externality for third parties and, given the regional bias in economic integration, this source of externality is more sizeable at the regional level.

Bilateral cooperation calls for international cooperation. On the other hand, global cooperation, no matter how desirable it can be, is inherently difficult because of the sheer number of parties involved. It follows that regional cooperation is often a good compromise between bilateral and global cooperation.

Third, it is often the case that countries that belong to the same region share similar specialization in trade. It follows that, in the face of external shocks, the desirable paths of their respective exchange rates are reasonably similar.

Fourth, countries from the same region often already have in place various mechanisms or institutions designed to organize consultations. This provides an infrastructure to deal with exchange rates.

Fifth, geographic closeness can lead producers to relocate in other countries of the same region if excessive exchange rate fluctuations prove to hurt their activities. Such relocations are inherently costly and unproductive. Regional efforts at limiting exchange rate fluctuations stand to reduce unproductive relocations.

4.5.2 How the Great Crisis is changing views

The question is how the Great Crisis may be changing the case for cooperation in East Asia. On the negative side, two observations are warranted. First, the sidelining of CMIM suggests that cooperation is more difficult than perhaps was anticipated. Clearly, if East Asian countries want to achieve more cooperation, they will have to strengthen or modify existing arrangements. Second, the European debt crisis has revealed that even deep arrangements may have flaws that backfire under specific circumstances. Put differently, it is likely that any cooperation arrangement, no matter how well crafted, may occasionally create more harm than good.

On the other hand, the crisis has added six new specific arguments in favor of monetary cooperation in East Asia. First, the adoption of the flexible inflation-targeting strategy—or similar approaches—by central banks did not prevent a deep monetary crisis. In particular, the view that exchange rates should matter for monetary policy making only in so far as they affect expected inflation is not acceptable any more. Central banks must concern themselves with their exchange rates and their impact on both domestic and foreign financial markets. Externalities are numerous and can have highly powerful effects. Going some way toward internalizing these effects has been shown to be clearly desirable.

Second, the crisis has also shown that in a low-inflation environment—likely to be preserved durably—interest rates can quickly reach the zero lower bound. At that stage, the only tool left, quantitative easing, strongly affects the exchange rate. This brings to the fore the issue of cooperation, both to avoid the deleterious consequences of perceived beggar-the-neighbor effects and to avoid bruising "currency wars".

Third, while it is desirable on a day-by-day basis, monetary cooperation is most important in crisis periods. This is why Chiang Mai came after the East Asian crisis, much as Europe started on its path to monetary unification after the collapse of the Bretton Woods system brought tensions into bilateral exchange rates. In the midst of crisis, there is no time for negotiations and for setting rules. Cooperation therefore must be specified *ex ante* in great detail, including procedures that can be triggered automatically in emergency situations. In particular, the link between CMIM and IMF programs implies that CMIM can be at most a secondary line of defense.

Fourth, the case for automaticity is enhanced by the fact that, at crisis times, political considerations may come to bear on policy decisions. Over the last two years, the tense, and highly politicized, debate between the PRC and the US on the renminbi flexibility issue has interfered with the objective of finding adequate solutions for regional bilateral exchange rates.

Fifth, the Europeans have now established a de facto European monetary fund. Already during the Greek crisis in May 2010, the collective intervention of other Eurozone countries was closely harmonized with the IMF program. What was deemed impossible in East Asia in 1997 is now becoming reality in Europe.

Sixth, as the likely more dynamic region in the world, East Asia can no longer depend for its growth prospects on strong exports to the developed countries, where huge public debts will have to be rolled back over a period that could extend to a generation. This rebalancing of demand will enhance the importance of the region's market for its future growth. This will make it more similar to Europe since the 1960s, and will include a strong concern toward internal exchange rate stability.

4.5.3 *Policy Implications*

If further integrative steps are deemed desirable, it is natural to start with the CMIM and deepen it gradually. A possibility is to include non-compulsory flexible basket pegging, an idea initially developed by Williamson (1999). This can be done in several ways. A first solution is to peg to a basket of non-regional currencies. The basket can be identical or specific to each country that joins the arrangement. This would completely stabilize regional bilateral rates if the basket is the same. If baskets are country-specific, the degree of intraregional exchange rate stability would still be high.

Another solution is to make up a basket of regional currencies, like the Asian monetary unit (AMU) proposed by Mori et al. (2002), Kuroda and Kawai (2003), Kawai and Takagi (2005), and Ogawa (2006). A variant is for each country to make its own basket of regional and possible external currencies. In both cases, as shown in Park and Wyplosz (2004), the nature of averaging implies that the practical difference between these arrangements is very small.[12]

Whatever the chosen solution, the allowed margins of fluctuation could be left to each country's discretion, but credibility of the arrangement requires that these margins be publicly announced. To be meaningful, the margins should not exceed a width of, say 15 percent. The arrangement should also include escape clauses that would specify first under which conditions the exchange rate can move out of the allowed margin of fluctuation and, second, when the declared parity can be changed. Both cases require that some mutual support be triggered, which in turn calls for surveillance.

Given the already agreed-upon swaps within the CMIM, the natural approach would be to expand their sizes. A better arrangement, still, would be to replace the swap agreements with an implicit pooling à la EMS, which would not specify *ex ante* limits. Obviously, the larger the amounts to be made available, the more important becomes the surveillance process. In the case when large disbursements were needed, conditionality would become necessary.

Taken together, the existence of larger support funds and the adoption conditionality implies the setting up of some version of an Asian monetary fund. The European decisions of May 2010 imply that such a regional mechanism is no longer controversial outside the region. Within the region, the approach could start as purely voluntary, an experimental coalition of the willing. It could be coupled with the newly created AMRO.

Such a deepening of exchange rate cooperation would not only stabilize regional bilateral exchange rates but could also alleviate the risk of disrupting capital flows. The Republic of Korea, for instance, has once again been subject to a sudden stop of inflows, followed by outflows that forced a deep depreciation. Other countries, like the PRC and Japan, have faced inflows that sharpen the choice between exchange rate stability and further unwanted accumulation of foreign exchange reserves. An arrangement that stabilized intraregional exchange rates would not necessarily stabilize regional currencies vis-à-vis

---

[12] A technical issue, with serious political implications, arises when pegging to a common basket of regional currencies. The "N-1 problem" relates to the fact that N currencies have only N-1 independent bilateral exchange rates. At least one currency must stay out of the basket pegging arrangement and that currency, if alone, would determine all other exchange rates, both bilaterally and vis-à-vis the rest of the world. In effect, it would be the anchor. If two or more currencies were to stay out, the basket's evolution would represent the weighted average evolution of these two or more currencies, while all others would still stabilize their bilateral rates. From an economic viewpoint, there is nothing inherently wrong with this arrangement, but the political aspects are bound to be delicate. If, as is likely, Japan elected to stay out, so would the PRC, which could induce the Republic of Korea to do so as well. The AMU, and the exchange rates of the ASEAN countries, would then be driven by the average evolution of the yen, the renminbi, and the won.

the dollar or the euro but it would reduce the natural tendency of markets to focus on one country at a time. A collective defense of intraregional parities stands to eliminate the existence of outliers that attract market attention. Even if disruptive flows occurred, deepened cooperation would reduce their distortionary impact on regional bilateral rates.

4.6 Conclusion

Crises are extreme experiments that reveal pre-existing weaknesses. Recent years have shown the limits of East Asian monetary cooperation, much as flaws in the European monetary union have become the source of deep turmoil. Europe's response seems to be to deepen integration, extending solidarity and collective oversight.[13] East Asian countries may draw two opposite conclusions. The first one is that the demands of monetary cooperation are more demanding than hitherto believed. The second one is that international financial instability is a permanent implication of globalization and that the regional defense mechanism ought to be strengthened.

Although they lead to strikingly opposite policy implications, both conclusions are warranted. In fact, they are not new. Since 1997–8, debates on monetary cooperation have been informed by these two views. The question is whether the most recent crisis, which originated outside the region, is changing the balance of arguments toward one of these views.

This chapter can be seen as making two main points. First, the likelihood of continuing exchange rate instability, including recurrent crises, strengthens the appeal of cooperation. Second, bad arrangements backfire at times of crises. Current arrangements in East Asia, the CMIM and EPRD now backed by AMRO, lie at the weak end of the spectrum of cooperation intensity; they provide little or no support but they do little or no harm. If East Asian countries, or a subset of them, conclude that monetary and exchange rate cooperation ought to be strengthened, then they should aim at more ambitious, but carefully crafted, steps.

Acknowledgments

This chapter was presented as a paper at the conference on "Financial Development and Integration in East Asia" held in Seoul on December 2–3, 2010. I am grateful for very helpful comments from the conference participants, especially from my discussants, Takatoshi Ito and Yiping Huang, and from anonymous referees.

---

[13] These are intentions. It remains to be seen whether the measures currently being discussed will achieve their aims.

References

Arnone, Marco, Bernard J. Laurens, Jean-François Segalotto, and Martin Sommer. 2009. "Central Bank Autonomy: Lessons from Global Trends." *IMF Staff Papers* 56(2): 263–96.

Bean, Charles. 2004. "Asset Prices, Monetary Policy and Financial Stability: A Central Banker's View." Speech given at the American Economic Association Annual Meeting, San Diego.

Bernanke, Ben S. 2002. "Asset-Price 'Bubbles' and Monetary Policy." Remarks before the New York Chapter of the National Association for Business Economics, New York.

Blinder, Alan, Thomas J. Jordan, Donald Kohn, and Frederic S. Mishkin. 2013. "Exit Strategy." *Geneva Reports on the World Economy* 15. Geneva: International Center for Monetary and Banking Studies.

Breedon, Francis, Jagjit S Chadha, and Alex Waters. 2012. "The Financial Market Impact of UK Quantitative Easing." *Oxford Review of Economic Policy* 28(4): 702–28.

Canzoneri, Matthew B., Robert E. Cumby, and Behzad T. Diba. 2001. "Is the Price Level Determined by the Needs of Fiscal Solvency?" *American Economic Review* 91(5): 1221–38.

Cecchetti, S. G., H. Genberg, J. Lipsky, and S. Wadhwani. 2000. "Asset Prices and Central Bank Policy." *Geneva Reports on the World Economy* 2. Geneva: International Center for Monetary and Banking Studies.

Cooper, Richard N. 1968. *The Economics of Interdependence*. New York: McGraw-Hill.

Cúrdia, Vasco, and Michael Woodford. 2010. "Conventional and Unconventional Monetary Policy." *Federal Reserve Bank of St. Louis Review*: 229–64.

Frankel, Jeffrey, and Shang-Jin Wei. 1995. "Emerging Currency Blocs." In *The International Monetary System: Its Institutions and Its Future*, edited by Hans Genberg. Berlin: Springer.

Genberg, Hand, and Dong He. 2009. "Monetary and Financial Cooperation Among Central Banks in East Asia and the Pacific." In *Exchange Rate, Monetary and Financial Issues and Policies in Asia*, edited by Ramkishen S. Rajan, Shandre Thangavelu, and Rasyad A. Parinduri. Singapore: World Scientific.

Gerlach, Stefan, Alberto Giovannini, Cédric Tille, and José Viñals. 2009. "Are the Golden Years of Central Banking Over? The Crisis and the Challenges." *Geneva Reports on the World Economy* 10. Geneva: International Center for Monetary and Banking Studies.

Hamada, Koichi. 1985. *The Political Economy of International Monetary Interdependence*. Cambridge, MA: MIT Press.

Hamada, Koichi. 1976. "A Strategic Analysis of Monetary Interdependence." *Journal of Political Economy* 84: 667–700.

Jeanne, Olivier, and Charles Wyplosz. 2003. "The International Lender of Last Resort: How Large Is Large Enough?" In *Managing Currency Crises in Emerging Markets*, edited by Michael P. Dooley and Jeffrey A. Frankel. Chicago: University of Chicago Press.

Kawai, Masahiro. 2002. "Exchange Rate Arrangements in East Asia: Lessons from the 1997–98 Currency Crisis." *Monetary and Economic Studies*, Institute for Monetary and Economic Studies, Bank of Japan, 20(S1): 167–204.

Kawai, Masahiro, and Shinji Takagi. 2005. "Strategy for a Regional Exchange Rate Arrangement in East Asia: Analysis, Review and Proposal." *Global Economic Review* 34(1): 21–64.

Kenen, Peter, Jeffrey Shafer, Nigel Wicks, and Charles Wyplosz. 2004. "International Economic and Financial Coordination: New Issues, New Actors, New Responses." *Geneva Report on the World Economy* 6. London: CEPR.

Krishnamurthy, Arvind, and Annette Vissing-Jorgensen. 2011. "The Effects of Quantitative Easing on Interest Rates: Channels and Implications for Policy." *Brookings Papers on Economic Activity* 43(2): 215–87.

Kuroda, Haruhiko, and Masahiro Kawai. 2003. "Strengthening Regional Financial Cooperation in East Asia." *PRI Discussion Paper Series* No. 03A-10, Policy Research Institute. Tokyo: Japanese Ministry of Finance.

Mori, Junichi, Maoyoshi Kinukawa, Hideki Nukaya, and Masashi Hashimoto. 2002. "Integration of East Asian Economics and a Step by Step Approach Towards a Currency Basket Regime." IIMA Research Report No. 2.

Ogawa, Eiji. 2006. "AMU and AMU Deviation Indicators." Research Institute of Economy, Trade and Industry, Tokyo.

Mundell, Robert A. 1961. "Optimum Currency Areas." *American Economic Review* 51: 509–17.

Park, Yung Chul, and Charles Wyplosz. 2004. "Exchange Rate Arrangements in East Asia: Do They Matter?" In *Monetary and Exchange Rate Arrangements in East Asia*, edited by Yonghyup Oh, Deo Ryong Yoon, and Thomas D. Willett, pp.129–60. Seoul: Korea Institute for International Economic Policy.

Park, Yung Chul, and Charles Wyplosz. 2010. *Monetary and Financial Integration in East Asia: The Relevance of European Experience*. Oxford: Oxford University Press.

Reinhart, Carmen, and Kenneth Rogoff. 2004. "The Modern History of Exchange Rate Arrangements: A Reinterpretation." *Quarterly Journal of Economics* 119(1): 1–48.

Reinhart, Carmen M., and Kenneth S. Rogoff. 2010. "Growth in a Time of Debt." *American Economic Review: Papers and Proceedings* 100: 573–8.

Svensson, Lars E. O. 2010. "Inflation Targeting." In *Handbook of Monetary Economics* 3, edited by Benjamin M. Friedman and Michael Woodford. Amsterdam: Elsevier.

Thornton, Daniel L. 2013. "An Evaluation of Event-Study Evidence on the Effectiveness of the FOMC's LSAP Program: Are the Announcement Effects Identified?" Federal Reserve Bank of St. Louis Working Paper No. 2013–033B.

Ueda, Kazuo. 2012. "Japan's Deflation and the Bank of Japan's Experience with Non-traditional Monetary Policy." *Journal of Money, Credit and Banking* 44(2): 175–90.

Walsh, Carl E. 2009. "Using Monetary Policy to Stabilize Economic Activity." Paper prepared for the Federal Reserve Bank of Kansas City's symposium *Financial Stability and Macroeconomic Policy*: Jackson Hole, Wyoming, August 20–22.

Williamson, John. 1999. "The Case for a Common Basket Peg for East Asian Currencies." In *Exchange Rate Policies in Emerging Asian Countries*, edited by Stefan Collignon, Jean Pisani-Ferry, and Yung Chul Park. London: Routledge.

5

A View from ASEAN

Chalongphob Sussangkarn and Worapot Manupipatpong

5.1 Introduction

Over the past decade and a half, East Asia has been hit by two major crises. The first originated from within the region in 1997 and the most recent crisis was the great financial crisis originating from the West. Both have had, and will continue to have, important impacts on regional financial cooperation in the region. The 1997 crisis led to many initiatives in finance, trade, and other areas, with ASEAN very much a part of almost all these initiatives. It is expected that the recent crisis will also lead to further and deeper cooperation in the region; some will be continuations of initiatives adopted in response to the 1997 crisis, and others are likely in response to the recent crisis and the challenges that the region will face in the future. Even though the great financial crisis has dented some earlier projects, it is still believed that greater cooperation can make the region stronger and more immune to future crises.

This chapter focuses on financial and monetary cooperation in East Asia after the recent crisis from the perspective of ASEAN. Of course, future cooperation will not start from scratch, but will build from initiatives that already exist in the region, deepening those that are regarded as particularly important in light of the most recent crisis. The chapter starts by describing the various financial and monetary cooperation initiatives that evolved prior to the recent financial crisis. This will provide a good understanding of the context within which the region found itself when it was hit by spillovers from the great financial crisis and of the various financial and monetary cooperation initiatives in existence at that time. Directions for deepening cooperation initiatives that already existed will be discussed, as will new financial and monetary cooperation initiatives to address new concerns arising from the crisis.

The next section briefly reviews financial and monetary cooperation in East Asia, mostly in ASEAN, prior to the 1997 Asian financial crisis. It reminds us that many areas of financial and monetary cooperation being now implemented or under discussion, such as financial safety nets or the promotion of more usage of regional currencies, were already discussed and implemented in ASEAN well before the Asian financial crisis. Section 5.3 discusses the financial cooperation initiatives that emerged after the Asian financial crisis. These extended beyond the ASEAN countries to East Asia more generally, first, because of the general dissatisfaction in East Asia about crisis resolution policies dictated by the IMF, and second on the basis that the greater financial resources of East Asia as a whole, compared to just within ASEAN, would make cooperation initiatives more effective. Section 5.4 discusses the impact of the great financial crisis on the ASEAN economies. Section 5.5 then looks at subsequent ASEAN perspectives on various East Asian regional financial and monetary cooperation. Section 5.6 concludes.

5.2 ASEAN Financial and Monetary Cooperation before the Asian Financial Crisis

ASEAN financial and monetary cooperation actually dates back to the 1970s. Following the Bali Summit in 1976,[1] the Committee on Finance and Banking (COFAB) and the ASEAN Swap Arrangement (ASA) were established in 1977. As one of the five committees under the ASEAN Economic Ministers (AEM) framework,[2] the COFAB promoted regional cooperation in the areas of finance, banking, capital market, taxation, customs, and insurance. It also facilitated intra-ASEAN trade and investment, including through measures such as avoidance of double taxation, the use of ASEAN currencies for intra-ASEAN trade and investment, and the ASEAN Reinsurance Corporation.

The initiative on the use of ASEAN currencies led to some relaxation of capital account restrictions in member countries. It also succeeded in promoting greater use of ASEAN currencies (mostly the Singapore dollar and Malaysian ringgit) in payment for intra-ASEAN trade. Lamberte (1991) noted an increase in the use of ASEAN currencies in the Philippines during 1986–9. While the main ASEAN currency bought by the Banko Sentral ng Pilipinas was the Singapore dollar, and to a lesser extent, the Malaysian ringgit, after 1987 there were also significant increases in purchases of the Brunei dollar,

---

[1] The Bali Concord adopted at the Summit expanded ASEAN cooperation in the economic, social, cultural, and political fields.
[2] The Bali Concord established the ASEAN Economic Ministers (mainly trade ministers) Meeting to strengthen regional economic cooperation, including working toward establishing preferential trading arrangements.

Thai baht and Indonesian rupiah. Yet the US dollar remained the main currency for settlement of intraregional trade. The percentage of trade transactions settled in regional currencies was relatively small, ranging from about 11 percent of total intra-ASEAN trade in Thailand to about 28 percent in Malaysia.

Regional cooperation in the area of taxation contributed to an increase in the number of bilateral agreements for the avoidance of double taxation among ASEAN countries. Customs cooperation also led to the adoption of the ASEAN Customs Code of Conduct in 1983. Furthermore, the ASEAN Insurance Commissioners focused their cooperation on harmonizing non-life insurance laws and unifying insurance statistics. Other cooperation activities under COFAB were limited to exchange of information and research and training activities on the issues of common interests.

The ASEAN Swap Arrangement (ASA) was established by five ASEAN central banks[3] to provide short-term (one to six months) liquidity assistance to members experiencing a temporary international liquidity problem. The initial size of the ASA was US$100 million. Each member contributed US$20 million and could request funding support up to twice its contribution (US$40 million).[4] The swap facility has been subsequently renewed and its size was first expanded in 1987 to US$200 million. After the 1997 Asian financial crisis, the ASA was again expanded in size and supplemented by swaps with the PRC, Japan, and the Republic of Korea to become the Chiang Mai Initiative (see section 5.3.2 and Chapter 2 of this volume).

In the broader regional context, the five ASEAN central banks who were original signatories to the ASA were also members of regional forums such as the South East Asian Central Banks (SEACEN) and the Executives' Meeting of East Asia-Pacific Central Banks (EMEAP).[5] The SEACEN Research and Training Centre was established in 1982 to promote a better understanding of financial, monetary, banking, and economic development matters and closer cooperation among its members in the area of research and training. EMEAP was established in 1991 as a high-level forum for central banks and monetary authorities in the East Asia and Pacific region to informally exchange information and views on economic and financial developments. Its first annual Governors' Meeting was held in 1996.

---

[3] The five central banks are Bank Indonesia, Bank Negara Malaysia, Bangko Sentral ng Pilipinas, Monetary Authority of Singapore, and Bank of Thailand.

[4] It was activated four times during 1979–81 by Indonesia (1979), Malaysia (1980), Thailand (1980), and the Philippines (1981).

[5] In addition to the five ASEAN members (Indonesia, Malaysia, Philippines, Singapore, and Thailand), other members of SEACEN include Myanmar, Nepal, Sri Lanka, Republic of Korea, Taipei,China, Mongolia, Brunei Darussalam, Fiji, Papua New Guinea, Cambodia, and Viet Nam. For EMEAP, there are six additional members including Australia; the PRC; Hong Kong, China; Japan; Republic of Korea; and New Zealand.

Not all ASEAN central banks were represented in these forums. It took the Asian financial crisis to get the ASEAN central banks and monetary authorities to officially form their own exclusive forum, the ASEAN Central Bank Forum (ACBF), in November 1997.

Before the Asian financial crisis ASEAN financial cooperation was carried out under the ASEAN Economic Ministers framework. Its various initiatives were focused mainly on facilitating intra-ASEAN trade and investment, with the exception of the ASA which was designed to promote a foreign exchange safety net. When the ASEAN Free Trade Area (AFTA) was established in January 1992, the ASEAN Economic Ministers in their Framework Agreements on Enhancing ASEAN Economic Cooperation encouraged stronger cooperation in finance and banking, specifically in the fields of capital market and free movement of capital, including further liberalization of the use of ASEAN currencies in trade and investment.

Regional financial cooperation was separated from the AEM and elevated to ministerial level just before the Asian financial crisis, when the Ministerial Understanding (MU) on ASEAN Cooperation in Finance was adopted at the first ASEAN Finance Ministers Meeting (AFMM) in Phuket, Thailand on March 1, 1997. The MU essentially defined the scope of financial cooperation, which included banking and finance, financial and capital markets, customs, insurance, taxation, and public finance. The MU also established the ASEAN Senior Finance Officials Meeting (ASFOM) to assist the AFMM in identifying and implementing regional finance cooperation initiatives and activities.[6] ASFOM replaced COFAB and took over its functions and areas of cooperation.

5.3 Financial and Monetary Cooperation after the Asian Financial Crisis

5.3.1 *Impetus for East Asian Regional Cooperation*

A few months after the first AFMM, Thailand effectively triggered the Asian financial crisis when it was forced to float the baht on July 2, 1997, after unsuccessful attempts by the Bank of Thailand to fend off speculative attacks against the national currency. Runs on some of its weaker financial institutions also forced Thailand to suspend fifty-eight finance companies during the second half of 1997. Having depleted almost all of its foreign exchange reserves, Thailand had to seek help from the IMF.[7] Other ASEAN countries—namely

---

[6] <http://www.asean.org/communities/asean-economic-community/item/ministerial-understanding-on-asean-cooperation-in-telecommunications-and-information-technology>.

[7] The lending package for Thailand was US$17.2 billion, of which US$4 billion came from the IMF's fund and the remaining contributions from countries in Asia and the Pacific, the World Bank, and the Asian Development Bank. See Sussangkarn (2002).

Malaysia, the Philippines, and Indonesia—came under speculative attacks shortly after the floatation of the Thai baht. Indonesia (and the Republic of Korea) also had to seek IMF support in November 1997. Malaysia did not seek IMF support but instead imposed controls on capital outflows. The Philippines was less affected by the crisis and received an extension of credit of US$1.1 billion from the IMF. The IMF also extended and augmented a credit to the Philippines to support its exchange rate and other economic policies (see Nanto (1998)).

The Asian financial crisis was a major financial shock to ASEAN and East Asia. It was too big for any regional financial cooperation initiative among ASEAN countries. For example, the size of the ASA at that time, US$200 million, was insignificant compared to the IMF programs for Thailand and Indonesia. Most ASEAN countries were weakened considerably by the Asian financial crisis in any case. However, the Asian financial crisis turned out to be an important push factor for economic cooperation and integration in East Asia as a whole. East Asia had little say in the crisis resolution measures, which were dictated by the IMF to those countries needing IMF assistance.[8] The imposed conditionality was very harsh and there were criticisms that these benefited financial institutions in the West to the detriment of the crisis-affected countries. Critics pointed to a number of areas, such as:[9]

- the harsh nature of the tight fiscal and monetary policies, with apparent disregard for their social or political consequences. The conditionality for the various countries tended to be of a "one size fits all" nature, therefore failing to differentiate between the different political and socio-cultural contexts;

- an unwillingness to allow non-market-based interventions such as controls on capital outflows, which were successfully used by Malaysia;

- an imposition of full guarantees for creditors of financial institutions (mostly foreign). There was also an imposition of relatively rapid structural reform measures, such as stringent financial standards and corporate restructuring, privatization of state-owned enterprises, and asset sales at what many considered as "fire sale" prices. These were regarded as mainly benefiting foreign banks and investment funds.

East Asia as a whole was financially strong prior to the crisis. It was a saving surplus region (about US$100 billion annually).[10] However, the surplus was

---

[8] For detailed discussions of the IMF program for Thailand, see Sussangkarn (2002).

[9] For various discussions, see for example, Sachs (1997), Stiglitz (1998), Feldstein (1998), Krugman (1998), UNCTAD (1998), Wyplosz (Chapter 4 in this volume), and Stiglitz (2002).

[10] ASEAN was however a deficit region; with a saving (current account) deficit of about US$16 billion–17 billion per year in the years leading up to the crisis.

mainly recycled back to the West while, when the crisis hit, the affected countries had to rely on huge inflows of short-term foreign debt to finance their abrupt payment deficits. In the three countries that went under IMF programs, the stock of short-term foreign debt rose to more than the amount of foreign reserves; this eventually led to the crisis. If East Asia had a better system of mutual self-help prior to the crisis, then it may be that the crisis could have been avoided. This was another rationale for the region to start the ASEAN+3 process, which brought together ASEAN and the PRC, Japan, and the Republic of Korea. This suited ASEAN, which emerged as the hub for the group. ASEAN+3 then promptly initiated financial cooperation initiatives such as the Chiang Mai Initiative (CMI), the Asian Bond Fund (ABF), and the Asian Bond Markets Initiatives (ABMI).[11] From cooperation on finance, the areas of cooperation expanded to trade and economic partnership agreements among various subgroups, and now there are many functional areas of cooperation under the ASEAN+3 umbrella, including ministerial-level meetings on areas such as agriculture, energy, and the environment. At the leaders' level, an annual East Asia Summit (EAS) includes India, Australia, and New Zealand in addition to the ASEAN+3 group; the US and the Russian Federation joined in 2011. So as a result of the 1997–8 crisis, economic cooperation in East Asia expanded to an extent that could hardly have been envisaged before the crisis.

5.3.2 Financial Cooperation Initiatives

Asian monetary fund. The first major proposal for East Asian financial cooperation did not get off the ground. In September 1997, Japan proposed setting up an Asian monetary fund (AMF), which would pool abundant Asian reserves that could be disbursed quickly to provide balance of payments support for crisis-hit economies. The original size of the fund was estimated at US$100 billion with half of the contribution from Japan and the remaining balance from the PRC; Hong Kong, China; the Republic of Korea; Australia; Indonesia; Malaysia; Singapore; Thailand; and the Philippines. Lipscy (2003) provides a detailed account of the development of the AMF. He refers to an idea called an "Asian Monetary Organization" with an initial size of US$20 billion developed by Japan in the fall of 1996 after the US/IMF bailout of Mexico raised some concern about possible US reluctance to contribute should a similar crisis happen in Asia. Observing IMF underfunding for the Thai bailout package, since about half of the total combined financial support for the three Asian countries came from bilateral donors who were mostly from the region, Japan tabled its AMF proposal, but the idea did not take off due to strong objection

---

[11] For discussions of rationales for East Asian financial cooperation, see Sussangkarn (2003).

from the US and the IMF on the grounds that such an arrangement would create moral hazard vis-à-vis the IMF, and possible double standards.[12] In addition, because prior consultations had been limited, support from within the region was weak.

In spite of the AMF setback, key players in the region continued to explore ideas for financial cooperation. At a meeting of Asian finance and central bank deputies in Manila, Philippines on November 18–19, 1997, the so-called "Manila Framework" was developed. This was to be "a new framework for enhanced Asian regional cooperation to promote financial stability". Given the involvement of the United States and the IMF at the meeting,[13] the ideas incorporated into the framework were not very radical and stressed the central role of the IMF. The Manila Framework explicitly acknowledged the need for any East Asian regional framework to be consistent with and supportive of the global framework. The official Summary of the Discussions stated:

> Deputies agreed on the need and desirability of a framework for regional cooperation to enhance the prospects for financial stability. This framework, which recognizes the central role of the IMF in the international monetary system, includes the following initiatives: (a) a mechanism for regional surveillance to complement global surveillance by the IMF; (b) enhanced economic and technical cooperation particularly in strengthening domestic financial systems and regulatory capacities; (c) measures to strengthen the IMF's capacity to respond to financial crises; and (d) a cooperative financing arrangement that would supplement IMF resources.

The Manila Framework was endorsed at a meeting of finance ministers from ASEAN; Australia; the PRC; Hong Kong, China; Japan; the Republic of Korea; and the United States in Kuala Lumpur, Malaysia on December 2, 1997. Work on the regional cooperative financing arrangement to supplement IMF resources continued. Since 1999, ASEAN countries have strengthened their cooperation with the PRC, Japan, and the Republic of Korea on the financial, monetary, and fiscal issues of common interest and self-help and support mechanisms in East Asia. The ASEAN+3 finance and central bank deputies (AFDM+3) held their first meeting in March 1999. In March 2000, the AFDM+3 explored ways to further strengthen regional self-help and support mechanisms in East Asia, including through a regional financing arrangement. Two months later, in May 2000, at the ASEAN+3 Finance Ministers Meeting (AFMM+3) in Chiang Mai, Thailand (back-to-back with the ADB Annual

---

[12] See Manupipatpong (2002).
[13] Represented were Australia; Brunei Darussalam; Canada; the PRC; Hong Kong, China; Indonesia; Japan; the Republic of Korea; Malaysia; New Zealand; the Philippines; Singapore; Thailand; and the United States. High-level representatives from the IMF, the World Bank, and the Asian Development Bank also attended the meeting.

Meeting), the ministers recognized "a need to establish a regional financing arrangement to supplement the existing international facilities" and agreed to "strengthen the existing cooperative frameworks among our monetary authorities through the 'Chiang Mai Initiative'. The Initiative involves an expanded ASEAN Swap Arrangement[14] that would include ASEAN countries, and a network of bilateral swap and repurchase agreement facilities among ASEAN countries, PRC, Japan, and Republic of Korea."[15]

Chiang Mai Initiative. The CMI and its evolution to the CMI Multilateralization (CMIM) are described in Chapter 2 of this volume. Further development of CMIM that would make it more useful to ASEAN countries are suggested in section 5.5 below.

Apart from the CMI, there were other important initiatives related to financial cooperation among ASEAN countries. The global surveillance process of the IMF was supplemented within ASEAN by the ASEAN Surveillance Process (ASP) after the 1997–8 crisis. This was meant to be an informal process based on a peer review system that would complement the regular surveillance by the IMF.

A unit was set up within the ASEAN Secretariat to assist with coordinating the work of the ASP and to prepare a series of semi-annual ASEAN surveillance reports. The ADB provides technical support for the operation of the ASP. The peer review of the ASP is conducted at the ASEAN Finance Ministers meeting, which is held twice a year. At the level of the ASEAN+3, surveillance is conducted through the Economic Review and Policy Dialogue (ERPD), which the ADB also supports. The ERPD is held at the Deputies' level twice a year to discuss economic and financial developments in the region and its outcomes are reported to the ASEAN+3 Finance Ministers Meeting, which is held annually.

The current surveillance mechanisms are still far from satisfactory. The resources to support them are very limited and the officials involved in these processes only carry out the tasks on a part-time basis alongside many other regular tasks. This is why an independent surveillance unit with full-time staff was set up to support the CMIM process. The so-called AMRO, located in Singapore, began its operations in 2011.

Another important area of cooperation is on developing the region's capital markets, particularly the bond markets. The idea is to promote the investment of the region's savings surplus within the region and provide more long-term

---

[14] The expanded ASEAN Swap Arrangement referred to the ASA, whose size was increased from US$200 million to US$1 billion, and whose membership was expanded to include all ten ASEAN member central banks.

[15] See the Joint Ministerial Statement of the 6 May 2000 meeting of ASEAN+3 finance ministers at <http://www.mof.go.jp/english/international_policy/convention/asean_plus_3/20000506.htm>.

development financing in place of the short-term foreign debt that deficit countries had to rely on prior to the 1997–8 crisis. Cooperation in this area has been through the ABMI of the ASEAN+3 group and the development of the Asian Bond Funds (ABF1 and ABF2) by central banks in the region. Chapter 2 of this volume describes these initiatives.

From an ASEAN perspective, these ASEAN+3 and East Asian initiatives complement ASEAN's own initiatives on regional monetary and financial integration. For example, the development of local currency bond markets through ABMI helps increase the width and depth of ASEAN local currency bond markets, while the region is also working toward promoting cross-border issuance of these bonds through bond (and equity) market linkages. CMI and CMIM provide additional liquidity supports to ASEAN beyond that provided under the ASA.

5.3.3 Trade and Investment Initiatives

It was natural that financial cooperation extend to trade and investment. Slow progress of the Doha round and the increasingly deeper economic linkages in East Asia from market-driven factors led to a proliferation of sub-regional trade and economic cooperation agreements in the region. Regional competition also played an important role, such as when the PRC proposed an ASEAN–PRC free trade area, then Japan had to follow suit. Most of these sub-regional agreements have ASEAN as a partner. So ASEAN free trade or comprehensive economic partnership agreements with each of the Plus Three countries (ASEAN–PRC, ASEAN–Japan, and ASEAN–Republic of Korea) have already been signed and are being implemented. Similarly, ASEAN–India and ASEAN–CER (Australia and New Zealand) agreements have been concluded. Apart from the sub-regional agreements, there are also numerous bilateral agreements.[16] Currently, there are proposals for agreements among various partners of ASEAN, such as between the Plus Three countries (the PRC, Japan, and the Republic of Korea), and even more ambitious proposals for an ASEAN+3 or ASEAN+6 FTA (including India, Australia, and New Zealand). Another approach is to start with a relatively clean FTA involving a few countries and enlarge the group as other countries become ready to join. This is the approach of the Trans-Pacific Partnership (TPP), which started in 2005 with four very small economies, Brunei Darussalam, Chile, New Zealand, and Singapore. It has attracted, interest from Australia, Japan, Malaysia, Peru, the United States, and Viet Nam.

Both market-driven factors and economic cooperation initiatives have led to a more integrated East Asia. ADB (2009) indicated that the share of

---

[16] See Chia (2010) for detailed discussions of trade and economic cooperation in East Asia.

intraregional trade in East Asia increased from about 42 percent in 1994–5 to about 48 percent in 2004–5. The closer integration on the trade side increases the importance of cooperation on the macroeconomic and financial side. Shocks and volatilities from one part can quickly transmit to other parts of the region. Of course, the region is also closely linked to the more advanced economies outside the region and cannot escape impacts from major shocks in these economies. This was clearly seen from impacts of the great financial crisis.

5.4 Impacts of the Global Financial Crisis on ASEAN Economies

5.4.1 The Context of the post 1997–8 Economic Adjustments

The post 1997–8 economic adjustments in ASEAN and other countries in East Asia set the context for how the region was affected by the great financial crisis. The salient features are briefly noted here.

A key adjustment in response to the Asian financial crisis was the (needed) large depreciation of the local currencies of the crisis-affected countries. Apart from the countries needing IMF support (Indonesia, the Republic of Korea, and Thailand), most of the other countries in the region experienced contagion and depreciating exchange rates. Being generally export-led economies, the export sectors were boosted and became the most important engine of growth for many countries.[17] The ratio of exports to GDP had increased during the post-crisis period for all East Asian countries, and more rapidly in recent years (see Table 5.1).

The East Asian export engine generated large current account surpluses and became an important part of the so-called "global imbalance." In the few years

Table 5.1. Ratio of exports of goods and services to GDP (current prices, %)

	1993–6	1997–2000	2001–4	2005–7
China, People's Rep. of	22.7%	21.5%	27.8%	40.0%
Indonesia	26.4%	39.3%	33.6%	31.5%
Korea, Rep. of	27.5%	39.0%	36.3%	40.3%
Malaysia	88.4%	112.5%	110.3%	114.8%
Philippines	35.5%	52.0%	50.0%	45.8%
Singapore	181.2%	185.0%	208.9%	262.6%
Thailand	39.5%	58.0%	66.6%	76.6%
Viet Nam	34.1%	48.2%	59.1%	73.2%
Japan	9.3%	10.8%	11.8%	16.5%

Source: World Bank, World Development Indicators (online through the Global Development Network).

---

[17] For a country like Thailand, one can almost say that export has remained the only engine of growth since the 1997–8 crisis.

leading up to the great financial crisis, the US deficit was about the same as the surplus of East Asia plus the major oil exporting economies. With the large surpluses in East Asia, it is not surprising that the amount of foreign reserves in the region increased substantially. By the end of 2008, the combined foreign reserves of East Asia reached about US$4.16 trillion, almost six times the amount prior to the 1997–8 crisis and accounting for about 55 percent of the world's foreign reserves. Most of these surpluses were invested in the West, mostly in the US, so they were basically recycled back to finance the major deficit country.

While higher foreign exchange reserves increase self-insurance against foreign exchange shortages, the large reserve accumulation in East Asia can be viewed more as an outcome of countries buying up the foreign exchange inflows resulting from the current account surplus and capital inflows to prevent their currencies from appreciating too much. This is understandable as export was the main engine of growth for many economies.

Another important area of post-crisis adjustment has to do with lessons learned as a result of the crisis and major financial reforms that were carried out subsequently. These led to improvements in prudential supervision and regulations, corporate governance, and generally to a more risk-averse financial system. This helped the region avoid significant exposures to the toxic sub-prime assets that led to the great financial crisis.

5.4.2 Impact of the Global Financial Crisis

Following the great financial crisis, capital-to-assets ratios did not change much in the risk-averse ASEAN banks (Table 5.2). The overall impact of the crisis was therefore quite limited, even though the region's stock markets suffered in line with global markets. But this was not surprising.

What was surprising was that some countries experienced severe foreign exchange liquidity shortages in spite of large foreign reserves. After the closure of Lehman Brothers, severe liquidity shortages in money markets in the US and other advanced economies led to a withdrawal of bank lending to emerging markets and a global liquidation of many of the portfolio investments

Table 5.2. Bank capital to assets ratio

	2005	2006	2007	2008	Change 2008 from avg. 2005–7 (%)
Indonesia	9.8	10.8	10.6	10.3	−0.1
Malaysia	7.7	7.6	7.4	8.0	0.4
Philippines	11.8	11.7	11.7	10.6	−1.1
Singapore	9.6	9.6	9.2	8.3	−1.2
Thailand	8.9	8.9	9.5	9.3	0.2

Source: IMF, Global Financial Stability Report, April 2010 and Bank of Thailand.

A View from ASEAN

Table 5.3. Foreign reserves and potential short-term liabilities (end of 2008)

	(1) Foreign exchange reserves (US$ billion)	(2) Short-term debt (by remaining maturity)	(3) Foreign holdings of stocks	(4) Foreign holdings of bonds	(5) Ratio of (1) to (2)+(3)+(4)
Republic of Korea	201.7	191.1	111.0	27.0	61.3%
Indonesia	50.9	33.2	18.0	7.1	87.3%
Malaysia	91.3	42.4	22.3	11.8	119.3%
Philippines	39.6	14.3	11.6	0.6	149.4%
Thailand	112.3	35.1	30.7	1.7	166.4%

Source: Chua (2009), quoted in Table 2 of Huang (2009).

held by investment funds. As a result, large amounts of foreign currencies (mostly US dollars) fled emerging markets, leading to severe liquidity shortages of US dollars. The situation for the Republic of Korea was particularly severe. Although it had more than US$200 billion of foreign reserves, it also had large amounts of short-term foreign debt and large foreign holdings of portfolio investment which could be easily liquidated to take money out of the country. The Republic of Korea's foreign reserves were not sufficient to cover short-term foreign debt and short-term contingent liabilities from foreign holdings of portfolio investment (see Table 5.3). To a lesser extent this was also the case for Indonesia, and Singapore too faced severe US dollar liquidity shortages. The foreign exchange shortages led to sizeable currency depreciations in the Republic of Korea and some other countries (see Figure 5.1).

Given East Asia's and ASEAN's dependence on exports, the biggest impact of the great financial crisis was through the export channel. Sharp declines in exports were experienced by ASEAN countries, starting around the last quarter of 2008. Weak demand from the US and Europe as well as some temporary shortages of trade financing explain these declines. Exports of most ASEAN countries contracted by between 8.2 and 30 percent in 2009 (Table 5.4). As a result, real GDP growth turned negative in 2009 for Thailand, Malaysia, Singapore, and Brunei Darussalam (Table 5.5). Indonesia and Viet Nam are less dependent on the export sector than other countries, and while their growth rates slowed down in 2009, they still managed to achieve reasonable growth. While GDP growth has recovered in all ASEAN countries since the first half of 2010,[18] the slow and fragile recovery in the advanced economies, particularly the US and EU, means that their consumer spending will remain sluggish for several years to come. Asian and ASEAN countries will therefore have to rely more on domestic and regional demand to sustain their economic growth.

[18] However, Thailand's growth for 2011 was severely affected by the flood toward the end of the year.

113

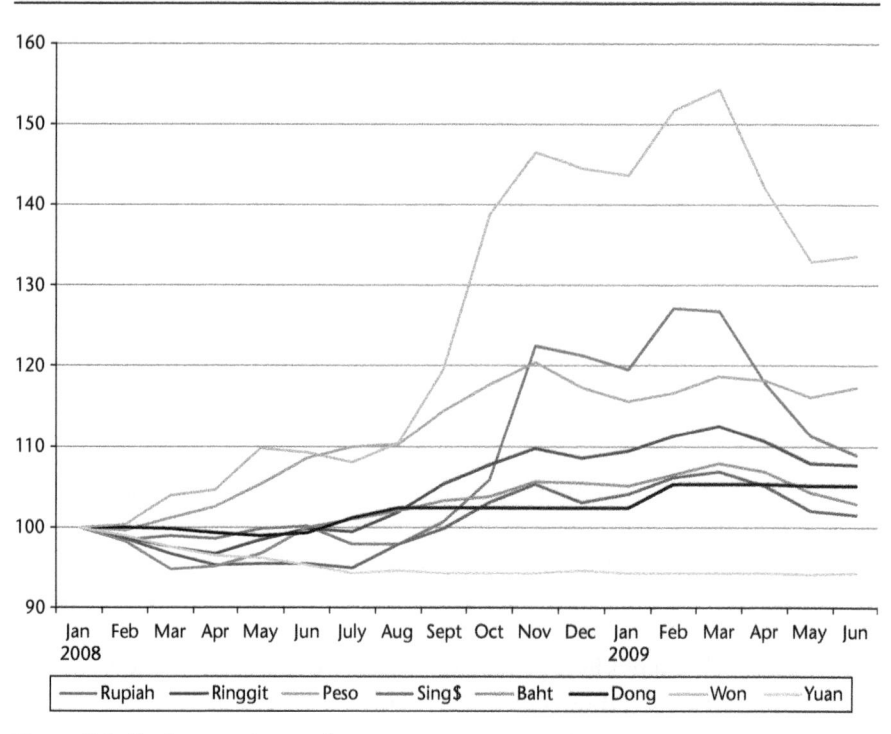

Figure 5.1. Exchange rate trends

Table 5.4. Total ASEAN trade, 2008–9 (value in US$ million; change in %)

	2008 Exports	2008 Imports	2009 Exports	2009 Imports	Year-on-year change Exports	Year-on-year change Imports	Year-on-year change Total trade
Brunei Darussalam	10,268.0	2,506.7	7,168.6	2,399.6	(30.2)	(4.3)	(25.1)
Cambodia	4,358.5	4,417.0	4,985.8	3,900.9	14.4	(11.7)	1.3
Indonesia	137,020.4	129,197.3	116,510.0	96,829.2	(15.0)	(25.1)	(19.9)
Lao PDR	827.7	1,803.2	1,237.2	1,725.0	49.5	(4.3)	12.6
Malaysia	194,495.9	144,298.8	156,890.9	123,330.5	(19.3)	(14.5)	(17.3)
Myanmar	6,620.6	3,794.9	6,341.5	3,849.9	(4.2)	1.4	(2.2)
Philippines	49,025.4	56,645.6	38,334.7	45,533.9	(21.8)	(19.6)	(20.6)
Singapore	338,175.9	319,780.3	269,832.5	245,784.7	(20.2)	(23.1)	(21.6)
Thailand	174,966.7	177,567.5	152,497.2	133,769.6	(12.8)	(24.7)	(18.8)
Viet Nam	61,777.8	79,579.2	56,691.0	69,230.9	(8.2)	(13.0)	(10.9)
ASEAN	977,536.9	919,590.5	810,489.2	726,354.1	(17.1)	(21.0)	(19.0)

Source: ASEAN Merchandise Trade Statistics Database (compiled/computed from data submission, publications and/or websites of ASEAN Member States)

Table 5.5. ASEAN real GDP growth, 2006–11

Country	Base year	2006	2007	2008	2009	2010	2011
Brunei Darussalam	2000	4.4	0.2	−1.4	−1.8	2.6	2.2
Cambodia	2000	10.8	10.2	6.7	0.1	6.0	6.4
Indonesia	2000	5.5	6.3	6.0	4.5	6.3	6.5
Lao PDR	1990	8.3	6.0	7.8	7.5	8.1	8.0
Malaysia	1987	5.8	6.6	4.8	−1.6	7.2	5.1
Myanmar	1990	13.6	13.1	12.0	10.3	10.6	10.4
Philippines	1985	5.3	7.4	4.2	1.1	7.6	3.9
Singapore	1995	8.6	8.5	1.8	−0.8	14.9	4.9
Thailand	1988	5.1	5.0	2.5	−2.3	7.8	0.1
Viet Nam	1994	8.2	8.5	6.3	5.2	6.8	6.0

Source: ASEAN Finance and Macroeconomic Surveillance Unit database.

5.5 ASEAN Perspectives on Post-Crisis Regional Financial and Monetary Cooperation

5.5.1 *Is East Asian Regional Cooperation still Relevant?*

The experiences through the great financial crisis have raised questions about the continued relevance of East Asian economic and particularly financial cooperation that have been built up since the Asian financial crisis. Many factors point to a possible lowering in importance of East Asian regional cooperation.

First, as indicated above, the sub-prime crisis led to large capital outflows from the region and some countries faced severe shortages of US dollars. However, it turned out that the CMI, which is a central feature of regional cooperation, was designed precisely to deal with this type of situation, though it played no role in assisting the countries with US dollar liquidity problems. While the amount available through the swaps may have been an issue, the main problem was the need for countries to be under an IMF program if they wanted to draw more than 20 percent of maximum swap lines. After the 1997–8 experiences, there was such a distrust of the IMF in the region that no government was willing to take the political risk by putting its country under another IMF program, even a Flexible Credit Line (FCL). Instead, the Republic of Korea and Singapore each arranged for swaps of US$30 billion with the US Federal Reserve to ease their liquidity pressures. Indonesia also requested a swap with the US Fed but was refused. Instead, it got a swap line from the PRC outside of the CMI and also increased its swap amount with Japan under the CMI. Given its limited role, it is easy to understand how countries might simply lose interest in the CMI and its future development.

Second, talk of possible decoupling of East Asia from the West prior to the sub-prime crisis was contradicted by the massive declines in exports from

Table 5.6. Intra-East Asian trade shares (%)

	2005–7 average		1994–5 average	
	Parts and components	Final products	Parts and components	Final products
Machinery	62.6	38.5	55.5	42.9
ICT products	68.5	34.4	59.8	36.4
Electrical goods	68.4	67.4	60.1	58.8
Motor vehicles	44.0	16.9	42.5	22.5

Source: Table 4 in Athukorala and Kohpaiboon (2009).

East Asia in the aftermath of the crisis. East Asia had been increasing its intraregional trade shares, yet much of the manufactures trade between East Asian countries is in parts and components, and this has been increasing over time. East Asia is still highly dependent on outside markets for its final products. In fact, the share of intraregional trade in manufactured *final* goods has been generally declining, indicating increasing dependence on the economic prospects of advanced economies in the West (see Table 5.6 for some key product categories). Thus, East Asia cannot ignore its trade linkages to the rest of the world and regional demand has to be significantly strengthened in order to serve as an engine of growth after the great financial crisis.

Finally, the G20 has now become the premier forum for economic discussions and cooperation in the global arena. There are six members of the East Asian Summit in the G20 including one member from ASEAN, Indonesia. For these G20 members, the global arena may provide more attraction than local regional forums, so the focus on regional meetings, such as the various ASEAN+ forums, may decline compared to before the great financial crisis. But it is important for ASEAN as a group that its views and positions are properly conveyed and represented, particularly on issues relevant to the region.

While these factors may indicate a reduced importance of regional mechanisms and initiatives, on the opposite side other considerations support continued regional cooperation and some even reinforce the need for more cooperation. First, instead of losing interest, ASEAN+3 continued to work on extending the CMI to the CMIM after the great financial crisis. In spite of the need to negotiate some very sensitive and tricky issues, such as each country's contribution and voting weight, agreement was reached in May 2009 with slight refinements in May 2010. The CMIM agreement came into force on March 24, 2010. This shows that ASEAN+3 is still willing to make the effort to strengthen its regional self-help and support mechanism. The regional surveillance unit to support CMIM, the so-called AMRO, was established in Singapore in April 2011 and the size of CMIM was expanded in May 2012. The total size is now US$240 billion, with 80 percent contributed by the Plus Three countries and 20 percent by ASEAN countries (see Chapter 2 in this volume for an extensive presentation of CMIM).

On the trade side, the region's exports and economic growth bounced back sharply in 2010 in spite of still sluggish economic growth and continued economic problems in the advanced economies. The bounce-back was generated mainly from sources of growth within the region. In the case of Thailand, exports grew by more than 27 percent in 2010, and continued to show strong growth of more than 20 percent in the first three quarters of 2011 until the country was hit by severe floods at the end of 2011 and beginning of 2012. The good export bounce-back showed that the region was capable of generating more intraregional export demand in spite of global sluggishness, particularly from the big economies of the PRC and India. So there still seems to be a lot of room for greater regional trade cooperation and integration to boost growth. However, as economic sluggishness in the advanced economies continued, the region could not fully escape the negative side-effects. In 2012 and 2013, growth of the big Asia economies, the PRC, and India slowed down. Exports and economic growth for most ASEAN economies also slowed down significantly. Greater regional trade integration may be able to boost regional growth somewhat, but a global recovery would be the key to a sustainable recovery of the region.

Finally, while there are six EAS countries represented in the G20, none can speak on behalf of the group. It has therefore been important that the ASEAN chair—who also chairs the ASEAN+3 Leaders Meeting and the EAS—continues to participate in G20 meetings, since he or she is the appropriate person to convey common views of the group (if any) to the G20. The G20 is actually complementary to the East Asian forums, and the East Asian meetings should be scheduled (as in 2010) to be slightly before the G20 meeting so that some positions for East Asia can be developed and later conveyed to the G20 by the ASEAN chair.

There are also many important areas for economic cooperation in light of developments since the great financial crisis. New growth engines for the region are being explored, including regional—particularly cross-border—infrastructures. The ADB has stressed the potential for better connectivity to boost Asia's growth. The governments of Japan and the PRC are also pushing along this path. Regional cooperation in this area could concern financing as well as cross-border agreements to improve the effectiveness of infrastructures. Finally, as the region cooperates and integrates more and more, the regional risk factors increase. This increases the need for more effective intraregional surveillance and macroeconomic cooperation or coordination. Some of the issues related to future financial and monetary cooperation in the region are further discussed below.

5.5.2 CMIM from ASEAN's Perspective

CMIM is covered in detailed in Chapter 2 of this volume. Here we briefly discuss CMIM from ASEAN's perspective. First it should be noted that the Plus Three countries are unlikely to need liquidity support from CMIM. The PRC and Japan have huge foreign reserves, and the Republic of Korea has rapidly built up its own reserves since the severe US dollar liquidity crunch after the closure of Lehman Brothers. But CMIM can be useful to ASEAN countries, particularly the less-developed members. This is particularly important given the unconventional monetary policies being pursued by the advanced economies. When these policies are wound down, there are likely to be large capital outflows from emerging market economies, including in ASEAN, and foreign exchange liquidity shortages may arise. If the situation becomes very severe, access to quick and sufficiently large liquidity support can prevent the situation from deteriorating into a foreign exchange crisis. Unfortunately, the current status of CMIM cannot yet provide sufficient support to deal with such a situation.

The size of CMIM, at US$240 billion, is large enough. But as of mid-2013, members could only draw up to 30 percent of their quotas without being under an IMF program. For example, Thailand could draw up to US$6.828 billion without an IMF link. This is rather small compared to the US$17.2 billion IMF package of 1997, or the swap of US$30 billion that the Republic of Korea agreed with the Federal Reserve during the great financial crisis. Of course, with the IMF linked portion included, Thailand could draw up to US$22.76 billion, which should be sufficient to meet most contingencies. However, if an IMF link is needed for sufficient funding then CMIM provides little added value as a regional self-help and support mechanism that can effectively deal with such a situation. The time and resources spent on developing CMIM as well as establishing AMRO seem to be rather wasteful. To be useful to ASEAN countries, the link to the IMF needed to be weakened or removed.

The unlinked portion was due to be increased to 40 percent in 2014. This ratio should increase even more as the regional surveillance capability of AMRO gets much stronger. Its capacity has been greatly strengthened since its establishment in April 2011, and there is now a plan to evolve AMRO into a full-fledged international organization. When this happens, the link to the IMF can be removed in cases of temporary liquidity shortages, which is the most likely scenario for most ASEAN member countries. If the situation turns out not to be temporary, but structural, such that CMIM support for, say, six to nine months cannot resolve the problem, then it would be possible to invoke the IMF link at that time (see Sussangkarn (2011)).

5.5.3 Growth Rebalancing and Regional Cooperation

The environment following the great financial crisis will require some adjustment in the growth strategies of various countries in ASEAN and East Asia. Growth in the advanced economies has been sluggish and is likely to remain so for a number of years, given continued financial problems in the Eurozone. Therefore, East Asia needs to rely less on exporting to the advanced economies in the West. Further regional economic integration can lessen reliance on Western markets. The potential for this can be seen by export growth patterns since 2010. In spite of sluggish growth in the US and Europe, exports of many countries in Asia rebounded in 2010, driven mainly by demand coming from within the region, particularly from the large economies such as the PRC and India. Apart from exports, other domestic growth drivers need to be promoted. Investment has been weak in many ASEAN economies for some time. Increasing domestic investment will probably need to be achieved through public sector initiated investment projects, particularly infrastructure projects. Greater domestic consumption can also be promoted. Regionally, cross-border investment can also increase regional demand, promote connectivity, and boost economic integration and regional growth.

Park (2009) suggests that people in Asia save more because of the poor quality or lack of public services such as health care, education, and social security, and the inability to smooth consumption over time. To stimulate domestic demand, he suggests reforms of social protection, public and private pension, public health care, and education systems and the creation of financial institutions specializing in household lending. The Asian Policy Forum (2010) further suggested that Asia would need to pursue structural reforms that reduce factor and resource market distortions, stimulate consumption, invest in education, and promote integration of Asian markets for goods and services and also that integrate financial markets so that Asian savings can be mobilized to fund investment needs in the region. Noting that the ratio of investment to GDP in ASEAN declined significantly after the Asian financial crisis, Kawai and Lee (2015) recommend that investment be promoted by increasing targeted public investment, particularly in infrastructure, and enabling environment for investment. They highlight the importance of infrastructure development in enhancing cross-border connectivity, which together with the expansion of intraregional trade can create greater trade and investment opportunities in the region.

A growth rebalancing strategy should therefore follow a two-prong approach. The first prong is to encourage greater consumption by enhancing access to key public services such as health care, education, and social security as well as financial services. The second prong is to stimulate investment, by both the public and private sectors, initially through greater public investment, preferably in infrastructure, improved investment climate, and closer integration of trade, investment, and financial markets.

ADB and ADBI (2009) estimated that Asia will need to invest almost US$8 trillion in national infrastructure over the next 11 years. In addition, another US$290 billion will be needed for cross-border projects in transportation and energy. Given such a huge investment requirement, the issue of financing is of great importance. This is also linked to the idea arising from the aftermath of the 1997–8 crisis that more of the large savings surplus in the region should be recycled as long-term development finance for the region. The development of the region's bond market is indirectly related to supplying long-term investment funds for infrastructure investment. Efforts to develop the Asian Bond Market through the ABMI and Asian Bond Funds should continue, as well as new initiatives that would make it easier for the private sector to raise funds through the Asian Bond Market. These will help to recycle more of the region's savings surplus for long-term financing of investment within the region and should help to make available more funding from within the region for infrastructure investment. In May 2012, ADB and ASEAN launched an ASEAN Infrastructure Fund (AIF). with an initial capital of US$485 million contributed mainly by ADB, Malaysia, and Indonesia. The amount is still very small, however, compared to the region's infrastructure needs, so the size of the fund needs to increase substantially and also possibly include the participation of the Plus Three countries.

5.5.4 Greater ASEAN Economic and Financial Integration

As East Asian countries integrate more and more with each other, and intraregional trade and investment play more important roles in driving regional growth, the importance of the populous economies (the PRC and India) will continue to increase. As these large economies become more dynamic and develop closer linkages with the rest of the region, the ASEAN countries will benefit from a stronger demand for their exports. But the smaller economies also fear that they will be overwhelmed by exports from these large economies, each with still a very large pool for relatively cheap semi-skilled labor. This is why the ASEAN countries attach priority to their own integration. The PRC and India have shown that "size does matter," and the only way for ASEAN countries to be able to compete on more equal terms with the PRC and India is to develop the main features of a single market and single production base. Only then can ASEAN offer the benefits of economies of scale comparable to (although still less than) the PRC and India.

ASEAN has of course embarked on economic integration for some time. The ASEAN Free Trade Area (AFTA) was proposed by the then Thai Prime Minister, Anand Panyarachun, in 1991, and was endorsed by the ASEAN leaders at the

Fourth ASEAN Summit in Singapore in January 1992. The implementation of AFTA has virtually been completed. By January 1, 2010, duties on 99.65 percent of all tariff lines under the Common Effective Preferential Tariff Scheme for the AFTA (CEPT-AFTA) were eliminated. For the newer ASEAN Member States (Cambodia, Lao PDR, Myanmar, and Viet Nam), tariffs on 98.96 percent of total lines were within the 0–5 percent range. ASEAN has also agreed on a more comprehensive agreement on trade in goods. The ASEAN Trade in Goods Agreement (ATIGA) came into force in May 2010. It is an improvement over the current AFTA-CEPT Scheme, since it consolidates all of ASEAN's existing initiatives, obligations, and commitments on intra-ASEAN trade-in-goods, including both tariff and non-tariff elements, into one single comprehensive agreement.

Intraregional trade in ASEAN has gradually improved over time. After the 1997–8 crisis, intra-ASEAN trade declined slightly and returned to the pre-crisis level by 2000, when under AFTA almost all imports among the ASEAN countries were subjected to no more than a 5 percent import tariff. Further reduction of tariffs in 2003, when nearly 80 percent of intra-ASEAN imports were not subject to import tariffs, led to a further increase in intraregional trade to 27 percent of total trade by 2008.

FTA utilization can still be improved, however. Kawai and Wignaraja (2010) summarize the outcome of an ADB survey of 551 Asian firms on their use of FTA preferences. The survey indicates that lack of information on the FTAs was the major reason for non-use, followed by low margins of preferences and delays and administrative costs associated with rules of origin.[19] They suggest promoting the use of FTA preferences through enhancing awareness of FTA provisions, margins of preferences at the product levels, and administrative procedures for rules of origin.

With the emergence of the PRC, and more recently India, ASEAN countries see the need to go beyond AFTA. The PRC's emergence raised many questions about ASEAN competitiveness. After the Asian financial crisis, the PRC quickly replaced ASEAN as the focal point for FDI and the manufacturing hub for labor-intensive products to feed the world market. In fact, even though the crisis gave some breathing room to many ASEAN industries in the form of large depreciations of their currencies, particularly against the Chinese yuan, the PRC's exports have increased much faster than ASEAN's since the crisis. In 2004 the PRC's exports overtook ASEAN's in value for the first time, and by 2007 were more than 50 percent larger.

The message for ASEAN is that in order to regain competitiveness it needs to integrate beyond AFTA to reduce the costs of doing business so that the region becomes more competitive and more attractive for foreign investment. The

---

[19] Other reasons include use of other schemes, such as export processing zones, and non-tariff measures in partner countries.

challenge from the PRC was the key push-factor that led ASEAN leaders to seriously consider further integration. At the ninth ASEAN Summit in Bali, Indonesia, in October 2003, the leaders agreed to set 2020 as the target for the formation of the so-called ASEAN Economic Community (AEC). This was moved up to 2015 at the twelfth summit in Cebu, Philippines, in January 2007 and the AEC Blueprint was adopted at the thirteenth ASEAN Summit in Singapore in November 2007, where the ASEAN Charter was also signed.

From the official statements, "AEC envisages the following key characteristics: (a) a single market and production base, (b) a highly competitive economic region, (c) a region of equitable economic development, and (d) a region fully integrated into the global economy."[20] The target to achieve this (or most of the main elements) is 2015. While many ASEAN countries are still apprehensive about the AEC, as they feel that increased intra-ASEAN competition may harm them, the AEC is essential otherwise all the ASEAN countries could become marginalized in the shadows of the giants of the region, the PRC and India, and also the more technologically advanced economies, such as Japan and the Republic of Korea. ASEAN countries need to understand that it is not AEC versus the status quo, but rather AEC or the risk of becoming marginalized within the region.

This risk is even more pronounced given the recent development of the Regional Comprehensive Economic Partnership (RCEP) under which ASEAN has been negotiating its trade and investment liberalization with Australia, the PRC, India, Japan, the Republic of Korea, and New Zealand since November 2012 with the target of concluding it by the end of 2015. The TPP, which started in 2005 with four economies, has since expanded to include eight more countries, including the US, Japan, Australia, and four ASEAN economies. An economically integrated ASEAN or AEC will enhance ASEAN competitiveness in their free trade negotiations whether conducted as a group (ASEAN+1, ASEAN+3, and RCEP) or individually (TPP).

ASEAN cooperation on finance and monetary issues has evolved along with cooperation on trade and investment. Apart from the ASEAN Surveillance Process noted earlier, ASEAN expanded its financial cooperation to areas of taxes, customs, and insurance with additional focuses on capital market development, monitoring of capital flows, and financial services liberalization. In August 2003, the ASEAN Finance Ministers developed the Roadmap for Monetary and Financial Integration of ASEAN (RIA-Fin) to implement the ASEAN Vision of achieving "a free flow of goods, services and investments, and a freer flow of capital" by 2020 (the year of the AEC target at that time).[21]

---

[20] <http://www.asean.org/communities/asean-economic-community>.
[21] <http://www.asean.org/news/item/joint-ministerial-statement-seventh-asean-finance-ministers-meeting-6-7-august-2003-makati-philippines-2>.

The RIA-Fin identified targets and milestones for financial integration in the areas of capital market development, capital account liberalization, financial services liberalization, and ASEAN currency cooperation. The RIA-Fin was adopted by the ASEAN Leaders at their summit in October 2003.

The RIA-Fin aims to achieve a free flow of financial services through successive rounds of negotiation under an enhanced positive list approach.[22] Capital market development and capital account liberalization aim to further develop and link capital markets in the region supported by greater capital mobility. Currency cooperation focuses on ways to further facilitate and promote intra-regional trade and deepen regional economic integration. However, at the current stage, cooperation on finance should not be viewed in isolation from the AEC goals. Financial cooperation should primarily aim at facilitating the ability of ASEAN to achieve the goal of becoming a single market and single production base. This will enhance ASEAN's competitiveness and allow it to compete on more equal terms with the PRC and India.

In the area of currency and exchange rates, the ASEAN Finance Ministers in 1998 endorsed the use of Bilateral Payments Arrangements (BPAs), as proposed by a special task force of the ASEAN central banks, in order to promote the use of regional currencies in intra-ASEAN trade. Under a BPA, when goods or services are traded internationally the exporter is paid in domestic currency by their country's central bank, through a designated commercial bank, and the importer pays their own central bank, again through a designated commercial bank, in their own domestic currency. The central banks settle the net amount due in an agreed currency on a periodic basis. Effectively, this arrangement converts commercial risk relating to trade into sovereign risk, as the central or government-appointed banks guarantee payments to their respective exporters. Bank Negara Malaysia (BNM) has been the most active in pursuing BPAs, concluding the first ASEAN BPA with the Philippines, and now has agreements with almost twenty countries, both within ASEAN and elsewhere. Thailand also has a BPA with Myanmar, through the Export-Import Bank of Thailand.

The issue of exchange rates has also been under discussion within ASEAN. Exchange rate stability reduces cross-border trade costs and therefore has a positive impact on bilateral and intraregional trade. This is confirmed by evidence from the euro in relation to intra-EU trade. Figure 5.2 presents one of the various estimates of the effects of euro on trade (Rose effect)[23]. Baldwin and Taglioni (2004) suggested that a currency union will have a greater Rose

---

[22] The positive list approach is enhanced by greater transparency through the inclusion of medium-term and long-term lists of sub-sectors and modes according to the country's readiness (and willingness) to open up.

[23] See Rose (2000).

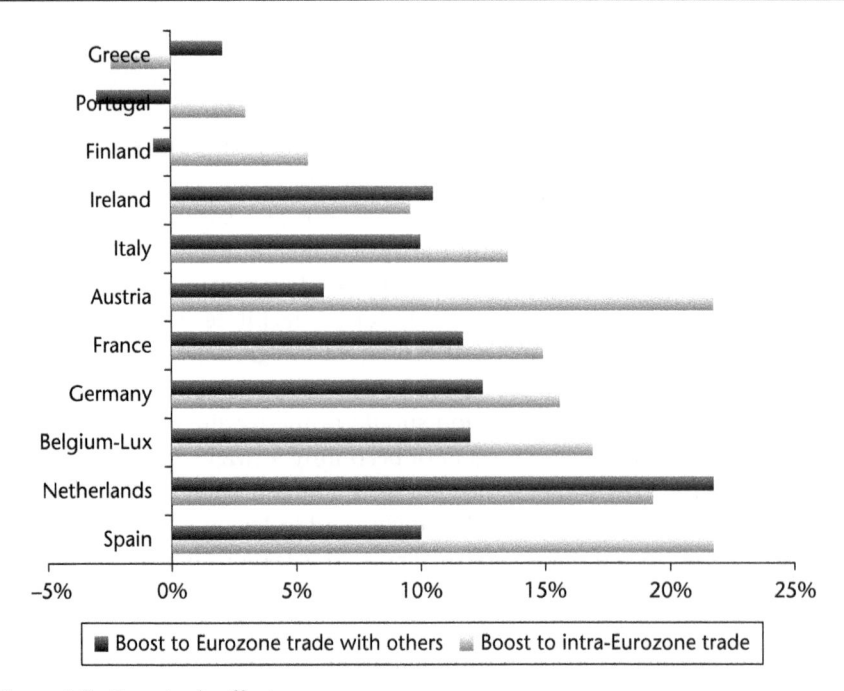

Figure 5.2. Euro trade effects
Source: Baldwin and Taglioni (2004), based on Micco et al. (2003), Table 8.

effect if countries are already tightly integrated on the real side and have more (tradable) sectors with imperfect competition and increasing returns.

The main objective is to explore some form of currency arrangement that could further facilitate intraregional trade and investment through greater exchange rate stability. At the same time, ASEAN countries agreed to work toward maintaining appropriate macroeconomic policies and foster greater macroeconomic convergence, as preconditions for closer monetary cooperation. The RIA-Fin certainly does not envision a currency union in ASEAN. An ASEAN Central Bank Forum Task Force conducted a study during 2001–2 to assess the suitability of a common currency for ASEAN. The analysis was based on the intensity of intraregional trade, the symmetry of shocks, the existence of a compensating adjustment mechanism, the similarity of business and social models, the presence of an anchor currency, political commitments, and institutional frameworks.[24] It concluded that various preconditions and institutions, such as greater macroeconomic convergence, a strong regional

---

[24] See Kuang and Singh (2003) and Guinigundo (2005).

institutional framework, and greater intraregional trade, would need to be in place first. The ASEAN Finance Ministers at their meeting in August 2003 concurred with the findings of the study and agreed to "focus first on areas of currency cooperation that could further facilitate and promote intra regional trade and deepen regional economic integration."[25]

Without going all the way to a common currency, some form of coordination of monetary and exchange rate policies that stabilized bilateral exchange rates among ASEAN currencies would still generate a positive impact on intraregional trade through reduction of trade costs. Based on an assumption of relative purchasing power parity, two countries that adopted common inflation targets would experience relatively more stable bilateral exchange rates. Empirically, Kuttner and Posen (2001) and Rose (2006) found lower exchange rate volatility among inflation targeters.

Eichengreen (2007) also came to a similar conclusion when he examined three approaches for monetary cooperation in Asia—exchange rate pegging, a parallel regional currency, and harmonized inflation targeting—against three criteria: robustness of capital mobility, compatibility with political circumstances, and congruence with modern monetary policy conduct. He suggested that, given the current financial, political, and technical constraints, harmonized inflation targeting is the best approach to promote exchange rate stability in Asia while laying the foundation for closer monetary cooperation and monetary unification at a later stage. Historically, it was difficult to maintain a pegged-rate regime with a deregulated financial system and an open capital account, and the adjustment cost could be large when it collapsed, such as during the Asian financial crisis. With most ASEAN exchange rate regimes under a managed float, with explicit or implicit inflation targeting regimes, a gradual convergence of the inflation targets of the various countries should lead to greater stability of their currencies.

The use of a parallel regional currency, such as an Asian Currency Unit (ACU),[26] could also eliminate exchange rate risks, but it would be effective only if widely accepted and used (by both the public and private sectors). Past efforts in gaining wide acceptance and sufficient market share for the parallel regional currency, learning from the experience of the European Currency Unit (ECU), were met with little success, and the existing levels of intraregional trade and investment, trade, and capital market structures in Asia may not yet provide enough incentive to switch from a national currency to the parallel regional currency. Ongoing problems in the Eurozone raise a lot of caution about the desirability of single currency blocs.

---

[25] <http://www.asean.org/communities/asean-economic-community/item/joint-ministerial-statement-seventh-asean-finance-ministers-meeting-6-7-august-2003-makati-philippines>.

[26] See discussions of an ACU in Kawai (2007).

5.5.5 ASEAN Concerns over Exchange Rates

Although the CMIM is the centerpiece of financial cooperation in the region, the issue of main concern to most ASEAN economies over the past few years, especially those with relatively open capital accounts, is not about the need for a foreign exchange liquidity support mechanism, even though this could still be very important in certain circumstances in the future. The risks have been from large capital inflows which create great difficulty for exchange rate and macroeconomic management in emerging market economies. Unconventional monetary policies adopted by the US and other advanced economies create excessive liquidity in the global currency markets and have huge spillover impacts on emerging market economies with relatively open capital accounts, such as those in ASEAN. As of the second quarter of 2013, many ASEAN economies have been facing large portfolio capital inflows to seek higher yields. This has led to currency appreciation and concerns about loss of competitiveness vis-à-vis economies with less open capital accounts, particularly the PRC.

The PRC's capital account is less open, so it is more shielded from portfolio capital flows. Of course, the PRC faces a lot of foreign currency inflows from its current account surplus and FDI inflows. It has, however, kept the yuan from appreciating significantly against the US dollar, in order to prevent potential large loss of export and employment. As this goes on, emerging market economies in ASEAN (and also elsewhere) will face huge negative spillover impacts from both the unconventional monetary policies in the US and other advanced economies and Chinese exchange rate policies. The PRC is an important trade partner of ASEAN, and the PRC is also a major competitor for many ASEAN economies in third countries' markets. So ASEAN will likely lose out. Given that export is the main engine of growth for many ASEAN countries, the appreciation of their currencies (against the US dollar and relative to the yuan) will hurt the competitiveness of their exports and, consequently, have an adverse impact on the growth potential of their economies. Instead of the PRC losing exports and employment, it will more likely be emerging market economies in ASEAN that suffer the fate.

Analyses in Thorbecke (2010) bear this out. He carried out an empirical investigation of labor-intensive exports from ASEAN (Indonesia, Malaysia, the Philippines, and Thailand) to twenty-five major importing countries between 1983 and 2007. It investigates how ASEAN exports are affected by incomes in importing countries, the bilateral exchange rate between ASEAN and importing countries (as a group) and also the bilateral exchange rate between ASEAN's competitors (such as the PRC) and importing countries. It finds that the exchange rate elasticities are generally high. A 10 percent appreciation in

ASEAN's currency would reduce its labor-intensive exports by about 20 percent, and a 10 percent depreciation of competitors' exchange rates would lead to a decline in ASEAN labor-intensive exports by between 11 and 14 percent. Thorbecke suggests these results imply that profit margins are fairly thin for labor-intensive exports and that changes in competitiveness through currency movements can have a significant impact on these exports. These results highlight the significance of the exchange rate issue within the region. Uncoordinated exchange rate policies can create significant "beggar-thy-neighbor" outcomes. For a region that is becoming more and more closely integrated, and consisting of countries that also compete with each other in third countries' markets, finding a way to foster closer cooperation and coordination of exchange rates should rank high on the regional financial cooperation agenda.

The exchange rate issue is very sensitive, however, and has become a global issue. An important question is the extent to which global or regional institutions and architecture are appropriate for dealing with this issue. The IMF has warned of currency wars. However, the 2010 annual meeting of the IMF/World Bank failed to reach any kind of consensus on this issue. The IMF was set up during a time of fixed exchange rates, so it will need a major re-engineering to become more relevant to exchange rate problems in the current financial environment. No serious move by major countries to redesign the global financial architecture can be seen at present. Tinkering with IMF quotas seems to be completely irrelevant for solving current global currency and financial problems. At the G20 level, many were disappointed with the results of the Seoul meeting. However, given the sensitivity and complexity of the issues, it was not surprising that more concrete outcomes on dealing with global imbalance and currency issues were not achieved.

Can the East Asian regional frameworks deal with some of these issues? ASEAN+3 is unlikely to be the appropriate forum for this as the PRC and Japan have taken completely different approaches to exchange rate management. The best possibility for serious discussion on this issue, at least from the ASEAN perspective, might be through a policy dialogue between ASEAN and the PRC. ASEAN should explain the negative spillover on its economies and urge the PRC to work more closely with it on exchange rate cooperation. If ASEAN currencies were to appreciate in line with the yuan, there would be much less concern among its business community. In fact, ASEAN countries may find that the best strategy under the current policy environment is to think about targeting their exchange rates to the yuan with some flexibility. This could be the start of what some foresee emerging in East Asia in the longer term, an implicit yuan bloc (for example, see Park and Song 2010).

Finally, dealing more effectively with exchange rate issues within the region needs more institution building. Up to 2011, the involvement of the ASEAN+3 central banks and monetary authorities in the ASEAN+3 Finance Ministers process was limited to the deputy governor's level (AFDM+3), whereas in ASEAN, in addition to having the deputy governors of ASEAN central banks as members of the AFDM, the past, present and future chairs (troika) of the ASEAN Central Bank Governors' Meeting have been participating in the ASEAN Finance Ministers Meeting. Greater involvement of central banks and monetary authorities at the governors' level is certainly needed for a serious and effective dialogue on exchange rate issues. Starting from 2012, central bank governors have regularly been participating in the ASEAN+3 Finance Ministers Meeting. This is certainly a good sign. Institution building is also needed for more effective regional surveillance, which will become more and more important as the region becomes more integrated and economic risks stemming from within the region increase. Making sure that AMRO can function effectively will be very important. In fact, AMRO should eventually evolve to become something like an Asian Monetary Organization (AMO) that could support CMIM as well as provide technical support to an integrated framework for the Finance Ministers and the Central Bank Governors processes. If this can be done, it will become the focal point for discussion of financial and monetary cooperation and development in the region. It will also lead to more effective regional surveillance and provide the institutional infrastructure for cooperation on exchange rate policies within the region. An AMO could also cooperate with global institutions such as the IMF, so that coordinated action in East Asia would be consistent with solving major issues at the global level, such as global imbalances, excessive volatile capital flows, and exchange rate movements. This should be the target for AMRO as it evolves into an international organization.

There will also be additional challenges on ASEAN economies as the unconventional monetary policies adopted by the US and other advanced economies begin to unwind. This was clearly seen around mid-2013 as expectation about the unwinding of the US QE3 increased. There were large capital outflows from emerging market economies, including in ASEAN. This led to currency depreciations and declines in foreign reserves. While the likelihood of rapid US QE unwinding has declined somewhat with the nomination of Janet Yellen as the next Chairperson of the US Federal Reserve, the unwinding in the US and elsewhere will inevitably happen. This will again strain exchange rate and macroeconomic management in many ASEAN economies. It becomes even more important that institutions such as AMRO and CMIM provide effective surveillance and liquidity support for countries needing the facility.

5.6 Conclusions

Prior to the Asian financial crisis in 1997, financial cooperation in East Asia was fairly limited, but was more intensive within ASEAN than elsewhere. This was not surprising as ASEAN was formed in 1967. Financial cooperation has gradually developed as one of many areas of economic cooperation. In the wider East Asian context there were no strong push-factors for major financial cooperation initiatives, though this changed with the occurrence of the Asian financial crisis. Dissatisfied with crisis measures required by the IMF and the limited amount of financial resources present in the region, East Asia began to develop deeper regional cooperation mechanisms. The ASEAN+3 group was formed, and various financial cooperation initiatives were initiated which eventually were extended to trade agreements and many other areas. ASEAN benefited from these regional cooperation initiatives, from the larger financial resources available in East Asia as a whole, and from the fact that many cooperation initiatives, such as the ASEAN+3 mechanism, and various ASEAN+1 free trade agreements, had ASEAN as the core partner.

The great financial crisis resulted in another major economic shock to the region. In this case, the crisis was a global one and the main arena of policy responses was at the global level. The G20 became the focal point for economic consultation and cooperation in the global context. While the regional cooperation initiatives that were developed after the Asian financial crisis played little role in the latest crisis, East Asia still pushed ahead to deepen these initiatives, such as the finalization of the CMIM together with the setting up of AMRO. Presumably, CMIM is believed to still be useful in the future, but the IMF link will need to be modified to make CMIM more practical and useful for countries in the region.

The great financial crisis also provided new rationales for further economic cooperation among East Asian countries. Too much reliance on markets in the West resulted in sharp declines in export and economic growth for most countries in the region as a result of the great financial crisis. As the Western economies are likely to remain sluggish for some time, a rebalancing toward more intraregional trade in East Asia and more domestic drivers of growth should provide a more resilient growth path. Investment, particularly in domestic and cross-border infrastructures, could play an important role in driving the region's growth, and there can be deeper financial cooperation initiatives to recycle more of the region's savings surplus to provide long-term financing for infrastructure investment. ASEAN has just started an infrastructure fund, but the amount is still small. This could be expanded in size and in membership to include other countries in East Asia.

Looking ahead to an East Asian region of closer and deeper economic integration, ASEAN will need to make sure that it remains an efficient and competitive bloc within the larger cooperation framework. The PRC and India clearly demonstrate the benefit of economic size. ASEAN is now working hard to implement the ASEAN Economic Community by 2015. This will be important to make ASEAN more of a single market and single production base, so that ASEAN can reap the benefits of scale economies similarly to those that can be achieved by the PRC and India. Financial cooperation to facilitate this will also be important. The aim is to reduce the cost of carrying out intra-ASEAN trade and investment so that the goal for ASEAN to become a single market and a single production base can become a reality. This also includes cooperation to reduce exchange rate volatility among ASEAN countries. Although a single ASEAN currency is not a realistic goal in the foreseeable future,[27] more convergence of monetary policy regimes, such as having similar inflation targets (explicit or implicit), should help to reduce exchange rate volatilities.

Exchange rate concerns extend beyond ASEAN. As many countries in East Asia are competitors in third countries' markets, relative exchange rate movements influence competitiveness. Of particular concern to many ASEAN countries is the so-called "currency war." US quantitative easing could have spillovers to emerging markets, encouraging more capital inflows and putting upward pressures on their currencies. At the same time, the relative inflexibility of the Chinese currency could lead to a loss of competitiveness for countries who are the PRC's competitors and who have more open capital accounts and a more flexible exchange rate regime. More consultation and cooperation on exchange rates in East Asia are clearly needed. This is important not just for the relative competitiveness among East Asian economies, but is also crucial for dealing with the global imbalance issue.

References

ADB. 2009. *Asian Development Outlook 2009*. Manila: Asian Development Bank.
ADB and ADBI. 2009. *Infrastructure for a Seamless Asia.* Manila: Asian Development Bank and Tokyo: Asian Development Bank Institute.
Asian Policy Forum. 2010. *Policy Recommendations to Secure Balanced and Sustainable Growth in Asia*. October, Asian Development Bank Institute.
Athukorala, Prema-chandra, and Archanun Kohpaiboon. 2009. "Intra-Regional Trade in East Asia: The Decoupling Fallacy, Crisis, and Policy Challenges." ADBI Working Paper No. 177. Tokyo: Asian Development Bank Institute.
Baldwin, Richard, and Daria Taglioni. 2004. "Positive OCA Criteria: Microfoundations for the Rose Effect." COE/RES Discussion Paper Series, No. 34, Hitotsubashi University, February.

---

[27] It may not be a desirable goal given the diversity of ASEAN countries' levels of development and the recent problems in the Eurozone.

Chia, Siow Yue. 2010. "Regional Trade Policy Cooperation and Architecture in East Asia." ADBI Working Paper No. 191. Tokyo: Asian Development Bank Institute.

Chua, Johanna. 2009. "Asia Macro Views: Asia—Reassessing FX Reserve Adequacy," 23 February. Citigroup.

Eichengreen, Barry. 2007. "Fostering Monetary and Exchange Rate Cooperation in East Asia." Working Paper, University of California, Berkeley, August.

Feldstein, Martin. 1998. "Refocusing the IMF." *Foreign Affairs* 77(2): 20–33.

Guinigundo, Diwa C. 2005. "Financial Cooperation Arrangements in the ASEAN." *Banko Sentral Review*, July, 5–16.

Huang, Yiping. 2009. "Strategies for Asian Exchange Rate Policy Cooperation." Paper presented at a conference on Asian Economic Integration: Financial and Macroeconomic Issues, organized by the East Asia Bureau of Economic Research, ANU, the Institute of World Economics and Politics, CASS, and the Institute of Asia-Pacific Studies. CASS. May 14. Beijing, People's Republic of China.

Kawai, Masahiro. 2007. "Toward a Regional Exchange Rate Regime in East Asia." ADBI Working Paper No. 68. Tokyo: Asian Development Bank Institute.

Kawai, Masahiro, and Jong-Wha Lee. 2015. "Chapter 1: Introduction and Overview." In *Rebalancing for Sustainable Growth: Asia's Postcrisis Challenge*, edited by Masahiro Kawai and Jong-Wha Lee. Heidelberg and New York: Springer.

Kawai, Masahiro, and Ganeshan Wignaraja. 2010. "Asian FTAs: Trends, Prospects, and Challenges." ADB Economics Working Paper Series No. 226. Manila: Asian Development Bank.

Krugman, Paul. 1998. "Saving Asia: It's Time to Get Radical." *Fortune*, September, 138(5): 74.

Kuang, Ooi Sang, and Sukhdave Singh. 2003. "The ASEAN Currency and Exchange Rate Mechanism Task Force." In *Regional Currency Areas and the Use of Foreign Currencies*, BIS Paper No 17, May. Basel: Bank for International Settlements.

Kuttner, Kenneth, and Adam S. Posen. 2001. "Beyond Bipolar: A Three Dimensional Assessment of Monetary Frameworks." *International Finance* 6: 369–87.

Lamberte, Mario B. 1991. "Structure and Prospects of ASEAN Financial and Banking Systems: A Perspective from the Philippines." Working Paper Series No. 91-05, Philippines Institute for Development Studies, April.

Lipscy, Phillip Y. 2003. "Japan's Asian Monetary Fund Proposal." *Stanford Journal of East Asian Affairs* 3(1): 93–104.

Manupipatpong, Worapot. 2002. "The ASEAN Surveillance Process and the East Asian Monetary Fund." *ASEAN Economic Bulletin* 19(1): 111–23.

Micco, Alejandro, Ernesto H. Stein, and Guillermo Luis Ordoñez. 2003. "The Currency Union Effect on Trade: Early Evidence from EMU." *Economic Policy* 18(37): 316–56.

Nanto, Dick K. 1998. "The 1997–1998 Asian Financial Crisis." CSR Report, February.

Park, Yung Chul. 2009. "The Global Economic Crisis and Rebalancing Growth in East Asia." Research Policy Brief No. 31. Tokyo: Asian Development Bank Institute.

Park, Yung Chul, and Chi-Young Song. 2010. "RMB Internationalization: Prospects and Implications for Economic Integration in East Asia." Paper presented at a conference on Financial Development and Integration in East Asia, Seoul, December 2–3.

Rose, Andrew K. 2000. "One Money, One Market: Estimating the Effect of Common Currencies on Trade." *Economic Policy* 15(30): 9–45.
Rose, Andrew K. 2006. "A Stable International Monetary System Emerges: Inflation Targeting Is Bretton Woods, Reversed." NBER Working Paper No.12711, November.
Sachs, Jeffrey D. 1997. "The Wrong Medicine for Asia." *New York Times*, November 3.
Stiglitz, Joseph. 1998. "Must Financial Crises Be This Frequent and This Painful?" McKay Lecture, Pittsburgh, Pennsylvania, September 23.
Stiglitz, Joseph. 2002. *Globalization and Its Discontents*. New York: W.W. Norton & Co.
Sussangkarn, Chalongphob. 2002. "Economic Crisis and Recovery in Thailand: The Role of the IMF." In *Asian Economic Recovery: Policy Options for Growth and Stability*, edited by Kong Yam Tan. Singapore: Singapore University Press.
Sussangkarn, Chalongphob. 2003. "East Asian Financial Cooperation: An Assessment of the Rationales." In *East Asian Cooperation: Progress and Future*, edited by Zhang Yunling. Beijing: World Affairs Press.
Sussangkarn, Chalongphob. 2011. "The Chiang Mai Initiative Multilateralisation: Origin, Development and Outlook." *Asian Economic Policy Review* 6(2): 203–20.
Thorbecke, Willem. 2010. "An Empirical Analysis of ASEAN's Labor-Intensive Exports." *Journal of Asian Economics* 21(6): 505–13.
UNCTAD. *1998 Trade and Development Report*. Chapter 4. New York and Geneva: United Nations.

6

A View from the People's Republic of China

Yongding Yu

6.1 Introduction

Regional monetary cooperation can be defined broadly to include options ranging from informal policy consultations to European-style monetary union (Volz 2010). Though the debate on the possibility of monetary cooperation in East Asia started in the early 1990s (Bayoumi and Eichengreen 1994), the first serious attempt at regional monetary cooperation by East Asian countries was mainly a result of the Asian financial crisis.

Though economic integration through trade and direct investment in East Asia was deep, region-wide monetary cooperation had never been on the agenda of the governments in the region until the Asian financial crisis struck. The crisis seemed to show that without monetary cooperation, individual East Asian countries stood no chance of meeting attacks by international speculators. The Asian countries were deeply disappointed by the performance of the International Monetary Fund (IMF) during the Asian financial crisis. The rescue packages provided by the IMF were too small and came too late. The IMF's conditionality was out of touch with local reality and caused undue pain for the recipient countries. The idea of regional monetary cooperation was initially raised by the governments in the region as an alternative or supplement to the role of the IMF as lender of last resort in an international financial crisis.

Regional monetary cooperation[1] in East Asia initially took the form of the establishment of a regional financial architecture that would function as a mutual assistance mechanism. The countries in the region with relatively

---

[1] The term "financial cooperation" has also been widely used in the literature. Here the terms "monetary cooperation" and "financial cooperation" are interchangeable.

good financial conditions would provide loans to those that did not have enough financial resources and might suffer a balance of payments crisis. Then, after the Asian financial crisis, the focus of the regional financial crisis shifted to the coordination of exchange rate arrangements.

Essentially, the establishment of a regional financial architecture is about pooling reserves of countries so that individual countries can fend off international speculative attacks without resorting to rescue packages provided by the IMF under strict conditionality or to accumulate foreign exchange reserves that are extremely costly. Though the Asian monetary fund proposed by the Japanese government failed to materialize, countries in the region have made progress in pooling reserves together within the framework of the Chiang Mai Initiative (CMI).

The issue of coordination of exchange rate arrangements was raised in the wake of the Asian financial crisis. During the crisis, competitive devaluations were one of the biggest worries in the region. After the crisis in the early 2000s, the East Asian countries redoubled their efforts to increase exports, hoping to promote economic growth and strengthen the international balance of payments position. The worsening of the US current account deficit mirrored Asian countries' success in exports. The United States started to put pressure on East Asian countries, and the PRC in particular, to appreciate their currencies.

Initially, the East Asian countries concentrated their efforts on stabilizing the intraregional exchange rates. This reflected their desire to avoid "beggar your neighbor" policies and, to some extent, to deepen economic integration. An Asian economic community, an Asian monetary union, and, further in the future, an Asian common currency were then envisaged. Later, following the increase in the pressure from the United States and the rapid increase in the PRC's trade surplus, exchange rate coordination in the region increasingly aimed at avoiding a loss in competitiveness against the renminbi (RMB) by other East Asian countries. On the other hand, the PRC was suspicious of the intentions of its East Asian neighbors as they pushed for greater coordination of exchange rate arrangements. Naturally, compared with the progress made in establishing a regional financial architecture, the progress in the area of exchange rate coordination has been much less significant.

During the 2008–9 global financial crisis, East Asia fared much better than during the Asian financial crisis. Their good fiscal and external positions enabled the Asian countries to absorb the impact of the global financial crisis that had originated in the United States. The Republic of Korea was the only noteworthy exception. During the crisis, East Asia's financial architecture was put to the test. Unfortunately, its performance was rather unimpressive.

From the beginning, East Asian monetary cooperation was inspired by the success of EMU and the euro. The European sovereign debt crisis seriously dampened—possibly even destroyed—the enthusiasm for a future Asian economic community, Asian monetary union, and Asian common currency. Regional monetary cooperation has become a journey without a destination. Bayoumi and Eichengreen (1994, 1) had argued that "[l]ooking into the future, the move toward regionally based free-trade areas in North America, East Asia, and South America may eventually prompt policy makers in these regions, as in Europe, to contemplate the creation of single regional currencies." Based on past experience with the promotion of regional monetary cooperation and the current crisis of the euro, East Asian economists have to ask themselves several questions. Is a single currency still a feasible objective? How should regional monetary cooperation proceed if there is still room for maneuver? What will be the most likely path toward a regional financial architecture and the coordination of exchange rate arrangements? In short, the question about regional monetary cooperation at the moment is: what should be the way forward?

The chapter attempts answer these questions from the PRC's perspective. The second section assesses the contribution of the CMI to East Asian countries' financial stability. The third section is about the movement of exchange rates in the region since the Asian financial crisis. Section 6.4 discusses the possibility of a regional coordination of exchange rate arrangements. Section 6.5 is about the PRC's attitude toward regional coordination of exchange rate arrangements and the evolution of the RMB exchange rate regime. Section 6.6 examines the progress in the internationalization of the RMB and its implication on regional currency coordination. In the seventh section, a possible way forward is discussed. The last section provides concluding remarks.

6.2 The Unimpressive Performance of the Chiang Mai Initiative and the Need for Improvement

The East Asian region as a whole ran a sizable savings surplus after the Asian financial crisis. By 2008, the region had accumulated more than US$4 trillion foreign reserves, compared with US$630 billion in 1997. One could argue that the need for a liquidity support mechanism for the region was no longer necessary. However, the global financial crisis shows that even with more than US$200 billion of foreign reserves, the Republic of Korea was not able to cover short-term foreign debt and short-term contingent liabilities, when they were quickly liquidated as a result of liquidity shortages in the US.

According to Sussangkarn (2011), the unimpressive performance of the CMI is attributable to two shortcomings in its design and in its more recent version, Chiang Mai Initiative Multilateralization (CMIM). First, the total size of multilateral swap agreements (US$120 billion) was far from enough. Second, the link with the IMF blocked the effective use of the financial facilities provided by the CMIM. The Republic of Korea was hit by liquidity shortage and a credit crunch at the beginning of the global financial crisis. Though it had access to US$18.5 billion under CMIM through its swap agreements, it could draw only US$3.7 billion (20 percent) without having to apply to an IMF program. Consequently, it had to be rescued by a swap line provided by the US Federal Reserve rather than by activating the swap agreements under the CMIM.

The lackluster performance of the CMIM can be explained partially by the nature of the shock that East Asian countries experienced in 2008–9. The global financial crisis was a debt crisis of the developed countries, and the US in particular. The brunt of the crisis was borne by the US. Except for the Republic of Korea, East Asia suffered mainly from collateral damage as external demand for their export sectors declined. On the other hand, the economic fundamentals of the countries in the region were much better than during the Asian financial crisis. During the global financial crisis, most countries in the region were not under speculative attacks and their own foreign exchange reserves were large enough to cushion external shocks. Few countries in the region needed any financial support.

Despite this unimpressive performance, most East Asian countries still regard the pooling of foreign exchange reserves as a worthy option which in the future will be of great benefit to countries in the region. In the face of dollar devaluation and possible high inflation, as a result of the monetization of public debts by the US and other developed countries, holding large amounts of dollar-denominated foreign exchange reserves will be increasingly costly. The CMI could reduce the need of individual countries in the region to hold an excessively large amount of dollar-denominated foreign exchange reserves and hence improve resource allocation.

Based on the experience during the global financial crisis, East Asian economists have put forward various suggestions for improving the CMIM. According to Sussangkarn (2011), the CMI mechanism first should be de-linked from the IMF. Second, the total size of the available resources should be raised to US $400 billion–500 billion from the current US$120 billion pool. Third, it should possible for other members of the East Asian community to participate in CMIM activities, even though they are not yet full contributing members. Fourth, the CMIM needs a strong ASEAN+3 Macroeconomic Research Office.

Strengthening of the CMIM is perhaps the most likely area where regional monetary cooperation could make important headway. For Ariff (2010), the CMIM is already a far cry from the aborted AMF. He does see a need for revisiting the AMF concept. And there is no reason why the AMF cannot complement the IMF, pretty much as the IMF could work alongside the European Union and European Central Bank in several crisis-hit countries in

Europe. CMIM can evolve into a much bigger regional 'lender of last resort' with much greater powers and resources. Drysdale and Armstrong (2010) criticize East Asian financial cooperation for being reactive and inward looking, focused on establishing a measure of independence from US dominance in the global financial system and attempting to build regional trade arrangements. For them, the important question is how can the regional architecture be restructured to relate effectively to the new global arrangements, such as the IMF and G20?

The PRC's interests in the creation of the regional financial architecture have been fading rather quickly since the global financial crisis. Since then, there have been very few, if any, discussions in the PRC on issues related to regional financial architecture. Political factors aside, there seem no obvious benefits that the PRC could reap from further enlargement and deepening of the regional financial architecture centered on CMI or CMIM. With more than US$3 trillion foreign exchange reserves, the PRC is highly unlikely to need financial help from its neighbors. What it does need is to dispose of a large part of its foreign exchange reserves in the form of US treasuries, to avoid possible heavy capital losses. But what can the regional financial architecture offer to help the PRC to achieve this objective? While it is not only affordable but also desirable for the PRC to make more contribution to CMIM, its holdings of US treasuries are too large to be diversified away and the help that CMIM can provide in this regard is limited. Furthermore, the PRC can reduce its dependence on dollar holdings through bilateral swap agreements, which would be much simpler and hence more effective, at least from its point of view.

The PRC was presented with such an opportunity when the Republic of Korea sought its help before obtaining liquidity support from the Fed. It could have both boosted regional financial cooperation and helped the PRC to reduce its holding of dollar assets. In my view, the PRC missed this opportunity because it feared that a US dollar devaluation would cause significant losses if it provided the Republic of Korea with dollar liquidity. Actually, this problem was not that difficult to overcome. The PRC could have negotiated with the Republic of Korea the terms of its support in a way that could have safeguarded the interests of both sides. For example, the dollar liquidity provided by the PRC could be have been denominated in RMB. The PRC was simply not prepared for such a circumstance and could not come up with a well-thought-out action plan for discussion at the time.

In recent years, territorial disputes and political differences among East Asian countries have further dampened the PRC's enthusiasm for continuing to develop regional financial architecture in the form of a deepened and enlarged CMIM, let alone for creating a regional institution in the form of the AMF.

The call for expansion of regional cooperation to include countries such as Australia, New Zealand, and India further complicated the issue and alienated the PRC. Any regional cooperation must be exclusive one way or another. If it is not aimed at "establishing a measure of independence from American dominance in the global financial system,"[2] why should East Asia take the trouble of creating an economic community and a regional financial architecture? Furthermore, what are the criteria for including some countries and excluding others? If ASEAN+3 is not the right grouping, and should be expanded, why not include the United States, Russian Federation, and many other countries together in the regional financial architecture?

For many Chinese economists, the call for the enlargement of the ASEAN+3 is simply an attempt to counterbalance the PRC's influence in the region. Now, political differences among key countries in the East Asian region are worsening continuously and are likely to linger in the foreseeable future. If countries in the region cannot reach the kind of political consensus achieved in the EU, how can East Asian regional cooperation can precede any further? In fact, the unity of the ASEAN+3 grouping is already in tatters. East Asian regionalism has become a thing of the past.

A noteworthy event reflecting the PRC's policy toward the regional financial architecture is the establishment of the BRICS Development Bank, which was announced in March 2013 by the leaders of the BRICS countries (Brazil, Russian Federation, India, PRC, and South Africa). The bank's goals are to provide funding for infrastructure projects and to create a "Contingent Reserve Arrangement." To deal with future financial shocks in emerging markets the five BRICS countries have committed to pool their individual reserves to create a foreign exchange fund worth US$100 billion. This is comparable to the CMIM's total size of US$120 billion of multilateral swap agreements, The PRC's enthusiasm in participating in the establishment of the BRICS Bank shows that eventual regional economic integration in East Asia is no longer a priority in its international economic policy agenda.

6.3 Exchange Rate Movements in East Asia since the Asian Financial Crisis

Before the Asian financial crisis, most East Asian currencies were more or less de facto pegged to the US dollar, except for Japan and the Philippines, which adopted a free float. McKinnon (2000) called these arrangements the East Asian dollar standard (EADS). While most Asian currencies were pegged to the US dollar, the yen started to depreciate in 1995. The exchange rate fell

---

[2] See Drysdale and Armstrong (2010).

from 80 yen against US$1 in 1995 to 140 yen against US$1 in 1998. The trend continued until April 2002.

During the Asian financial crisis, most East Asian currencies depreciated significantly against the US dollar. At the time, the main worry was competitive devaluation among East Asian countries. However the nightmare did not materialize, thanks to the PRC's resisting the temptation to devalue the RMB.

In early 2002, as a result of a worsening current account deficit, the US dollar began its so-called "strategic devaluation." At the same time, the US government started to press Asian countries to stop intervening and to allow their currencies to appreciate. In fact, as a result of the Asian financial crisis, East Asian countries began to run current account surpluses with the aim of building up foreign exchange reserves as well as boosting growth. But because the PRC ran an increasingly large current account surplus while its economy grew strongly, the RMB's peg to the dollar became the focal point of pressure. The RMB was de-pegged from the US dollar on July 21, 2005 and started to slowly appreciate.

During the global financial crisis, most East Asian countries, except for Japan and the Republic of Korea, intervened heavily in their foreign exchange markets. The RMB was re-pegged to the dollar, as was the Malaysian ringgit, in September 2008. After five years without intervening, the Japanese government resumed its interventions in the foreign exchange market, and many countries in the region followed suit in late 2008. The RMB was again de-pegged from the US dollar on June 19, 2010, immediately followed by the Malaysian ringgit. The People's Bank of China (PBOC) continues its intervention to control the pace of RMB appreciation against the US dollar.

It is fair to say that, whatever the paths of evolution of exchange rates of individual countries, there was no coordination of exchange rate policy whatsoever in the region. According to McKinnon, despite the large devaluation of most Asian currencies and a proclaimed shift to floating during the Asian financial crisis, both the affected countries of East Asia and those not affected have since returned to formal or informal dollar pegging. Almost all the central banks in the region actively intervene in foreign exchange markets and most interventions are aimed at preventing appreciation rather than depreciation against the dollar. Indeed, Figure 6.1 shows that the East Asian currencies generally fluctuated less against the US dollar than against the yen and euro over the last decade.

During the Asian financial crisis, beside the RMB all East Asian currencies devalued against the US dollar in nominal terms. Since the early 2000s, most East Asian currencies have tended to appreciate against the dollar. The process was interrupted only temporarily during the global financial crisis (Figure 6.2). Yet, the movements of East Asian currencies against the euro is not that different from the changes against the dollar (Figure 6.3).

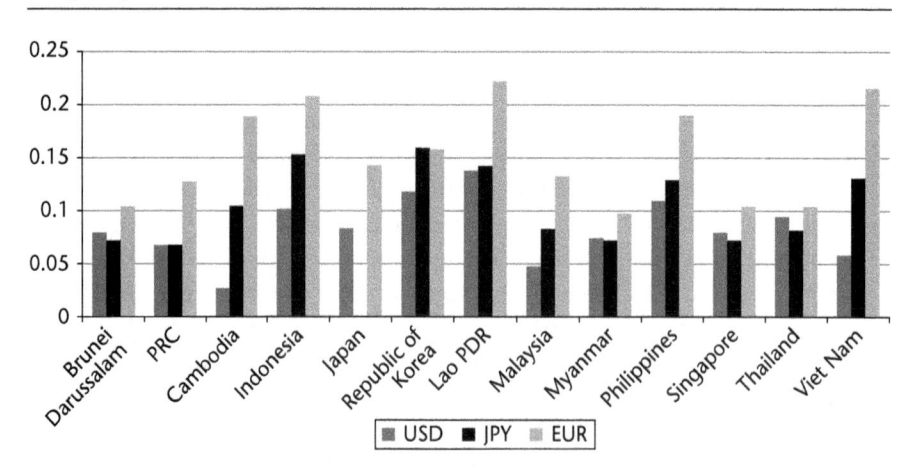

Figure 6.1. The fluctuations of ASEAN+2 currencies against the US dollar, yen, and euro
Notes: 1. Time horizon is from January 1999 to August 2010; 2. The vertical axis represents the monthly standard deviation of the exchange rate relative to the average of other exchange rates over the entire period from 1999 to 2010.
Source: Xu Qiquan.

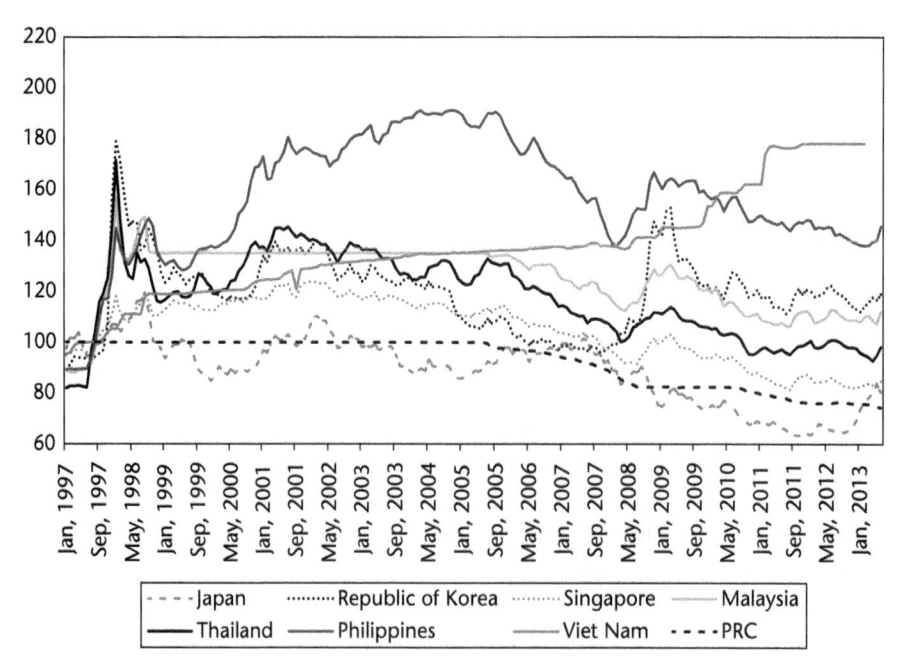

Figure 6.2. Fluctuation of East Asian currencies against the US dollar
Note: 1997 =100.
Source: IMF, Xu Qiyuan, Institute of World Economics and Politics, Chinese Academy of Social Sciences.

A View from the People's Republic of China

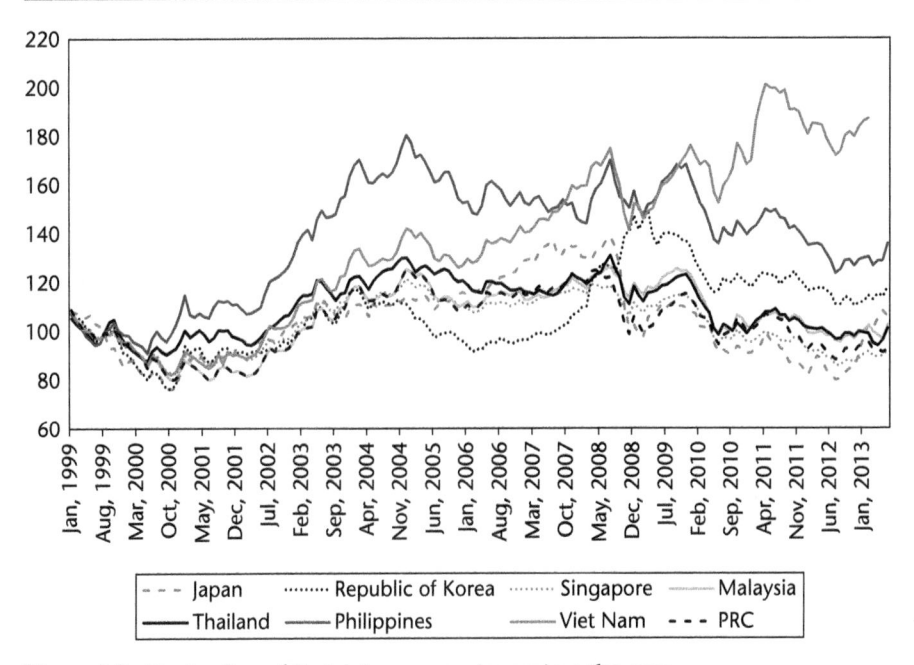

Figure 6.3. Fluctuation of East Asian currencies against the euro

Note: 1999 =100.

Source: IMF, Xu Qiyuan, Institute of World Economics and Politics, Chinese Academy of Social Sciences.

Table 6.1. Weights of currency changes in East Asian currencies explained by the US dollar, euro, and yen

	Singapore dollar	Rupiah	Baht	Brunei dollar	Dong	Philippine peso	Yuan	Won
US dollar	0.70	0.88	0.81	0.79	0.98	0.90	0.99	0.86
Euro	0.14	0.10	0.15	0.08	0.10	0.04	0.01	0.09
Yen	0.22	0.16	0.09	0.17	0.01	0.13	0.01	0.13

Note: Samples are relevant exchange rates of all trading days from January 1, 1999 to November 4, 2010. Due to certain irregularities, the Malaysian ringgit is not included in the calculation. The rolling regressions are made on sample groups, each of which consists of 60 periods. The coefficients in the table are the average values of the estimates of the groups. From the rolling regression, it was found that the weight of the Japanese yen in explaining changes in exchange rates of the rest of East Asian currencies has been decreasing since the 2007 sub-prime crisis, especially after late 2008.

Source: Xu Qiyuan, Institute of World Economics and Politics, Chinese Academy of Social Sciences.

However, based on the approach developed by Frankel and Wei (1993), when all exchange rates are expressed in a stable third currency, the Swiss franc, a rolling regression indicates that changes in East Asian currencies can indeed be explained overwhelmingly by the changes in the US dollar (Table 6.1).

The differences between the results of the two approaches can be explained by the different nature of the calculations. The first is about the correlation between the *levels* of each East Asian currency and the US dollar, euro, and yen, respectively. The second is about the correlation between *changes* in each East Asian currency and the changes in the US dollar, euro, and yen, respectively. If the euro moves up and down against the US dollar, it is entirely possible that the correlation between accumulated changes in each East Asian currency and the euro is lower than the correlation between the accumulated changes in each Asian currency and the changes in the US dollar, even though changes in East Asian currencies follow the changes in the US dollar more closely.

The empirical evidence shows that, even though the basic trends are the same, exchange rates in the region have never moved in concert against the dollar, euro, or yen or any other reference currency. However, despite the lack of concerted action in exchange rates, intraregional trade has never been seriously harmed since the end of the Asian financial crisis. In fact, since the early 2000s, the growth rates of exports of the main economies in the region have been quite impressive and highly synchronic (Table 6.2).

During the global financial crisis, exports of all the countries in the region suffered serious setback. But after the crisis, the East Asian economies rebounded strongly without any coordination in their exchange rate policies. This once again indicates that, for East Asian countries, export growth is more elastic with respect to growth of the US and Europe than with respect to changes in prices. This implies that the coordination of exchange rate arrangements in the region is not that important for the countries' trade and growth.

It is worth noting that despite the lack of coordination after the Asian financial crisis and during the global financial crisis, no East Asian country complained about exchange rate policies in neighboring countries. Nor was there competitive devaluation in the region. All countries seemed satisfied with the status quo regarding intraregional exchange rate arrangements. Recently, to revive the Japanese economy, the Abe government has fired "three arrows." As a result, the Japanese yen has fallen drastically. However, on the whole, the responses of East Asian countries have been muted, which further shows that the importance of exchange rate coordination in the region has receded.

6.4 Options for the Coordination of Exchange Rate Arrangements in East Asia

Despite the fact that the coordination of exchange rates in the region is perhaps not that important, it is perceived as necessary to promote regional economic integration. Basically, there are three possible exchange rate regimes

Table 6.2. Trade growth of East Asian economies, 1996–2012 (%)

	Brunei Darussalam	PRC	Hong Kong, China	Indonesia	Japan	Cambodia	Republic of Korea	Lao PDR	Myanmar	Malaysia	Philippines	Singapore	Thailand	Viet Nam
1996	13.4	3.3	3.5	7.8	3.9		11.3	12.5	-3.7	3.4	19.0	5.6	0.7	12.8
1997	-1.0	12.1	4.6	16.0	-3.0		-3.8	5.2	38.0	0.7	16.4	0.4	-6.1	0.6
1998	-34.5	-0.3	-9.6	-20.4	-17.2	1.1	-35.5	-13.4	28.5	-16.6	-4.1	-16.6	-18.9	10.9
1999	40.8	11.3	-1.4	-1.3	11.0	10.1	28.4	-9.4	-8.2	14.1	13.5	5.2	11.7	29.9
2000	31.4	31.5	17.3	28.3	21.9	14.6	34.0	3.6	16.5	20.1	8.2	20.6	20.3	3.7
2001	-24.5	7.5	-5.7	-11.7	-8.0	47.0	-12.1	-4.1	30.5	-10.2	-10.3	-12.7	-3.1	16.9
2002	44.4	21.8	4.3	-6.8	-3.4	10.7	7.8	-9.9	2.5	7.0	7.9	1.6	4.6	24.6
2003	6.4	37.1	11.8	18.3	13.6	10.4	17.6	6.7	-15.2	4.7	4.6	12.6	17.6	28.7
2004	9.4	35.7	16.4	19.0	18.7	24.7	25.5	34.9	0.0	27.4	8.3	33.2	22.1	18.4
2005	-100.0	23.2	11.0	29.4	13.3	23.0	16.4	33.4	25.5	10.5	7.6	18.5	19.8	22.6
2006		23.8	10.6	13.2	12.6	20.9	18.4	35.3	24.5	14.2	15.1	18.8	13.7	31.1
2007	-0.5	23.4	9.3	14.6	6.9	11.6	15.3	2.5	34.2	10.5	7.6	18.5	19.8	28.9
2008	23.9	17.8	5.5	26.5	23.1	22.8	22.0	25.4	17.3	10.4	1.6	17.0	20.3	-11.4
2009	-23.0	-13.8	-11.4	-20.1	-27.8	-10.4	-25.8	0.7	-1.2	-21.0	-23.3	-21.6	-19.3	22.8
2010	21.4	34.8	23.6	37.5	25.8	16.5	31.7	51.4	21.9	29.3	30.6	28.5	32.7	28.8
2011		22.4	10.8	28.7	23.3	37.0	23.3	21.2	36.0	14.4	2.1	17.0	19.6	14.7
2012		6.2	3.8	0.5	3.7	18.3	-11.9	10.5	-1.1	2.0	4.4	1.7	5.1	

Source: CEIE database.

in East Asia: peg to the US dollar or the Japanese yen, coordinate exchange rate arrangements, or free-floating. Various forms of arrangement for coordination of exchange rates have been discussed.

Before the Asian financial crisis, except for the Japanese yen and the Philippine peso, East Asian currencies were pegged to the US dollar. However, it is highly unlikely that there will a common arrangement in the future. It is hard to imagine that the Japanese yen would be pegged to the US dollar. With the yen fluctuating widely against the dollar, the policy of pegging would be bound to lead to macroeconomic instability in Asia's developing countries. As pointed out by Kwan (2001), since the Plaza Accord in 1985 there has been a clear tendency for economic growth in Asia to accelerate when the yen appreciates and to decelerate when the yen depreciates. In fact it was the weakening of the yen that led to a marked deterioration in Asia's export performance and current account balances in 1996, which in turn led to the Asian financial crisis.

Kwan (2001) once proposed the creation of a yen block. However, since 2002, due to a worsening current account deficit and continuous fall in interest rates, the dollar entered a long period of depreciation, which reached more than 40 percent before a reversal in 2008. The current strength of the US dollar is likely to be temporary. The depreciation of the dollar since 2002 helped to boost US exports. If it were not for the European sovereign debt crisis, the dollar would have resumed its long-term depreciation trend. On the other hand, the Japanese yen has been strong on the whole in the 2010s, hitting a record high of 76.52 yen against US$1 in March 2011. Obviously, with a strong yen and a lackluster Japanese economy, a yen block is not an attractive option.

If the countries in the region decide to coordinate their exchange rate arrangements, they have five options from which to choose:

- peg to a common currency basket consisting of the dollar, euro, and yen, with the same weight for all countries (John Williamson);
- peg to different currency baskets but consisting of the dollar, euro, and yen, with different weights for individual countries (Soko Tanaka);
- peg to similarly defined currency baskets consisting of extraregional as well as intraregional currencies, either excluding or including their own currencies (Kawai);
- peg to a common currency basket consisting only of regional currencies;
- create an Asian monetary system, equivalent to the EMS, with (1) an exchange rate mechanism (ERM) consisting of a grid of bilateral exchange rate bands between each of the member currencies, and (2) an ACU, equivalent to the ECU (Ogawa).

According to Williamson (2005), there would be significant advantages for both East Asia and the rest of the world if the countries of East Asia were to adopt a basket of currencies as the numeraire of their exchange rates, instead of using the US dollar. It is generally agreed that if the Asian countries had pegged to a basket rather than pegged to the dollar, and if the currencies in the basket had moved in opposite directions against the domestic currency, they would not have had to intervene so heavily. Consequently, the Asian economies that were under attack by international speculators would not have had to cave in after having exhausted their foreign exchange reserves (Yoshino et al. 2004).

Williamson (2005) pointed out further that "[i]t would be particularly advantageous to them if they were all to adopt the same basket. Such a basket would prevent variations in extraregional exchange rates from disrupting the East Asian economies by altering effective exchange rates and the relative competitiveness of the different countries of East Asia."

A common basket of currencies would minimize the possible disruption to the intraregional economic relationship. But is it really so important for the countries of East Asia to maintain fixed exchange rates against each other at the expense of each currency's stability against a major currency outside of the region, say the US dollar? Furthermore, because different economies in the region are very different in terms of trade structure and policy objectives, the preferred weights of the currencies in the basket are different. How can the member countries reach an agreement on the weights of the composition currencies in the common basket? The inclusion of the Japanese yen is also a problem, because, according to Williamson, a country should use a basket numeraire that includes its own currency. Last but not least, a basket numeraire would "leave traders in the participating countries without a mechanism for ascertaining the local currency value of trade contracts that will mature only in the future." (Williamson 2005).

As mentioned earlier, another option is to peg to different currency baskets consisting of dollar, euro, and yen only, but with different weights for individual countries. This avoids the question of how to decide the weights for individual composition currencies in the basket to the satisfaction of all member countries. But it seems that this option would reduce the role of the basket in stabilizing effective exchange rates and hence promoting trade integration among the countries in the region. However, according to Park and Wyplosz (2004), own basket pegging provides a similar stabilization effect as baskets with common weights. This is an issue worth further exploration.

Even without any of the above-mentioned problems, in the absence of a central financial authority in the region or some other institutional arrangement, how can this currency basket for regional currencies be decided, maintained, and adjusted properly?

If neither a peg to a single currency nor to a basket of currencies is feasible, how about a parallel currency? Japanese economists insist that the ACU is not intended to create an ECU-like currency unit to be officially used, but to provide a useful indicator of currency movements in East Asia. However, this is an approach that resembles the ECU. As pointed out by Eichengreen (2007, 13), "the ECU never acquired a significant role in the business of the European Community and in the EMS in particular," because "it was unattractive to move to the ECU in the absence of evidence that others were prepared to do likewise." Despite all its advantages as a parallel currency, because it is not clear where the ACU is intended to lead it has failed to attract much interest in the rest of East Asia. The dilemma for its initiators is that if the ACU is a step toward the Asian common currency, it is still too early for East Asian leaders to contemplate it. Hence "constructive ambiguity" is necessary. However, because of the ambiguity, the ACU cannot obtain the momentum necessary to attract interest in a parallel currency. It is likely that its fate will be similar to that of the ECU.

6.5 The PRC's Attitude toward Regional Coordination of Exchange Rate Arrangement and the Unilateralist Evolution of the Renminbi Exchange Rate Regime

The PRC is relatively positive in participating in swap agreements within the framework of the CMIM and has committed a large amount of money to the regional common pool of foreign exchange reserves. But the PRC's attitude toward the regional exchange rate coordination was ambiguous, and now is passive, to say the least.

According to Wyplosz (2010), "[t]he idea of establishing an Asian monetary unit (AMU) is intimately linked to the view that exchange rate fluctuations within (East) Asia are more troublesome than exchange rate fluctuations relative to the rest of the world." This argument applies to the PRC's attitude toward the coordination of exchange rate arrangements in the region, which is, to a large extent, decided by the PRC's assessment of the relative importance of the stabilization of intraregional exchange rates vis-à-vis the stabilization of the exchange rate of the RMB against the US dollar.

The United States is the PRC's most important trade partner. Even though the share of intraregional trade between the PRC and its East Asian neighbors is higher than that between the PRC and the US, the bulk of intraregional trade is organized by multinationals and the most important final destination of the products is the US, though final products may depart from ports in different countries in the region. Indeed, regional trade in East Asia is to a large extent intra-enterprise within the same multinationals. A common practice is that multinationals import parts and components from other countries, or even from factories of the same multinationals located in these countries. After processing and assembling, the final products are re-exported to Europe and the United States. With this production pattern, negative impacts due to changes in exchange rates on profitability of multinationals can be offset automatically. This was one of the main reasons why, during the Asian financial crisis, the PRC eventually decided to maintain the RMB's de facto peg to the US dollar instead of devaluing the RMB.

Furthermore, since multinationals have strong price-setting ability, via transfer pricing and so on, any negative impact of exchange rates on profitability can be minimized.[3] The intra-enterprise cross-border trade organized by a multinational is much less sensitive to exchange rate fluctuations among host countries where different segments of a production process are located.

Last but not least, because of the its position as the core international reserve currency, the US dollar is used by the PRC as well as other East Asian countries (excluding Japan) as a unit of account, invoice currency, settlement currency, vehicle currency, and reserve currency. The lion's share of the PRC's foreign assets is denominated in US dollars, while the PRC's foreign liabilities are denominated mostly in RMB. An appreciation of the RMB vis-à-vis the US dollar will worsen the PRC's net international investment position (NIIP) automatically. Therefore, NIIP consideration makes the PRC even more reluctant to allow the RMB to appreciate against the US dollar. This perhaps is true of other East Asian countries. In short, interregional stability of exchange rates vis-à-vis the US dollar is more important than intraregional stability of exchange rate among East Asian currencies.

The PRC runs a large trade surplus with the United States. In contrast, it has run trade deficits against the rest of East Asia for most of the years in the past decade. Therefore, in my view, there is no strong case for the countries in the region to argue for stabilizing exchange rates or even fixing exchange rates among their currencies, if it comes at the expense of individual countries' exchange rate stability against the US dollar.

For the PRC—rightly or wrongly—to maintain a stable, if not fixed, exchange rate against the US dollar is more important than to maintain stable exchange rates against the currencies of other countries in the East Asian region. From the perspective of trade and economic growth, it seems that there is no reason why the PRC should be more worried about exchange rate

---

[3] There is a large literature explaining why the exchange rate pass-through elasticity is less then unity when a multinational firm exports intermediate goods to its foreign subsidiary. It is argued that measured exchange rate pass-through elasticity may reflect within-firm transfer pricing between domestic and foreign subsidiaries rather than final product pricing (Hegji 2003).

fluctuation vis-à-vis the rest of East Asia than vis-à-vis the rest of the world in general, and the US in particular.

Thanks to the PRC's strong international balance of payments position, pressure on the RMB suddenly turned from depreciation to appreciation in 2003. Initially, the PRC resisted the international pressure. Many economists argued that the PRC should not de-peg from the US dollar and that allowing the RMB to appreciate even by 1 percent would lead to disastrous consequences for the economy.

The PRC's policy was geared toward reducing RMB appreciation pressure. In order to reduce this pressure, the PRC tried to encourage capital outflows by adopting a policy of "stricter control over capital inflows and looser control over capital outflow." Among the measures taken or tried, but eventually shelved, were permitting limited purchases of foreign equities by Chinese residents via the so-called Qualified Domestic Institutional Investors (QDII), and the so-called plan of "through train," which allowed PRC retail investors to buy shares in Hong Kong, China directly via the Bank of China's trading system. Because RMB appreciation expectations were strong, these policies have done little to reduce appreciation pressure.

The only feasible instrument left for the government to maintain the peg was central bank intervention in the foreign exchange market. As a result, the PRC's foreign exchange reserves started to increase exponentially. The increase in foreign exchange reserves heightened inflation pressure and caused increasingly more welfare losses, an issue elaborated upon later. Following the passage of time, it became increasingly clear that the cost of maintaining the peg was too high and would grow even higher.

After some initial hesitation, the PRC adopted an exchange rate regime of managed floating with reference to a basket of currencies on July 21, 2005. Since then the RMB exchange rate against the US dollar has started to climb up gradually. When the global financial crisis struck, the RMB had already appreciated by some 20 percent vis-à-vis the US dollar. RMB appreciation was interrupted by the global financial crisis in the second half of 2008. The peg to a basket resumed on June 21, 2010. At the time of writing, the RMB exchange rate against the US dollar has appreciated by more than 30 percent in real terms.

The PRC's basket consists of extraregional and intraregional currencies. The introduction of the new exchange rate regime was aimed at making the RMB exchange rate more flexible as well as at allowing the PBOC to manage its nominal effective exchange rate in line with the PRC's general economic situation. On the one hand, the PBOC would set a target for the "tolerable rate of appreciation" against the basket of currencies in each year. On the other hand, the PBOC has to calculate the RMB exchange rate vis-à-vis the

US dollar in line with the given nominal effective exchange rate. The actual central rate of the RMB exchange rate against the US dollar is then derived.

Initially, the floating band of the RMB exchange rate against the US dollar was less than 0.5 percent below or above the central parity rate. On April 16, 2012, the PBOC widened the band to 1 percent. It is worth noting that the central parity rate of the RMB against the US dollar is not based on the exchange rate at the closing time of the market on previous business day; instead it is determined on the basis of the above-mentioned procedure before the opening time of the market on each business day.

The new exchange rate regime helped the PRC to reduce its current account surplus-to-GDP ratio from some 10 percent in 2007 to 2.8 percent in 2011, while the negative impact of the appreciation on the PRC's exports and its unemployment was moderate.

However, the gradualist approach has its cost. The "twin surpluses" continue, As a result, foreign exchange reserves have been increasing steadily. In 2003 when the debate on RMB appreciation began, the PRC's foreign exchange reserves were about US$400 billion. Now they stand at US$3.6 trillion. However, in 2003, the price of crude oil was generally under US$30 a barrel, and the price of gold was less than US$400 an ounce. Since then, prices for crude oil and gold have increased to more than US$120 a barrel and US$1,600 an ounce, respectively. The value of the PRC's foreign exchange reserves in terms of purchasing power has shrunk greatly and may shrink further in the future due to higher interest rates, inflation or dollar devaluation. By running a current account surplus, the PRC is parking its excess savings in US government securities. However, if US government securities are no longer a reliable store of value, one cannot help but wonder why the PRC authorities do not just buy products from exporters and throw them into the Atlantic and Pacific oceans.

It is worth emphasizing that the PRC's exchange rate policy and policy debate since 2003 reflected both US pressure on the PRC and the PRC's domestic situation. During the protracted process of RMB appreciation, regional cooperation has played no role whatsoever. Complaints about the PRC's approach toward RMB appreciation in the rest of East Asia have been muted. Yet, are there any incentives for the PRC to participate in the coordination of regional exchange rate arrangements? The answer should be yes, if the coordination is aimed at establishing an Asian monetary union and the PRC is convinced that this objective is achievable (Yu 2006).

First, the PRC believes in a tri-polar world consisting of North America, the euro area, and ASEAN+3. The PRC believes that this new world order will provide a better guarantee for world peace and prosperity than under the US hegemony.

Second, East Asian people suffered greatly before and during the Second World War. Although reconciliation among East Asian nations has been achieved since the war, relationships among the nations, especially between Japan and the PRC, are far from satisfactory. Mutual suspicion and apprehension are still deeply rooted. Rising nationalism may have serious consequences. The European experience shows that political reconciliation lies in economic integration. If regional monetary cooperation eventually leads to an Asian monetary union and an Asian common currency, the possibility of hostilities and wars among East Asian countries will be buried once for all.

Third, the current international financial system is characterized by the fact that the US dollar—a national currency—is the key international reserve currency. The system gives the US the privilege of financing its external debts through IOUs or through the printing press and collecting offshore seigniorage. An emerging Asian monetary union, together with the European Monetary Union, will impose necessary discipline on the US government and US monetary authority (Yu 2006), and change the international monetary system fundamentally to the benefit of the world.

Unfortunately, the European sovereign debt crisis has dealt a fatal blow to the euro but also to the aspirations in the East Asian region for an Asian currency. The euro crisis shows that the euro will not survive without a fiscal union, which means that member countries have to surrender their fiscal sovereignty. However, to create an Asian monetary union and an Asian currency supported by a fiscal union is simply impossible in East Asia, because of the political and economic differences in the region. Without a clear vision for the final destination, it is difficult to draw a road map for Asian monetary cooperation. Without a final destination and a road map, the regional monetary cooperation that East Asian governments can contemplate has to be in specific areas and on specific issues on an ad hoc basis. Under these circumstances, the incentive for the PRC to participate in the coordination of exchange rate arrangements in the region will be even less than before.

6.6 Renminbi Internationalization and Its Implication for Regional Monetary Cooperation

Since the global financial crisis, while the RMB exchange rate is still the major concern of the PRC's decision-makers, the safety of its huge foreign exchange reserves has belatedly become a serious concern.

The near collapse of Fannie Mae and Freddie Mac horrified many in the PRC. Some Chinese economists have started to discuss the necessity of diversifying the PRC's foreign exchange reserves and the possibility of transferring part of the dollar-denominated assets into SDR-denominated assets. The deepening of the discussion led to the realization of the importance of reform of the international monetary system. The discussion culminated in Governor Zhou's proposal for the creation of a supranational currency. The international response to Governor Zhou's call was overwhelming and the PRC government was quick to distance itself from the proposal. A spokesman for the Ministry of Foreign Affairs wasted no time in dismissing the proposal as personal. The reason for this attitude perhaps is that the PRC government did not wish to disturb the current international order.

If the coordination of exchange rate arrangements in the region cannot do very much to help the PRC to reduce RMB appreciation pressure, and the reform of the international monetary system is too complicated to contemplate, what else can the PRC do to maintain a slow pace of RMB appreciation on the one hand and protect the value of the PRC's foreign exchange reserves on the other? It is against this backdrop that RMB internationalization was suggested as a possible solution.

The newly found enthusiasm for RMB internationalization also comes from the fact that unlike the reform of the international financial architecture and the promotion of regional monetary cooperation, RMB internationalization is an issue for which the PRC can set an agenda on its own without being constrained by external conditions. In early 2009, RMB internationalization was formally launched.

There are many potential benefits from RMB internationalization for the Chinese economy. First, it reduces exchange rate risks for Chinese exporters. Second, it improves the funding efficiency of Chinese financial institutions and hence increases their international competitiveness. Third, it increases cross-border trade by lowering transaction costs. Fourth, it reduces the need for holding the US dollar as a medium of exchange and a store of value and hence reduces the seigniorage paid to the US.[4]

The PRC government has made important progress in internationalizing the RMB since its launch. First, when the PRC announced the Pilot RMB Trade Settlement Scheme (PRTSS) in early 2009, RMB trade settlement was negligible. It accounted for some 9 percent of total trade settlements in the PRC by the end of 2011.

Second, RMB-denominated assets held by non-residents have increased significantly. RMB deposits held by Hong Kong, China residents grew exponentially between late 2010 and late 2012. The PRC government and major financial institutions as well as companies in Hong Kong, China have issued sizable RMB-denominated bonds.

---

[4] Seigniorage amounts to the return on the extra assets (real and financial) that a country is able to acquire because of the external holdings of its currency, less the interest paid on the assets in which foreigners invest their holdings and less any extra administrative costs arising from the international role of its money. See Pearce (1981, 389).

Third, the holding of the RMB as reserve currency by foreign central banks has increased via currency swap arrangements between the PBOC and foreign central banks. Mutual holding of government bonds with foreign central banks has also increased.

However, the internationalization of the RMB has faced various hurdles. Capital account liberalization is one of them. Although the internationalization of a currency is not tantamount to capital account liberalization and full convertibility, the degree of internationalization is conditional on the degree of capital account liberalization and convertibility. Most steps of RMB internationalization are predicated upon corresponding steps of capital account liberalization, which in turn is constrained by the inflexibility of interest rates and the exchange rate of the RMB. There are other necessary conditions too. For example, to encourage non-residents to hold RMB assets, not only must the RMB be convertible but also the PRC must have a deep and liquid financial market. Even if all necessary conditions have been met, the network externality is still a difficult hurdle to overcome. Japan's slow progress in yen internationalization is a case in point.

The progress so far was based to a large extent on expectations of further RMB appreciation. One cannot help but wonder whether foreign exporters will still accept the RMB as a settlement and investment currency when these expectations disappear. Another question is what is the best way for the PRC, as a current account surplus country, to provide its trade partners RMB liquidity? To provide the RMB via import settlements but without being able to "recycle" the RMB via exports is equivalent to borrowing from non-residents. In fact, RMBs provided by the PRC via import settlement are held either as deposits or used to purchase RMB-denominated bonds by non-residents. As a result, RMB internationalization leads to further increases in foreign exchange reserves held by the Chinese monetary authority, which is still reluctant to allow the RMB to appreciate according to market forces.

The increase in holding of RMB-denominated assets such as RMB deposits and RMB-denominated bonds by non-residents is one of the most acclaimed achievements of RMB internationalization. However, the PRC has already attracted too much foreign capital over the past thirty years, and had to translate a large proportion of the capital inflows into US dollar-denominated foreign exchange reserves. The PRC does not need to attract more capital inflows, independently of the currencies in which these inflows are denominated. In short, many achievements of RMB internationalization turn out to be contrary to the original intentions.[5]

---

[5] A more detailed discussion on RMB internationalization is provided in Yu (2012).

Ideally, the PRC should encourage foreign investors to sell RMB-denominated bonds (Panda bonds) to Chinese investors. Panda bonds suit the PRC's desire for reducing the appreciation pressure as well as the exchange rate risks. Unfortunately, when the RMB is still undervalued and the PRC's capital market still lacks depth and liquidity, it is difficult to persuade non-residents to issue RMB-denominated liabilities. A few foreign firms in Hong Kong, China sold some Panda bonds. But the motivation of the issuance is certainly not entirely economic. During the global financial crisis, due to liquidity shortage and credit crunch many economies were badly in need of US dollars. At the time, they could issue Panda bonds and then use the RMB proceeds to buy dollars from the PRC. The Fed's swaps with many central banks eliminated the necessity. The so-called Dim Sum bonds that are denominated in RMB and sold by companies with business in the PRC to Hong Kong, China residents benefit the PRC as well as the Hong Kong, China residents. But the scale of the bonds is limited due to various constraints.

RMB internationalization can be either a positive or a negative factor for regional monetary cooperation. On the one hand, RMB internationalization reflects the PRC's intention to go its own way to safeguard its own interests, given the lack of interest in the coordination of regional exchange rate arrangements. Fortunately, RMB internationalization does not yet conflict with other possible options, such as the creation of a regional common currency. But the creation of an RMB bloc, as the result of RMB internationalization, may come at the expense of coordination of exchange rate arrangements in the region. On the other hand, RMB internationalization has opened new channels for regional monetary cooperation.

6.7 Way Forward for Regional Monetary Cooperation in East Asia

Regional monetary cooperation initially represented a desire to learn from the successful experience of Europe. In the wake of the Asian financial crisis, progress could be attributed to the awareness of the need for liquidity and to distrust of the IMF's willingness to provide such liquidity during a major crisis. Once East Asian countries fully recovered from the crisis and started to run current account surpluses, the coordination of exchange rate arrangements in the region essentially aimed at fairly sharing the burden of appreciation. Coordination was implicitly aimed at persuading or pressing the PRC to allow the RMB to appreciate more aggressively, while the aspiration for deepening regional economic integration has played an important role.

Since the global financial crisis and the European sovereign debt crisis, East Asia has faced a very different situation. First, with all major developed countries entering prolonged recession, the export-led growth model is no longer viable. East Asia as a whole has had to shift its growth paradigm to rely on domestic demand. As a result, competitiveness has become less of a concern. For example, after its gradual appreciation since 2005, the RMB is approaching equilibrium value. In fact, the RMB could even devalue according to the non-deliverable forward (NDF) market. Some other macroeconomic variables are becoming more important. As Eichengreen (2007) suggested, things such as inflation targeting and macroeconomic policy cooperation could become the focus of regional monetary cooperation in place of the coordination of exchange rate arrangements.

Second, as a result of the deepening of the euro crisis and possibly the worsening of the US public debt crisis, East Asian countries may face further capital outflows due to liquidity shortage, the need for capital injection, and commercial bank deleveraging. At the same time, there is also the opposite possibility that large amounts of capital will flow into the region out of desperation or safe-haven demand. To minimize the impact of large capital-flow fluctuations on financial stability of the individual countries, regional supervision and regulation of capital flows will become extremely important.

Third, due to the fact that almost all US foreign liabilities are denominated in US dollars and that the bulk of its foreign assets are denominated in local currencies, the possibility of East Asian countries suffering huge capital losses is very high. How to safeguard the value of US$4 trillion of foreign exchange reserves and other foreign assets is a huge challenge that the East Asian region is facing. Countries in the region should minimize their holdings of US dollars and adjust the currency structure of their foreign assets and liabilities. Regional cooperation is essential to carry out such adjustments.

On March 13, 2012, the PRC gave Japan the go-ahead to buy 65 billion yuan (US$10 billion) of government bonds. In May 2012 the PRC and Japan decided to start direct currency trading. These are two important developments. In particular, direct currency trading might signal a new direction for regional monetary cooperation. The elimination of US dollars from Sino-Japanese bilateral trade and financial transactions will help the bilateral yuan/yen exchange rate market, and thereby reduce transaction costs and lower exchange rate risks. For the PRC, the decision is a boost to the use of the RMB as a settlement currency for trade and financial transactions.

It seems that, faced with this new situation, East Asia can forget about the more ambitious goals of regional monetary cooperation for the time being and make more efforts to achieve some less ambitious but more feasible and urgently needed objectives. For example, the region can:

- improve the CMIM and reduce the need for further accumulation of foreign exchange reserves aimed at fending off speculative attacks;

- encourage a wider use of local currencies for invoicing and settlement in place of the US dollar for trade and financial transactions in the region;
- issue and hold more local currency denominated bonds and speed up the development of Asian bond markets;
- prepare for a coordinated exit from US government securities without causing undue impact on the market;
- translate interregional East Asian current account surpluses into intraregional FDI;
- coordinate their activities in participating in the rescue of the euro and the reform of the international monetary system.

6.8 Concluding Remarks

East Asian countries have been struggling with the issue of regional monetary cooperation for more than a decade. Unfortunately, progress has been very slow and frustrating. A lack of leadership and strong political will has been a key obstacle. Without a clear answer to the question of whether East Asia wishes to form an Asian economic community and AMU, regional monetary cooperation will never go very far. On the one hand, East Asia has made important progress in regional monetary cooperation in the form of the CMIM. On the other hand, unilateralism in the area of exchange rate coordination prevailed over regionalism.

The global financial crisis has failed to confirm the necessity of and benefits from regional monetary cooperation. The European financial crisis has dealt a fatal blow to the aspiration for an Asian monetary union and an Asian common currency. With consensus on the final destination of regional monetary cooperation shattered, a road map for cooperation has become impossible. Regional monetary cooperation will be more ad hoc in the foreseeable future. RMB internationalization reflects the PRC's frustration and intention to go its own way to safeguard its own interests.

Following the global financial crisis and the European sovereign debt crisis, East Asia is faced with new challenges. The global economy may have entered a long-drawn out recession. The export-led growth model is no longer viable. East Asia as a whole has to shift its growth paradigm to rely on domestic demand. East Asian countries may have to face more external shocks such as sudden changes in the direction of capital flows. It is highly likely that, as they respond to economic stagnation, central banks in the US and Europe will speed up the operation of printing presses with dire consequences for the real value of foreign exchange reserves, into which East Asians have packed their savings to prepare for the coming aging societies.

While it may have to give up on its desire to eventually create an Asian monetary union and an Asian common currency, East Asia should not give up its efforts toward regional monetary cooperation. However, how to do so requires further exploration. Perhaps, the wider use of local currencies in trade and financial transactions in the region in place of the US dollar represents a new way forward.

Acknowledgments

The author is very grateful for the research assistance provided by Xu Qiquan, Dong Yan, and Zhang Lin with of the Institute of World Economics and Politics, Chinese Academy of Social Sciences.

References*

Ariff, Mohamed. 2010. "Comment on 'International and Regional Cooperation: Asia's Role and Responsibilities.'" *Asian Economic Policy Review* 5(2): 174–75.

Bayoumi, Tamin, and Barry Eichengreen. 1994. *One Money or Many?* Princeton, NJ: International Section, Department of Economics, Princeton University.

Drysdale, Peter, and Shiro Armstrong. 2010. "International and Regional Cooperation: Asia's Role and Responsibilities." *Asian Economic Policy Review* 5(2): 157–73.

Eichengreen, Barry. 2007. *Fostering Monetary and Exchange Rate Cooperation in East Asia.* Berkeley: University of California Press.

Frankel, Jeffrey A., and Shang-Jin Wei. 1993. "Trade Blocs and Currency Blocs." NBER Working Paper 4335, April§.

Hegji, Charles E. 2003. "A Note on Transfer Prices and Exchange Rate Pass-Through." *Journal of Economics and Finance* 27(3): 396–403.

Kwan, Chi Hung. 2001. *Yen Bloc: Toward Economic Integration in Asia.* Washington, DC: Brookings Institution Press.

McKinnon, Ronald I. 2000. "After the Crisis, the East Asian Dollar Standard Resurrected: An Interpretation of High-Frequency Exchange Rate Pegging." Economic Department, Stanford University. <http://web.stanford.edu/group/siepr/cgi-bin/siepr/?q=system/files/shared/pubs/papers/pdf/credpr88.pdf>.

Park, Yung Chul, and Charles Wyplosz. 2004. "Exchange Rate Arrangements in Asia: Do They Matter?" In *Monetary and Exchange Rate Arrangements in East Asia*, edited by Yonghyup Oh, Deo Ryong Yoon, and Thomas D. Willett, pp. 129–60. Seoul: Korea Institute for International Economic Policy.

Pearce, David W. 1981. *The Macmillan Dictionary of Modern Economics.* London: Macmillan.

---

* The Asian Development Bank recognizes China by the name People's Republic of China.

Sussangkarn, Chalongphob. 2011. "The Chiang Mai Initiative Multilateralization: Origin, Development and Outlook." *Asian Economic Policy Review* 6(2): 203–20.

Volz, Ulrich. 2010. *Prospects for Monetary Cooperation and Integration in East Asia.* Cambridge, MA: MIT Press.

Williamson, John. 2005. "A Currency Basket for East Asia, Not Just China." Policy Brief No. 05-1. Washington, DC: Institute for International Economics, July.

Wyplosz, Charles. 2010. "An Asian Monetary Unit?" In *The Future Global Reserve System, An Asian Perspective*, edited by Jeffrey D. Sachs, Masahiro Kawai, Jong-Wha Lee, and Wing Thye Woo. Manila: Asian Development Bank.

Yoshino, Naoyuki, Sahoko Kaji, and Ayako Suzuki. 2004. "The Basket-Peg, Dollar-Peg, and Floating: A Comparative Analysis." *Journal of the Japanese and International Economies* 18(2): 183–217.

Yu, Yongding. 2006. "The Roadmap for East Asian Financial Cooperation." Speech at the International Conference on Regional Monetary Cooperation, 29 October, Osaka.

Yu, Yongding. 2012. "Revisiting the Internationalization of the Yuan." ADBI Working Paper No. 366. Tokyo: Asian Development Bank Institute.

7
A View from Japan

Masahiro Kawai

7.1 Introduction

In recent years, East Asia has seen rapid advances in market-driven economic integration through cross-border trade, investment, and finance. Following Japan, the Asian newly industrialized economies (NIEs)—Hong Kong, China; the Republic of Korea; Singapore; and Taipei,China—and middle-income Association of Southeast Asian Nations (ASEAN) member states, the People's Republic of China (PRC) is the most recent participant in this integration process. This growing trade and foreign direct investment (FDI) integration has led to the formation of a regional production network, with supply chains throughout East Asia.[1] Japanese multinational corporations, with significant presence in the region thanks to their advanced technological capabilities, have played a key role in creating and supporting these production supply chains. Financial integration has also progressed, albeit to a more limited extent than trade and FDI integration, due to limited financial market development and opening in many developing economies in the region.

Reflecting such rising economic integration through trade, FDI, and finance, macroeconomic interdependence has deepened in East Asia. The high and rising degree of economic interdependence in East Asia suggests that it is increasingly important for the region's economies, including Japan, to avoid disruptive exchange rate volatility and to achieve intraregional exchange rate stability.[2] The reason is that intraregional currency stability is

---

[1] In this chapter, East Asia includes the so-called ASEAN+3 countries (the ten ASEAN member states plus the PRC; Japan; and the Republic of Korea); Hong Kong, China; Taipei,China; and India.

[2] Some key policy makers in East Asia are even more vocal about the need to create a monetary union in the region (e.g. Chino 2004; Kuroda 2004). The recent Eurozone financial crisis clearly revealed a much more challenging task in forging a regional monetary union than previously thought.

conducive to more active trade and FDI and thus the more efficient workings of the supply chains.

In reality, however, the region remains characterized by diverse, uncoordinated exchange rate arrangements. Japan and the PRC, the two dominant countries in East Asia, have respectively adopted an exchange rate regime akin to a pure float and a tightly managed United States (US) dollar-based regime. Most other economies—except for the small open economies of Brunei Darussalam and Hong Kong, China, both of which have adopted currency board systems—employ intermediate regimes of managed floating with the US dollar as the most important anchor currency. However, it is becoming a challenge to maintain intraregional rate stability through the traditional policy of dollar pegs, so it would be desirable to develop a regional framework for exchange rate policy coordination in East Asia. The PRC aggressively pursues renminbi (RMB) internationalization and may wish to create a RMB-based monetary system in the region. From a Japanese perspective, the yen could hopefully be a major currency for the region's monetary policy coordination as it is the region's only convertible—particularly reserve—currency.

A group of international experts (Angeloni et al. 2011; Eichengreen 2011; Subramanian 2011) holds the view that the RMB will play the role of a dominant international currency in Asia. Indeed, building on an impressive economic performance, the PRC authorities have adopted a strategy to internationalize the RMB using a two-track approach: the first is to promote the international role of the RMB through its use in trade and investment settlements, the establishment of offshore markets for bank deposits and bonds in Hong Kong, China, and bilateral currency swap arrangements; and the second is to achieve capital account convertibility through gradual liberalization of international capital and financial flows. According to this view, East Asia will be an RMB zone where substantial amounts of trade and investment transactions are conducted in RMB. On the other hand, another group of economists is much less optimistic about the prospect of RMB internationalization. The PRC faces enormous economic, social, and political challenges domestically, and it is by no means certain that the RMB will become the most prominent international currency in East Asia. According to this second view, over the next decade or two at least it is highly unlikely that the RMB can establish itself as a credible international currency with full capital account convertibility. Or even if RMB internationalization is successful, it may take much longer for the RMB to grow to an international currency parallel to the US dollar and the euro than optimists expect. Under this scenario, there is a case for developing a basket of East Asian currencies—such as an Asian currency unit (ACU)—as the region's common reference currency. If the second view is more valid than the first, creating an ACU would be desirable not only for the PRC and Japan but also for East Asia as a whole.

This chapter focuses on Japan's strategy for Asian monetary integration and asks the following questions:

- What has been the problem with Japan's initiative to internationalize the yen?
- What should Japan do to promote intraregional exchange rate stability?
- What are the steps for strengthening foundations for regional exchange rate policy coordination? What types of institutional support are needed for this purpose?
- What are the most serious impediments to such steps?

Essentially, Japan faces three major policy challenges when promoting intraregional exchange rate stability. First, intraregional rate stability requires some convergence of exchange rate regimes in East Asia, and the most realistic option is for the region's emerging economies to adopt similar managed floating regimes—rather than a peg to an external currency. This means a move by major emerging economies—particularly the PRC—to a more flexible regime vis-à-vis the US dollar, which is in their interests as well as of the region as a whole. Second, given the limited degree of the yen's internationalization and the lack of the RMB's (or the prospect of its rapid) full convertibility, the emerging East Asian economies may wish to create a regional monetary anchor through a combination of some form of national inflation targeting and a currency basket system. For example, the special drawing rights (SDR) or an SDR-plus currency basket (i.e. a basket of the SDR and emerging East Asian currencies) could be suitable for their exchange rate target, Third, if the creation of a stable regional monetary zone is desirable, the region must have a country or countries assuming a leadership role in this endeavor. There is no question that Japan and the PRC are such potential leaders, and their close collaboration is essential. Japan may also wish to transform Tokyo into a world-class international financial center and further internationalize the yen in order to play a joint leadership role with the PRC.

The chapter is organized as follows. Section 7.2 reviews the recent developments of Japan's exchange rate, its current account balance, and real economic activity. Section 7.3 discusses Japan's policy challenges in the areas of exchange rates, yen internationalization, and relationships with other East Asian economies. Section 7.4 explores Japan's strategy for East Asian monetary integration from the perspectives of transforming Tokyo into an international financial center, creating an ACU as Asia's regional currency basket, and supporting regional financial and currency stability. It also identifies policy steps for exchange rate policy coordination that could lead to stable intraregional exchange rates. Section 7.5 provides concluding remarks.

7.2 The Japanese Yen and the Current Account

7.2.1 *Yen Appreciation*

The Japanese yen has been appreciating in terms of both nominal and real (effective) exchange rates as a trend over the last 40 years. This chronic appreciation trend has been a defining feature even during the periods of the "lost decade" of the 1990s, the global financial crisis of 2007–9, and the post-triple disaster in 2011. In addition, despite the pressures from an aging population and rapidly rising public debt, the yen remained strong rather than collapsed. The launch of Abenomics in 2013 reversed this trend, but it remains to be seen whether this is long-lasting or short-lived. We first examine why the yen appreciation trend persisted until late 2012 and then discuss the recent yen depreciation under Abenomics.

FACTORS BEHIND YEN APPRECIATION

One important factor behind the nominal appreciation of the yen is Japan's low inflation or deflation, which has reduced Japan's prices relative to those in the US over time. Figure 7.1 plots the nominal yen/US dollar exchange rate and the relative producer price index (PPI) and consumer price index (CPI) between Japan and the US. The downward trends of the relative prices on average match the appreciation trend of the yen. Japan's relative price decline reflects the relative tightness of Japanese monetary policy vis-à-vis the US.

A factor behind the real yen appreciation trend is the persistent current account surplus (see next subsection). Waves of yen rate appreciation seem to be associated with changes in the current account balance; with a rising current account surplus the yen tended to appreciate, and vice versa. This phenomenon is consistent with what McKinnon (2005) called "conflicted virtue," that is, as Japan ran current account surpluses by saving more than investing domestically and thus accumulated net external assets, the real exchange rate tended to appreciate and reduce the yen value of net external assets, thereby inducing further savings, current account surpluses, and yen appreciation.

Noteworthy is the fact that, even during the global financial crisis of 2007–9 and the post-triple disaster period of 2011, the yen appreciated.

Surprisingly, the global financial crisis initially caused the US dollar to appreciate against most currencies, except the yen. The reason for the US dollar appreciation was that cash-short US financial firms repatriated massive amounts of US dollar liquidity back to the US from the rest of the world, putting upward pressure on the dollar.[3] In Asia, for example, the Republic of Korea saw

---

[3] There were carry trades between the US dollar and most other currencies in the form of borrowing in low-cost US dollar instruments and investing in higher-yield currencies during

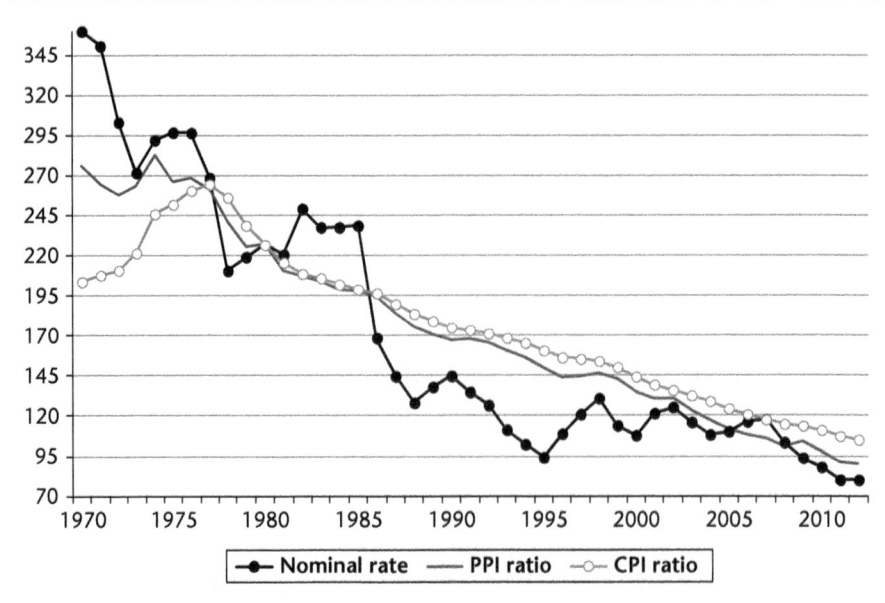

Figure 7.1. Nominal yen appreciation matched by relative price deflation
Source: International Monetary Fund, International Financial Statistics.

rapid liquidity outflows, sharp currency depreciation, and a large loss of foreign exchange reserves, experiencing a mini-won crisis. There was, however, no significant liquidity repatriation from Japan to the US; instead, there was an unwinding of yen carry trades—that is, reversals of capital outflows from Japan to high-yield countries and repatriations of funds back to Japan—causing yen appreciation.[4]

There may have been a safe-haven effect as well; the Japanese economy was not growing, but its growth prospect was deemed better than those of the crisis-affected US and Europe—given the latter's problems, such as deep banking sector problems and sharp economic contractions—and thus attracted fund flows to Japan. When the US Federal Reserve adopted an easy monetary policy, particularly quantitative monetary easing in March 2009, the US dollar began to depreciate and the yen continued to appreciate.[5]

2002–7. The global financial crisis caused a rapid unwinding of these carry trades, a massive repatriation of funds back to the US, and a consequent appreciation of the US dollar.

[4] The short-term yen interest rate was near zero and, as a result, there were no carry trades of borrowing in US dollar and investing in yen. There were, however, carry trades between the yen and several currencies in Asia and the Pacific—such as the won, the Australian dollar, and the New Zealand dollar—and the US dollar, in the form of borrowing in yen and investing in these currencies. The unwinding of the yen carry trades caused appreciation of the yen.

[5] Soon after this first round of quantitative easing (QE1) policy was introduced, US dollar liquidity started to flow out of the US to the rest of the world, particularly to emerging

Following the triple disaster of the Great East Japan Earthquake in March 2011, the yen once again appreciated with the expectation of Japanese insurance firms' repatriation of their funds from their investment destinations abroad. Together with the further deepening of the Eurozone financial crisis, the yen continued to appreciate, breaking the historical record reached in April 1995. The monthly average exchange rate reached 76.8 yen/US dollar (September 2011) while the previous peak was 83.7 yen/US dollar (April 1995).

PUBLIC DEBT AND THE YEN

Despite the pressures from an aging population and the rising public debt, the yen remained strong. The general government public debt-to-GDP ratio reached 224 percent (for gross debt) and 137 percent (for net debt) at the end of 2013 (OECD, *Economic Outlook*, No. 96 database) and has continued to rise. The consensus view is that the fiscal position and public debt are clearly unsustainable, although the market has not shown any sign of concern. Indeed, the government's net debt interest payments were only 1.0 percent of GDP in 2013, while the OECD average was 2.0 percent of GDP.

There are several factors underlying this favorable market reaction. First, most sovereign debt, particularly long-term Japanese government bonds (JGBs), is held by Japanese investors, and foreign ownership is only about 10 percent. This prevents flight of investment, particularly by Japanese banks, away from sovereign debt to foreign financial assets. Second, the current account is still in surplus, implying that Japan does not have to rely on foreign borrowing to finance fiscal deficits. This provides market confidence that further debt issuance can still be financed domestically without much difficulty. Third, room exists for substantial fiscal consolidation through an increase in the consumption tax rate, which is currently only 8 percent.[6] Japan could raise the consumption tax rate to 20 percent, which is the norm in Western European countries, thereby generating a total tax revenue of 55 trillion yen (roughly 11 percent of GDP) and contributing to fiscal consolidation.[7]

However, the issue is one of multiple equilibria. Once market participants lose confidence in the sustainability of public debt for some reason—for example, the current account turning into a deficit—they may start selling

---

economies with strong growth prospects. This put upward pressure on the currencies of these economies as well as Japan.

[6] The government raised the consumption tax rate from 5% to 8% in April 2014 but has decided to postpone the timing of the next rate hike to 10% (originally scheduled for October 2015) until April 2017.

[7] In Japan, government total outlays as a share of GDP are not particularly high; they were 43% in 2013, roughly the same as the OECD average of 42%. In contrast, government revenues were low at 33% of GDP in 2013, while their OECD average was 37% of GDP. Thus, the first challenge for Japan in its efforts at fiscal consolidation would be to raise government revenues.

debt instruments for fear of capital loss, forcing the JGB price down and the interest rate up. In this sense, expectations can be self-fulfilling. Such market developments would further increase fiscal deficits by magnifying interest payments on JGBs, threaten the health of the banking system as many banks hold massive amounts of sovereign debts, and likely cause a financial and economic crisis.

THE PRC'S INDUSTRIALIZATION AND JAPAN'S TRADE STRUCTURE

The rapid emergence of the PRC as a large, low-cost supplier in the world economy may have created a deflationary impact on the rest of the world, particularly Japan, and yen appreciation pressure. Hirakata et al. (2014) analyze empirically the impact of a supply shock in emerging economies on Japan's inflation rate, using the panel instrumental variable method developed by Auer and Fischer (2010). They find that the impact on Japan was deflationary and that it was more deflationary in Japan than in the US and Europe.

Hirakata et al. (2014) also examine the impact of the PRC's supply shock on the yen rate by using a three-country dynamic stochastic general equilibrium (DSGE) model, which replicates the trade relationships among Japan, the PRC, and the US and the existing exchange rate arrangements.[8] Using simulation analysis, they find that a positive supply shock to the PRC's final goods sector stimulates its production of final goods and its imports of parts and components from Japan, generates trade surpluses in Japan and the PRC and a trade deficit in the US, and causes the yen to appreciate vis-à-vis the US dollar. The yen appreciates largely because Japan runs a trade surplus against the US, as the nominal value of the RMB cannot appreciate against the US dollar because of the fixed exchange rate assumption. In Japan and the US, price deflation takes place and Japan's deflation is more severe than US deflation.

The observation of a long-term yen appreciation trend is consistent with these simulation results. They support the view that the rise of emerging economies in the global economy, represented as persistent supply shocks, would lead to yen appreciation when Japan is a competitive producer of parts and components for Asia's supply chain countries and adopts a free float for the yen, while the US dollar is an anchor currency for many emerging economies.

---

[8] The model assumes vertical specialization of trade between Japan and the PRC: Japan produces and exports highly sophisticated parts and components to the PRC; the PRC produces final manufactured goods, by assembling parts and components, and then exports final goods to Japan and the US; and the US has no advantage in the production of parts and components or final goods. The model also assumes that the central banks of Japan and the US set the respective policy interest rates following the Taylor rule, while the central bank of the PRC pegs the currency to the US dollar.

LAUNCH OF ABENOMICS AND YEN DEPRECIATION

The second Abe Cabinet, formed at the end of 2012, adopted "Abenomics" comprising "three arrows" to revitalize the Japanese economy: a combination of aggressive monetary policy easing by the Bank of Japan (BOJ), flexible fiscal policy (a fiscal stimulus), and structural reforms to boost Japan's productivity. The new BOJ Governor, Haruhiko Kuroda, implemented aggressive monetary policy easing of a "different dimension" in April 2013—called quantitative and qualitative easing (QQE)—to achieve an inflation target of 2 percent in two years.

One important way of making monetary policy effective was to affect asset prices through the expectations channel, backed by its behavior. That is, even before the BOJ QQE policy was announced, Japanese stock prices had begun to rise and the yen rate had begun to depreciate in late 2012 when the victory of the Liberal Democratic Party in the general election was widely anticipated. Governor Kuroda then indicated that there was a fundamental regime change in monetary policy making to create a sustained rate of inflation of around 2 percent so that people should start behaving differently.

As a result, 2013 saw a reversal of yen movements toward depreciation and a rise in stock prices. Although these new trends were adversely affected in May 2013 by Federal Reserve Board Chairman Bernanke's indication of QE tapering, they subsequently recovered and returned in the new direction. It is noted that yen rate and stock price movements have been closely related. There is a strong indication that the stock market surge in Tokyo and the yen depreciation trend have been driven primarily by foreign investors, particularly foreign hedge funds. The new yen depreciation trend will likely be sustained over a long period.

7.2.2 Japan's Current Account

PERSISTENT CURRENT ACCOUNT SURPLUSES

Japan has experienced sizable current account surpluses since the 1980s (Figure 7.2) although the size of the surplus has fluctuated over time in a cyclical way. The current account balance improved sharply from a small deficit (1.1 percent of GDP) recorded in 1980 to a large surplus (4.2 percent of GDP) reached in 1986. The balance then declined toward 1990 and began to widen substantially again from a moderate surplus (2.1 percent of GDP) in 2001 to a record large surplus (4.8 percent) in 2007, followed by a trend decline afterward.

There has been a shift in the composition of the current account surplus. In earlier years, a substantial part was from the goods trade balance, while the services trade balance has long been in deficit at a relatively stable level of

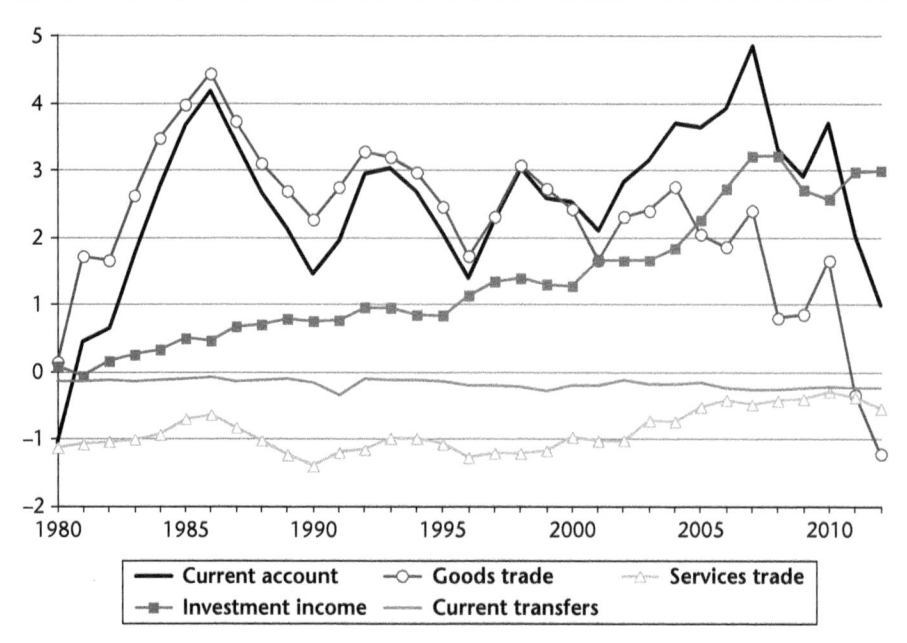

Figure 7.2. Japan's current account and its composition (% of GDP)
Source: Bank of Japan, Balance of Payments Statistics; Cabinet Office.

1 percent of GDP. In more recent years, the source of the current account surplus has shifted to a surplus in net investment income, which has reached around 3 percent of GDP, far exceeding a surplus in the goods trade balance. The large investment income surplus is a result of the accumulation of net external assets, which have risen significantly from a mere 2.5 trillion yen (1 percent of GDP) in 1980 to 296 trillion yen (62 percent of GDP) in 2012. It is expected that Japan will continue to earn a high level of net investment income from abroad, while its size can rise or fall as a share of GDP depending on the yen's exchange rates against the US dollar and other major currencies in which the assets are held.

The surplus in the goods trade balance has been on a declining trend since the eruption of the global financial crisis. In 2011, the goods trade balance registered a deficit for the first time since the last deficit in 1963 (0.2 percent of GDP), mainly due to the increased imports of liquefied natural gas (LNG), petroleum, and other sources of energy for electricity power generation, required by the stoppage of almost all nuclear power reactors following the failure of Tokyo Electric Company's Fukushima Daiichi Nuclear Power Plant in March 2011. The deficit was also partly due to the reduced exports of manufacturing products following the disruptions of supply chains hit by the tsunami in the Tohoku area and a rapid yen rate appreciation.

IMPACT OF REAL YEN APPRECIATION ON NET EXPORTS

Movements in the real exchange rate have played a significant role in promoting adjustment of the current account. To quantify the impact of real exchange rate changes on external rebalancing, Kawai and Takagi (2015) consider a vector autoregressive (VAR) model of Japanese net exports as a percentage of GDP, Japan's real GDP growth less world GDP growth (RY), and Japan's real effective exchange rate (REER), and examine the impact of the REER shock on net exports.[9] The estimated VAR model reveals several points. First, the estimated coefficient of the lagged RY and REER variables have the expected (negative) signs, suggesting that faster growth in Japan or real yen appreciation causes net exports to decline, though only the estimated coefficient of one-period lagged REER is statistically significant. Second, the negative impact of a REER shock on net exports lasts for up to only three years, while about 20 percent of the variance of net exports can be explained by the variance of the REER during the current period, with the percentage increasing to 50 percent in three years before declining to 40 percent.

These findings indicate that changes in the real effective exchange rate have a statistically significant, predictable impact on Japan's net exports, though the impact is temporary and lasts only for about three years. They also suggest that Japan's external balance over the medium to long term depends largely on the fundamental determinants of domestic savings and investment, independently of cyclical or transitory factors.

PROSPECTS FOR JAPAN'S CURRENT ACCOUNT

In considering the future prospects for Japan's current account, three fundamental factors—net savings of the public, the corporate, and the household sector—need to be examined.

First, given the large gross public debt amounting to 224 percent of GDP, the public sector is expected to go through significant fiscal consolidation to maintain debt sustainability. Fiscal consolidation is expected to be achieved mainly through increases in tax revenues and partly through containment of public expenditures. This is the only way to avoid the kind of sovereign debt crisis observed in Greece in 2010–11. This suggests that public sector net savings will likely increase in the future, contributing to an increase in national savings over investment.

Second, the corporate sector has had positive net savings since the second half of the 1990s. It had accumulated large retained earnings to the tune of 300 trillion yen by March 2013. This was largely due to the need for the corporate sector to repay debt incurred during the period of asset price bubbles

---

[9] A qualitatively similar result was obtained using the current account balance instead of net exports. However, the estimated model fits considerably better when net exports are used.

in the late 1980s; and low corporate domestic investment because of stagnant domestic economic activity,[10] a shift of manufacturing production abroad, and the prospective population decline. Once the Japanese economy recovers from the "two lost decades," corporate investment is expected to recover as well, thereby reducing corporate net savings.

Third, the household sector has experienced a trend decline in net savings since the 1990s. This declining trend can largely be explained by demographic changes—in particular, increases in the aged population and declines in the working-age population. Net savings have declined despite the presence of counterbalancing factors, such as greater future uncertainty associated with debt sustainability concerns and the declining trust in social safety nets due to the deterioration of public finances. Even when these concerns abate under the scenario of fiscal consolidation, the household sector net savings are expected to further decline.

The increase in public net savings will be offset by a decline in corporate and household net savings, with an ambiguous impact on overall national net savings or the current account balance. Under the reasonable scenario that the demographic factors eventually dominate the fiscal consolidation factor, current account surpluses will likely vanish and deficits may even emerge. Given that the net investment income balance will remain positive, this implies that the goods trade balance is expected to further deteriorate to deficits in the future. Thus, the Japanese economy will depend increasingly on the non-tradable goods sector for domestic production and employment and investment income from abroad, while focusing on higher value-added manufacturing activities.

7.2.3 Impact of Yen Appreciation on the Japanese Economy

YEN APPRECIATION AND JAPANESE MANUFACTURING

Real effective yen appreciation has had a significant negative impact on the Japanese manufacturing sector and its overall economic activity, while yen depreciation has had a positive impact. The global financial crisis and the Eurozone financial crisis were associated with rapid yen appreciation, aggravating negative impacts on the Japanese economy. The business sector was hit by the high yen in recent years. However, according to the yen's overall real effective exchange rate (REER) index, published by the Bank for International Settlements (BIS) and based on relative CPIs, the yen was still about 35 percent lower in 2012 than the previous peak in 1995 and

---

[10] Japan's corporate investment as a ratio of GDP has been declining as a trend since the early 1990s. Its net investment (i.e. gross investment net of capital depreciation) became negative in 2009.

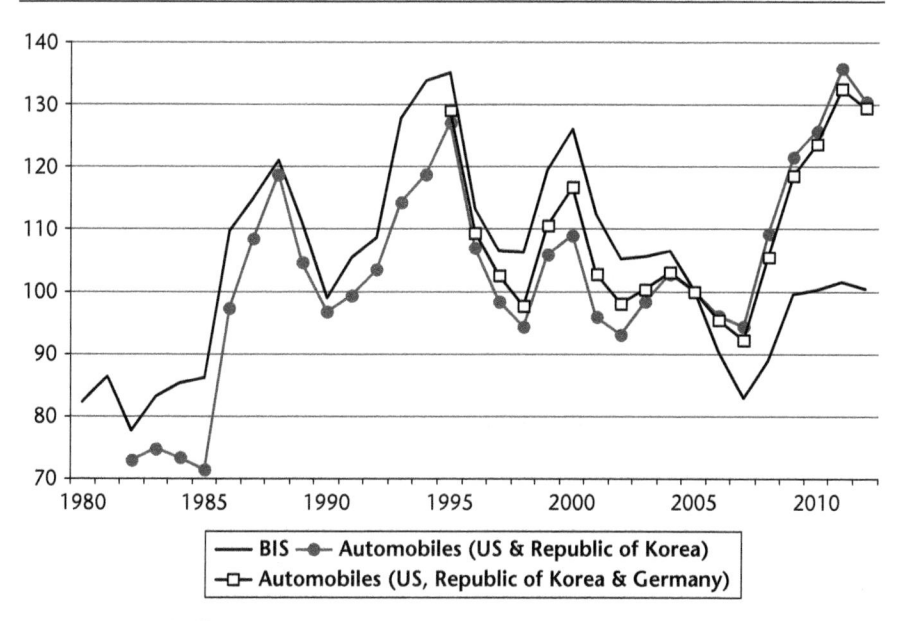

Figure 7.3. Real effective exchange rates of the yen, BIS data, and for automobiles
BIS = Bank for International Settlements, US = United States.
Sources: BIS; national data for the US, Germany, and the Republic of Korea.

25 percent lower than in around 2000 (Figure 7.3). This begs the question why the real effective yen rate facing the manufacturing sector was considered "high."

Part of the answer is that the BIS REER index, based on relative CPIs, may not adequately capture the difficulties of some manufacturing firms. First, the manufacturing firms were accustomed to a low yen from the early 2000s until 2007, which may have caused difficulties for firms in adjusting to the new, high yen rate environment. Second, the real REER constructed for the automobile sector based on producer prices suggests that the recent level of the yen was as high as in 1995. Many auto firms, including big and competitive ones like Toyota, lost money in domestic production for exports. Once the auto sector was severely hit, there were large negative spillover effects on the wider, auto-related sectors (steel, tires, glass, electronics, etc.), dampening overall manufacturing activities.

The business sector has long been concerned with the hollowing out of Japanese manufacturing—that is, a relocation of production bases abroad and a loss of domestic employment. Several sectors, such as electronics and electric appliances, which had already exited from Japan, were hardly affected by the high yen. However, competitive sectors that continue to stay home, such as automobiles and technology- and knowledge-intensive sectors, were severely affected.

IMPACT ON THE NON-TRADABLE AND THE TRADABLE GOODS SECTOR

The ratio of non-tradable to tradable goods production has been moving largely in a way consistent with the movements of real effective exchange rates. Figure 7.4 depicts this ratio, using both nominal and real GDP data. The ratio exhibits an upward trend, implying a de-industrialization trend toward the non-tradable (or services) sector. The fact that the nominal data indicate a steeper trend than the real data suggests that the relative price of non-tradables to tradables has tended to rise over time.

The movements of the non-tradable-to-tradable goods production ratio around the upward trend line appear to have responded to the REER changes; real yen appreciation stimulated the production of non-tradable goods relative to the production of tradable goods, while real yen depreciation had an opposite impact. For example, in 1985–94 when the yen sharply appreciated as a trend, the ratio of non-tradable-to-tradable goods production (expressed as an index) rose from 95 to 115. During the pre-global financial crisis episode of yen depreciation between 2002 and 2008, the ratio declined from 130 to 112.

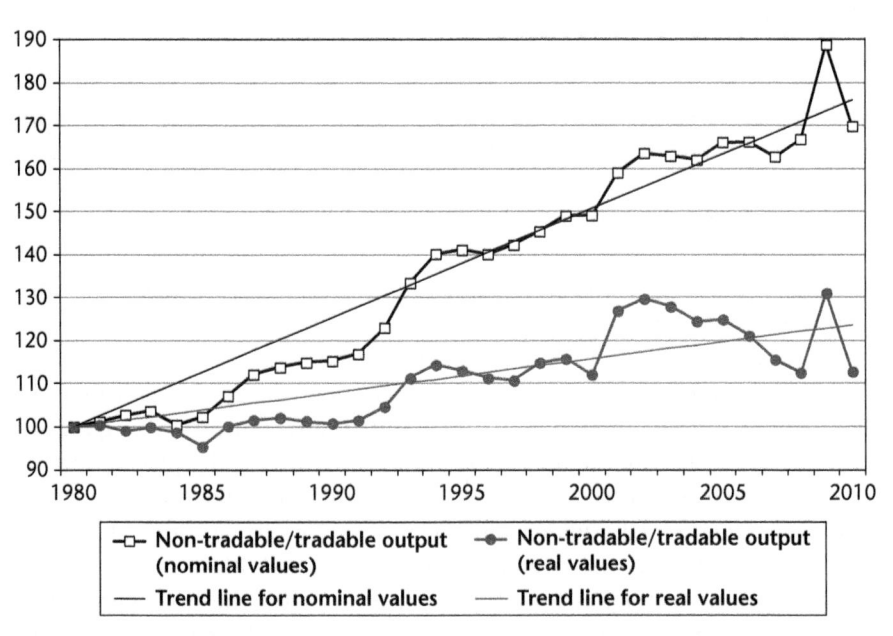

Figure 7.4. Production of non-tradable goods relative to tradable goods, nominal and real, 1980 = 100

Note: The tradable goods sector includes agriculture, mining, and manufacturing industries, while the non-tradable goods sector includes other sectors (construction, electricity, gas, water, wholesale and retail trade, banking and insurance, real estate, transportation, telecommunication, and services).

Source: Constructed from data published by the Cabinet Office, Government of Japan.

The key to current account adjustment is a shift in resources between the tradable and the non-tradable goods sector. Essentially, a higher real value of the yen raises the relative price of non-tradable goods, thus encouraging their production and causing a shift of resources away from the production of tradable goods. As long as the economy is always in full employment, with a smooth shift of resources (in particular labor) between sectors, REER changes should not pose a significant problem for the economy. In reality, however, the economy's adjustment to REER appreciation tends to be more difficult than to real depreciation.

7.3 Japan's Yen Policy

7.3.1 *Foreign Exchange Market Intervention*

PREVENTING RAPID YEN APPRECIATION

To prevent rapid yen movements, the Japanese authorities intervene in the foreign exchange market from time to time. According to the data published by the Ministry of Finance, Japan has intervened mostly to purchase foreign currency—that is, to prevent rapid yen appreciation (Figure 7.5). The exception was 1998 when the authorities intervened to sell foreign currency to prevent rapid yen rate depreciation. During the period from January 2003 to March 2004, there were massive interventions totaling more than 35 trillion

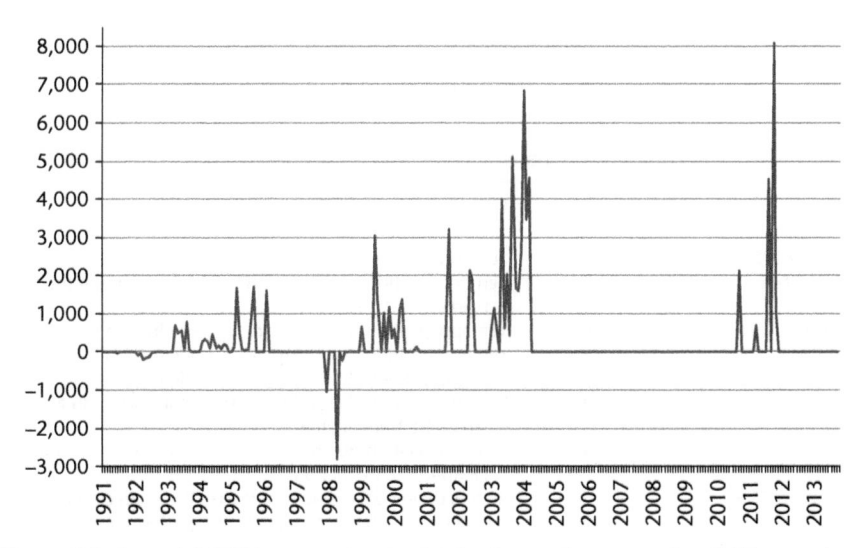

Figure 7.5. Japan's MOF intervention in the foreign exchange market (billion yen)
MOF = Ministry of Finance.
Note: Positive and negative numbers indicate purchases and sales, respectively, of foreign currency with the yen
Source: Japanese Ministry of Finance, official website.

yen, to stem rapid yen appreciation and to contain price deflation through the provision of yen liquidity into money markets. Between April 2004 and August 2010, there was a six-year absence of intervention until September 2010 when intervention resumed. The recent intervention in October 2011 was a record high, reaching more than 8 trillion yen as monthly intervention volume.

Intervention has often, but not always, been sterilized. Intervention has been mostly unilateral, without coordination with the US or other authorities. Table 7.1 provides information on coordinated intervention, which turns out to be relatively rare. As intervention tends to be more effective when coordinated with other authorities, the effectiveness of intervention has likely been limited in exerting lasting impact or stopping rapid currency movements, but it has given signals to the market that the authorities are concerned about the pace and speed of yen movements. These signals have likely had a smoothing effect on the rate movements, lowering the speed of yen movements and avoiding a free fall of the target currency concerned.

In the face of rapid yen appreciation, more fundamental policies than currency market interventions are needed to prevent it. These include proactive monetary policy to address Japan's persistent price deflation—and thereby contain yen appreciation—and the creation of an environment in which more capital outflows take place so that the yen does not appreciate and even depreciates. The first arrow of Abenomics—introduced by the BOJ in April 2013 in the form of aggressive quantitative and qualitative easing of monetary policy—has been successful in generating CPI inflation and a weak yen. Capital outflows through portfolio investment and FDI abroad

Table 7.1. Internationally coordinated intervention for the yen

Period	No. of days	Episodes
February 1987	1	Yen appreciation (Louvre Agreement)
January–February 1992	3	Yen depreciation together with low performance in the stock market
April–June 1993	4	Yen appreciation due to Japan–US trade friction
May–June 1994	2	Yen appreciation due to Japan–US trade friction
November 1994	2	Yen appreciation due to Japan–US trade friction
March–May 1995	4	Yen appreciation due to the Mexican currency crisis and Japan–US trade friction
July–August 1995	3	Yen appreciation due to the Mexican currency crisis and Japan–US trade friction
November 1997	5	Rupiah depreciation due to spread of the Asian currency crisis
June 1998	1	Yen depreciation due to Japan's non-performing loan problem
September 2000	1	Euro depreciation
March 2011	1	Yen appreciation in the aftermath of the Great East Japan Earthquake

Source: Press releases by the Japanese Ministry of Finance and other media sources.

will likely prevent further appreciation of the yen, but these have yet to take place.

ADDRESSING THE VOLATILITY OF THE YEN AGAINST EMERGING ASIAN CURRENCIES

Japan in principle adopts freely floating exchange rates with occasional currency market intervention, while many East Asian economies tend to manage exchange rate movements to varying degrees. Until the Asian financial crisis of 1997–8, many emerging economies in East Asia had maintained de jure or de facto US dollar peg regimes, but the post-Asian financial crisis period exhibited a greater diversity in exchange rate regimes (Kawai 2008). The two giant economies in the region, Japan and the PRC, have adopted different exchange rate regimes: Japan a freely floating exchange rate regime and the PRC a heavily managed regime targeted at the US dollar. Other countries operate intermediate exchange rate regimes, mostly managing their rates to avoid excessive volatility. In a sense, the region has seen some convergence toward greater exchange rate flexibility, except in the PRC. This convergence, however, has not reduced exchange rate volatility between the yen and emerging East Asian currencies.

When East Asian currencies become more flexible, there could be an even greater volatility of the yen rate against such currencies. An example is the case of the won. The yen rate against the won has moved in a very volatile manner (Figure 7.6). The won was strong before the global financial crisis but, following the Lehman collapse, depreciated sharply from 907 won/US dollar (October 2007) to 1,483 won/US dollar (November 2008). As a result, the won/yen rate moved from 7.6 won/yen in mid-2007 to above 15.5 won/yen at the end of 2008 and in early 2009. The extent to which the yen appreciated against the won during the global financial crisis was massive in comparison to the yen's movements against other currencies. This large fluctuation is greater than the yen/won movements observed during the Asian financial crisis of 1997–8. Such a large exchange rate volatility is counterproductive to trade and investment given the high and rising economic interdependence between the two countries.

7.3.2 Yen Internationalization

Even though Japan liberalized its capital account in the mid-1980s, the country has not been successful in fully internationalizing the yen, even in East Asia. Reversing the initial policy stance of limiting the international use of the yen, Japan's Ministry of Finance began to promote yen internationalization in the 1990s. However, Japan's large economic and financial size globally has not

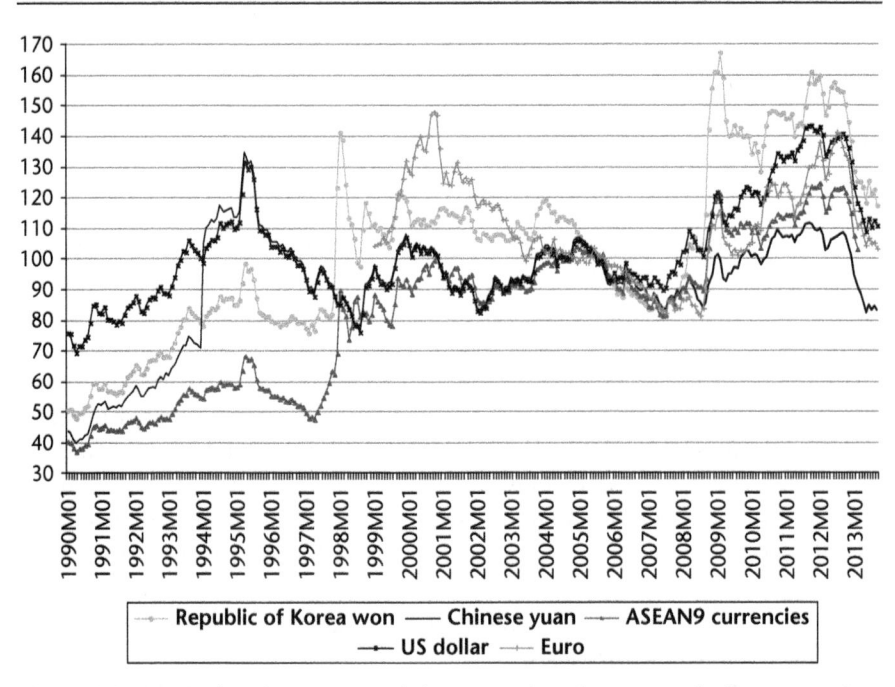

Figure 7.6. Nominal exchange rates of the yen against the won and other currencies

Note: ASEAN9 currencies refer to a weighted average of the exchange rates of nine ASEAN countries: Brunei Darussalam, Cambodia, Indonesia, Malaysia, Philippines, Singapore, Thailand, and Viet Nam, against the Japanese yen. GDP shares are used as weights. Note: An increase is Japanese yen appreciation.
Source: International Monetary Fund, International Financial Statistics, CD-ROM.

been matched with a commensurate increase in the use of the yen as an international currency.

INTERNATIONAL USE OF THE YEN

Table 7.2 summarizes the currency compositions of foreign exchange trading in the world's major markets from April 1989 to April 2013. The table indicates that the share of foreign exchange trading involving the US dollar has declined somewhat over the 24-year period, though it remains the most dominant currency globally at 87 percent in 2013. The euro share has declined as a trend from 38 percent in 2001 to 33 percent in 2013, perhaps due to the Eurozone debt and banking crisis in 2011–12. The share of the yen also declined from 27 percent in 1989 to 23 percent in 2013, but is making a good recovery from the trough of 17 percent recorded in 2007. Its share is still higher than the share of the pound sterling, which was 12 percent in 2013. The share of the RMB in the global currency markets has risen substantially since the mid-2000s and achieved the number 9 position at 2.2 percent in 2013, exceeding the shares of all other Asian currencies such as the Hong Kong dollar, the Singapore dollar, and the won.

Table 7.2. Currency distribution of reported foreign exchange market turnover[a] (% shares of average daily turnover in April)

	1989	1992	1995	1998	2001	2004	2007	2010	2013
United States dollar	90.0	82.0	83.3	86.8	89.9	88.0	85.6	84.9	87.0
Euro	—	—	—	—	37.9	37.4	37.0	39.1	33.4
Japanese yen	27.0	23.4	24.1	21.7	23.5	20.8	17.2	19.0	23.0
Pound sterling	15.0	13.6	9.4	11.0	13.0	16.5	14.9	12.9	11.8
Deutsche mark	27.0	39.6	36.1	30.1	—	—	—	—	—
French franc	2.0	3.8	7.9	5.1	—	—	—	—	—
ECU and other EMS currencies	4.0	11.8	15.7	17.3	—	—	—	—	—
Australian dollar	2.0	2.5	2.7	3.0	4.3	6.0	6.6	7.6	8.6
Swiss franc	10.0	8.4	7.3	7.1	6.0	6.0	6.8	6.3	5.2
Canadian dollar	1.0	3.3	3.4	3.5	4.5	4.2	4.3	5.3	4.6
Mexican peso	—	—	—	0.5	0.8	1.1	1.3	1.3	2.5
PRC renminbi	—	—	—	0.0	0.0	0.1	0.5	0.9	2.2
New Zealand dollar	—	0.2	0.2	0.2	0.6	1.1	1.9	1.6	2.0
Emerging economy currencies[b]	—	8.8	8.5	13.4	15.1	15.4	20.2	19.7	20.3
All currencies	200.0	200.0	200.0	200.0	200.0	200.0	200.0	200.0	200.0

Notes: [a]Because two currencies are involved in each transaction, the sum of the percentage shares of individual currencies totals 200% instead of 100%. Data are adjusted for local and cross-border double-counting.
[b]Defined as the sum of emerging economy currencies.
Source: Bank for International Settlements, Triennial Central Bank Survey: Foreign Exchange Turnover (various issues).

The very high weight of the US dollar in foreign exchange market trading suggests that it plays the role of a vehicle currency, mediating exchanges of various currencies. For example, conversion of the yen into won is done typically through the US dollar, first converting the yen into dollars and then the dollars into won. This vehicle-currency role of the US dollar is usually explained by the low transaction costs, due to economies of scale and network externalities of the dollar; people prefer to use the US dollar because almost everyone else uses it as well. There is no sign that the yen has been functioning as a vehicle currency in the world's foreign exchange markets.

Data for currency compositions of foreign exchange reserves held by all International Monetary Fund (IMF) reporting countries show that the share of the US dollar, which was about 50 percent in the early 1990s, rose to 72 percent in 2001 and then declined to 61 percent in 2013 (IMF, *Currency Composition of Official Foreign Exchange Reserves* database). The share of the euro rose substantially from 18 percent in 1999 to 28 percent in 2009 before slightly declining to 24 percent in 2013. The share of the yen declined from a peak of 8.5 percent in 1991 to a mere 4 percent in 2013. The yen and pound sterling are the close third and fourth largest reserve currencies in the world, respectively, following the US dollar and the euro. The share of the US dollar used to be high among developing countries, but has become higher among industrialized countries since 2003. Though not much information is available about the reserve currency role of the RMB, the total size of the People's Bank of China's bilateral currency swap arrangements suggests that the value of global

RMB reserves would be in the range of US$30 billion to US$60 billion, accounting for at most 1 percent of global foreign exchange reserves. Thus the RMB is not yet one of the major global reserve currencies.

Table 7.3 summarizes the relative size of currency areas.[11] It indicates that the area of the world economy covered by the US dollar has been stable at 54 percent, though it rose to 60 percent in 1995–9 before declining to the historical norm. The share of the Eurozone has risen from 25 percent to 31 percent between the 1970s and the most recent period, 2005–7. The yen area has declined slightly from 9 percent to 8 percent over the last 37 years. The pound sterling area has declined from 9 percent to 5 percent. The size of the US dollar area is much larger than that of the Eurozone area, because many developing countries regard the US dollar as the most important global anchor. The yen area is only slightly larger than the weight of the Japanese economy in the world, reflecting a small number of countries assigning weights to the yen in their exchange rate policies. The yen area outside Japan is only 1 percent of the world economy and, thus, the yen cannot be said to be a full-fledged global or regional anchor currency.

LIMITING FACTORS OF THE YEN'S INTERNATIONAL CURRENCY ROLE

The weight of the Japanese yen as an international currency has been limited both in comparison to the US dollar and the euro, and relative to the size of the Japanese economy. The yen has not been playing a major role as international nominal anchor to which other countries may peg or stabilize the value of their currencies. Several explanations can be given for the limited role of the yen as an international currency.

First, use of the yen in invoicing Japan's trade has been limited due to the country's specific trade structure. Japan has been dependent on the US as its

---

[11] The relative size of currency areas was computed in the following way. First, we identify a currency or a currency basket each country in the world has chosen as a nominal anchor. To do this, we extended the work by Frankel and Wei (1994) and Kawai and Akiyama (1998) to determine whether each country's exchange rate is affected by the currencies of major industrialized countries, such as the US dollar, the euro, pound sterling, the yen, and a few regional currencies, using monthly observations and the Swiss franc as a numeraire. Though it is possible that the RMB began to play an important role in the exchange rate policies of some Asian economies from the second half of the 2000s (Kawai and Pontines 2015), we do not consider this possibility in this exercise. Prior to the introduction of the euro in January 1999, the Deutschmark and the French franc were used instead of the euro. The statistically significant coefficients were interpreted as the weights assigned by the authorities to the corresponding currencies in their exchange rate stabilization policies. Second, GDP measured at 2005 purchasing power parity was used to estimate the economic size of the currency areas for the US dollar, the euro, pound sterling, and the yen. For example, for a country pegging its exchange rate to a particular international currency, its entire economy is classified as belonging to the currency area formed by this particular currency. If a country assigns some weights to a basket of major or regional currencies, its economy is divided according to these weights and distributed to the corresponding currency areas. Before 1999, we assumed that Germany and France formed a future Eurozone.

Table 7.3. Estimated shares of currency areas of major currencies, 1970–2007 (%)

	US dollar area			Euro area			Yen area			Pound sterling area			Unallocated
	United States	Other	Total	Eurozone	Other	Total	Japan	Other	Total	United Kingdom	Other	Total	
1970–4	26.7	27.2	54.0	12.5	12.8	25.2	9.3	0.0	9.3	5.4	3.5	8.9	2.7
1975–9	25.8	27.8	53.6	11.9	15.4	27.3	9.3	1.6	10.9	4.9	1.6	6.4	1.8
1980–4	25.0	26.7	51.8	11.4	13.9	25.3	9.5	2.2	11.7	4.4	2.3	6.7	4.4
1985–9	25.5	27.3	52.8	10.7	9.4	20.0	9.6	0.5	10.2	4.4	1.8	6.2	10.8
1990–4	22.7	32.7	55.4	9.7	13.5	23.2	9.1	0.5	9.6	3.7	1.3	5.1	6.7
1995–9	23.5	36.4	59.9	11.3	10.8	22.1	8.5	2.4	10.9	3.7	0.9	4.6	2.5
2000–4	22.9	31.6	54.5	17.7	11.1	28.8	7.4	3.1	10.5	3.6	0.5	4.1	2.2
2005–7	21.7	32.8	54.6	16.1	14.3	30.5	6.7	1.0	7.7	3.4	1.5	4.9	2.3

Notes: 1. Computations are based on gross domestic product at 2005 purchasing power parity.
2. The euro area prior to 1999 is defined by Germany and France and after 1999 consists of the Eurozone member countries.
3. The figure for 1995–9 is the weighted average of the 1995–8 and 1999 data.

Source: Author's computation.

major export market of manufactured products and on imports of large quantities of resources (minerals, fuels, raw materials, and basic commodities) for its industrial production. Trade with the US and trade in resources tend to be dollar denominated, reducing the use of the yen.

Second, substantial trade has been carried out by Japanese trading companies and multinational manufacturing corporations with the capacity to marry US dollar-denominated exports and imports and minimize currency risks. From the perspective of Japanese multinational corporations (MNCs) which conduct global business, yen invoicing is not particularly important for intra-firm trade or trade in parts and components (from Japan to emerging Asia) and finished manufactured products (from emerging Asia to Japan). As a result, they have only limited interest in denominating trade in yen.

Third, the size of Japanese imports, particularly of manufactured products, has been relatively small. In recent years, manufactured imports have risen in value and seen rising yen invoicing ratios. However, the lack of horizontal intra-industry trade—in similar but differential products to satisfy consumer preference for diversity—between Japan and emerging Asia may have prevented yen invoicing.

Fourth, Japanese money and capital markets, particularly for treasury bills and other private short-term instruments, used to be less liquid than markets in New York or London. The lack of market infrastructures with a global standard and the perceived overregulation in Tokyo money and capital markets have been pointed to as severe impediments to an expanded use of the yen. As a result of these impediments in the Tokyo markets, foreign monetary authorities and private investors have been reluctant to use yen instruments to carry out international trade and investment transactions.

Fifth, Japan has been the only developed economy in Asia: most of Japan's neighbors have been developing and emerging economies which are basically dollar-area economies. These economies have had little incentive to use the yen, as they tended to maintain stable exchange rates vis-à-vis the US dollar. In contrast, European countries were more or less at a similar stage of economic development in the 1960s and 1970s, and their economic interdependence—particularly through horizontal intra-industry trade and FDI—gave an incentive to invoice a high proportion of intra-European trade in their own national currencies. After the introduction of the euro, many European countries naturally selected the euro as an invoicing currency. This type of symmetric relationship has not been developed in Asia, and as a result, most of Japan's trade with emerging Asian economies has been invoiced primarily in the US dollar.

Finally, a prolonged period of economic and financial stagnation in Japan during the 1990s prevented the yen from being used as an international currency. Damaged by the banking crisis, Japanese banks were paralyzed in advancing international businesses and the internationalization process of the yen stopped as a result. In addition, the size of the Japanese economy, measured in terms of the yen or the US dollar, hardly grew during this period, which also hurt the relative use of the Japanese yen as an international currency.

7.3.3 Importance of Intraregional Exchange Rate Stability for Japan

INTEGRATION THROUGH TRADE AND FOREIGN DIRECT INVESTMENT

The expansion of intraregional trade in East Asia over the last few decades has been remarkable. The share of East Asia's intraregional trade in its total trade has risen to more than 50 percent in recent years. This share is higher than for the North American Free Trade Agreement (NAFTA) area, though still lower than for the European Union.

The main driver behind economic integration through trade is the intraregional business activity of multinational manufacturing corporations (MNCs), initially those from Japan and then from Europe and the US. These MNCs have formed closely organized production networks and supply chains across East Asia, linked with the global market. These arrangements have emerged as a result of each MNC's business strategy of attempting to divide its whole production process into several subprocesses and locating these in different countries according to their comparative advantage—defined by factor proportions and technological capabilities. Such business arrangements have created vertical intra-industry trade within East Asia in capital equipment, parts and components, other intermediate inputs, semifinished goods, and finished manufactured products.

These trends accelerated in the wake of the Plaza Accord in 1985, when Japanese MNCs, compelled to cope with the high cost of domestic production due to the steep appreciation of the yen, began to relocate their production facilities to emerging East Asia—initially in the Asian NIEs, later in middle-income ASEAN member states (such as Indonesia, Malaysia, the Philippines, and Thailand), and more recently in the PRC. Facing rising domestic costs, NIE firms soon began also investing in middle-income ASEAN economies and later in the PRC. In recent years, not only global MNCs from developed economies (such as Japan, Europe, and the US), but also firms from the NIEs (the Republic of Korea in particular) and advanced ASEAN member states (such as Malaysia and Thailand) have been providing FDI to other ASEAN members (including Cambodia, Lao PDR, and Viet Nam) and to the PRC, contributing to the formation of a web of regional supply chains.[12] Japanese firms are now expanding these supply chains to India.

---

[12] See Kawai and Urata (1998) and Fukao et al. (2003) who found that FDI played a significant role in the rapid increase in vertical intra-industry trade in East Asia.

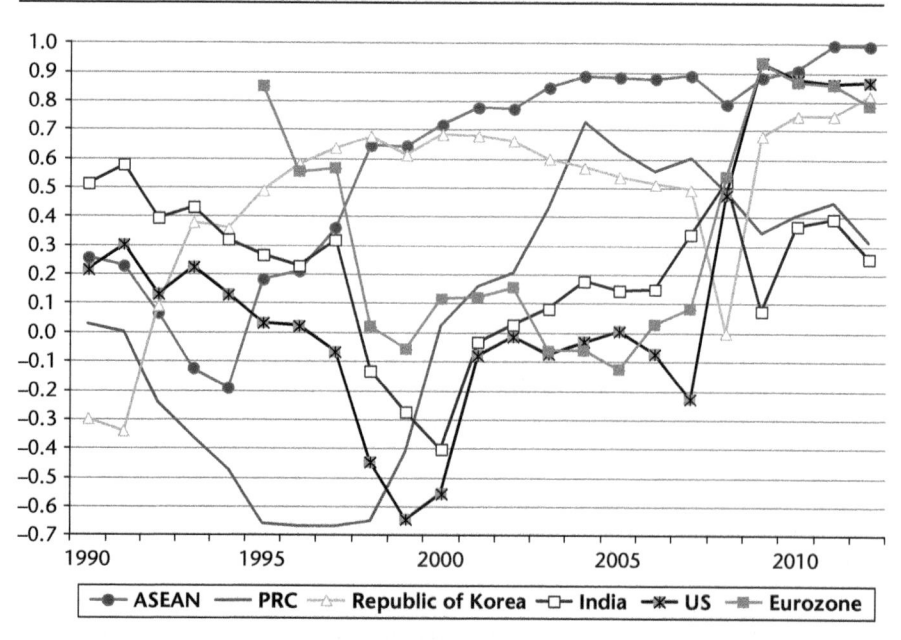

Figure 7.7. Correlation of GDP growth rates between Japan and major economies

Notes: 1. Correlation coefficients are calculated using ten-year moving windows. For example, the data for 1990 are the correlation coefficients for the period 1981–90.
2. Data for 2011 and 2012 are estimates and projections, respectively, made by the International Monetary Fund.

Source: Constructed using data from International Monetary Fund, World Economic Outlook, April 2013.

An important consequence of this growing trade and FDI integration is the heightened macroeconomic interdependence and business cycle co-movements within East Asia. The rolling ten-year moving correlations of GDP growth rates between Japan and emerging Asian economies (Figure 7.7) exhibit a rising trend of correlations or business cycle synchronization. The correlations with ASEAN have been rising persistently and are particularly high, while the correlations with the PRC have been declining in recent years, after having risen significantly from the mid-1990s to the mid-2000s. Overall, Japan's economic interdependence with emerging Asia has risen to a high level.

LACK OF EXCHANGE RATE POLICY COORDINATION
Given the heightened interdependence of the economies in the region, it may be argued that Japan and emerging Asian economies can benefit by stabilizing intraregional exchange rates through policy coordination. Japan and all supply chain countries would prefer intraregional exchange rate stability to instability.

Hayakawa and Kimura (2009) empirically investigated the relationship between exchange rate volatility and international trade, focusing on East Asia. They found that intra-East Asian trade was discouraged by exchange rate volatility more seriously than trade in other regions. They also found that an important source of this discouragement was in intermediate goods trade within supply chains, which accounted for a significant proportion of East Asian trade and was more sensitive to exchange rate volatility than other types of trade. Essentially, trade in parts and components within supply chain countries, including Japan, would benefit from intraregional exchange rate stability.

In addition to intraregional exchange rate stability, Japan also regards emerging Asia's financial stability as vital. The reason is that Japanese MNCs have developed extensive business operations in emerging Asia—particularly in ASEAN economies—and a large-scale financial crisis can have significant, negative business impacts on these MNCs. From this perspective, Japan took initiatives to support crisis-affected countries during the Asian financial crisis, beginning with Thailand, Indonesia, Malaysia, and the Republic of Korea. Japan took the lead in creating the ASEAN+3 processes to promote regional financial cooperation. During the more recent global financial crisis, Japan expanded bilateral currency swaps with the Republic of Korea to stabilize the currency markets and supported Indonesia for preparation of fiscal funding at a difficult time.

7.4 Japan's Strategy for Asian Monetary Integration

Japan's interest is to promote a stable monetary zone in Asia, with the yen as Asia's most important international currency. However, given that the PRC's economic growth will continue over the next decades, its trade, investment, and financial activities will expand rapidly, and the RMB has a strong potential to rise as the region's most prominent international currency in the long run. Thus, the yen may eventually be overshadowed by the RMB. To avoid this, Japan needs a clear strategy to substantially improve the yen's international role and to lead Asian monetary integration. Even if the RMB does not become a dominant international currency in East Asia, due to the PRC's domestic economic, social, and political problems, its rising economic size will certainly expand the RMB's international role. In response, it is in Japan's interest to pursue its own domestic reforms to further open its economy and intensify its collaboration with its East Asian neighbors—including the PRC—to create an Asian monetary zone, while promoting Japan's commercial and economic interests.

This chapter argues that a single national currency is unlikely to replace the US dollar as the dominant international currency in East Asia, at least over the next several decades. Without currency cooperation, the East Asian monetary system will likely be fragmented with the US dollar, the yen, the RMB, and (in the future) the Indian rupee playing their competing roles. With currency cooperation, East Asia can come up with a better monetary system. Thus, there is a case for Japan, the PRC, and other ASEAN economies to cooperate to seek intraregional currency stability through regional monetary cooperation. For example, they can develop a regional currency basket, composed of the yen, the RMB, the won, the baht, the ringgit, the rupiah, and others, as a currency unit for Asia. The Indian rupee could join the unit as well.

7.4.1 Transforming Tokyo into a Competitive International Financial Center

THE DECLINE OF TOKYO AS AN INTERNATIONAL FINANCIAL CENTER

In the late 1980s, London, New York, and Tokyo were the top three global financial centers, and Tokyo was challenging the leading role of New York in global finance (Cassis 2005). Today, however, London and New York are the only two genuinely global financial centers despite the global financial crisis that revealed problems of financial industries and regulatory failures in the US and the United Kingdom. Other centers—such as Hong Kong, China; Singapore, Tokyo; and Zurich—are national or regional centers and, according to the Global Financial Centres Index (Long Finance 2012), are not likely to challenge the dominance of London and New York. A view is even emerging that if a third global financial center is to develop, it is most likely to be Shanghai, which could surpass the regional financial centers of Tokyo, Singapore, and Hong Kong, China.

The weakness of Tokyo as an international financial center is often identified as the lack of a business-conducive regulatory environment and of available expertise and talent (see Yeandle et al. 2005; IBA Japan 2007). Tokyo's global ranking as an international financial center declined due to the bursting of the asset price bubble in the early 1990s, the subsequent banking sector difficulties, and the two decades of economic stagnation. According to the recent ranking of international financial centers reported in Table 7.4, however, Tokyo has gradually risen from around tenth in 2007 to fifth in 2013.

Tokyo's ranking as number five, however, does not quite match the size of Japan's economy, domestic financial assets, net external assets, or its potential. Given that Japan has the world's third largest GDP, the largest pools of savings liquidity in Asia, a "world-class city" with a dynamic urban environment supported by the best public transport system and infrastructure, a high degree of public safety, and a highly educated, literate workforce (IBA Japan 2007), Tokyo has the potential to rank among the top three centers globally.

Table 7.4. Ranking of global financial centers, March 2007–September 2013

Financial center	Mar 2007	Sep 2007	Mar 2008	Sep 2008	Mar 2009	Sep 2009	Mar 2010	Sep 2010	Mar 2011	Sep 2011	Mar 2012	Sep 2012	Mar 2013	Sep 2013
London	1	1	1	1	1	1	1	1	1	1	1	1	1	1
New York	2	2	2	2	2	2	1	2	2	2	2	2	2	2
Hong Kong, China	3	3	3	4	4	3	3	3	3	3	3	3	3	3
Singapore	4	4	4	3	3	4	4	4	4	4	4	4	4	4
Tokyo	9	10	9	7	15	7	5	5	5	6	5	7	6	5
Zurich	5	5	5	5	5	6	7	8	8	8	6	5	5	6
Boston	14	12	11	11	9	18	14	13	12	12	11	11	8	7
Geneva	10	7	7	6	6	9	8	9	9	13	14	9	7	8
Frankfurt	6	6	6	9	8	12	13	11	14	16	13	13	10	9
Seoul	43	42	51	48	53	35	28	24	16	11	9	6	9	10
Toronto	12	13	15	12	11	13	12	12	10	10	10	10	12	11
San Francisco	13	14	12	17	17	17	15	14	13	9	12	12	13	12
Chicago	8	8	8	8	7	8	6	7	7	7	7	8	11	14
Sydney	7	9	10	10	16	11	9	10	10	15	16	15	19	15
Shanghai	24	30	31	34	35	10	11	6	5	5	8	24	19	16
Shenzhen	—	—	—	—	—	5	9	14	15	25	32	38	32	27
Dublin	22	15	13	13	10	23	31	29	33	43	46	49	49	56

Notes: 1. The table lists financial centers that have been ranked among top 10 globally during the sample period.
2. Shenzhen cannot be ranked in and before March 2009 due to insufficient information.

Source: *The Global Financial Centres Index*, various issues (London: Long Finance, 2001–13).

Japan has not been able to maximize its economic and financial potential to become a truly global financial center. As a result, Tokyo has been overtaken by Singapore and Hong Kong, China as Asia's international financial center, and Shanghai is rapidly catching up with Tokyo, with the sixteenth ranking globally in 2013.[13]

TOKYO'S CHALLENGES AND OPPORTUNITIES

For Japan, where the population is rapidly aging, demand for better financial services is growing because of the need to maximize the rates of return on wealth and secure sufficient income for post-retirement. So far, Japan has invested mostly in bonds and equities in developed country markets, with limited investment in emerging Asia. Given the dynamic growth opportunities in emerging Asia, Tokyo can actively intermediate Japan's massive savings for emerging Asia's investment, particularly for infrastructure development. Tokyo can also provide attractive financial services related to emerging Asia's businesses, such as settlements of emerging Asian currencies (like the RMB and the won) and issuance of emerging Asia's local currency bonds. Attracting more listings in the Tokyo Stock Exchange from emerging Asia remains a challenge. The development of private banking and asset management, as in Zurich and Geneva, for Japanese wealth-holders is also key. This, however, requires a substantial change in public policy toward greater openness, business-friendly climates, and the provision of supporting market infrastructure for financial services.[14] Japanese private financial firms have huge business potential if they can accumulate regional financial information and knowledge, and analytical and innovation capabilities.

Building on the advantages referred to earlier, Tokyo could overcome its weaknesses. The regulatory and supervisory reforms undertaken so far since the creation of the Financial Services Agency (FSA) are laudable, but the FSA alone cannot make Tokyo a world-class international financial center.[15] The Ministry of Finance (MOF), the BOJ, and the FSA must work together to formulate a comprehensive strategy for transforming Tokyo into a competitive, global financial center that can compete against Singapore; Hong Kong,

---

[13] With the hype of the PRC's economic growth and high expectations of Shanghai as a global financial center, Shanghai in September 2011 ranked fifth, surpassing Tokyo, although its ranking has come down to a lower level in recent years. Shenzhen, once ranked fifth in September 2009, surpassing Tokyo and even Shanghai, has also come down to a much lower ranking recently.

[14] If Tokyo could intermediate emerging Asia's savings for the region's investment, it would be even better, but this would not be easy.

[15] Since the separation of the Banking Bureau and Securities Bureau from the MOF and the establishment of the FSA, the official attempt to further internationalize the yen and to make Tokyo an international financial center has been divided between the MOF and the FSA. Unfortunately, no persistent collaborative efforts in these areas have been made among the authorities, including the BOJ, for a long time.

China; and a future Shanghai. The MOF and the BOJ together can put in place a market infrastructure to make Tokyo an attractive venue for conducting Asia-related financial businesses. The FSA could further improve the country's regulatory framework—or make its "better regulation" even better—by strengthening the core principles of consistency, effectiveness, efficiency, and transparency. The current regulatory philosophy is often criticized as too restrictive, non-responsive, and business-unfriendly despite improvements, and it is under pressure to change to one that nurtures competition and innovation.

The transformation of Tokyo into a competitive international financial center will certainly enhance the role of the yen as an international currency.

TOKYO AS A CATALYST FOR MORE EFFICIENT FINANCIAL MARKETS FOR ASIA

An additional reason for the need to forge a comprehensive strategy to transform Tokyo into a world-class international financial center is that without it Japan's financial services may start migrating elsewhere—to Hong Kong, China; Singapore; and Shanghai—and the international use of the yen might further decline. The rapid rise of the PRC may transform Shanghai into the largest Asian financial center—and, over the next ten to fifteen years, a global one—if the PRC government commits to completing market-oriented reforms, including financial market liberalization, capital account opening, and the creation of a market-based regulatory regime.[16]

Healthy competition among Asian financial centers—particularly Tokyo, Shanghai, Singapore, and Hong Kong, China—can help improve the quality of Asia's financial intermediation services, facilitate Asian financial integration, and expand financial businesses in Asia. Developing a truly global financial center in Asia—particularly in its time zone—is beneficial for Asian savers and investors as well as for global financial players as it allows diversification of global financial transactions into the tripolar regions (Europe, North America, and Asia) and reduces risks associated with time zone differences. In this sense, Japan's effort to improve Tokyo's role as a competitive international financial center is important not only for Japan, but also for Asia and the world, as it encourages healthy competition among Asian cities to develop and deepen the respective financial markets, which benefits all consumers of financial services globally.

---

[16] The PRC authorities have decided to establish a Shanghai Free Trade Zone intended to make Shanghai a competitive international financial center in the near future. The immediate prospect for India is not so bright. The consensus view is that India will remain an inexpensive back office and information technology center and develop its own national financial center, like Mumbai, but it will not challenge the existing top international financial centers (Z/Yen Limited 2005).

7.4.2 Strengthening Regional Financial Cooperation

The Asian financial crisis of 1997–8 and its spread across the region revealed several important lessons: financial systems and economic conditions were closely linked across East Asia, the IMF should not be relied upon alone for crisis management, and a regional self-help mechanism should be created to effectively prevent and manage financial crises. Based on this recognition, the Government of Japan proposed the creation of an AMF in 1997, but this attempt was aborted because of the objections by the US and the IMF, and the lack of support by the PRC.[17] Despite such a setback, the ASEAN+3 finance ministers—the ten ASEAN member states plus the PRC, Japan, and the Republic of Korea—embarked on several new initiatives for regional financial cooperation in 2000:

- regional economic surveillance (Economic Review and Policy Dialogue, ERPD);
- regional liquidity support system (Chiang Mai Initiative, CMI); and
- local-currency bond market development (Asian Bond Markets Initiative, ABMI).

ECONOMIC REVIEW AND POLICY DIALOGUE AND CHIANG MAI INITIATIVE MULTILATERALIZATION

The ERPD is a regional economic surveillance process to promote macroeconomic and financial stability and prevent a financial crisis in the region. The ASEAN+3 authorities created a surveillance unit, the AMRO, in Singapore and from May 2012 expanded the ASEAN+3 process by including the central bank governors in addition to the finance ministers. The CMI, as a regional liquidity support facility, started as a combination of a network of bilateral currency swap agreements among the members and the ASEAN Swap Arrangement. Then, the CMI was multilateralized in March 2010 to become the CMIM, with its total size set at US$120 billion, which was raised to US$240 billion in May 2012. The ERPD is now considered an integral part of the CMIM.

---

[17] In the aftermath of the Thai baht crisis, Japan took an initiative to support Thailand by organizing a Thai rescue meeting in August 1997 in Tokyo, where the so-called "friends of Thailand" agreed on a financial support package. Thereafter, Japan, with support from the "friends of Thailand," proposed in September to establish an AMF to supplement IMF resources for crisis prevention and resolution. Its idea was to pool foreign exchange reserves of the East Asian economies, amounting to US$100 billion, which could be mobilized to deter currency speculation or to contain a currency crisis in a member economy. The US and the IMF objected to Japan's proposal on the grounds of moral hazard and duplication. They argued that an East Asian country hit by a currency crisis would bypass the tough conditionality of the IMF and receive easy money from the AMF, thereby creating potential for moral hazard; and that an AMF would be redundant in the presence of an effective global crisis manager, the IMF. The PRC did not express any view, which meant a lack of support for the proposal.

The global financial crisis of 2007–9 demonstrated the need to strengthen East Asia's regional financial cooperation. While the crisis impacted many East Asian economies primarily through the trade channel, it also created shortages of international liquidity in a few countries, such as the Republic of Korea and Indonesia. The Republic of Korea encountered sudden capital flow reversals in the aftermath of the Lehman collapse in September 2008 and saw a rapid loss of foreign exchange reserves and sharp currency depreciation.[18] Unwilling to go to the IMF or the CMI for liquidity support, the authorities in the country chose to secure a US$30 billion currency swap line from the US Federal Reserve System. This had an immediately positive, stabilizing impact on the financial and foreign exchange markets in Seoul. In addition, Japan and the PRC also provided bilateral currency swap lines for the Republic of Korea, which also contributed to the restoration of market confidence. In 2009, the low won helped exports recover and reserves to rise to almost US$250 billion by September. The won began gradually to restore its value.

One of the reasons the Republic of Korea did not go to the CMI for liquidity assistance in the fall of 2008 was that sufficient funds would have had to be linked with an IMF program. This would have created political problems within the country due to the "IMF stigma" stemming from its program and actions in the 1997–8 financial crisis. Another reason was that the authorities considered the turbulence in the fall of 2008 not quite a crisis, and the CMI was not designed for non- or near-crisis situations. The Republic of Korea was fortunate in being able to secure a US Federal Reserve currency swap line, but Indonesia was rejected by the Federal Reserve.[19] This illustrates the importance of strengthening the regional financing arrangement to make it accessible to countries that are fundamentally sound but are facing liquidity shortages due to external shocks. To address this problem, the total size of the CMIM was expanded to US$240 billion and in May 2012 a new facility, the CMIM Precautionary Line (CMIM-PL), was introduced to prevent a crisis from taking place.[20]

---

[18] The Bank of Korea lost large amounts of foreign exchange reserves, which fell from US$264 billion in March to just below US$200 billion in November. The won started to depreciate rapidly, from a strong 907 won–US dollar recorded in October 2007 to 1,483 won–US dollar in November 2008.

[19] Although Indonesia did not face a currency crisis in the aftermath of the Lehman collapse, it had some difficulty funding its fiscal needs internationally and the rupiah depreciated sharply. To cope with potential financial turbulence, the country obtained US$5.5 billion in 2009 through a "standby loan facility"—or "deferred drawdown options"—with the funds provided by Japan, Australia, the Asian Development Bank, and the World Bank. Thus, multilateral development banks and bilateral agencies played a critical role in helping Indonesia secure contingency financial resources for budgetary support.

[20] The existing CMIM began to be called the CMIM Stability Facility (CMIM-SF) to distinguish it from the CMIM-PL. The maturity period of the CMIM-SF was extended from 90 days to: (i) one year

An important feature of the CMIM is that crisis-affected members requesting short-term liquidity support can immediately obtain financial assistance up to an amount equivalent to 30 percent of the maximum amount that could be borrowed,[21] and that the remaining 70 percent is provided to the requesting member under an IMF program. Thus, the CMIM is closely linked with an IMF program and its conditionality. The CMIM's link with the IMF was designed to address the concern that the liquidity shortage of a requesting country may be due to fundamental policy problems, rather than a simple liquidity problem, and that the potential moral hazard problem could be significant in the absence of rigorous conditionality. Essentially, the CMI (or CMIM) has long been intended for crisis lending and hence has required conditionality. The lack of the region's capacity to formulate and enforce effective adjustment programs in times of crisis was a major reason for requiring the CMIM to be linked to IMF programs.[22]

NEXT AGENDAS: ECONOMIC REVIEW AND POLICY DIALOGUE, ASEAN+3 MACROECONOMIC RESEARCH OFFICE, AND CHIANG MAI INITIATIVE MULTILATERALIZATION

An important challenge is to strengthen the effectiveness of regional economic surveillance supported by AMRO in order to reduce, and ultimately dismantle, the CMIM's IMF link so that ASEAN+3 member economies can use the CMIM in both crisis and near-crisis situations without IMF programs. The key is to create conditions to promote further IMF delinking. For this purpose, AMRO should become a strong permanent secretariat for regional economic surveillance and liquidity support to address financial and currency turmoil so that lending conditionality, independent of IMF programs, can be formulated in the event of CMIM-SF activation.

More concretely, this chapter recommends the following actions:

- further reduce the CMIM's IMF link over time, ultimately to zero;
- clarify rules for activating CMIM lending—including the newly introduced precautionary lending facility (CMIM-PL)—and eschew policy conditionality in the event of externally or herd behavior-driven financial turbulence or crisis;

---

with two renewals, totaling up to three years if linked to IMF programs; and (ii) six months with three renewals, totaling up to two years if IMF-delinked.

[21] Initially, the IMF-delinked portion of the CMI was 10% and it was raised to 20% in May 2005 and then to 30% in May 2012. This portion may be further raised to 40% in the future if conditions are met.

[22] Japan and the PRC, as potential creditor countries, argue that the CMIM's IMF link is essential. Potential debtor members of ASEAN+3, such as Malaysia, believe that the CMIM should not be linked to IMF programs.

- provide AMRO with adequate resources to make it a strong international institution having the analytical expertise and policy experience to improve the quality of regional economic surveillance (ERPD), activate the CMIM, and formulate conditionality independent of the IMF;
- further enlarge the size of the CMIM or increase the maximum amount of liquidity that each member economy—other than Japan and the PRC—can borrow so that a sufficient amount of liquidity could be secured for economies in need;
- ensure that the precautionary facility (CMIM-PL) can be used at times of a near-crisis independent of IMF arrangements;
- move beyond the simple "information sharing" stage to a more rigorous "peer review and peer pressure" stage, and eventually to a "due diligence" stage, to improve the quality of economic surveillance; and
- consider expanding membership to include Australia, India, and New Zealand.

Once these actions are taken, a new de facto AMF would emerge, capable of conducting effective surveillance, providing international liquidity in the event of a crisis or near-crisis, and formulating and monitoring policy conditionality. However, it could take some time to achieve these, The CMIM for precautionary purposes should be activated flexibly, that is, without conditions during the transition period, in the event of the type of financial turbulence that the Republic of Korea experienced in the fall of 2008.

At the same time, the IMF and AMRO/CMIM can develop a coordination framework to strengthen complementarities and create synergies. This is because CMIM resources are unlikely to be sufficient to cope with a large-scale crisis or a region-wide crisis involving several economies and thus the AMRO will have to work with the IMF. While the European financial crisis provides a model for coordination between the global and regional financial safety nets, Asia will have to develop its own model for such coordination. Japan can play a pivotal role in bridging them in a coherent way.

7.4.3 Creating an Asian Currency Unit

DOLLAR, YEN, RENMINBI, OR A BASKET?
Even when there is a strong case for exchange rate policy coordination in East Asia, the issue is how a mechanism can be introduced to achieve such coordination in the region. There are at least two ways. One is for each economy to stabilize its currency to a common major international currency or a common basket of major international (and emerging East Asian) currencies. The other way is for these economies to jointly create a regional, cooperative system

such as the "Snake" or Exchange Rate Mechanism (ERM) in Europe. Given that economic (particularly structural) convergence among the East Asian economies is not sufficiently advanced, that fiscal policy and financial supervision and regulation—key factors identified as a result of the recent Eurozone financial crisis—are not adequately coordinated, and that political relationships are not sufficiently mature to support the creation of a tightly coordinated exchange rate system, the second option is harder to pursue, at least for now, and the first option appears more realistic. Only with sufficient economic convergence—and with strong political consensus—can East Asia move to the stage of joint exchange rate stabilization.

The experience of the global financial crisis and Asia's diverse economic relationship with the major economies of the world have shown that the traditional practice of choosing the US dollar as the region's monetary anchor is no longer the best policy. An obvious alternative is to choose the yen, the RMB, or their combination as a monetary anchor, given the size and importance of Japan and the PRC in East Asia.

While the RMB's international role will rise over time with the PRC's strong growth performance and trade expansion, decades may have to pass before it becomes a fully convertible international currency that is equivalent to the US dollar, the euro, or the yen.[23] Some East Asian economies—particularly those with strong trade ties with the PRC—may consider pegging their currencies to the RMB as desirable from a trade perspective, but many other economies with increasingly open capital accounts will have limited incentive to do so because of the lack of the RMB's role in international clearance, financing, and liquidity holding, and the lack of transparent rules-based institutions. It may take a long time for the PRC to establish a truly independent, credible central bank, to put in place effective prudential and supervisory frameworks governing its financial systems, and to implement the rule of law.

Other East Asian economies, however robust their monetary policies, are too small for their currencies to take on a meaningful international role. This clearly makes it desirable—even necessary—to introduce a mechanism for

---

[23] For the RMB to be widely held and utilized in third countries, the PRC economy must become fully open with respect to trade, investment, and finance. It was the openness and liquidity of US financial markets that heightened the dollar's international role and that made foreign investors willingly hold dollar-denominated assets. In addition, the US provided transparent, rules-based institutions that would protect private property and enable market participants to resolve any disputes based on law. If the RMB is to play a significant role as an international currency, the PRC must liberalize its capital account, remove its exchange controls, and build deeper and more liquid financial markets. In addition, it needs to significantly improve the quality of domestic institutions. Practically speaking, this is not going to happen any time soon. A precondition for capital account convertibility is that the country must complete its transition to a market economy and establish a sound and resilient financial sector. The PRC is still far from a free market economy, with extensive problems in its state-dominated banking system and underdeveloped capital markets. At a minimum, completing this transition will require another 10–20 years.

intraregional exchange rate stability based on a currency basket, as no single currency is capable of playing a dominant monetary anchor role at least in the foreseeable future.

A CASE FOR A CURRENCY BASKET SYSTEM

From Japan's perspective, a currency basket system is an attractive and viable direction to suggest for emerging East Asian economies, as the yen alone cannot become the region's key currency. A reasonable compromise would be for the yen to play a prominent role in the currency basket of emerging Asian economies. Three options may be considered for the region's currency basket:

- the SDR comprising the US dollar, the euro, pound sterling, and the yen;
- an SDR-plus (SDR+) currency basket comprising the US dollar, the euro, pound sterling, the yen, and emerging East Asian currencies; or
- an ACU—a basket of East Asian currencies including the yen, the RMB, the won, the baht, the ringgit, etc.

The first two of these options would not require a substantial degree of policy coordination, since they rely on external nominal anchors. The third option requires either a certain degree of monetary policy coordination or a few major country central banks pursuing a form of inflation targeting together with soft exchange rate stabilization, in order to establish a regional nominal anchor. The first option is the simplest and the third the most complex. One of the advantages of the second option is that it would be easier to move to the third option at a later stage by reducing weights on the dollar, the euro, and pound sterling to zero.[24]

Japan's interest would be to maintain its monetary policy autonomy through free floating of the yen and enjoy relative stability of the yen against emerging Asian currencies. Pursuit of free floating is particularly important as long as the BOJ adopts QQE and, after its success, reverses its monetary policy toward tightening. The yen rate can be relatively stable against currencies of emerging East Asian economies, including the PRC, if they choose any one of these currency baskets as a reference currency. By so doing, emerging Asia could also enjoy more stable effective exchange rates, with less susceptibility to dollar–yen fluctuations than a standard US dollar-based system. Singapore has been managing its exchange rate in an SDR+ framework (the second option) as its basket apparently includes the US dollar, the euro, pound sterling, the yen, the RMB, and other regional currencies.

---

[24] An SDR+ currency basket is also defined as a basket of the US dollar, the euro, pound sterling, and an ACU (which is a currency basket of the yen and other Asian currencies). If the weights on the dollar, the euro, and pound sterling become zero, the SDR+ basket becomes an ACU.

An SDR+ currency basket would be particularly suited to the PRC as the country may be hesitant to adopt a freely flexible exchange rate regime unless it is ready for advanced liberalization of capital accounts. Until then, an SDR+ basket system would serve the PRC well in maintaining a certain degree of exchange rate stability while allowing sufficient rate flexibility against the US dollar—particularly given the need for rebalancing in both countries. This system can protect the PRC and East Asia as a whole against the possibility of sharp changes in the value of the US dollar.

USING AN ASIAN CURRENCY UNIT FOR POLICY DIALOGUE AND COORDINATION

An ACU would be useful at least in four ways (Kawai 2009):

- a statistical indicator summarizing the collective movement of Asian currencies,
- an accounting unit for operations of regional financial cooperation mechanisms,
- a currency basket used by the market, and
- an official unit of account for exchange rate policy coordination.

To support the ongoing process of market-driven economic integration in East Asia, a more systematic, coordinated approach is clearly useful. The creation of an ACU serves this purpose in various ways.[25]

The first is the introduction of intensive policy discussions on exchange rate policy as a part of regional economic and financial surveillance. The objective is to cultivate a culture that views the exchange rate as not merely a national concern but also a regional matter, and intensify discussions among policy makers in order to reach a consensus regarding the implications of large currency misalignments within East Asia. An ACU index could be used as a benchmark, a tool to measure the value of East Asian currencies as a whole against external currencies—such as the US dollar and the euro—as well as the degree of divergence of each currency's value from the regional average set by the ACU. Once the PRC adopts a more flexible exchange rate regime, both the ACU index movements and the divergence indicators of component currency values would be able to provide more meaningful information.

---

[25] ASEAN+3 (plus Hong Kong, China) is a natural starting point for constructing an ACU because of its active financial cooperation efforts, including ERPD and CMIM. The ACU could be used as an index for monitoring exchange market developments, as accounting units for denominating operations of the CMIM and AMRO, as a private sector denomination for Asian bond issuance, bank deposits and loans, and trade invoicing, and as official units for currency market intervention. See papers included in Chung and Eichengreen (2007), particularly Chai and Yoon (2009); Kawai (2009); and Moon and Rhee (2009).

The second is the introduction of informal policy coordination to achieve both greater exchange rate flexibility vis-à-vis the US dollar and improved exchange rate stability within East Asia. Most emerging East Asian economies have adopted managed floating and the PRC may join this group by using a basket of SDR+ currencies as a loose reference, while economies with sufficient rate flexibility (such as Japan and the Republic of Korea) may continue their practices. By moving to a managed float policy targeted at an SDR+ currency basket (as is currently practiced in Singapore), the emerging economies could enhance the degree of extraregional exchange rate flexibility and intraregional stability. The currency weights in the basket could vary across economies, at least initially. How strictly national authorities wished to maintain the value of their currency in line with the basket currency could depend in each case on country conditions and preferences. National monetary authorities could maintain most of their autonomous policy making by combining an appropriately defined inflation targeting policy and a basket-based managed floating policy (Kawai and Takagi 2005). One advantage of this approach is that it does not require significant macroeconomic and structural convergence among the countries.

To be ready for such soft policy coordination, the region's authorities must become more serious about policy dialogue over capital flows, exchange rates, and macroeconomic management, using a set of economic and financial data, including an ACU index. Greater convergence of exchange rate regimes would be desirable to achieve a degree of intraregional rate stability, starting with similar managed floating regimes based on an SDR+ basket and then moving to an ACU-based basket once sufficient convergence has been achieved. With sufficient structural and economic convergence among East Asian economies, countries with floating currencies—such as Japan and the Republic of Korea—may eventually move to ACU-based systems. It is thus important for Japan to successfully achieve mild inflation (such as 2 percent), restore sustained growth, and normalize its monetary policy.

7.5 Conclusion

In view of the technology hub of Asia's production network and supply chains, it is in the interest of Japan to have intraregional exchange rate stability across the supply chain countries, including Japan itself. Securing financial stability in emerging East Asia is equally vital as the Japanese MNCs have established extensive business operations throughout the region and thus benefit from uninterrupted economic growth.

Despite the desirability of intraregional exchange rate stability, currently no coordination mechanism exists for exchange rate policies across East Asia as each economy pursues its own domestic objectives. An important strategy for Japan would be to support soft exchange rate policy coordination based on a gradual, step-by-step approach. The objective would be to encourage the region's major economies to move toward adopting greater exchange rate flexibility against the US dollar and, at the same time, increasingly achieving greater intraregional exchange rate stability.

It is indeed natural for an expanding and increasingly integrated East Asia to create its own monetary zone because the relative economic size of the US—the provider of the global international currency, the US dollar—will continue to shrink and the US Federal Reserve will continue to focus on domestic, not global nor East Asian, macroeconomic stability concerns in setting its monetary policy. While the PRC authorities may wish to see the RMB become East Asia's dominant international currency to rival the US dollar, the euro and the yen, there is a reasonable possibility that this will not happen, at least in the foreseeable future because of the country's significant domestic economic, social, and political problems. From a Japanese perspective, it would be desirable for the yen to be chosen as the region's most dominant anchor and reserve currency, but this is unlikely. This line of thinking leads to a case for policy cooperation between Japan and the PRC to secure Asia's monetary stability.

Japan has been cooperating with the PRC and other ASEAN+3 members to enhance regional policy dialogue (ERPD), set up AMRO, multilateralize and strengthen the CMI, and make progress on Asian bond market development. The recent agreement between Japan and the PRC, also including the Republic of Korea, to mutually hold each other's sovereign debt as part of foreign exchange reserves is another sign of cooperation. The global financial crisis has been a catalyst for such developments.

If Japan wants to assume a leadership role in creating a stable monetary zone in Asia, it needs to make significant efforts at the national and regional levels and further strengthen financial cooperation. Practical steps that Japan could take include restoring sustained economic growth through Abenomics, transforming Tokyo into a globally competitive international financial center, further strengthening regional economic and financial surveillance (ERPD and AMRO) and regional financial safety nets (CMIM), creating an ACU index, and launching serious policy discussions focusing on exchange rate issues to achieve intraregional exchange rate stability.

First, all three arrows of Abenomics must be fully implemented and fiscal consolidation pursued. While the first arrow (aggressive monetary policy easing, called QQE) has made significant progress, the third arrow (a set of structural reforms for restoring growth) has yet to be implemented and the second arrow (flexible fiscal policy) must be targeted to support the growth strategy. In addition, medium-term fiscal consolidation needs to be embarked on to ensure sovereign debt sustainability under the mounting pressure of rising old age-related expenditures.

Second, the MOF, the BOJ, and the FSA must work together to upgrade Tokyo as a truly international financial center that can compete against Hong Kong, China; Singapore; and a rising Shanghai. This would include creating enabling conditions for establishing infrastructure and environmental investment funds for emerging Asia; currency settlement arrangements for emerging Asian currencies (such as the RMB and the won); and markets for emerging Asian currency instruments, such as RMB-denominated bonds—all in Tokyo. Japan should support RMB internationalization and its greater rate flexibility.

Third, Japan needs to strengthen its support for ERPD, AMRO, and the CMIM to ensure that financial and currency stability in emerging East Asia will be preserved. Japan can guide ERPD to focus on exchange rate policies and capital flow management among the finance ministers and central bank governors. Japan can take the lead in providing sufficient resources for AMRO so that it can function as an effective surveillance institution, and in reducing the CMIM's link with the IMF over time, ultimately to zero, so that a de facto AMF will be created.

The creation of an ACU index is a step toward more systematic, coordinated institution-building in East Asia that can support the ongoing process of market-driven economic integration. ASEAN+3 and Hong Kong, China will be a natural starting point to construct an ACU and India can join later. Once introduced and operative, the ACU can act as an important tool in regional economic surveillance, facilitate soft exchange rate policy coordination, help deepen Asian financial markets, and contribute to further monetary and financial cooperation.

Fourth, Japan can continue to promote global macroeconomic and financial stability, particularly through the IMF. Japan as a member of the Group of Seven has long been engaged with other major developed countries in managing the global economy and finance through the provision of various types of global public goods. While playing this role, Japan can be a bridge between the global and regional financial architectures, for example, by ensuring consistency and complementarity between the IMF and a future AMF.

References*

Angeloni, Ignazio, Agnes Benassy-Quere, Benjamin Carton, Zsolt Darvas, Christophe Destais, Jean Pisani-Ferry, Andre Sapir, and Shahin Vallee. 2011. *Global Currencies for*

* The Asian Development Bank recognizes China by the name People's Republic of China.

Tomorrow: A European Perspective. Bruegel Blueprint Series, Volume XIII, and CEPII Research Reports. Brussels: Bruegel.

Auer, Raphael Anton, and Andreas M. Fischer. 2010. "The Effect of Low-Wage Import Competition on US Inflationary Pressure." *Journal of Monetary Economics* 57: 491–503.

Cassis, Youssef. 2005. *Capitals of Capital: A History of International Financial Centres, 1780–2005*. Geneva: Pictet & Cie.

Chai, Hee-Yul, and Deok Ryong Yoon. 2009. "Connections between Financial and Monetary Cooperation in East Asia." In *Fostering Monetary and Financial Cooperation in East Asia*, edited by Duck-Koo Chung and Barry Eichengreen, pp. 29–50. Singapore: World Scientific.

Chino, Tadao. 2004. "Consider a Single Asian Currency." *Asian Wall Street Journal*, June 1.

Chung, Duck-Koo, and Barry Eichengreen, eds. 2007. *Toward an East Asian Exchange Rate Regime*. Washington, DC: Brookings Institution.

Eichengreen, Barry. 2011. *Exorbitant Privilege: The Rise and Fall of the Dollar and the Future of the International Monetary System*. Oxford: Oxford University Press.

Frankel, J., and S. J. Wei. 1994. "Yen Bloc or Dollar Bloc? Exchange Rate Policies of the East Asian Economies." In *Macroeconomic Linkages: Savings, Exchange Rates and Capital Flows*, edited by T. Ito and A. Krueger. Chicago: University of Chicago Press.

Fukao, Kyoji, Hikari Ishido, and Keiko Ito. 2003. "Vertical Intra-industry Trade and Foreign Direct Investment in East Asia." *Journal of the Japanese and International Economies* 17(4): 468–506.

Hayakawa, Kazunobu, and Fukunari Kimura. 2009. "The Effect of Exchange Rate Volatility on International Trade in East Asia." *Journal of the Japanese and International Economies* 23(4): 395–406.

Hirakata, Naohisa, Yuto Iwasaki, and Masahiro Kawai. 2014. "Emerging Economies' Supply Shocks and Japan's Price Deflation: International Transmissions in a Three-Country DSGE Model." ADBI Working Paper Series No. 459 (February). Tokyo: Asian Development Bank Institute.

International Bankers Association of Japan (IBA). 2007. "Recommendations to Promote Tokyo as a Global Financial Center." March 16. Tokyo.

Kawai, Masahiro. 2008. "Toward a Regional Exchange Rate Regime in East Asia." *Pacific Economic Review* 13(1): 83–103.

Kawai, Masahiro. 2009. "An Asian Currency Unit for Regional Exchange Rate Policy Coordination." In *Fostering Monetary and Financial Cooperation in East Asia*, edited by Duck-Koo Chung and Barry Eichengreen, pp. 73–112. Singapore: World Scientific.

Kawai, Masahiro, and Shigeru Akiyama. 1998. "The Role of Nominal Anchor Currencies in Exchange Rate Arrangements." *Journal of Japanese and International Economies* 12 (4): 334–87.

Kawai, Masahiro, and Victor Pontines. 2015. "The Renminbi and Exchange Rate Regimes in East Asia." In *Renminbi Internationalization: Achievements, Prospects and Challenges*, edited by Barry Eichengreen and Masahiro Kawai. Washington, DC: Brookings Institution.

Kawai, Masahiro, and Shinji Takagi. 2005. "Strategy for a Regional Exchange Rate Arrangement in East Asia: Analysis, Review and Proposal." *Global Economic Review* 34(1): 21–64.

Kawai, Masahiro, and Shinji Takagi. 2015. "Japan's Current Account Rebalancing." In *Transpacific Rebalancing: Implications for Trade and Economic Growth*, edited by Barry P. Bosworth and Masahiro Kawai, pp. 119–47. Washington, DC: Brookings Institution.

Kawai, Masahiro, and Shujiro Urata. 1998. "Are Trade and Direct Investment Substitutes or Complements? An Empirical Analysis of Japanese Manufacturing Industries." In *Economic Development and Cooperation in the Pacific Basin: Trade, Investment, and Environmental Issues*, edited by Hiro Lee and David W. Roland-Holst, pp. 251–93. Cambridge: Cambridge University Press.

Kuroda, Haruhiko. 2004. "Transition Steps in the Road to a Single Currency in East Asia. A paper delivered to the ADB Seminar 'A Single Currency for East Asia—Lessons from Europe.'" Jeju, May 14.

Kuroda, Haruhiko, and Masahiro Kawai. 2002. "Strengthening Regional Financial Cooperation." *Pacific Economic Papers* No. 332 (October). pp. 1–35.

Long Finance. 2007–. The Global Financial Centres Index. March and September. London: Z/Yen Limited.

McKinnon, Ronald I. 2005. *Exchange Rates under the East Asian Dollar Standard: Living with Conflicted Virtue*. Cambridge, MA: MIT Press.

Montiel, Peter J. 2004. "An Overview of Monetary and Financial Integration in East Asia." In *Monetary and Financial Integration in East Asia: The Way Ahead, Volume 1*, edited by the Asian Development Bank, pp. 1–52. Basingstoke: Palgrave Macmillan.

Moon, Woosik, and Yeongseop Rhee. 2009. "Financial Integration and Exchange Rate Coordination in East Asia." In *Fostering Monetary and Financial Cooperation in East Asia*, edited by Duck-Koo Chung and Barry Eichengreen, pp. 51–72. Singapore: World Scientific.

Subramanian, Arvind. 2011. *Eclipse: Living in the Shadow of China's Economic Dominance*. Washington, DC: Peterson Institute for International Economics.

Yeandle, Mark, Michael Mainelli, and Adrian Berendt. 2005. *The Competitive Position of London as a Global Financial Centre*. November. London: Corporation of London.

8

A View from the Republic of Korea

Yung Chul Park and Chi-Young Song

8.1 Introduction

The 1997–8 Asian financial crisis marked a watershed in regional economic cooperation and integration in East Asia. It brought to the fore the need for closer cooperation and coordination in policy among the countries in the region in preventing future crises. Realizing this need, the thirteen countries from the region that include ASEAN10, the People's Republic of China (PRC), Japan, and the Republic of Korea—a group known as ASEAN+3—agreed to establish as a first step toward regional cooperation a system of bilateral currency swaps, under the Chiang Mai Initiative (CMI). It was designed to provide liquidity support to member countries suffering from short-run balance of payment problems. Two years later, ASEAN+3 launched another program—the Asian Bond Markets Initiative (ABMI)—for the integration of East Asia's regional capital markets.

Unlike the PRC and Japan, the Republic of Korea could be both a potential lender to and borrower from the CMIM. As a relatively small open economy, it would benefit more from regional economic stability. It could also serve as a mediator between the PRC and Japan on a wide range of issues on which the two countries cannot agree. Not surprisingly, there was a general consensus that the Republic of Korea should play an active role in promoting ASEAN+3 as a framework for regional integration in East Asia. However, the 2008 global financial crisis has changed this consensus. It has called for a review of the Republic of Korea's exchange rate policy and its strategy for regional financial and monetary cooperation within ASEAN+3.

The financial crisis of 2008 was the first market test of the effectiveness of CMIM. The outcome has not been reassuring. Although it was in dire need of liquidity in 2008, the Republic of Korea simply did not consider approaching the CMIM. In fact none of the ASEAN+3 members suffering from a liquidity shortage did. Neither the PRC nor Japan were prepared to offer any liquidity assistance.

From the beginning, the role of ASEAN+3 has been constrained by a leadership problem stemming from the lack of cooperation between the PRC and Japan—the two dominant economies—which have not seen eye to eye on many regional issues. It has hampered the expansion and consolidation of the CMIM. The leadership issue has become more tenuous with the rise of the PRC as a global economic power, making cooperation between the PRC and Japan more complicated and hence casting doubt on the future role of ASEAN+3. In this new setting, the Republic of Korea finds a dwindling room for mediation between the conflicting interests of the PRC and Japan.

The purpose of this chapter is to analyze the role of the Republic of Korea in promoting financial and monetary cooperation in East Asia. This requires a careful examination of the Republic of Korea's experience with managing the liquidity crisis of 2008, which has a direct bearing on charting a strategy toward regional economic integration. For this reason, section 8.2 analyzes macroeconomic developments that had begun with an economic downturn early in 2008, which was followed by financial turmoil exacerbated by a liquidity crunch in the second half of 2009 before financial stability returned in the second quarter of 2009. This analysis is then complemented by a review of the causes and consequences of the liquidity crisis and the manner in which the Republic of Korea's policy authorities responded to it during this period. Section 8.3 discusses the choice of an appropriate exchange rate regime in the Republic of Korea. Here it is argued that despite its limitations the Republic of Korea will continue to weakly manage its otherwise freely floating rate, resorting to foreign exchange market interventions and capital controls whenever a surge in or reversal of capital inflows caused by sudden changes in market expectation and speculation threatens financial stability. Section 8.4 examines prospects for and the role of the Republic of Korea in monetary and financial cooperation in East Asia. Section 8.5 concludes.

8.2 Policy Response to Economic Downturn and Liquidity Crisis: August 2007–June 2010

8.2.1 *Eruption and Resolution of a Liquidity Crisis: October 2008–March 2009*

At the beginning of the US sub-prime crisis it was widely believed that, unlike other emerging market economies, the Republic of Korea was well poised to deflect or adjust to the crisis without incurring much damage. It had built up a cushion of foreign exchange reserves exceeding US$260 billion at the end of

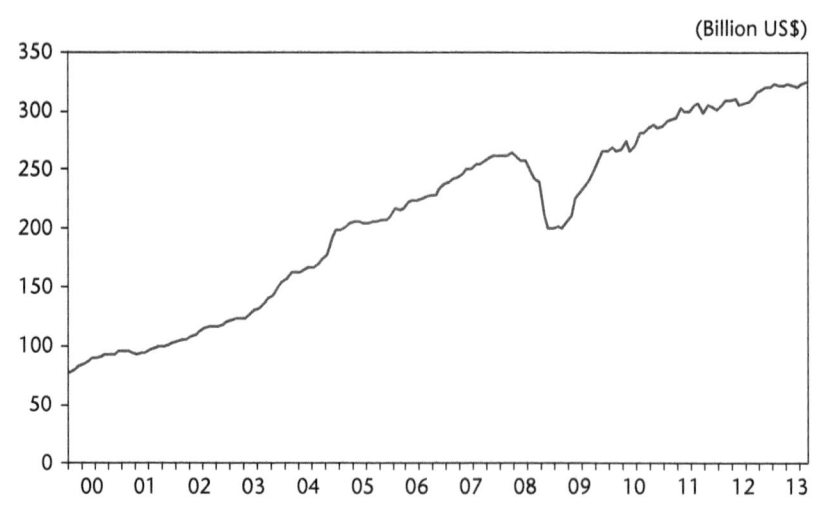

Figure 8.1. Trend of foreign exchange reserves in the Republic of Korea
Source: Bank of Korea: Economic Statistics System, <http://ecos.bok.or.kr/>.

2007 (see Figure 8.1), which was seen to be excessive to many, especially as it had strengthened its economic fundamentals through an extensive economic reform since the 1997–8 financial crisis.

Since Republic of Korea financial institutions did not hold sizable amounts of US toxic assets, the outbreak of the US sub-prime crisis itself did not impinge on their soundness or disrupt the Republic of Korea's stock market. It was also expected that the flexible exchange rate system would provide a first line of defense.[1] Yet, unlike other emerging economies in the region, the Republic of Korea could not avoid a severe US dollar liquidity crunch, which provoked a series of speculative attacks on its currency. In retrospect, the Republic of Korea was hit harder than other economies in the region as it was the only country unable to ward off a run on the central bank foreign exchange reserve without securing additional foreign currency liquidity from the central banks of the US, the PRC, and Japan (Park 2010).

RECESSION AND LIQUIDITY CRISIS

The global financial crisis did not reach the Republic of Korea until the last quarter of 2008; much of the growth slowdown during the first three quarters was brought on by a weak domestic demand, which was in part caused by the tighter stance of monetary and fiscal policy elected by the Republic of Korea's policymakers to arrest rapidly rising prices.

---

[1] According to the IMF's revised classification of the foreign exchange rate arrangement, the Republic of Korea's exchange rate system in 2008 and 2009 was classified as free floating (IMF 2010).

However, on top of the slowdown, a current account deficit in the first half of 2008 worsened the prospect of the Republic of Korea's economy even before it was hit by a liquidity crisis in the third quarter of 2008.

As the US sub-prime crisis spread to other parts of the world, foreign investors and lenders began retreating from East Asia to deleverage and increase the share of safe assets in their portfolios. Compared to the rebalancing of their portfolios elsewhere in Asia, foreign investors divested themselves relatively more of their Republic of Korea financial asset holdings, because they were led to believe that the deterioration in some financial market indicators made the Republic of Korea much more vulnerable to a financial crisis than other emerging economies. Since the Republic of Korea's financial markets were relatively larger and more liquid than those of East Asia's other emerging economies it was also easier for investors to pull out of the Republic of Korea. The share of foreign investment in the stock market capitalization was close to 31 percent at the end of 2007. A year later it fell below 27 percent.

Foreign banks had also become more averse to renewing their short-term loans to the Republic of Korea's financial institutions until they saw an improvement in the current account and better growth prospects in the early months of 2009. After the demise of Lehman Brothers in September 2008, the Republic of Korea's banks were increasingly hard-pressed as they rolled over their short-term foreign currency loans. At the lowest point in November, the renewal rate fell to below 40 percent (see Appendix, Table 8A.1). The decline in the rollover rate led to large capital outflows and a deficit on the financial account in addition to a current account deficit of US$7 billion, leading to an almost 20 percent loss of foreign exchange reserve.

Not surprisingly these deficits brought about a dollar liquidity shortage and subsequently curtailed the availability of foreign currency (mostly US dollar) loans. Reflecting the worsening of the liquidity crisis, both the sovereign spread and credit default swap (CDS) premium began a steep rise. At the height of the crisis, on October 27, the debt spread reached 751 and the CDS premium 700 basis points (Figures 8.2 and 8.3), crushing foreign investors' confidence in the Republic of Korea's economy.

The crisis hit hard both the stock and the foreign exchange markets. After breaking the 2,000 level in October 2007, stock prices measured by the Republic of Korea Composite Stock Price Index (KOSPI) began a sharp slide, falling below 1,000 by November 2008. The plunge reflected one of the worst performances among East Asia's stock markets (Figure 8.4).

The nominal exchange rate, which had remained below 1,000 won per US dollar during the first quarter of 2008, began a sharp depreciation in April to reach the height of 1,513 won per US dollar on November 24. Among the East Asian currencies the Republic of Korea's won lost most in value vis-à-vis the US dollar in 2008 (Figure 8.5).

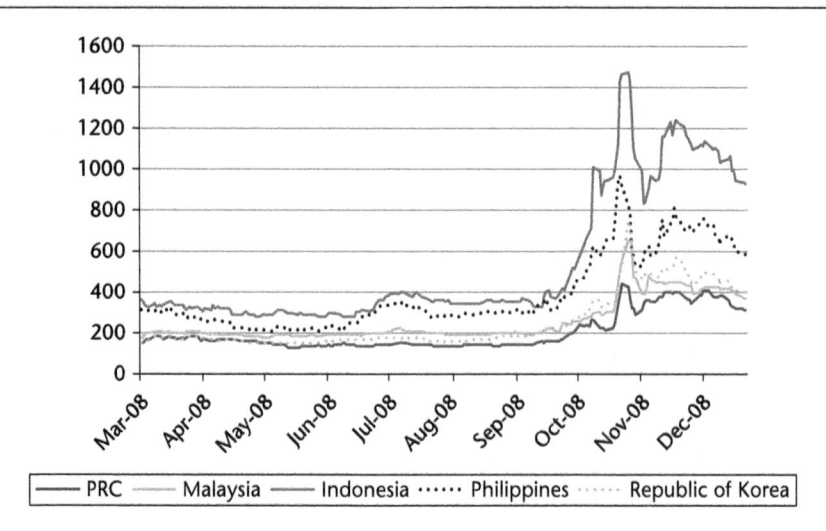

Figure 8.2. Sovereign spreads: foreign currency denominated sovereign bond spreads (vs. US Treasury note)
Source: Korea Center for International Finance.

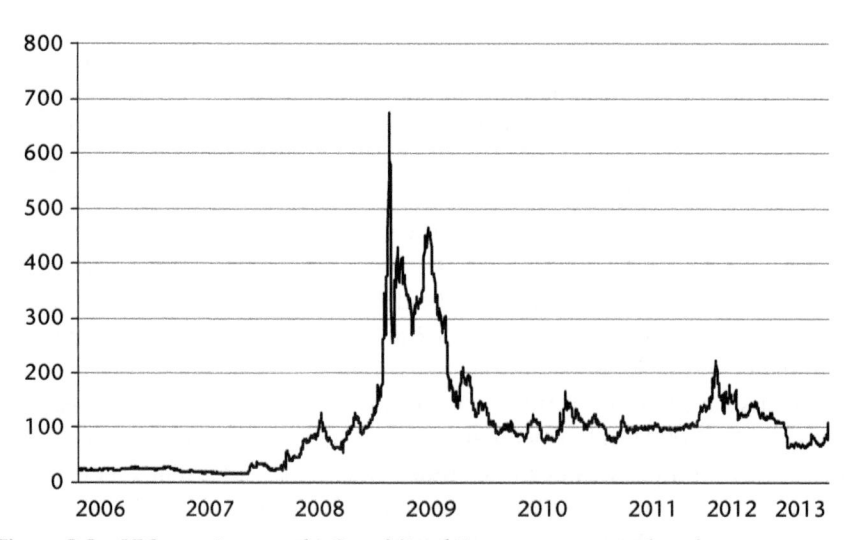

Figure 8.3. CDS premium on the Republic of Korea government bond
Note: 1. Credit default swap premium on the Republic of Korea government five-year foreign exchange stabilization bond.
Source: Bloomberg.

A View from the Republic of Korea

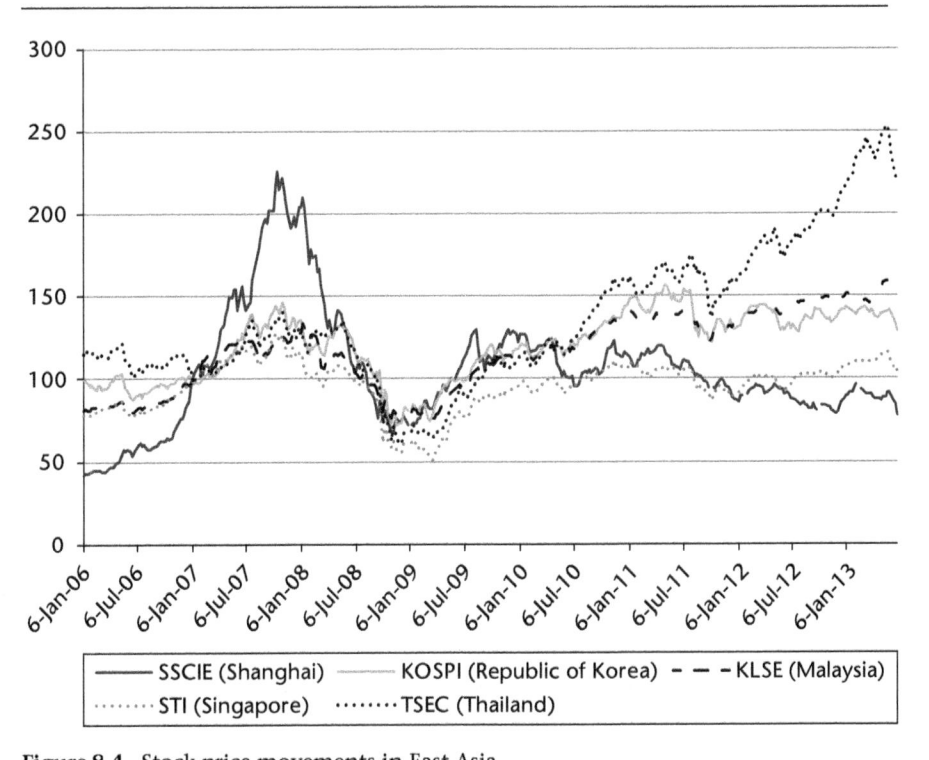

Figure 8.4. Stock price movements in East Asia
Source: Asia Regional Integration Centre of ADB, Economic and Financial Indicators Data Base, <http://aric.adb.org/macro_indicators.php>.

The high degree of instability of the exchange rate stems from two features of the won–dollar market in the Republic of Korea. One feature is that it is relatively small and shallow as the number of market participants is limited. On average, the volume of daily foreign exchange trading was less than 1.9 percent of GDP in 2007. Because of its small size and lack of liquidity, the market was overwhelmed by a series of external shocks that followed the collapse of Lehman Brothers. Another feature is that changes in the won/dollar exchange rates have been closely linked to changes in stock prices, which have been wide, and have been translated into equally large changes in the foreign exchange rate (see Figure 8.6).

There is no universally accepted definition of a currency crisis. But when a currency depreciates by more than 45 percent over a six-month period (July–November), and almost 22 percent over a month as it did in the Republic of Korea in October 2008, it must have come under a speculative attack and its downfall would be sure to trigger a financial crisis.

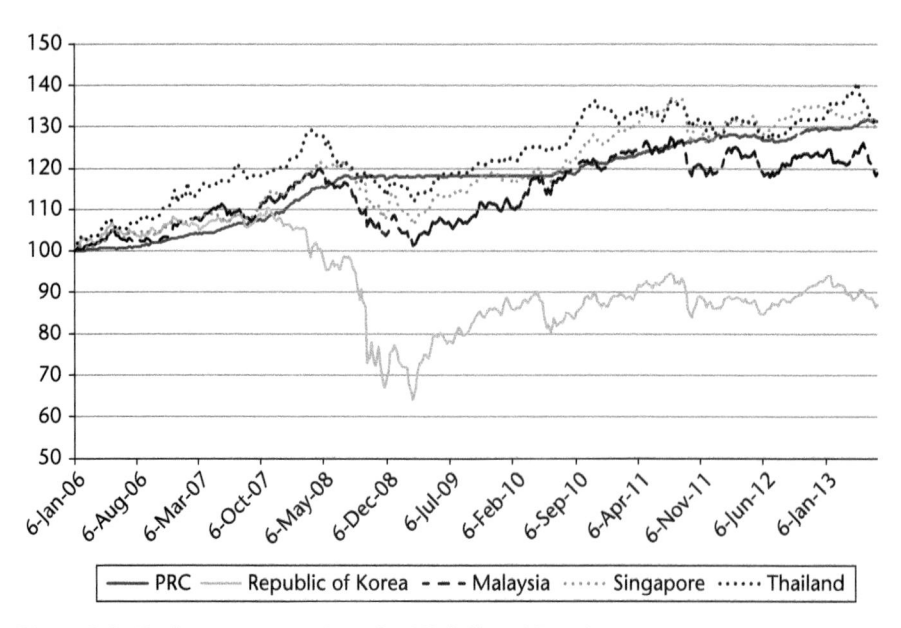

Figure 8.5. Exchange rates against the US dollar of East Asian economies

Notes: 1. An increase indicates nominal appreciation of the local currency against the US dollar.
2. January 2006 = 100.

Source: Asia Regional Integration Centre of ADB, Economic and Financial Indicators Data Base, http://aric.adb.org/macro_indicators.php.

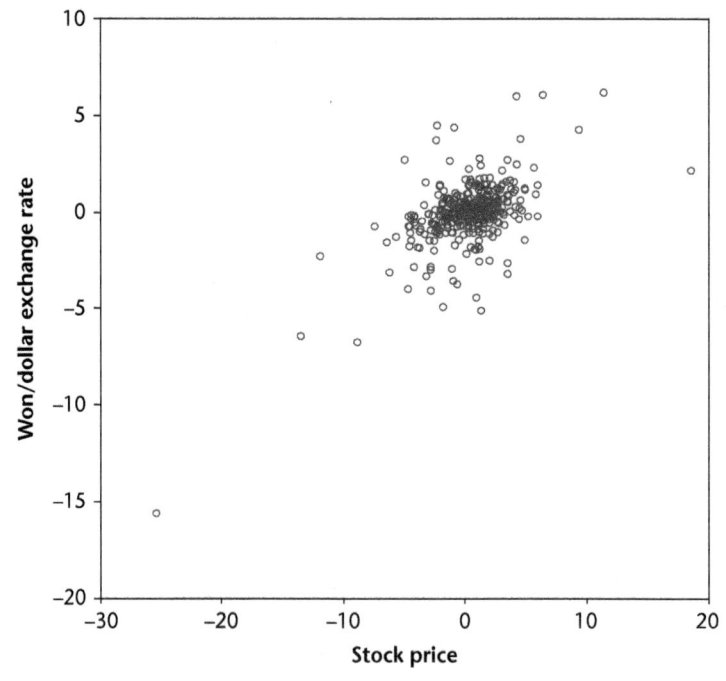

Figure 8.6. Changes in stock price and exchange rates in the Republic of Korea

Notes: 1. Rate of changes in weekly average of won/dollar exchange rate and KOSPI. 2. The sample period from January 2006 to December 2012.

Source: Bank of Korea.

CAUSES OF THE CRISIS

At the beginning of the crisis, the combination of structural vulnerabilities of the economy and deterioration in macroeconomic indicators frightened foreign lenders and investors who rushed to the exit en masse. Were these factors serious enough to pose systemic risk to the economy in general and the financial system in particular?

Park (2010) identifies a number of structural weaknesses of the Republic of Korea's economy which were often claimed by foreign analysts to have been at the root of the liquidity crisis. On the real side of the economy, the main culprit was vanishing export markets. The concentration of exports in a limited number of manufactures and producers was another cause of the deeper recession. In 2007, 57 percent of total exports were shipped by four industries—automobile, shipbuilding, electronics, and chemicals. Over the past decade, the top ten export products comprised more than 65 percent of the Republic of Korea's total exports as shown in the Appendix, Table 8A.2. The ten largest industrial groups made up 80 percent of the Republic of Korea's total exports in 2007. A setback in export earnings would then undermine the financial health of groups that constitute the backbones of the Republic of Korea's economy. The global demand for manufactures is more income-elastic than other categories of exportables and hence more sensitive to cyclical fluctuations of the global economy. As shown by Blanchard (2009), compared to countries with a diversified mix of export products, those with a heavy concentration in a limited number of manufactured export goods were hit harder by the 2008 global financial crisis.

These vulnerabilities of an export-led regime were exacerbated by the deterioration in a number of macroeconomic and financial indicators—the emergence of a current account deficit in the first half of 2008, a sharp increase in short-term external debt as a percentage of foreign exchange reserves, and a rise in banks' loan-deposit ratio.[2] While there are doubts as to whether these indicators are reliable measures of systemic risk, compared to other emerging economies in East Asia they had worsened much more in the Republic of Korea.

These macroeconomic woes were further aggravated by a substantial increase in both maturity and currency mismatches in the balance sheets of banks and other financial institutions and by an undisciplined capital account liberalization.[3] The latter set off massive capital outflows in the

---

[2] An overall risk ranking of emerging economies constructed by the HSBC in terms of the three indicators placed the Republic of Korea as the third most vulnerable country to a currency crisis among emerging economies. See *The Economist*, February 15–21, 2009.

[3] After the 1997 Asian financial crisis, the Republic of Korea's financial regulatory authorities instituted a number of prudential regulatory measures to minimize the incidence of the two balance sheet mismatches, but as the banking industry engaged in asset transformation of

form of portfolio investments abroad by the Republic of Korea's institutional and private investors in 2006 and 2007, the bulk of which were financed by short-term external borrowing (Park 2010). Cumulatively all these fragilities appeared serious enough to trigger an overreaction on the part of foreign investors, placing the Republic of Korea in a crisis zone by the end of September 2008.

8.2.2 Crisis Management and Macroeconomic Policy

Faced with dwindling export markets, dollar liquidity shortage, and the prospect of a long drawn-out recovery, the Republic of Korea's government set out to implement a three-pronged strategy for crisis management: expansionary monetary and fiscal policy, free floating with the addition of foreign exchange reserves, and a swift restructuring of ailing banks and firms. The Bank of Korea lowered its base rate and the fiscal authorities introduced two fiscal stimulus packages for 2009: the first package in the original budget amounted to about 2 percent of GDP and the second, approved in April, to 1.7 percent of GDP.

As a trade-off for stimulating domestic demand, there was a high probability that expansionary monetary and fiscal policies would worsen the current account and induce capital outflows. This led the authorities to refrain from intervening in the foreign exchange market in the belief that a large depreciation would moderate the deterioration of the current account and generate expectations of appreciation. At the same time they sought to prevent speculative attacks by replenishing foreign exchange reserves through external borrowing and currency swaps with the US, the PRC, and Japan. As it did before and during the 1997 Asian financial crisis, the Republic of Korea's government sought to restore foreign investors' confidence by issuing sovereign guarantees on new foreign loans maturing before the end of June 2009 up to US$100 billion on October 12, 2008. Similar guarantees had failed to allay fears of financial meltdown at the beginning of the Asian crisis in 1997 and they failed again.

As in 1997, the market reactions were indifferent. Only when the Republic of Korea secured a swap line amounting to US$30 billion from the US Fed on October 30 did the foreign exchange market settle down somewhat, but not for very long. The exchange rate shot up to 1,513 won per dollar three weeks after the swap was announced (Figure 8.7). The swap was apparently not enough to remove uncertainties surrounding the Republic of Korea's ability

---

short-term liabilities into long-term assets and was unable to borrow from abroad in the domestic currency these restrictions were not effective (Park 2010).

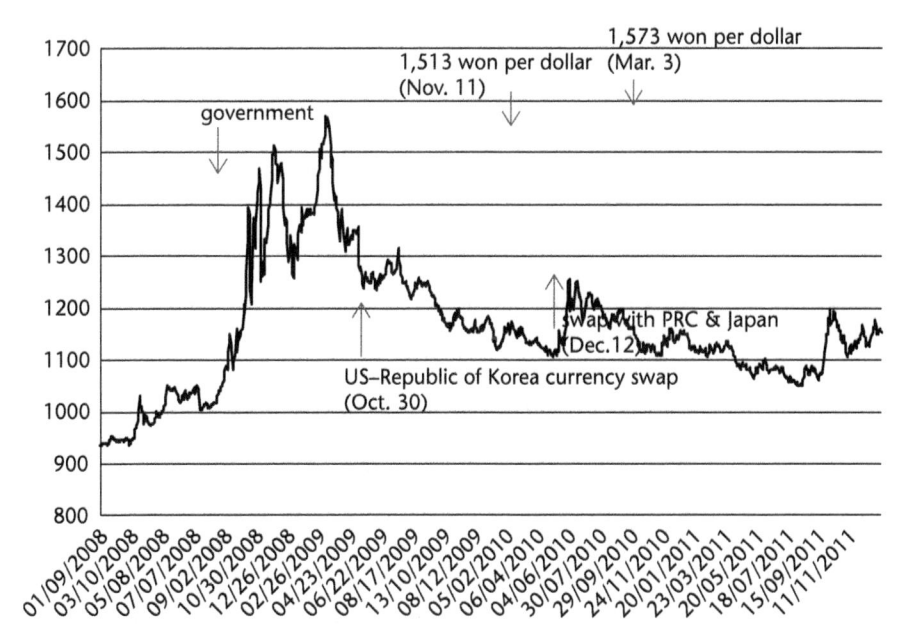

Figure 8.7. Fluctuations of the won/dollar exchange rate since the breakout of the global financial crisis
Source: Bank of Korea, Economic Statistics System, <http://ecos.bok.or.kr/>.

to service its foreign debt in view of large amounts of bonds held by foreign investors maturing and foreign loans to be renewed in the first quarter of 2009 at banks. The Republic of Korea subsequently succeeded in arranging won currency swaps with the central banks of both the PRC and Japan, each amounting to an equivalent of US$30 billion on December 12, 2008.[4]

These additional swaps together with the renewal of the Fed swap and a stronger current account than expected appear to have calmed down the market for a while. But thereafter the exchange rate was on a roller coaster, shooting up to 1,573 won per dollar on March 3, 2009 before subsiding below to 1,300 won at the end of June 2009.

Was this three-part strategy effective? Several pieces of evidence, including a substantial improvement in the current account and positive growth in the first two quarters of 2009, suggest that it was successful. More importantly, for all practical purposes the liquidity crisis was over by the end of the first quarter of 2009. Which measure of the three-part strategy was more effective in turning around the crisis? Most analysts would agree that the US Fed played

---

[4] Japan was reported to have been reluctant to offer a yen–won swap line. It asked the Republic of Korea to approach the IMF as a condition for the swap. The swap line was included in the CMI Japan–Republic of Korea bilateral swap.

a catalytic role in improving the market sentiments on the prospect of the Republic of Korea's economy.

8.3 Regime Choice for the Republic of Korea's Exchange Rate Policy

Like many other emerging economies, the Republic of Korea has a relatively large menu of choices for its exchange rate regime. It could stay with managed or independently floating or shift to either free floating or to pegging to a basket consisting of the currencies of its major trading partners. As discussed in the previous section, the crisis experience raises some doubts about the efficiency of free floating in heading off external financial shocks and stabilizing domestic financial markets. Basket pegging appears to be no more realistic an option. This assessment leaves managed floating as the most appropriate choice. This is because in managed floating the exchange rate is essentially market-determined, but the monetary authority has the room to change the level without specifying a particular exchange rate path or target.

8.3.1 Free Floating

When the crisis broke out late in 1997, upon IMF recommendation the Republic of Korea adopted a flexible exchange rate system as a means of stemming capital outflows and restoring a current account balance. Since then, according to the IMF assessment of exchange rate regimes of its members, the Republic of Korea's system had been classified as independently floating. In this regime, the exchange rate is market-determined as in managed floating, but the monetary authority may intervene in the foreign exchange market mostly to reduce the amplitude of fluctuations.

In 2009, the IMF reclassified the Republic of Korea's de facto exchange regime as floating instead of free floating.[5] According to the IMF's new definition, independent and managed floating are subsumed under a single category. In this classification floating does not mean total abstinence from market intervention. Several pieces of evidence suggest that since the introduction of independent floating the Republic of Korea's authorities have not been averse to intervening in the foreign exchange market rather frequently to induce depreciation or prevent appreciation of the Republic of Korea won. For this reason, the Republic of Korea's exchange regime is closer to managed floating.

---

[5] See IMF (2010).

A View from the Republic of Korea

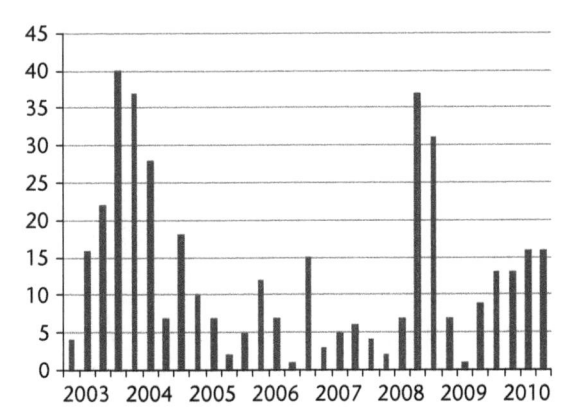

Figure 8.8. Frequency of the Republic of Korea's interventions in the won/dollar foreign exchange market

Note: 1. The year of 2010 includes the months from January to September.
Source: Park and Kim (2008) and author's estimates.

The monetary authority has intervened not only to prevent excessive depreciation or appreciation of the won/dollar exchange rate or to reduce its volatility around the trend, but on many occasions to improve the Republic of Korea's export competitiveness (Park and Kim 2008). Prima facie evidence for this type of intervention includes a large accumulation of foreign exchange reserves, which amounted to almost US$300 billion at the end of 2010. This evidence is also corroborated by estimates of the frequency of intervention, as shown in Figure 8.8 and in Table 8A.3 in the Appendix, which roughly correspond to stability indices devised by Bayoumi and Eichengreen (1998) and Baig (2001) in Figure 8.9, where lower indices correspond to more intensive interventions in the foreign exchange market by the authorities.[6]

The frequency of market interventions together with a visual inspection of the data suggest that the Republic of Korea's authorities had actively been engaged in stabilizing the Republic of Korea's real effective exchange rate between 2002 and 2004, as shown in Figure 8.10. For the next three years, until 2007, the frequency declined considerably as the Republic of Korea authorities were trying to engineer a gradual appreciation of the won to trim a growing surplus on the current account.

The crisis was a bitter reminder that the Republic of Korea did not have many places to turn to for dollar liquidity when it needed this most. It also underscored the need to hold a large amount of foreign exchange reserves for

---

[6] Following Bayoumi and Eichengreen (1998), the foreign exchange rate flexibility is estimated as follows: Index = SDEX/(SDEX+SDREV) where SDEX = standard deviation of exchange rate changes, and SDREV = standard deviation of the ratio of changes in foreign reserves divided by lagged base money.

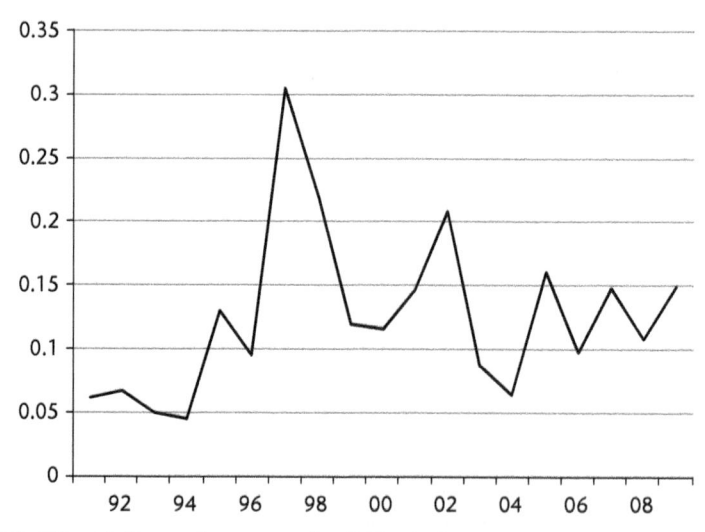

Figure 8.9. Won/dollar exchange rate flexibility index
Source: Author's estimates based on Bayoumi and Eichengreen (1998).

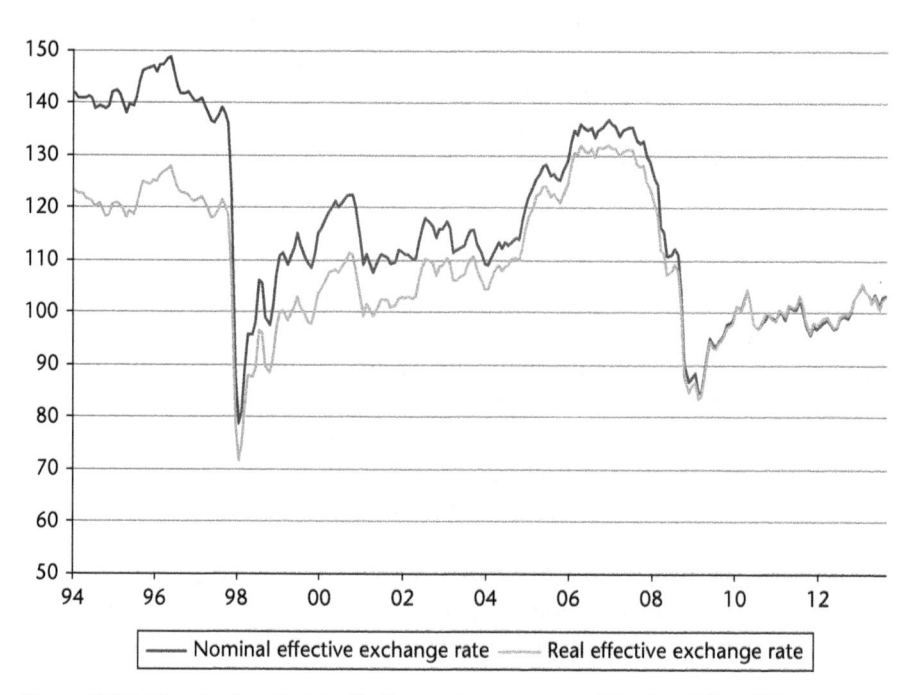

Figure 8.10. Nominal and real effective exchange rates of the Republic of Korea won
Note: 1. The rise of the index indicates appreciation.
Source: BIS.

self-insurance, which may have influenced the Republic of Korea's policy of generating current account surpluses even after stability returned to the foreign exchange market in the second half of 2009.

8.3.2 Limitations of Free Floating

The Republic of Korea's experience with liquidity crisis management presents another piece of evidence that free floating may not moderate capital outflows once a crisis breaks out. As is well known, a run on reserves may occur in the presence of extrapolative expectations that put the nominal exchange rate on an implosive trajectory.[7]

A depreciation of almost 50 percent over a three-month period until November 2008 did not stop speculators from dumping their holdings of the local currency. Currency speculators did not stop selling the won after it had clearly depreciated below its long-run equilibrium. In fact they did not seem to care to know what the long-run value of the currency was when the country was steeped in a crisis. Under these circumstances, there is no reason to believe that a further depreciation could have stopped capital outflows.

A large depreciation is often seen as symptomatic of structural problems that could undermine a country's ability to service foreign debt. This perception often induces foreign exchange traders to assess higher risk premiums on foreign exchange markets, which then work through asset markets to cause further nominal depreciation without corresponding changes in macroeconomic economic variables (Duarte and Stockman 2005). They then sell more the currency in the expectation of further depreciation. The herding among incompletely informed traders then realizes the expectation of depreciation.

Destabilizing speculation is likely to occur more often in small open economies where the relatively small size of the foreign exchange market exacerbates the volatility of the exchange rate. To large foreign private and institutional investors, their exposure to an individual emerging economy like the Republic of Korea often accounts for a very small share of their total investments. But to a small emerging economy with shallow and illiquid domestic financial markets, financial investments of these foreign investors can be large, beyond its absorptive capacity, and dictate movements of local financial prices including the exchange rate. Global investors continuously

---

[7] Behavioral economists have long argued that human beings tend to be too confident of their own abilities and tend to extrapolate recent trends into the future—a combination that may contribute to bubbles. Lansing (2006) develops an asset pricing model where extrapolative expectations can generate excess volatility of stock prices, time-varying volatility of returns, long-horizon predictability of returns, bubbles driven by optimism about the future, and sharp downward movements in stock prices that resemble market crashes. All of these features appear to be present in long-run US stock market data.

reappraise their investment risks and adjust their regional and country exposures in response to changes in market conditions at the regional and country level, making it difficult to predict when they will move in or out of the regional and specific country's financial markets.

When foreign investors decide to reduce their exposure to East Asia's emerging economies, they often liquidate their holdings of financial instruments without discriminating between countries and securities. Their withdrawal may represent a small portfolio adjustment, but it could have a large impact on these countries' small and illiquid domestic financial markets, causing an unbearably large change in financial prices including the foreign exchange rate. For instance, before the US sub-prime crisis erupted, foreign investors accounted for almost 35 percent of the Republic of Korea's stock market capitalization. At the end of 2008 the share declined to below 27 percent. Few countries could withstand such a large decline without endangering the stability of domestic financial markets.

8.3.3 Basket Pegging

If free floating is not a viable regime, could the Republic of Korea adopt an alternative system from a variety of basket pegging arrangements? This choice is not going to be any more acceptable than free floating because of the PRC factor.

The PRC has become the Republic of Korea's largest trade partner, accounting for more than 20 percent of the Republic of Korea's total exports (2012), which is more than the combined share of both the US and Japan. The large share means that if the Republic of Korea were to adopt a basket pegging, the renminbi (RMB) would have a lion's share of the basket, and in fact more than its trade weight if the Republic of Korea's small traders are excluded from the basket.

According to a recent study by Jeong (2009), more than 70 percent of the Republic of Korea's total exports to the PRC in 2008 consisted of intermediate products. The proportion has been declining since 2005, when it reached an all-time high of 82 percent, but is still one of the highest among the PRC's trade partners. At the same time the PRC has been the Republic of Korea's major source of imports of intermediate products with a share of almost 64 percent in 2008.

Prema-chandra and Menon (2010) show that trade in parts and components is not sensitive to changes in relative prices, implying that changes in the exchange rate may not be effective in restoring balance in the current account in countries belonging to the network trade such as the Republic of Korea. Under these circumstances, a basket pegging would mostly dictate that the Republic of Korea stabilize its currency against the RMB—that is, it would end up pegging to the RMB.

To examine this possibility—the extent to which the won/dollar exchange rate responds to changes in the RMB/dollar exchange rate—the following

Table 8.1. Effects of change in the RMB/US dollar exchange rate on East Asian currencies

Variables	Indonesia (rupiah/US$)	Republic of Korea (won/US$)	Malaysia (ringgit/US$)	Philippines (peso/US$)	Singapore (S$/US$)	Taipei,China (NT$/US$)	Thailand (baht/US$)
Δx_{t-1}	−0.050	−0.031	−0.007	−0.061	−0.056	0.057	−0.173**
	(−1.388)	(−0.812)	(−0.194)	(−1.671)	(−1.690)	(1.696)	(−5.109)
Δx_{t-2}	−0.089*	0.053				0.005	0.168*
	(−2.480)	(1.380)				(0.140)	(4.998)
ΔRMB_t	0.105	0.619**	0.505**	0.232*	0.491**	0.433**	0.478**
	(0.611)	(4.357)	(5.652)	(1.933)	(6.172)	(5.741)	(4.404)
ΔYen_t	0.065*	0.008	0.005	−0.051	0.133**	0.120**	0.146**
	(2.062)	(0.029)	(0.321)	(−0.690)	(9.128)	(8.559)	(7.282)
D-W	1.981	2.017	2.043	2.003	2.024	1.992	2.023
R^2	0.017	0.035	0.044	0.008	0.180	0.158	0.166

Note: 1. Figures in parentheses indicates t-statistics. 2. **, *: significant at 1% and 5% level, respectively. 3. We do not report the estimates of constant term for sparing spaces. 4. D-W: Durbin-Watson Statistics.
Source: Park and Song (2011).

autoregressive equation is estimated using daily data for the period from July 22, 2005 to the end of June 2008 during which the PRC was on managed floating:

$$\Delta x_t^i = c + \sum_{k=1}^{m} \beta_k \Delta x_t^i + \beta_{m+1} \Delta RMB_t + \beta_{m+2} \Delta Yen_t + \epsilon_t,$$

where x_t^i is the dollar exchange rate of the ith country at time t, and RMB_t and Yen_t are the RMB/dollar and yen/dollar exchange rates. All variables are in natural logarithms. The more recent period is excluded to remove the impact of the global economic crisis on regional currency movements and to avoid a sample bias caused by the PRC's return to dollar pegging.

The estimation results in Table 8.1 show that the sign of the coefficient of the RMB/dollar exchange rate is positive and statistically significant. A 1 percentage change in the RMB/dollar exchange rate leads to a 0.62 percent change in the won/dollar exchange rate during the sample period.[8] Even in a floating regime, the won has moved closely with the RMB. This close association has prevailed because, given the vertical intra-industry trade integration, other things being equal, an appreciation of the RMB would reduce the PRC's exports to the Republic of Korea. However, it is not clear what would happen to the PRC's imports from the Republic of Korea. Vertical integration in trade suggests that the PRC's imports might fall rather than increase. But even in

---

[8] It should also be noted that the co-movements of the dollar exchange rates of these sample countries with the RMB/dollar exchange rate could result partly from the shocks to the US economy that changed the overall value of the US dollar vis-à-vis the other currencies, including those of East Asian economies.

this case, if the dollar exchange rate of the Republic of Korea won remained unchanged, the PRC's imports of intermediate products from the Republic of Korea in RMB would be cheaper and hence would fall less than otherwise.

At the same time, the Republic of Korea would be able to cut into the PRC's export markets in the US and Europe. For these reasons, the market expects an RMB appreciation to improve the Republic of Korea's current account and drive up the value of the won vis-à-vis the US dollar. Because of this market reaction, the dollar exchange rates of the PRC and the Republic of Korea are likely to move together. Once a basket pegging is adopted, the movements of the two currencies would be much closer than in the case of floating.

The increase in intra-industry trade with and geographical proximity to the PRC suggest that the Republic of Korea may benefit from forming a currency union with the PRC, but as shown by Park and Song (2011), exogenous shocks are asymmetric. Neither the demand nor the supply shocks of the two countries are highly correlated. Global shocks account for one-third of output variations in the PRC, while regional shocks cause relatively large variations in domestic output in the Republic of Korea. This asymmetry may decline over time as consumption and capital goods increase as a share of intra-industry trade between the two countries. Nevertheless, if the Canada–US relation on the exchange rate arrangement is any guide, the Republic of Korea is highly unlikely to eschew its current regime of free floating in favor of basket pegging.

8.3.4 *A Weakly Managed Floating*

If neither free floating nor basket pegging is a workable exchange rate regime, the Republic of Korea would benefit most from a weakly managed floating—free floating with a prudential system of capital control and foreign exchange market intervention. In this regard, Canada's experience with free floating is instructive for the Republic of Korea's regime choice.

Canada and the US share the same open border and cultural heritage, and use the same language. More than 75 percent of Canada's exports were shipped to and more than 51 percent of its imports originated in the US in 2009. In many economic respects, the PRC is to the Republic of Korea what the US is to Canada. Yet, Canada does not appear to believe that it is in its interest to form a currency union with the US. Citing the asymmetry of shocks and the loss of monetary independence, Murray (2000) argues against the creation of a Canada–US monetary union. Thiessen (2000) and Dodge (2005) also question the economic viability of such a union on the ground of losing monetary independence.

For a similar reason, monetary independence, which may symbolize and help protect the Republic of Korea's political independence, will eventually dictate the Republic of Korea's decision to stay with free floating. However the exchange regime will not be a pure floating: it will be complemented by intervention in the foreign exchange market, and capital controls whenever a large increase in or sudden reversal of capital inflows caused by changes in market expectations threatens financial stability.[9] The Republic of Korea has also been exploring the possibility of internationalizing its currency, with the expectation that such a transformation would help the country to borrow from abroad in its own currency.

8.4 Prospects for Regional Monetary and Financial Integration in East Asia: the Role of the Republic of Korea

8.4.1 Overview

Since the 2008 global financial crisis, a number of developments in and outside the region have weakened the momentum for and reduced the scope of economic integration in East Asia. One such development has been a leadership vacuum. Neither the PRC nor Japan is willing or prepared to lead the integrationist movement in East Asia.

As the second largest and most advanced economy in the region, Japan was at the forefront of mobilizing regional efforts to garner political and public support for regional economic integration. It was Japan that advocated the creation of an Asian monetary fund during the 1997–8 Asian financial crisis. Japan also took the lead in launching the ABMI and campaigned for the introduction of a regional currency unit à la Ecu as a way of stabilizing bilateral exchange rates of the members of ASEAN+3. However, in recent years, deflation, a strong yen, slow growth, and political instability have prevented Japan from assuming a greater regional role in East Asia.

The PRC has also shown a lack of interest in regional economic integration, but for a different reason. Unlike Japan, it has been increasingly preoccupied with its global rather than its regional role. Not only for economic but also for strategic reasons, the PRC's policy-makers have traditionally placed greater emphasis on integration with its neighboring economies such as ASEAN member states than either Japan or the Republic of Korea. The PRC's business cycle is rather asynchronous so that it is not likely to reap a large benefit from participating in East Asia's regional integration (Park and Song 2011).

Furthermore, as Eichengreen (2009) points out, the PRC might not have to participate in or lead promotion of any regional arrangements to attain greater political and economic influence in the region. Instead of trying to emulate the European approach to regional integration, all it has to do is wait. The

---

[9] The IMF also sees the need for resorting to capital control to mitigate the impact of large speculative capital inflows and outflows. See Ostry et al. (2010).

longer it waits, the greater will be its economic position in the region. Eventually the large export market the PRC presents to other member states of ASEAN+3 will be an incentive strong enough to bring them into the fold of the PRC.

As for other members of ASEAN+3, including the Republic of Korea, the failure of the CMIM as a regional liquidity support system during the 2008 global financial crisis has not inspired much confidence in the future role of ASEAN+3. It may be also true that the Eurozone crisis has made the ASEAN+3 members realize that the costs of regional monetary cooperation would be much higher than often claimed, and more so in a region characterized by a higher degree of heterogeneity in country profiles than in Europe. More than anything, however, the emergence of a free-trade area in the region where the PRC will be the hub and its RMB will be the dominant trade invoicing and settlement currency will determine the future of ASEAN+3.

8.4.2 Emergence of an ASEAN+New3 RMB Area

In recent years, the PRC has taken concrete steps to internationalize the RMB.[10] At an early stage, the RMB is expected to be used in invoicing and settling trade mostly with its neighboring economies in Southeast Asia. A deepening of intraregional trade integration centered on the PRC will increase the usage of the RMB as an invoicing currency. This in turn will expand intraregional trade. Trade integration and RMB internationalization will reinforce each other to lay the groundwork for the creation of an RMB area among the thirteen economies in East Asia (the ten ASEAN countries, the PRC, Taipei,China, and Hong Kong, China): an "ASEAN+New3".

RMB internationalization is likely to follow a three-stage process. First, it will be used as a currency for pricing and settlement of bilateral trade. Then will come RMB denomination of globally traded financial instruments. At the third stage, reserves will be held in RMBs. Over time with the PRC's rapidly growing economy and a large share in global trade, the RMB may acquire an international status commensurate with its economic weight and trade scale.

However, some find the elevation of the RMB to a full-fledged international currency as hardly promising. They argue that unless the PRC is prepared to open its financial markets and to make its currency fully convertible, the RMB may never obtain a global status. They also point out that as a group the thirteen economies hardly qualify for membership in a monetary union. In some of these economies, anti-Chinese feelings run deep and the growing assertiveness of and territorial disputes with the PRC may have aggravated

---

[10] This section draws on Park and Song (2011).

these sentiments and alienated some economies. However, a series of recent developments in trade in the region appear to have ameliorated these adverse conditions and changed for the better the future prospect of the RMB.

In economic relations, ASEAN and Taipei,China, which the PRC regards as its natural and rightful sphere of influence with strategic interests, are increasingly integrated with the PRC through the formation of FTAs—ASEAN–PRC FTA and Preferential Trade Agreement (PTA) between the PRC and Taipei,China. In addition, the PRC has been playing a leading role in the development of the Greater Mekong Subregion (GMS). The informal networks of ethnic Chinese traders throughout East Asia have served as a conduit for the booming trade between the PRC and ASEAN.

Even before the PRC–ASEAN FTA entered into force at the beginning of 2010, total trade of ASEAN with the PRC was growing at a double-digit rate, and has since increased at a phenomenal rate. Compared to 2009, ASEAN's total exports to the PRC in 2011 rose more than 72 percent and imports by 61 percent. As a result, the share of the PRC in ASEAN's total exports rose to 12 percent in 2011 from less than 10 percent in 2009. If Taipei,China were to join the ASEAN–PRC FTA, a larger free trade area with the PRC as the hub would come into existence with a combined GDP of US$10.8 trillion in 2011. Total exports of the "ASEAN+New3" economies amounted to US$3.9 trillion in the same year. As a whole the group imported a lot less, running a current account surplus of US$364 billion, equivalent to 78 percent of the US trade deficit, in 2011. The ASEAN+New3 FTA would also be supported by two regional financial centers—Hong Kong, China and Singapore—and an emerging center in Shanghai.[11]

In the beginning, it is expected that the Chinese planners will aim at promoting the RMB as a regional rather than a global currency. This strategy has several appealing features for them and might be the most realistic and expedient approach. One such feature is that the formation of an RMB area is likely to be a natural evolutionary outcome of trade integration with its neighboring countries. Another is that the PRC will need to deregulate and open its financial markets, but the extent of financial liberalization and opening required for the regionalization will not be as extensive as for global internationalization. All the PRC might have to do is to supply an adequate amount of offshore RMB liquidity and create financial instruments in RMB that investors can invest in.

---

[11] The economic interests that bind the economies together have guided them to leave politics out of economics. It would not be as unrealistic as it may sound to expect that by reinforcing free trade in the region, internationalization of the RMB would unleash strong market forces that would establish its position as a credible regional currency. Park and Song (2011) argue that the same market forces would pave the way for the formation of a currency area among the thirteen economies in East Asia.

8.4.3 Prospects for Regional Integration in East Asia

Japan has also established a comprehensive economic partnership agreement with ASEAN. It has been sending an increasingly large share of its exports to the PRC. Yet it is inconceivable that it would ever eschew free floating to participate in any RMB area or for that matter to join any regional monetary cooperation led by the PRC with the RMB as an anchor currency. In Japan's view the emergence of an RMB area is likely to be a divisive development that could derail—if not bring to an end—regional economic integration led by ASEAN+3. As noted earlier, it is hard to conceive that the Republic of Korea would join an RMB area. This means that if the PRC succeeds in broadening and deepening its economic and political relations with ASEAN to create an RMB area but fails to find a new modality of monetary cooperation with Japan and the Republic of Korea, ASEAN+3 could lose its rationale.

Global financial market participants have been and will continue to be dismissive of the importance of the CMIM as a regional supplier of liquidity, simply because it is too small to prevent contagion of a regional crisis. The G20 has been exploring the possibilities of creating a global liquidity safety net that strengthens the role of both the IMF and regional arrangements such as the CMIM as its components. Would this new initiative gather momentum for regional economic cooperation in East Asia? The answer will depend on the structure agreed by the G20 members. Barring any new G20 initiative, the CMIM as a regional liquidity support system might be relegated to a symbolic arrangement.

In view of differences in their interests, there will not be any renewed efforts to resuscitate the existing regional initiatives among the members of ASEAN+3. Unlike in 1997, most of the countries weathered the 2008 global economic crisis better than expected and as a result, they do not see the need to create a large regional institution now that the IMF has established new lending facilities such as FCL and PCL.

The lack of interest in regional economic integration led by ASEAN+3 does not necessarily mean the demise of the integrationist movement in East Asia. Despite the setback in the ASEAN+3 process, policy-makers from the PRC, Japan, the Republic of Korea, and some of the members of ASEAN realize the importance of stabilizing their bilateral exchange rates, and more so with the increase in intraregional trade. There has been a long protracted discussion on creating a three-country FTA involving the PRC, Japan, and the Republic of Korea. The Republic of Korea is committed to negotiating an FTA with the PRC and is likely to resume its negotiations with Japan.

Once the PRC, Japan, and the Republic of Korea made headway in forming a three-country FTA, there would be greater private sector pressure for the stability of intraregional exchange rates. Even before the creation of a three-country FTA, the PRC, Japan, and the Republic of Korea could consider less formal exchange rate policy cooperation.[12]

8.5 Concluding Remarks

East Asia is at the crossroads in its quest for regional financial cooperation and integration. The members of ASEAN+3 have lost much of their earlier enthusiasm for moving forward with the CMIM and ABMI—the two pillars of the ASEAN+3-led integrationist movement—in the wake of the 2008 global economic crisis. Except the Republic of Korea, all other members of ASEAN+3 weathered the 2008 global economic crisis much better than expected and may not see the need of expanding the CMIM. This lack of interest has been compounded by the leadership problem.

The PRC and Japan have not been able to work out their differences in many regional issues, failing to provide leadership vital to East Asia's integrationist movement. The Eurozone crisis may have made many East Asia's leaders realize the size of the tasks lying ahead of their commitment to regional economic integration.

In the meantime, the PRC has embarked on internationalizing the RMB, which is directed to ensuring its acceptance as a key regional currency, rather than a global medium of exchange, to be used mostly in its neighboring economies—the ASEAN states; Hong Kong, China; and Taipei,China. The PRC is likely to follow this regionalization route because it requires less extensive financial liberalization that would promote the RMB as a global currency, and because these economies constitute a region with which the PRC needs to cement tighter economic relations.

RMB internationalization is expected to lay the groundwork for forming an RMB area among the thirteen economies including the ASEAN member states, the PRC, Taipei,China, and Hong Kong, China. The emergence of such a currency area would weaken a sense of solidarity and cohesiveness of ASEAN+3 as a regional cooperative arrangement. This would in turn undermine both the rationale and cooperative efforts for moving forward with the ASEAN+3 initiatives such as the CMIM and ABMI, simply because neither Japan nor the Republic of Korea could join the new RMB area.

---

[12] One suggestion is to establish a scheme of joint intervention of the PRC, Japan, and the Republic of Korea in their foreign exchange markets, using their own reserves, when one of the three currencies displays an excessive appreciation or depreciation. This scheme would not mean the creation of an ERM but would be an ad hoc arrangement to be activated when one of the markets of the three countries came under destabilizing speculation. For this purpose the CMIM could be restructured for short-term lending not only for crisis management but also for exchange rate stabilization; alternatively a new stabilization fund could be created.

References*

Baig, Taimur. 2001. "Characterizing Exchange Rate Regimes: Post-Crisis East Asia." IMF Working Paper No. 01/152.

Bayoumi, Tamin, and Barry Eichengreen. 1998. "Exchange Rate Volatility and Intervention: Implications of the Theory of Optimum Currency Areas." *Journal of International Economics* 45(2): 191–209.

Blanchard, Oliver. 2009. "Emerging Market Countries in the Crisis." A keynote address delivered at the World Bank ABCDE, Seoul.

Dodge, David. 2005. "Monetary Policy and the Exchange Rate." Remarks by the Governor of the Bank of Canada to the Canada China Business Council, Beijing, People's Republic of China, June 2.

Duarte, Margarida, and Alan C. Stockman. 2005. "Rational Speculation and Exchange Rates." *Journal of Monetary Economics* 52(1): 3–29.

Eichengreen, Barry. 2009. "The Dollar Dilemma." *Foreign Affairs* 88(5): 53–68.

IMF. 2010. *Annual Report on Exchange Arrangements and Exchange Restrictions, 2010.* Washington, DC: International Monetary Fund.

Jeong, Whan-Woo. 2009. "Changes in the Commodity Structure of Trade between Korea and China in 2008 and their Implications." Institute for International trade, Korea International Trade Association (in Korean).

Lansing, Kevin. 2006. "Lock-in of Extrapolative Expectations in an Asset Pricing Model." *Macroeconomic Dynamics* 10(3): 317–48.

Murray, John. 2000. "Why Canada Needs a Flexible Exchange Rate." *North American Journal of Economics and Finance* 11(1): 41–60.

Ostry, Jonathan D., Atish R. Ghosh, Karl Habermeier, Marcos Chamon, Mahvash S. Qureshi, and Dennis B. S. Reinhardt. 2010. "Capital Inflows: The Role of Controls." IMF Staff Position Note SPN/10/04, International Monetary Fund.

Park, Haesik, and Youngdo Kim. 2008. "Co-movement of the Korean Won and the Japanese Yen and Its Effect on the Korean Exports." KIF Financial Research Report 2008–05, Korea Institute of Finance (in Korean).

Park, Yung Chul. 2010. "Global Economic Recession and East Asia: How Has Korea Managed the Crisis and What Has It Learned?" Working Paper No. 409, Economic Research Institute, Bank of Korea.

Park, Yung Chul, and Chi-Young Song. 2011. "RMB Internationalization: Prospects and Implications for Economic Integration in East Asia." *Asian Economic Papers* 10(3): 42–72.

Prema-chandra, Athukorala, and Jayant Menon. 2010. "Global Production Sharing, Trade Patterns, and Determinants of Trade Flows in East Asia." Working Papers on Regional Economic Integration No. 41. Manila: Asian Development Bank.

Thiessen, Gordon. 2000. "The Conduct of Monetary Policy When You Live Next Door to a Large Neighbor." Remarks by the Governor of the Bank of Canada to the Canadian Society of New York, March 9.

---

* The Asian Development Bank recognizes China by the name People's Republic of China.

Appendix

Table 8A.1. Rate of renewal of foreign loans at the Republic of Korea banks (Unit: US$100 million)

Classification		2007	2008	2008 1/4	2/4	3/4	4/4	2009 1/4
Short-term	Total borrowing	764.6	795.8	208.6	270.6	237.7	86.3	33.3
	Due for repayment	739.8	957.9	210.3	270.8	250.9	235.9	38.7
	Rollover rate (%)	103.4	83.1	99.2	99.9	94.7	36.6	86.2
Long-term	Total borrowing	162.6	134.5	28.6	75.0	23.8	7.2	41.3
	Due for repayment	72.5	131.5	18.5	38.6	34.8	39.6	1.8
	Rollover rate (%)	224.3	102.3	154.6	194.3	68.4	18.2	2,320.80
Total	Total borrowing	927.2	930.3	237.2	345.6	261.5	39.5	74.6
	Due for repayment	812.3	1,089.5	228.9	309.5	285.8	275.6	40.4
	Rollover rate (%)	114.1	85.4	103.6	111.7	91.5	33.9	184.6

Source: Bank of Korea, Economic Statistics System, <http://ecos.bok.or.kr/>.

Table 8A.2. Exports by principal commodity, 2007

Classification	Amount (US$ billion)	Ratio (%)
Total	3,714.90	100.0
Semi-conductor	390.5	10.5
Non-line telephony apparatus	291.9	7.9
Display	167.2	4.5
Computer	137.9	3.7
Car	497.1	13.4
Chemicals	368.2	9.9
Irons, steel products	315.9	8.5
Machinery	287.0	7.7
Ship and boat	268.6	7.2
Petroleum, petroleum product	242.1	6.5

Source: Bank of Korea, Economic Statistics System, http://ecos.bok.or.kr/.

Table 8A.3. Frequency of the Republic of Korea's interventions in the won/US dollar foreign exchange market (number of days)

Year	2003	2004	2005	2006	2007	2008	2009	2010
Intervention	82	90	24	35	18	77	30	51

Note: 1. The year 2010 includes the period from January to October.
Source: Park and Kim (2008) and author's estimates.

Index

Abenomics 3, 20, 22, 87, 142, 161, 165
  yen policy 46, 172
aging populations
  Japan 22, 161, 163, 168, 184
  Republic of Korea 23
AMRO *see* ASEAN+3: Macroeconomic Research Office
ASEAN (Association of Southeast Asian Nations) 102–32
  Asian financial crisis
    cooperation after 105–11
    cooperation before 103–5
  bond markets 40, 110
  Central Bank Forum (ACBF) 105
  Central Bank Governors' Meeting 128
  CMI/CMIM 6, 37, 38
  current account 13
  Customs Code of Conduct 104
  Economic Community (AEC) 23, 122, 123
  Economic Ministers (AEM) 103, 105
  exchange rate regimes 3–4, 46
  finance and central bank deputies
    (AFDM) 128
    AFDM+3 128
  Finance Ministers 109
  Finance Ministers Meeting
    (AFMM) 105, 128
  Free Trade Area (AFTA) 105, 120–1
  free trade agreements 8, 105, 120–1, 217
  GDP growth rates 180
  global financial crisis 23, 111–28
  growth 12
  inflation 13
  Infrastructure Fund (AIF) 120
  Insurance Commissioners 104
  international reserves 6
  and Japan
    agreements 110, 218
    ASEAN Economic Community 122
  and PRC 110, 122, 123
    dominance 10
    Free Trade Area 121, 217
    RMB internationalization 8
    trade 217

Regional Comprehensive Economic Partnership (RCEP) 32–3
Reinsurance Corporation 103
Secretariat 34
Senior Finance Officials Meeting
  (ASFOM) 105
  and Republic of Korea 110, 122
surveillance 71, 109
Surveillance Process (ASP) 109
Swap Arrangement (ASA) 35, 36, 37 n. 14, 103, 104, 105, 106, 110, 186
Trade in Goods Agreement (ATIGA) 121
triangle trade 26
US financial crisis 3, 4
ASEAN+3
  Asian Bond Markets Initiative (ABMI) 41
  Asian currency unit 192 n. 25
  Asian financial crisis 107
  Bond Market Forum 41 n. 18, 43
  bond markets 43
  CMI/CMIM 71, 116–17
  current account 44
  enlargement calls 138
  exchange rates 48–9, 127–8
  finance and central bank deputies
    (AFDM+3) 108–9
  Finance Ministers Meeting 109, 128
  Japan's viewpoint 181, 218
    Asian financial crisis 107
    leadership issue 199
  leadership issue 199, 215, 216
  Macroeconomic Research Office (AMRO)
    6, 80, 109, 116, 118, 128, 136, 186
  Asian monetary fund 98
  ERPD 33–5
  exchange rate policy coordination 49
  Japan's viewpoint 188–9
  potential disintegration 3
  PRC's viewpoint 138, 149
    Asian financial crisis 107
    leadership issue 199
  prospects 218
  regional financial cooperation
    initiatives 186

Index

ASEAN+3 (cont.)
  Republic of Korea's viewpoint 107, 198, 199
  surveillance see Economic Review and Policy Dialogue
ASEAN+New3 216–17
ASEAN5 16, 21
Asian Bond Funds (ABF1 and ABF2) 41, 107, 110, 120
Asian Bond Markets Initiative (ABMI) 41, 107, 110, 120, 186, 198, 215
Asian common currency 134, 135, 146, 150, 155, 156
Asian currency unit (ACU) 125, 146, 159, 189–93
  index 48
Asian Development Bank (ADB)
  and AMRO 34
  ASEAN
    Infrastructure Fund 120
    Surveillance Process 109
  CMI 35
  connectivity, importance for growth 117
  ERPD 34
Asian economic community 134, 135
Asian financial crisis (1997–8) 2, 198
  aftermath 72
  ASEAN 102
    cooperation after crisis 105–11
    cooperation before crisis 103–5
    depreciation 111
  banking reform 69
  bond markets 40
  causes 16
  CMI 97, 135
  epicenter 20
  exchange rates 46, 47, 79, 82, 125, 134, 173
    PRC's viewpoint 138–42
  financial integration 71
  fiscal policy 18
  inflation targeting 72
  Japan's viewpoint 186
    Asian monetary fund 215
    support for crisis-affected countries 181
    yen 144
  lessons 153
  monetary cooperation mechanisms 92–3
  PRC's viewpoint 72, 133, 147
    exchange movements since crisis 138–42
  reserves pooling 5
  savings 120
  Republic of Korea's viewpoint 106, 181, 200, 206, 208
Asian monetary fund (AMF) 98, 107–8, 134, 136, 186
  PRC's viewpoint 107, 137, 186
  Japan's viewpoint 107, 134, 189, 215
  Republic of Korea's viewpoint 107

veto 5
Asian monetary organization (AMO) 128
Asian monetary system 144
Asian monetary union 134, 135
Asian monetary unit (AMU) 97–8
  European public debt crisis, lessons from 88, 89
  Japan's viewpoint 98 n. 12
  PRC's viewpoint 98 n. 12, 146, 149
  Republic of Korea's viewpoint 98 n. 12
asset price misalignments 82
Association of Southeast Asian Nations see ASEAN entries
Australia
  ASEAN agreements 110
  Asian monetary fund 107
  CMIM 189
  East Asia Summit 107
  free trade agreements 8
    RCEP 32, 122
    TPP 33, 110, 122
  Manila Framework 108
  PRC's viewpoint 138
  RMB internationalization 8
  US-led global financial stability 69
Austria 64 n. 9
auto sector, Japan 169

baht
  baht crisis 186 n. 17
  fluctuations
    against euro 140, 141
    against US dollar 140, 141
    against yen 140, 141
  global financial crisis 114
  RMB/US dollar exchange rate, effects on 213
balance of trade
  global financial crisis 24
  PRC 147
Bali Summit (1976) 103
Bank for International Settlements (BIS)
  and AMRO 34
  global financial crisis 61, 63, 64–6
  yen's real effective exchange rate index 168–9
Bank Indonesia 18
Bank Negara Malaysia (BNM) 123
Bank of England 16, 85, 87
Bank of Japan (BOJ)
  Abenomics 87, 165, 172
  Asian monetary integration, Japan's strategy for 184–5
  East Asian monetary policy 85
  global financial crisis 18, 22
  quantitative and qualitative easing 13–14, 46, 165, 172, 191

224

Index

Bank of Korea 4, 18, 187 n. 18, 206
Bank of Thailand 105
Banko Sentral ng Pilipinas 103–4
Belgium 69
Bermuda 64 n. 9
Bernanke, Ben 165
Bilateral Payments Arrangements (BPAs) 123
bond markets 40–4, 71
   ASEAN 109–10
   development of Asian bond market 41–3
   East Asia 43–4, 155
   global financial crisis 120
   Japan 40, 42
      Japanese government bonds (JGBs) 7, 154, 163, 164
   local-currency 40–1
   PRC 40, 151–2, 153
   Republic of Korea 40, 42
Brazil 69
Bretton Woods system, collapse 97
BRICS Development Bank 138
Brunei Darussalam
   CMI/CMIM 36, 38
   currency fluctuations against US dollar, euro, and yen 140, 141
   exchange rates 159
   global financial crisis 113, 114, 115
   trade growth 143
   Trans-Pacific Partnership 33, 110

Cambodia
   ASEAN Economic Community 23
   ASEAN Free Trade Area 121
   CMI/CMIM 36, 38
   currency fluctuations against US dollar, yen, and euro 140
   global financial crisis 114, 115
   intraregional trade 179
   trade growth 143
Canada
   bond market 42
   exchange rate regime 214
   global financial crisis 62
   TPP 33
   and the US
      global financial stability 69
      trade between 214
capital accounts
   ASEAN 103, 126
   Asian currency unit 190
   PRC 126, 152
   Republic of Korea 205
capital controls 47–8
   Malaysia 106
   Republic of Korea 215
capital flows
   ASEAN 126

East Asia 154
   global financial crisis 13, 17, 20
   Japan 172–3
   PRC 148, 152
   Republic of Korea 205–6, 211
capital markets
   regulation 57, 58
   US-led global financial stability 70
capital-to-assets ratios, ASEAN 112
Chiang Mai Initiative (CMI) 5, 35–7, 71, 79, 107, 109, 110, 134, 186, 198
   Asian financial crisis 97
   ERPD 34
   global financial crisis 115
   IMF stigma 39
   Multilateralization see Chiang Mai Initiative Multilateralization
   origins 104
   PRC's viewpoint 135–8
Chiang Mai Initiative Multilateralization (CMIM) 5–6, 37–40, 71, 80, 110, 116–17, 126
   ASEAN's perspective 118
   Asian monetary organization 128
   ERPD 34–5
   European public debt crisis, lessons from 92–3, 95, 96, 97, 98
   and the IMF 97
   improvements 154
   Japan's viewpoint 186–9
   PRC's viewpoint 135–8, 146
   Precautionary Line (CMIM-PL) 37–8, 187, 188, 189
   prospects 218
   restructuring 219 n. 12
   Republic of Korea's viewpoint 198–9, 216
   Stability Facility (CMIM-SF) 37, 38, 187–8 n. 20
   surveillance see ASEAN+3: Macroeconomic Research Office
Chile 33, 110
China see People's Republic of China (PRC)
Chinese yuan see renminbi
Clearstream 43
Colombia 64 n. 9
Committee on Finance and Banking (COFAB) 103, 104, 105
Common Effective Preferential Tariff Scheme for the AFTA (CEPT-AFTA) 121
competitiveness
   European public debt crisis 83
   global financial crisis 16
consumer price index (CPI), Japan 161, 172
consumption tax, Japan 163
Coordinated Portfolio Investment Survey (CPIS) 61, 62, 63
corporate savings, Japan 167–8

225

Index

Costa Rica 64 n. 9
credit default swap (CDS)
  global financial crisis 16
  premium, Republic of Korea 201, 202
Credit Guarantee and Investment Facility (CGIF) 41, 41 n. 18
credit market
  international financial integration 53
  PRC 18
credit ratings 54, 55–6, 58–9, 60, 64, 65–6, 67
crude oil prices 149
currency baskets
  Japanese viewpoint 160, 182, 189–93
  PRC's viewpoint 144–5, 148
  Republic of Korea's viewpoint 212–14
currency swaps *see* swaps
currency union members 60, 61
current accounts
  Asian financial crisis 139
  East Asia 88, 155
  European public debt crisis 88
  exchange rate regimes 44, 46
  global financial crisis 20–1
    ASEAN 111–12
    international financial integration 53, 57, 58–9, 60
  Japan 44, 161, 163, 165–8
    non-tradable and tradable goods sector 171
    persistent surpluses 165–6
    post-crisis period 21
    prospects 167–8
    yen appreciation, impact on net exports 167
  PRC 44, 46, 126, 149
    post-crisis period 21–2
    pre-crisis period 12, 13
  Republic of Korea 46, 201, 205, 206, 207, 208, 211
  US 13
customs union 8, 72
Cyprus 64 n. 9
Czech Republic 64 n. 9

decoupling theory 2
deflation, Japan 161
Democratic Party (US) 70
Democratic People's Republic of Korea, PRC's support 10
Democratic People's Republic of Korea, support for 10
Denmark 69
Dim Sum bonds 153
domestic investment, ASEAN 119
dong *see* Vietnamese dong
dot-com crash 13–14, 24, 28

East Asia Summit (EAS) 107, 116, 117
economic rebalancing *see* growth rebalancing
Economic Review and Policy Dialogue (ERPD) 6, 33, 34–5, 80, 109, 186
  Japan's viewpoint 186–8, 189
Estonia 55, 64 n. 9
euro 134
  ASEAN+2 currency fluctuations 140
  caution about single currency blocs 125
  currency area, relative size 176, 177
  East Asia's role in rescue of 155
  East Asian currency fluctuations 141, 142
  European public debt crisis 87, 94, 135, 150
  exchange rates 139
    versus the yen 174
  international reserves 175
  international use 174
  intra-EU trade 123–4
  as invoicing currency 178
Euroclear 43
Europe
  banking sector 69, 70
  bond market 42, 43
  East Asian exports to 2, 113, 142
  Exchange Rate Mechanism 190
  global financial crisis 20, 21, 113, 119
  inflation targeting 71
  intra-European trade 178
  and PRC, trade between 147
  quantitative easing 3
  recession (2011) 24
  single market 72
  triangle trade 26
  US-led global financial stability 69, 70
European Central Bank (ECB)
  European public debt crisis, lessons from 86, 87
  swap arrangements 93
  global financial crisis 16
  and the IMF 136
European Currency Unit (ECU) 125, 146
European Financial Stability Fund (EFSF) 94–5
European Monetary Union 134, 150
European public debt crisis 1, 4–5, 9, 10, 134–5, 153–4
  East Asian exchange rates 88–92
  exchange rates 47
  FDI 30
  financial supervision and regulation 190
  impact 150
  Japan 98
    exchange rates 83
    exports 90
    swap arrangements 93
    yen appreciation 163, 168
  lessons 79–101, 158 n. 2, 216
    changing views 96–7

Index

monetary policy and exchange rate 81–5
monetary policy in low-inflation
  environment 85
  policy implications 97–9
  regional cooperation 95–6
  strategic dominance 85–8
model for coordination between global and
  regional financial safety nets 189
monetary cooperation 92–5
  East Asia 92–3
  Europe 94–5
PRC 7, 98
  exports 91
  swap arrangements 93
Republic of Korea 4, 98
  current account 88
  exchange rates 83
  swap arrangements 93
European Stability Mechanism (ESM) 94–5
European Union (EU)
  FDI 29, 30
  free trade agreement with Republic of
    Korea 10
  and the IMF 136
  imports from East Asia by production stage
    (1995–2012) 25, 27
  intra-EU trade 123–4, 179
Eurozone
  crisis *see* European public debt crisis
  exchange rates 9
  FDI 29
  GDP growth rates 180
  global financial crisis 119
  monetary fund 6
  PRC's viewpoint 149
  public debt instruments 7
  travails 49
Exchange Rate Mechanism (ERM) 190
exchange rates 44–9, 158–9
  ASEAN 111, 114, 123–4, 125, 126–8
  Asian currency unit 189–93
  Asian financial crisis 79, 82, 111, 114, 134
  Brunei Darussalam 159
  against euro 9
  European public debt crisis, lessons from 80,
    81–5, 86, 95, 96, 97–9
    East Asian exchange rates during the
      crisis 88–92
    Europe 94
    exports 91–2
    regional cooperation 95–6
  floating 47–8
  global financial crisis 16, 17
  Hong Kong, China 159
  Japan 44, 46, 72, 127, 159, 160, 173
    cooperation 3–4, 219
    exports 167

global financial crisis 17
intervention 171–3
intraregional stability, importance 179–81
policy coordination, lack of 180–1
see also Japanese yen
non-compulsory flexible basket pegging 97
policy coordination 48–9
PRC 44–6, 72, 126, 127, 159, 160, 173, 204
  cooperation 3–4, 219
  coordination attitude 146–50
  coordination opportunities 142–6
  global financial crisis 17
  post-Asian financial crisis 138–42
  RMB internationalization 7, 150–3
  RMB regime 146–50
regimes 44–6, 72
regional stability 2–4, 5, 9
SDR exchange rate 54, 55–6, 57, 58–9, 60,
  62, 64, 65–6, 67
Republic of Korea 46, 82, 200, 204, 208–15
  basket pegging 212–14
  cooperation 4, 219
  crisis management 206
  free floating 208–12
  global financial crisis 17
  interventions in won/dollar
    market 209, 221
  liquidity crisis 201–3
  nominal and real effective exchange
    rates 209, 210
  weakly managed floating 214–15
  won/dollar exchange rate flexibility
    index 209, 210
US crisis 2–4
  against US dollar 9, 201, 204
  US-led global financial stability 70
Executives' Meeting of Asia-Pacific Central
  Banks (EMEAP) 34 n. 9, 104
bond markets 41, 43
Export-Import Bank of Thailand 123
exports
  ASEAN 111, 112, 113, 114, 117, 119, 126–7
  destination by production stage
    (1995–2012) 24–7
  European public debt crisis, lessons from 88,
    89–92, 97
  export-led strategy 2
  global financial crisis 14, 15–16, 24
    ASEAN 113, 114, 117
    post-crisis period 20, 21, 115–16,
      120, 121
  growth 142, 143
  Japan 2, 167, 178
  PRC 12, 121, 149, 212, 213, 217
  Republic of Korea 15, 16, 205, 212,
    213–14, 221
  Thailand 117

227

Index

Factory Asia 26, 27
Fannie Mae 6, 150
FDI *see* foreign direct investment
Federal Reserve
  East Asian monetary policy 85
  European public debt crisis, lessons
    from 86, 87
  exchange rates 88
  swap arrangements 93
  global financial crisis 16
  quantitative easing 3, 47, 48, 85, 88,
    128, 165
  RMB internationalization 153
  swaps 66–9
    Indonesian request 115, 187
    Singapore 115
    Republic of Korea 6, 18, 39, 115, 118, 136,
      187, 206–8
  Yellen 128
  yen appreciation 162
financial globalization 4
Financial Services Agency (FSA), Japan 184–5
fiscal policy
  cooperation, challenges 87
  European public debt crisis, lessons
    from 87–8, 94
fiscal stimulus 17–20
Flexible Credit Line (FCL) 218
flight to quality 16
foreign assets, net 60, 61
foreign direct investment (FDI) 27–30
  East Asian integration 158
  intraregional 155, 179–80
  Japan 27, 173
  patterns 27–9
  PRC 121, 126
  sources and destinations 29–30
  Republic of Korea 4
  triangle trade 26
foreign exchange reserves *see* international
    reserves
France 69
Freddie Mac 6, 150
free trade agreements (FTAs) 8, 30–3
  ASEAN 110
  Japan 8, 32
    RCEP 32, 122
    with Republic of Korea and PRC 218
    TPP 33, 110, 122
  PRC 8, 32
    RCEP 32, 122
    with Republic of Korea and Japan 218
    TPP 33
  RCEP 32–3, 122
  scope 31–2
  Republic of Korea 8, 10, 32
    with PRC and Japan 218

    RCEP 32, 122
    TPP 33
  TPP 32, 33, 110, 122

G20 *see* Group of Twenty
GDP *see* gross domestic product
Global Financial Centres Index 182, 183
global financial crisis 1, 134, 153–4
  ASEAN 102
  impacts 111–15
  post-crisis cooperation 115–28
  Asian currency unit 190
  CMIM 136, 198–9
  East Asian integration, prospects for 218
  economic stimulus responses 17–20
    fiscal policy 18–20
    monetary policy 18
  exchange rates
    cooperation 4
    regimes 46
  exports 142
  FDI 28, 30
  free trade agreements 30
  impacts 11, 14–17
    financial channel 16–17
    trade channel 15–16
  international financial integration 52–78
    baseline domestic model 56–9
    cross-country differences in crisis
      severity 54–6
    importance of international financial
      linkages 59–68
    policy implications and
      interpretation 68–73
    research data 77–8
    research methodology 76
  international reserves 6–7
  Japan 139
    current account 166
    deflation 15, 17
    exports 15, 16
    fiscal policy 18, 19
    international financial integration 52, 55,
      61, 62, 63, 65, 66, 67
    monetary policy 18
    post-crisis period 20, 21, 22, 117
    pre-crisis period 170
    support for crisis-affected countries 181
    yen appreciation 161, 168
  need for regional financial cooperation 187
  post-crisis developments and
    challenges 20–3
    economic rebalancing 20–2
    economic recovery 20
    macroeconomic policy 22–3
  PRC's viewpoint 137, 139
    exports post-crisis 121

Index

fiscal policy 19
international financial integration 52, 55, 61, 62, 63, 66, 69
monetary policy 18
post-crisis period 21–3, 117, 119, 120, 121, 122
RMB exchange rate against US dollar 148
RMB internationalization 153
pre-crisis macroeconomic conditions 12–14
Republic of Korea 4, 134, 137, 161–2, 187, 198
  capital flows 17
  CMIM 216
  exports 15, 16
  fiscal policy 19
  impact 14
  international financial integration 52, 55, 61, 62, 63, 65
  international reserves 113, 135
  Japan's support 181
  post-crisis period 23
  potential short-term liabilities 113
  recession and liquidity crisis 201
  swap with Federal Reserve 115, 118, 136, 187
  won/dollar exchange rate fluctuations 207
  trade patterns 23–7
  US dollar appreciation 161–2
global payments imbalances 11–12, 13
gold prices 149
Greater Mekong Subregion (GMS) 217
Great Moderation 80, 83, 89
Greece 86, 87, 94, 97, 167
gross domestic product (GDP)
  ASEAN 23, 111, 113, 115
  global financial crisis 14, 15, 24, 117
    ASEAN 113, 115
    fiscal policy 19, 20
    international financial integration 54, 55–6, 58–9, 60, 62, 64, 65–6, 67
    per capita GDP, natural logarithm of 57, 58–9
  pre-crisis levels 12
  Japan 14, 20, 180
  PRC
    capital investment relative to 22
    current account surplus relative to 12, 13
    global financial crisis 16
    growth rates 180
    investment relative to 3
  Republic of Korea 180
Group of Twenty (G20) 116, 117, 127, 137
  prospects for East Asian integration 218
growth patterns
  ASEAN economies 23
  bond markets 40
  global financial crisis 16

  Japan 13–14
  PRC 12
  see also growth rebalancing
growth rebalancing 2–3, 8, 9, 11–12
  ASEAN 119–20
  European public debt crisis 80
  global financial crisis 20–2
  PRC 2–3, 7, 12, 21–2

Herstatt Risk 44
Hong Kong, China
  ASEAN+New3 216–17
  Asian monetary fund 107
  banking sector 70
  CMIM 37 n. 13, 38
  Dim Sum bonds 153
  European public debt crisis, lessons from 93
  exchange rates 44, 72, 159
  as financial center 182, 184, 217
  Manila Framework 108
  Panda bonds 153
  RMB internationalization 8, 151, 159
  through train plan 148
  trade growth 143
Hong Kong dollar, international use 174

Iceland 55
imports
  European public debt crisis, lessons from 88
  global financial crisis 15, 24, 114
  Japan 178
  PRC 212, 213–14, 217
  RMB internationalization 152
  Republic of Korea 212, 213
India
  ASEAN 110, 121, 123
    Economic Community 122
  Asian financial crisis 72
  bond market 42
  CMIM 189
  East Asia Summit 107
  financial centers 185 n. 16
  free trade agreements 8
    ASEAN 121
    RCEP 32, 122
  GDP growth rates 180
  global financial crisis 69, 117, 119, 120
  Japanese supply chains 179
  and PRC 10, 138
    RMB internationalization 8
Indonesia
  ASEAN Infrastructure Fund 120
  ASEAN Swap Arrangement 104 n. 4
  Asian financial crisis 106, 181
  Asian monetary fund 107
  Bank Indonesia 18
  bond market 42

229

Index

Indonesia (*cont.*)
  CMI/CMIM 36, 38
  European public debt crisis, lessons from
    current account 88
    exports 90
    swap arrangements 93
  exchange rates 17, 46
  exports 126
  G20 116
  global financial crisis 187
    bank capital to assets ratio 112
    exports 15, 114
    fiscal policy 19
    GDP 113, 115
    impact 14
    imports 114
    international financial integration 55
    international reserves and potential short-term liabilities 113
    Japan's support 181
    swap agreements 115
  inflation targeting 71
  intraregional trade 179
  monetary policy and exchange rate 82
  sovereign spread 202
  trade growth 143
  see also Indonesian rupiah
Indonesian rupiah
  currency fluctuations against US dollar, euro, and yen 140, 141
  global financial crisis 114
  RMB/US dollar exchange rate, effects on 213
inflation
  European public debt crisis, lessons from 81–3, 85, 86, 96
  global financial crisis 13, 15
  Japan 161, 172
    Abenomics 165
  PRC 13, 148
  Republic of Korea 71
  targeting 71–2, 125, 154
infrastructure development
  ASEAN 119–20
  and bond markets 40–1
insurance market 40
interest rates
  European public debt crisis, lessons from 81–2, 85, 96
  global financial crisis 16, 18
  Japan 162 n. 4, 164
  PRC 152
international capital markets, financing via 60, 61
International Monetary Fund (IMF) 72, 137
  and AMRO 34
  ASEAN Surveillance Process 109
  Asian financial crisis 105, 106, 107, 107, 115, 133, 153, 186
    Republic of Korea 208
  Asian monetary fund 108, 186
  capital controls 47
  CMI 5–6, 35, 37, 187
  CMIM 37, 38–9, 71, 93, 97, 118, 136, 188, 189
    Stability Facility 188 n. 20
  ERPD 34
  EU 136
  European Central Bank 136
  European public debt crisis, lessons from 94–5, 97
  exchange rates 44, 127
  Flexible Credit Line 218
  G20 218
  global financial crisis
    ASEAN 115
    international financial integration 61, 62, 69
  Manila Framework 108
  Mexican bailout 107
  PCL 218
  Republic of Korea 208
  stigma 39, 187
  support avoidance in East Asia 5
  surveillance 80, 109
  Thailand 38–9
international reserves 9, 71, 154
  accumulation 5
  ASEAN 112
  Asian financial crisis 72, 135, 139
  Chiang Mai Initiative *see* Chiang Mai Initiative
  currency compositions 175
  European public debt crisis, lessons from 93
  global financial crisis 6–7, 135, 136
    ASEAN 112, 113
    international financial integration 60, 61
  Japan 118
  pooling 5–6
  PRC 6–7, 118, 137, 148, 149, 150, 151
    global financial crisis 18
    RMB internationalization 7, 152
  Republic of Korea 6, 16, 17, 39, 47, 118, 187, 199–200, 205, 206, 209
  US dollar 150
investment
  ASEAN 119
  FDI *see* foreign direct investment
  Japan 166
Ireland 55, 94
Italy 87, 94

Japan 158–97
  Abenomics 3, 20, 22, 87, 142, 161, 165
    yen policy 46, 172

Index

ASEAN
  agreements 110, 218
  Economic Community 122
ASEAN+3 181, 218
  Asian financial crisis 107
  leadership issue 199
Asian monetary fund 107, 134, 189, 215
Asian monetary integration strategy 181–93
  Asian currency unit 189–93
  strengthening regional financial cooperation 186–9
  Tokyo as international financial center 182–5
Asian monetary unit 98 n. 12
banking sector 69, 70
bond market 40, 42
  Japanese government bonds (JGBs) 7, 154, 163, 164
CMI/CMIM 35, 37, 37 n. 12, 37 n. 13, 38, 109, 118, 186–9
currency fluctuations
  against euro 140, 141
  against US dollar 140
current account 44, 161, 163, 165–8
  non-tradable and tradable goods sector 171
  persistent surpluses 165–6
  post-crisis period 21
  prospects 167–8
  yen appreciation, impact on exports 167
earthquake and tsunami (2011) 20, 163, 166
East Asian leadership issue 215
European public debt crisis 98
  exchange rates 83
  exports 90
  swap arrangements 93
exchange rates 44, 46, 72, 127, 159, 160, 173
  cooperation 3–4, 219
  exports 167
  global financial crisis 17
  intervention 171–3
  intraregional stability, importance 179–81
  policy coordination, lack of 180–1
  see also Japanese yen
exports 2, 167, 178
FDI 27, 173
free-trade agreements 8, 32
  RCEP 32, 122
  with Republic of Korea and PRC 218
  TPP 33, 110, 122
GDP growth rates 14, 20, 180
global financial crisis 139
  current account 166
  deflation 15, 17
  exports 15, 16
  fiscal policy 18, 19

  international financial integration 52, 55, 61, 62, 63, 65, 66, 67
  monetary policy 18
  post-crisis period 20, 21, 22, 117
  pre-crisis period 170
  support for crisis-affected countries 181
  yen appreciation 161, 168
as global player 9
government bonds (JGBs) 7, 154, 163, 164
government indebtedness 7
household savings 168
Indonesian swap 115
inflation 161, 172
  Abenomics 165
labor market 22
macroeconomic developments 13–14
Manila Framework 108
manufacturing sector 168–9
Ministry of Finance (MOF) 171, 173, 184–5
monetary policy 85
non-tradable and tradable goods sector 170–1
and PRC
  Asian monetary integration strategy 181, 185
  direct currency trading 154
  free trade agreement 218
  relationship between 150
  RMB internationalization 8, 10
  trade between 218
producer price index (PPI) 161
as regional leader 160
and Republic of Korea
  free trade agreement 218
  swaps 187, 206, 207
tradable goods sector 170–1
trade 158
  growth 143
  structure 164
  triangle 26
and the US
  financial crisis 3–4
  global financial stability 69, 70
  trade between 176–8
see also Bank of Japan (BOJ); Japanese yen
Japanese yen
  Abenomics 142
  appreciation 161–5
  PRC's industrialization and Japan's trade structure 164
  factors behind 161–3
  impact on economy 168–71
  impact on exports 167
  non-tradable and tradable goods sector 170, 171
  prevention 171–3
  public debt 163–4

231

Index

Japanese yen (*cont.*)
　ASEAN+2 currency fluctuations 140
　Asian currency unit 189–91
　Asian financial crisis 138–9
　Asian monetary integration, Japan's strategy for 181, 185
　Asian monetary unit 98 n. 12
　currency area, relative size 176, 177
　depreciation 165
　　non-tradable and tradable goods sector 170, 171
　East Asian currency fluctuations 141, 142
　as East Asia's only convertible currency 159
　European public debt crisis 88
　exchange rates 46, 139, 144, 145
　　versus emerging Asian currencies 173
　global financial crisis 16–17, 20, 22
　internationalization 152
　international reserves 175
　policy 171–81
　　foreign exchange market intervention 171–3
　　intraregional exchange rate stability, importance of 179–81
　　yen internationalization 173–9
　US financial crisis 3
　volatility versus emerging Asian currencies 173
　yen block proposal 144

Koizumi government 14
Korea Composite Stock Price Index (KOSPI) 201
Kuroda, Haruhiko 22, 165

Lao PDR
　ASEAN Economic Community 23
　ASEAN Free Trade Area 121
　CMI/CMIM 36, 38
　currency fluctuations against US dollar, yen, and euro 140
　European public debt crisis 90
　global financial crisis 114, 115
　intraregional trade 179
　trade growth 143
Latvia 55, 64 n. 9
Lehman Brothers 14, 18, 22, 44, 46, 56, 112, 201, 203
Li Keqiang 22
London, as international financial center 182
Louvre agreement (1985) 87–8

Maastricht Treaty 94
macroeconomic policy cooperation 154
Malaysia
　ASEAN currencies 104
　ASEAN Infrastructure Fund 120

ASEAN Swap Arrangement 104 n. 4
Asian financial crisis 106, 181
Asian monetary fund 107
Bilateral Payments Arrangements 123
bond market 42
CMI/CMIM 36, 37 n. 12, 38
European public debt crisis, lessons from 93
exchange rates 17, 46, 204
exports 126
global financial crisis
　bank capital to assets ratio 112
　exchange rates 17
　exports and imports 114
　fiscal policy 18
　GDP 113, 115
　international financial integration 55
　international reserves and potential short-term liabilities 113
intraregional trade 179
sovereign spread 202
stock price movements 203
trade growth 143
Trans-Pacific Partnership 33, 110
see also Malaysian ringgit
Malaysian ringgit
　fluctuations
　　against euro 140, 141
　　against US dollar 140
　　against yen 140
　global financial crisis 114, 139
　intra-ASEAN trade 103
　RMB/US dollar exchange rate, effects on 213
Manila Framework 108
manufacturing sector
　Japan 168–9
　Republic of Korea 205
Mexico
　bond market 42
　global financial crisis 64n9
　Trans-Pacific Partnership 33
　US/IMF bailout 107
middle-income trap 22
Ministerial Understanding (MU) on ASEAN Cooperation in Finance 105
monetary policy
　European public debt crisis 81–5, 87, 96
　global financial crisis 17–18
moral hazard, and Asian monetary fund 108
multinational corporations (MNCs)
　bond markets 40
　East Asian intraregional trade 179
　Japan 158, 178, 179, 181
　PRC 146–7
Multiple Indicator Multiple Cause (MIMIC) model 53, 55, 57–8, 60, 61, 63, 66, 76
Myanmar
　ASEAN Economic Community 23

232

Index

ASEAN Free Trade Area 121
Bilateral Payments Arrangements 123
CMI/CMIM 36, 38
currency fluctuations against US dollar, yen, and euro 140
European public debt crisis, lessons from 90
global financial crisis 114, 115
trade growth 143

N-1 problem 98 n. 12
Netherlands 69
net international investment position (NIIP) 147
New York, as international financial center 182
New Zealand
  ASEAN agreements 110
  CMIM 189
  East Asia Summit 107
  free trade agreements 8
    RCEP 32, 122
    TPP 33, 110
  and PRC 138
non-deliverable forward (NDF) market 154
non-tradable goods sector
  growth rebalancing 2–3
  Japan 170–1
North America
  bond market 42, 43
  PRC's viewpoint 149
North American Free Trade Agreement (NAFTA) 72, 179

oil prices 13, 15, 149

Panda bonds 153
Panyarachun, Anand 120
parallel currencies 146
PCL 218
pension market 40
People's Bank of China (PBOC)
  exchange rates 148–9
  global financial crisis 18
  international reserves 6, 175–6
  RMB appreciation against US dollar 139
  swap arrangements 152
  trading system 148
People's Republic of China (PRC) 133–57
  ASEAN 110, 123
    Economic Community 122
    Free Trade Area 121, 217
    RMB internationalization 8
    trade 217
  ASEAN+3 138, 149
    Asian financial crisis 107
    leadership issue 199
  ASEAN+New3 RMB area 216–17
  Asian currency unit 192

Asian financial crisis 72, 133, 147
  exchange movements since 138–42
Asian monetary fund 107, 137, 186
Asian monetary unit 98 n. 12, 146, 149
banking sector 69, 70
bond markets 40, 151–2, 153
business cycle 215
capital account 126, 152
CMI/CMIM 35, 37, 37 n. 12, 37 n. 13, 38, 109, 118, 135–8, 146
currency fluctuations
  appreciation 134
  against euro 141
  against US dollar 140
  against US dollar, yen, and euro 140
current account 44, 46, 126, 149
  post-crisis period 21–2
  pre-crisis period 12, 13
East Asian leadership issue 215–16
European public debt crisis, lessons from 7, 98
exports 91
swap arrangements 93
exchange rates 44–6, 72, 126, 127, 159, 160, 173, 204
  cooperation 3–4, 219
  coordination attitude 146–50
  coordination opportunities 142–6
  global financial crisis 17
  post-Asian financial crisis 138–42
  RMB internationalization 7, 150–3
  RMB regime 146–50
exports 12, 121, 149, 212, 213, 217
FDI inflows 121, 126
free trade agreements 8, 32
  RCEP 32, 122
  with Republic of Korea and Japan 218
  TPP 33
future of monetary cooperation 153–5
GDP
  capital investment relative to 22
  current account surplus relative to 12, 13
  global financial crisis 16
  growth rates 180
  investment relative to 3
global financial crisis
  exports post-crisis 121
  fiscal policy 19
  international financial integration 52, 55, 61, 62, 63, 66, 69
  monetary policy 18
  post-crisis period 21–3, 117, 119, 120, 121, 122
  RMB exchange rate against US dollar 148
  RMB internationalization 153
as global player 9
growth

233

Index

People's Republic of China (PRC) (*cont.*)
   pre-crisis period 12
   rebalancing 2–3, 7, 12, 21–2
  as hegemon 9
  Indonesian swap 115
  industrialization 164
  inflation 13, 148
  international reserves 6–7, 118, 137, 148, 149, 150, 151
   global financial crisis 18
   RMB internationalization 7, 152
  intraregional trade 179
  and Japan
   Asian monetary integration strategy 181, 185
   direct currency trading 154
   free trade agreement 218
   relationship between 150
   RMB internationalization 8, 10
   trade between 218
  Manila Framework 108
  power 10
  Preferential Trade Agreement with Taipei,China 217
  regional leadership potential 160
  SDR+ currency basket 192, 193
  Shanghai as financial center 182, 184, 185, 217
  and Republic of Korea
   swaps 187, 206, 207
   trade 212, 213–14
  sovereign spread 202
  stock price movements 203
  trade
   with ASEAN 217
   growth 143
   with Japan 218
   triangle 26
  unemployment 149
  and the US 138
   debate over renminbi flexibility 97
   financial crisis 2–3
   global financial stability 70
   industrialization 164
   international reserves 7
   public debt crisis 154
   trade between 146, 147
  as world power, Asian versus non-Asian predictions 2
  see also People's Bank of China; renminbi
Peru 33, 110
Philippines
  ASEAN currencies 103–4
  ASEAN Swap Arrangement 104 n. 4
  Asian financial crisis 106
  Asian monetary fund 107
  Banko Sentral ng Pilipinas 103–4
  Bilateral Payments Arrangements 123
  bond market 42
  CMI/CMIM 36, 38
  exchange rates 17, 46
  exports 15, 114, 126
  global financial crisis
   bank capital to assets ratio 112
   exports 15, 114
   GDP 115
   imports 114
   international reserves and potential short-term liabilities 113
  inflation targeting 71
  intraregional trade 179
  sovereign spread 202
  trade growth 143
  see also Philippines peso
Philippines peso
  fluctuations
   against euro 140, 141
   against US dollar 140, 141
   against yen 140, 141
  global financial crisis 114
  RMB/US dollar exchange rate, effects on 213
pilot RMB Trade Settlement Scheme (PRTSS) 151
Plaza Accord (1985) 87–8, 144, 179
Plus Three countries *see* Japan; People's Republic of China; Republic of Korea
Portugal 94
pound sterling
  currency area, relative size 176, 177
  international reserves 175
  international use 174
protectionism 83
public and publicly-guaranteed debt (PPG) 66

Qualified Domestic Institutional Investors (QDII) 148
quantitative and qualitative easing (QQE)
  European public debt crisis, lessons from 85
  Japan 13–14, 46, 165, 172, 191
quantitative easing (QE)
  European public debt crisis, lessons from 96
  exchange rates, pressure on 3
  Japan 13–14
  US 3, 47, 48, 85, 88, 128, 165

real estate market 20
Regional Comprehensive Economic Partnership (RCEP) 32–3, 122
regional trade
  European public debt crisis 89–91, 95, 96
  global financial crisis 115–16
regional trade agreements, ASEAN 110–11
relocation 96

Index

renminbi (RMB)
  appreciation 12
  area 3, 4
  ASEAN+3 216
  ASEAN+New3 216–17
  Asian currency unit 189–91
  Asian financial crisis 139
  Asian monetary unit 98 n. 12
  currency baskets 212
  currency fluctuations against US dollar, euro, and yen 141
  equilibrium value 154
  exchange rates
    coordination 134
    evolution of regime 146–50
    global financial crisis 114
    with US dollar 212–13
    with yen 174
  flexibility debate between the PRC and US 97
  global financial crisis 18, 139
  internationalization 7–8, 10, 150–3, 159, 174, 181, 190, 216
    Japan's viewpoint 218
    Republic of Korea's viewpoint 8, 10, 218
  international reserves 6, 175–6
  non-deliverable forward market 154
  re-pegging 3
  as settlement currency 154
  yuan bloc 127
Republic of Korea 198–221
  ASEAN
    agreements 110
    Economic Community 122
  ASEAN+3 107, 198, 199
  Asian currency unit 193
  Asian financial crisis 106, 181, 200, 206, 208
  Asian monetary fund 107
  Asian monetary unit 98 n. 12
  banking sector 69–70
  bond market 40, 42
  CMI/CMIM 35, 37, 38–9, 71, 109, 118, 198–9, 216
  currency fluctuations
    against euro 141
    against US dollar 140
    against US dollar, yen, and euro 140
  current account 46, 201, 205, 206, 207, 208, 211
  European public debt crisis, lessons from 4, 98
    current account 88
    exchange rates 83
    swap arrangements 93
  exchange rates 46, 82, 200, 204, 208–15
    basket pegging 212–14
    cooperation 4, 219
    crisis management 206
    free floating 208–12
    global financial crisis 17
    interventions in won/dollar market 209, 221
    liquidity crisis 201–3
    nominal and real effective exchange rates 209, 210
    weakly managed floating 214–15
    won/dollar exchange rate flexibility index 209, 210
  exports 15, 16, 205, 212, 213–14, 221
  foreign loans renewal rate 201, 221
  free trade agreements 8, 10, 32
    with PRC and Japan 218
    RCEP 32, 122
    TPP 33
  GDP growth rates 180
  global financial crisis 4, 134, 137, 161–2, 187, 198
    capital flows 17
    CMIM 216
    exports 15, 16
    fiscal policy 19
    impact 14
    international financial integration 52, 55, 61, 62, 63, 65
    international reserves 113, 135
    Japan's support 181
    post-crisis period 23
    potential short-term liabilities 113
    recession and liquidity crisis 201
    swap with Federal Reserve 115, 118, 136, 187
    won/dollar exchange rate fluctuations 207
  inflation targeting 71
  international reserves 6, 16, 17, 39, 47, 118, 187, 199–200, 205, 206, 209
  intraregional trade 179
  and Japan
    free trade agreement 218
    swaps 187, 206, 207
  loan–deposit ratio 205
  macroeconomic policy 206–8
  Manila Framework 108
  monetary policy 82
  policy response to downturn and liquidity crisis 199–208
    crisis management and macroeconomic policy 206–8
    liquidity crisis 6, 199–206
  and PRC
    swaps 187, 206, 207
    trade 212, 213–14
  regional monetary and financial integration 215–19
  RMB internationalization 8, 10, 218
  stock market 201, 203, 204, 212
  swaps

Index

Republic of Korea (*cont.*)
   Japan 187, 206, 207
   PRC 187, 206, 207
   US 6, 18, 39, 115, 118, 136, 187, 206–8
   trade growth 143
   see also Bank of Korea; Republic of Korea won
Republic of Korea won
   Asian monetary unit 98n12
   currency fluctuations against US dollar, euro, and yen 141
   European public debt crisis 89
   exchange rate
     global financial crisis 114
     regimes 46
     against yen 173, 174
   global financial crisis 4, 114, 187
   internationalization 215
   international use 174
   RMB/US dollar exchange rate, effects on 212–14
   yen conversion to 175
Republican Party (US) 70
repurchase agreements 71
reserves *see* international reserves
ringgit *see* Malaysian ringgit
RMB *see* renminbi
Roadmap for Monetary and Financial Integration of ASEAN (RIA-Fin) 122–3, 124
Romania 64 n. 9
Rose effect 123–4
rupiah *see* Indonesian rupiah
Russian Federation 107, 138

savings
   ASEAN 119, 120
   Japan 161, 167–8
Second World War 150
seigniorage 151 n. 4
shadow banking sector 20, 22
Shanghai, as financial center 182, 184, 185, 217
Singapore
   AMRO 34
   Asian monetary fund 107
   banking sector 70
   CMI/CMIM 36, 38
   European public debt crisis 93
   exchange rates 17, 46, 72, 204
   as financial center 182, 184, 217
   free trade agreements 31
     TPP 33, 110
   global financial crisis
     bank capital to assets ratio 112
     exchange rates 17
     exports 15, 114
     fiscal policy 18

     GDP 113, 115
     imports 114
     international reserves 113
     post-crisis period 21
     swap with Federal Reserve 115
   SDR+ currency basket 191, 193
   stock price movements 203
   trade growth 143 *see also* Singapore dollar
Singapore dollar
   fluctuations
     against euro 140, 141
     against US dollar 140, 141
     against yen 140, 141
   global financial crisis 114
   international use 174
   intra-ASEAN trade 103
   RMB/US dollar exchange rate, effects on 213
social security, ASEAN 119
Southeast Asian Central Banks (SEACEN) 104
sovereign spreads 202
   PRC 202
   Republic of Korea 201
Spain
   European public debt crisis 87, 94
   global financial crisis 64 n. 9
special drawing rights (SDR) 150, 160
   exchange rate 54, 55–6, 57, 58–9, 60, 62, 64, 65–6, 67
   Japan's viewpoint 191
   SDR+ currency basket 191–2, 193
Stability and Growth Pact 94
stock markets
   ASEAN 112
   global financial crisis 54, 55–6, 58–9, 60, 64, 65–6, 67, 112
   Japan 165, 184
   price movements (2006–13) 203
   Republic of Korea 201, 203, 204, 212
strategic dominance 85–8
swaps 71
   ASEAN Swap Arrangement (ASA) 35, 36, 37 n. 14, 103, 104, 105, 106, 110, 186
   credit default swap (CDS)
     global financial crisis 16
     premium, Republic of Korea 201, 202
   European public debt crisis 93
   international financial integration 66–9
   Japan 181
   PRC 152
   Republic of Korea 6, 18, 181, 206–8
   see also Chiang Mai Initiative; Chiang Mai Initiative Multilateralization
Sweden 69
Swiss franc 83
Swiss National Bank 87
Switzerland
   banking sector 69

Index

European public debt crisis, lessons from 93
Zurich as financial center 182
see also Swiss franc

Taipei,China
  ASEAN+New3 216–17
  European public debt crisis, lessons from 88, 90, 92
  global financial crisis
    exchange rates 17
    exports 15, 16
    international financial integration 55
    post-crisis period 21
  Preferential Trade Agreement with PRC 217
  RMB internationalization 8
  RMB/US dollar exchange rate 213
tariffs, ASEAN 121
taxation
  ASEAN 104
  Japan 163, 167
Thailand
  ASEAN currencies 104
  ASEAN Swap Arrangement 104n4
  Asian financial crisis 105, 181
  Asian monetary fund 107
  Bilateral Payments Arrangements 123
  CMI/CMIM 36, 38–9, 118
  European public debt crisis 88, 91
  exchange rates 17, 46, 204
  exports 91, 114, 126
  flood (2011) 113 n. 18, 117
  global financial crisis
    bank capital to assets ratio 112
    exchange rates 17
    exports and imports 114
    GDP 113, 115
    international financial integration 55
    international reserves and potential short-term liabilities 113
    post-crisis period 117
  inflation targeting 71
  intraregional trade 179
  RMB/US dollar exchange rate 213
  stock price movements 203
  trade growth 143
  see also baht
through train plan, PRC 148
Tokyo, as international financial center 182–5
Tokyo Electric Company 166
Tokyo Stock Exchange 184
trade
  Japan 158
    growth 143
    structure 164
    triangle 26
  liberalization 72–3

PRC
  with ASEAN 217
  growth 143
  with Japan 218
  triangle 26
  Republic of Korea 143
  surpluses 15
  see also regional trade
transfer pricing 147
Trans-Pacific Partnership (TPP) 22, 32, 33, 110, 122
"triangle trade" 26, 27

UBS 87
Ukraine 55
United Kingdom (UK)
  Bank of England 16, 85, 87
  European public debt crisis 83
  global financial crisis 55, 62
  London as international financial center 182
  monetary policy 85
  see also pound sterling
United States (US)
  Asian financial crisis 139
  Asian monetary fund 108, 186
  Asian monetary union 150
  banking sector 69
  bond market 42, 43
  and Canada
    exchange rate regime 214
    trade between 214
  challenges to US-led global financial stability 68–70
  CMI/CMIM 5–6, 35, 136
  current account 13, 134
  East Asian exports to 142
  East Asian monetary and financial cooperation 70–3
  East Asia Summit 107
  European public debt crisis 88
  export-led strategy in East Asia 2
  Fannie Mae 6, 150
  FDI 29, 30
  financial crisis
    exchange rate cooperation 2–4
    Republic of Korea 4, 199–200, 201, 212
  Freddie Mac 6, 150
  free trade agreements
    RCEP 33
    with Republic of Korea 10
    TPP 33, 110, 122
  GDP growth rates 180
  global financial crisis 112, 134
    ASEAN exports 113
    ASEAN reserves 112
    CMIM 136

Index

United States (US) (*cont.*)
    international financial integration 52, 53, 61–4, 66, 67, 68–70
        post-crisis period 20, 21, 119
        pre-crisis period 112
        Republic of Korea reserves 135
    global payments imbalance 11–12
    hegemony 149
    imports from East Asia by production stage (1995–2012) 25, 27
    international financial system 150
    and Japan
        financial crisis 3–4
        global financial stability 69, 70
        trade between 176–8
    Manila Framework 108
    Mexican bailout 107
    monetary policy 85, 126
        normalization 46
    New York as international financial center 182
    and PRC 138
        debate over renminbi flexibility 97
        financial crisis 2–3
        global financial stability 70
        industrialization 164
        international reserves 7
        public debt crisis 154
        RMB exchange rate regime 149
        trade between 146, 147
    public debt instruments 9
    quantitative easing 3, 47, 48, 85, 88, 128, 165
    triangle trade 26
    US government securities 149, 155
    US treasuries 16, 17, 137
    see also Federal Reserve; US dollar
US dollar
    ASEAN+2 currency fluctuations 140
    Asian currency unit 189–91
    Asian financial crisis 138, 139
    currency area, relative size 176, 177
    East Asia 154, 155
        currency fluctuations 140, 141, 142
        exchange rates (2006–13) 204
    European public debt crisis 88–9
    exchange rates 9, 44, 46, 47, 139, 144
        East Asia 204
        against RMB 139, 146, 147–8, 149, 212–14
        against won 212–14
        against yen 174
    global financial crisis 113
        ASEAN 115
        depreciation of East Asian currencies 16
        dollar appreciation 161–2
    as international currency 7, 150, 174, 175
    international reserves 175
    intra-ASEAN trade 104
    PRC
        reserves 7
        RMB appreciation 6
        RMB exchange rate against 139, 146, 147–8, 149, 212–14
        RMB internationalization 151, 153
        RMB pegged to 18
        use of dollar 147
    strategic devaluation 139
    yen internationalization, limiting factors 178
US government securities 149, 155
US treasuries 16, 17, 137

value chains 85
Venezuela 64 n. 9
Viet Nam
    ASEAN Economic Community 23
    ASEAN Free Trade Area 121
    CMI/CMIM 36, 38
    European public debt crisis 90
    global financial crisis
        exports and imports 114
        GDP 113, 115
    intraregional trade 179
    trade growth 143
    Trans-Pacific Partnership 33, 110
    see also Vietnamese dong
Vietnamese dong 114, 141
    fluctuations
        against euro 140, 141
        against US dollar 140
        against yen 140

wealthy man curse 6
won *see* Republic of Korea won
World Bank
    and AMRO 34
    exchange rates 127
    Global Development Finance data set 66
    global financial crisis 61, 66
World Trade Organization (WTO), free trade agreements 31
    TPP 33

Xi Jinping 22

Yellen 128
yen *see* Japanese yen
yuan *see* renminbi

Zhou, Xiaochuan 150
Zurich, as financial center 182